Exhibited by Candlelight

Sources and Developments in the Gothic Tradition

Edited by
Valeria Tinkler-Villani
and Peter Davidson,
with Jane Stevenson

Amsterdam - Atlanta, GA
1995

ISBN 90-5183-832-8 bound (CIP)

Cover design: Hendrik van Delft

© Editions Rodopi B.V.
   Amsterdam - Atlanta, GA 1995

Printed in The Netherlands

Exhibited
by
Candlelight

Sources and Developments
in the Gothic Tradition

STUDIES IN LITERATURE 16

Series Editors
C.C. Barfoot - M. Buning - A.J. Hoenselaars
W.M. Verhoeven

CONTENTS

LIST OF ILLUSTRATIONS

EXHIBITED BY CANDLELIGHT: INTRODUCTION

It may be apposite to begin by citing S.T. Coleridge's suspicious reaction, in his *Table Talk*, to Gibbon's *Decline and Fall of the Roman Empire*, which we would not perceive as a Gothic text:

> When I read a chapter in Gibbon, I seem to be looking through a luminous haze or fog; figures come and go, I know not how or why, all larger than life, or distorted and discoloured; nothing is real, vivid, true; all is scenical, and, as it were, exhibited by candlelight.

What Coleridge, whose own literary ambitions were differently directed, sees in Gibbon is expressive distortion, the atmosphere of dream, chiaroscuro: above all, the making of a dramatic picture (which is what he means by *scenical*). These are markers which to us, denote the Gothic. In fact, this passage suggests that it denotes something much larger and more fundamental: an anxious, irrational, subjective aspect of eighteenth-century European writing which is not only at odds with the Augustan, rationalist side of eighteenth-century literature, but alien to the new Romanticism which the authors of the *Lyrical Ballads* were doing so much to create.

In terms of writers of Gothic fiction, the Brontës, Mrs Gaskell and George Eliot, as women, and Hogg as a peasant, are fed by "hunger, rebellion and rage" as Matthew Arnold put it (speaking of Charlotte Brontë) in reaction against a world they used, courted, and sometimes quite clearly despised. It is this dark undertow of raw and uncivilized feeling, however edited for presentation in such cosy contexts as Dickens's *Household Words* and *Blackwood's Magazine*, which is defined as Gothic in papers such as those of Shelston, Mack and Kauhl.

It is a Gothic which has come a long way: a politicized Gothic — its mythic, static, visual and dreamlike qualities are now seen as the voice of writers alienated from the mainstream. Perhaps the normative quality of this might become clearer if we gave some brief attention to some novels which have been left out: William Beckford's *Vathek* (1786), as successful a "wild tale" as Walpole's *Otranto*, and somewhat later, the novels of Sir Walter Scott.

Gothic, many writers on the Gothic agree, is a state of mind, not directly requiring dependence on tropes of European medievalism and anti-catholic propaganda: if Maskull on Tormance and Dracula in the Hammer Studios' pasteboard Transylvania are within a Gothic mode of perception, there is nothing to exclude *a priori* Beckford's fantasy of an *Arabian Nights* Middle East. Perhaps the problem is that whether consciously or not, the Gothic mode (even in the violent hands of Matthew Lewis) is now perceived as redemptive. The villainous Monk of Lewis's novel achieves nothing worse than rape and murder: Vathek is wholly successful in corrupting the innocence of those who fall into his company, in a landscape of virtually unrelieved viciousness and despair. Compared with the desolate cynicism of *Vathek*, the novels treated as Gothic in this work are relatively cheerful. *Wuthering Heights* achieves a final peace. Dracula does not succeed in permanently corrupting Lucy Westenra. People die in Gothic novels, but the good remain good: they are not damned as Nouronihar is by association with Vathek. The despair inherent in *Vathek* is something which the Gothic as now defined has turned away from.

Scott presents a problem of quite a different order. Such novels as *The Antiquary* and *The Bride of Lammermoor* offer the reader antiquarianism, the use of the tableau, of ritual, mythic and folktale elements urgently present in the structure of the narrative. Why has he not been regularly cited as a Gothic writer? On one level, perhaps too simply, one might suggest that he is not politically correct. In so far as the Gothic is now politicized, it is bound to exclude Scott who, though steeped in the oral lore of his native land, was overtly centrist and pro-establishment in all his political instincts and in every page he wrote. Scott is not in the least interested in subversion: thus, his Gothic machinery is not used to Gothic ends. It is the opposite problem to Beckford. If Beckford questions too deep, too recklessly, Scott does not on this level question at all. His friend Hogg's realization of the sheer complexity of peasant perceptions, for which the Gothic mode offered the only acceptable literary dress, was something inconsistent with a politics which believed in making the world safe for the Duke of Buccleugh and his like.

Scott's *The Antiquary* (1816) is a crucial anti-text for the study of the Gothic — relating to Gothic texts much as Eco's *Foucault's Pendulum* does to postmodernism — a novelistic equivalent to a crucial historical work, *Mesmerism and the End of the Enlightenment*, or, as Scott in effect predefines it, "Mesmerism; the end of the enlightenment". *The Antiquary* is anti-Gothic in a way which *Northanger Abbey* is not, and does not try to be. Jane Austen revises the Gothic perceptions of that lovable goose,

Catherine Moreland (see Lamont's paper in this volume) but does not wholly undercut them: there are reasons to fear the power of a General Tilney, even if they are not the reasons which Catherine believes she has found. In *The Antiquary*, Scott offers such quintessentially Gothic elements as reading the past, Ossianic Gaels, Mesmerists, lost inheritances, family secrets, magic, Germans, uppity women, and sinister Catholics — and all are relegated to the margins of relevance in a novel genuinely anxious to underscore the belief that the enlightenment is not even questioned, far less threatened, by any such peeping and muttering from the shadows in the corners of society. Society is based on reason, unionist politics and primogeniture. It is in the excesses of dismissal that Scott becomes really interesting. He equates the literary mode of the Gothic with political and social subversion in a way which is comparable with the assumption shared by most of the contributors to the current volume, though it would have surprised most Gothic novelists as much as it would gratify the most fashion-led contemporary critic.

The interest in the Gothic is perhaps more lively now than it has ever been. As a result, this volume appears in a growing arena of discourse which attempts to clarify some issues, to bring to light new material and shed light on new aspects of recognized material, and to study historical contexts or analyse recurrent motifs. Nevertheless, many of the studies collected here reveal remarkable cohesion, with their authors seeming to be concerned with one main cluster of issues. To begin with, one important strand in the Gothic which is confirmed in these papers is the central function of the visual: Ann Radcliffe, as is well known, uses particular paintings as reference-points, and a number of writers draw on representations — visual or written — of famous views, such as the Rialto (see Helga Hushahn for some examples). More specifically, Gothic is a way of viewing: Fuseli's paintings and drawings, mentioned by Johnson, or Piranesi's *Vedute di Roma* and his *Carceri* present ways of seeing which are profoundly suggestive. In fact, like the eighteenth-century theatre with the scenery of Loutherbourg, the Gothic novel finds its natural climax in a tableau: in "The Old Nurse's Tale", for example, discussed by Shelston, father, jealous sisters and hapless baby are held in a frozen moment — a presence from the past, a spectral apparition explaining the present and the real. Similar, though at a further stage on the time scale, are the Hammer Studios' visualizations of Dracula, which give reality to the presence of the undead. The Gothic, therefore, makes use of ways of communicating with the reader that go beyond the word on the page, and which, in addition, call into play the passions — including, or, in fact, primarily, sexual passion, as Robert Druce demonstrates. This aspect of Gothic writing is not peculiar to the group of texts so defined: as De Voogt has emphasized, writings we think of as Gothic grows out of a continuum of eighteenth-century discourse.

Continuity with the past is a further strand in the Gothic that receives particular attention in these texts, which, at times indirectly, worry about the sources of the Gothic and how these sources are in fact connected with the origin of personal existence, of personal history, of history and existence. In this respect, on the most obvious level the Gothic as a genre appears as a form of literary outlawry. Women writers like the Brontës, Mrs Gaskell and George Eliot, and Hogg as a peasant, for example, have in common their alienation from a male, middle-class, urban literary élite. All of them have access to the alternative creative tradition of ballads, oral culture, fairy-stories, primitive peasant superstitions. This is the tradition from which much of the eighteenth-century Gothic derived in the first place (particularly when it came to be enriched by the more colourful and sexual tales of the Arabian Nights). This is not just a Gothic which requires a post-Freudian, post-Jungian reading of texts which on so many levels invite such treatment (and receive it in a number of these papers), but a Gothic which offers a voice for writers who cannot fit themselves into the perceptions of the dominant group: those, as Johnson's paper suggests, who perceive gaps.

Not only Johnson, but many other writers focus on gaps, void spaces, locked trunks; for this is the paradox of the Gothic as it emerges from these texts: the writers' concern with the continuity of the present with the past (personal and general) finds its most worrying moments in the discovery of real and unreal gaps which leads to the recreation of such gaps in the structure of the tale (as in Borges's story, quoted by Johnson). What this, in its ultimate analysis, leads the writer, and the reader, to explore is the whole issue of Punter's "questionable source". This search for clarification becomes most obvious in the proliferation of epithets so many contributors use in order to define and clarify the way the Gothic works. David Punter's "heroic gothic" is at one end of a scale of which the opposing end is occupied by Robert Druce's "porno-gothic"; but whether this scale traces the description of a particular aspect of the Gothic, or the nature of the writer's intention, or the envisaged response of the reader is a question which would be difficult to determine with any degree of certainty.

There are many areas of the Gothic which are not covered by the studies collected in this volume, mainly to do with the historical forms the presence of the Gothic has assumed, or its details. But these essays do contribute to a continuing exploration and clarification of the main core of Gothic. For, in the end, what Gothic represents is the possibility for new forms of the unreal to enter and change whatever has become mainstream literature; it is a way of writing just as much as a way of reading; it is a mode, more than a form or genre, which allows the fantastic, the horrific, the supernatural (that is, the world of the mind) to enter and impregnate the real, making the reader respond to the text as if it were reality. In fact, one basic question which could be developed further is to what extent the Gothic exists in postmodernism (as D'haen convincingly argues), or, rather, to what extent fantastic postmodernism testifies to the presence of the Gothic is a new shape, a process which will continue even when POMO is dead. For from its first beginnings in the eighteenth century, "Gothic" has always referred to a dynamic type of literature, which reflects what is most active, developing and changing in the literary, social and cultural developments of the times in which it is written. I conclude by going back to the many combinations of words the writers of these papers have resorted to; some are borrowed from previous studies, such as Westerweel's reference to "imperial gothic"; but others appear for the first time in these papers, coined as a result of the present authors' reflections on how the Gothic mode works on literature — or perhaps more correctly (as C.C. Barfoot's essay shows), *in* literature, working through it as a leavening yeast.

Peter Davidson
Jane Stevenson
Valeria Tinkler-Villani

Editorial Note

Most of the essays collected in this volume are based on papers delivered at a conference on *The Gothic: Sources and Developments*, organized by the English Department of Leiden University in October 1991. A number were commissioned specifically for this volume. Once more we would like to thank the British Council and the Leiden Faculty of Letters for their financial support for the conference.

GAPS AND GOTHIC SENSIBILITY:
WALPOLE, LEWIS, MARY SHELLEY, AND MATURIN

"When you look into the abyss, the abyss also looks into you"[1]

Borges got it right. In "There Are More Things" (1975), a short tale dedicated to the memory of H.P. Lovecraft, his narrator, having dreamed of a minotaur slumbering in a Piranesian labyrinth, awakens with foreboding and spends the following days on an inexorable path — spiralling ever inward towards the centre of his attentions.[2] His goal is the Casa Colorada of his childhood reminiscence, which had formerly belonged to an uncle but had been transformed by its elusive new owner — becoming something alien and sinister; something frightening to the builders; something no one dared enter. One night, impelled by curiosity and driven by a storm, he discovers himself beside its fence. Trying the gate he finds that it opens, and that the door of the house is ajar. He takes the plunge: he enters the realm of the indescribable. And it is indescribable:

> Let me explain myself. To see a thing one has to comprehend it. An armchair presupposes the human body, its joints and limbs; a pair of scissors, the act of cutting .... None of the meaningless shapes that that night granted me corresponded to the human figure or, for that matter, to any conceivable use. I felt revulsion and terror. In one of the corners, I found a ladder which led to the upper floor. The spaces between the iron rungs, which were no more than ten, were wide and irregular. That ladder, implying hands and feet, was comprehensible, and in some way this relieved me .... The nightmare that had foreshadowed the lower floor came alive and flowered on the next .... I now recall a sort of long

---

1. Nietzsche, cited as an epigraph in Stephen King's *Misery*, London, 1987.

2. Jorge Luis Borges, "There Are More Things" (1975), in *The Book of Sand*, trans. N.T. di Giovanni, Penguin, 1982, 42.

operating table, very high and in the shape of a U, with round
hollows at each end. I thought that maybe it was the bed of the
house's inhabitant, whose monstrous anatomy revealed itself in this
way, implicitly, like an animal's or a god's, by its shadow.

We are, one might suspect, at the beginning of a revelation. But this is
where the author chooses to end the story, leaving his narrator on the
penultimate rung of the ladder, in wide-eyed anticipation of the slow,
oppressive, and two-fold beast that has entered the house and is
lumbering up the ramp towards him.

Borges's strategy is to leave us with a gapped structure. On what
Barthes would have called the sequential level,[3] its narrative is
fragmented, open — consciously unfinished. On the actantial level its
narrator is distanced from us by the non-disclosure of the tale he seems
to have lived to have failed to relate. Here, too, the main object of his
initial interest — the owner, Max Preetorius — remains little more than
a name, while the house's mysterious inhabitant is not described at all.
And the interplay within and between these levels is complemented, on
the indicial level, by the themes of unfinishedness, uncertainty, otherness,
and unimaginableness, which whirl round in the head of the reader after
the closing of the book.

Such a stratagem — such uncertainty — is, of course, pure Borges (as
is the satiric edge which glimmers behind the pastiche). But the motifs
of the story — dreams within labyrinthine dreams, the paradoxical
interface of an alien dimension, the bizarre interior, the open ending —
reach back too, through Lovecraft, to a tradition of thought which
extends to the inception of the Gothic itself as a literary genre. And
despite the fact that Borges has finessed them to his own ends — thereby
revealing the extent of his own immersion in that tradition — they belong
to the common stock of the working Gothic novelist.

Where are we to look if we wish to trace the sources of this
concatenation of motivic fragments, this aesthetic of incompleteness
which makes the Gothic so much at home in the postmodern world? One
answer might be to follow its paths back through the history of ideas
itself — most especially in the dealings of the latter with psychology —
from Lacan and Jung, through Freud and Breuer to those early
practitioners of psychic uncertainty, Maxime de Puységur and Franz
Anton Mesmer (or perhaps even further, into the eighteenth-century
exponents of the alchemical art). Another might be to trace the history

---

3. Roland Barthes, "Introduction to the Structural Analysis of **Narratives**"
(1966), in *Image-Music-Text*, trans. Stephen Heath, London, 1977, 79-124.

of images — the shifting iconospheres — of these motifs in their
movement from surrealism to its precursors in the irrational dream
paintings of Johannot, Kinninger, Goya, and Fuseli. From architecture
we could pursue Borges's bizarre interior through the nineteenth-century
Gothic revival to the work of Gibbs, Walpole's Strawberry Hill, or the
drawings of Piranesi himself. Even in the Anglo-American branches of
Gothic literature we could watch their shift and reassemblage in a
backward-leading textual tradition, running via, say, Stoker, Wilde,
Stevenson, Le Fanu, and Poe. We could trace them through the codifiers
of fragmented sensibility: De Quincey, Coleridge, and that group —
comprising Mary and Percy Bysshe Shelley, Dr Polidori, Matthew
Lewis, and Byron — whose sojourn at Geneva, Lake Leman, and the
Villa Deodati in the early summer of 1816 was instrumental in the
production of *Frankenstein* (1818), *Prometheus Unbound* (1820), and *The
Vampyre* (1819). Or further still: into Lewis's own novel, *The Monk*
(1796), Ann Radcliffe's *The Mysteries of Udolpho* (1794), *The Italian*
(1797), and Walpole's *The Castle of Otranto* (1764). Such an undertaking
would be vast — indeed, inexhaustible — as well as presumptuous for a
solitary writer. So I shall set limits, concentrating here on the English
Gothic revival from, roughly speaking, 1764-1820 (a privileged period
in the growth of these motifs). And I shall attempt to bring them into
focus by considering their function with respect to one small but telling
component of the Gothic aesthetic: the idea of the gap.

What is a gap? Let us test its senses. In English the word signifies a
breach. On a physical level it may be in a hedge or wall or, on a larger
scale, through strata, as in a gorge or pass. In this sense it takes its
meaning ultimately from the Old Norse *gapa* (MHG *gaffen*): a chasm or
abyss (which is also etymologically cognate with the "gape" we might
expect from Borges's narrator at the end of his tale). Because, too, such
breaches occur through almost every stage of the sediment of the lived,
the word comes to take on its more general range of meanings: signifying
an unfilled space or interval, a blank, a break in continuity.

It is to this latter sense that Wolfgang Iser, one of our finest
connoisseurs of the subject, leans in his informal typology of its
occurrence in literary texts.[4] For him, human experience outside
literature is gapped and the creation of fiction in our everyday lives is,
on one hand, a sort of knowing surrogate for what we know we cannot
know; and on the other, a means of filling some sort of psychic vacancy

---

4. Wolfgang Iser, *The Implied Reader* (1972), Baltimore: Md., 1974, 300.

created by the rejection or transformation of old belief systems. Approaching the text itself, the reader may perceive a space between techniques of presentation and the reality presented (as in the use of irony, for instance); discontinuities in the author's placement and juxtaposition of parts of the text; or, on the level of character, breaches of knowledge between character and character or character and the reader. In all these areas, Iser argues, the gaps in the text are there to be filled by the reader "in his own way".[5] In this sense, the imaginative involvement of the reader in the text through such lacunae becomes a crucial part of the act of reading itself: for any literature, in any language.

But that is not to say that different periods, genres, and cultures do not favour different kinds of gapping. It is notable and comprehensible, for instance, that Iser should settle on Faulkner, Beckett and Joyce as exponents of these techniques, for the use of space in the novel — as Joseph Frank long ago pointed out[6] — is a hallmark of the modernist aesthetic. Equally, it is clear from Frank, and beyond, that the idea of the gap enjoyed a special and explicit status in the Gothic novel from its very inception in English culture — an almost unprecedented deliberacy about the breaks and discontinuities in the form, an implied self-consciousness which was, in itself, something of a generic indicator.

We could test this assertion by glancing at four very different but nonetheless representative works of the period: *The Castle of Otranto*, *The Monk*, *Frankenstein*, and Maturin's *Melmoth the Wanderer* (1820). In no case do we have to look far to find gapped structures on the indicial level. From Walpole we need only recall the subterraneous caverns or the climactic ruining of the Castle of Otranto itself.[7] From Lewis we may remember Lorenzo's vision of an "abyss" opening to swallow Ambrosio, and the real "abyss" in which Agnes is later imprisoned;[8] from Mary Shelley, the "ruined castles hanging on the precipices" as well as the ice-caves and "ridges of inaccessible

---

5. *Ibid.*, 280.

6. Joseph Frank, "Spatial Form in Literature: An Essay in Three Parts", *Sewanee Review* (1945), 221-40, 433-56, 643-53.

7. Horace Walpole, *The Castle of Otranto. A Gothic Story* (1764), ed. W.S. Lewis, London, 1969, 25-28, 108.

8. Matthew Lewis, *The Monk* (1796), ed. Howard Anderson, London, 1973, 28, 367.

precipices" inhabited by Frankenstein's monster.[9] From Maturin we could bring to mind the ruined lodge and gapped walls around the approach to old Melmoth's house and the "abyss of fire" into which a mother watches her children falling;[10] or Alonzo di Monçada's descent into the formless darkness of the passages beneath the monastery in which he has been confined (191-215). In each of these cases, the idea of brokenness, of the fragmentary, imparts a colour to our imaginative response which extends beyond the locality of the verbal surface.

A similar effect is visible on the actantial level. Without playing too much on the etymological contiguity between "gap" and "gape" it is worth at least reminding ourselves that — from the empty eye-sockets of Walpole's skeletal Hermit;[11] through Radcliffe's Schedoni to Lewis's Monk, Ambrosio; to the "yellow, watery, but speculative eyes" of Frankenstein's monster (9), and the physiognomy of Melmoth the Wanderer himself — the gape does imply a type of psychic space which had been little explored in English literary tradition before the Gothic revival. In fact, these novels raise the topic of psychic space itself in a new way: the eyes signifying a terrible unfathomableness and blankness akin to the "fixed stare" of the hypnotized patient as examined from the quasi-mystical perspectives of Mesmer and respectabilized as a subject for scientific investigation by Braid in the following century.[12]

The concern of the Age with mesmerism and trance was, on another level, little more that the tip of that wider interest in dream and the subconscious which was to contribute so much to the development of psychology. Strikingly, the actants of these novels engage so prominently in waking dreams or nightmares that their state of mind appears to become part of the action of the texts themselves. Victor Frankenstein begins to question the boundaries between his life and dream (178). He implicates us in his nightmares (58, 184). He loses himself in reverie (172). He communes with his lost loved ones through the medium of sleep (204). In his last hours, Melmoth the Wanderer climactically (though disappointingly) dreams of falling down a precipice (539), and in this way supplies us with the imaginative surrogate for an event that

9. Mary Shelley, *Frankenstein, or The Modern Prometheus* (1818), ed. M.K. Joseph, Oxford and New York, 1980, 94, 155, 148.

10. Charles Maturin, *Melmoth the Wanderer* (1820), ed. Douglas Grant, Oxford and New York, 1989, 9, 52.

11. *The Castle of Otranto*, 102.

12. Thomas H. Leahey, *A History of Psychology: Main Currents in Psychological Thought*, Englewood Cliffs: NJ, 1980, 158.

we are not able to witness due to his absence at the end of the novel. So, too, in the same work, Monçada the Spaniard is forced — in collaboration with the reader — to listen to the nightmares of the parricide with whom, in the subterraneous darkness, he is attempting his escape from the monastery in which he has been confined. "Emotions are my events", says the parricide to Monçada (199-202, 204), and it seems that on this level the gapped structures of dreams and altered states of consciousness are a substitute for action itself, deferring the actantial to the indicial and consequently redefining the role of psychology as a functional element in the structure of the narrative.

It is, however, on the sequential level that gapping most obviously presences itself as a feature of the Gothic texture. Maturin's sustained and deliberate text slowly ensnares us in the illusion of fragmentariness, so that we find ourselves at the heart of the novel in the tale of Guzman's family — which is an interruption in "The Tale of the Indians", found in the manuscript of a Jew in hiding within a secret place at the centre of a larger hiding place — in a tale told to John Melmoth (who has just been reading a similar manuscript) by the shipwrecked Monçada (399 ff.). The two main "manuscripts" themselves carry a great deal of the narrative weight of the novel, but characteristically they both break or become illegible at the most important points, so that the convolutedness and incoherence of the whole become a part of the deliberate design.

Mary Shelley was less devious than this, her *Preface* to *Frankenstein* maintaining the barrier between fiction and reality. But even so, she presented her material in an epistolary form, distancing her reader from her material through self-embedded letters. Hence the monster, at the centre of the novel, narrates his nightmares to his creator in a story told by his creator to Captain Walton, reported in a letter sent by the Captain to his sister from the unstable environs of the North pole (137).

Despite the fact that Lewis's novel is formally more conservative than the others, its intricate double plotting whirls the reader through a labyrinth of often inconsistent turns and changes, punctuated by the intrusion of ballads (a form which, Thom Gunn reminds us, takes much of its strength from its implicative lacunae).[13] No doubt some of its caveats result from the fact that its author (like the author of *Frankenstein*) was adolescent, writing — as even the fair copy of the manuscript reveals — in some haste and (unlike Mary Shelley) without

---

13. Thom Gunn, "Hardy and the Ballads", *Agenda*, 10 (1972), 19-46.

adequate revision.[14] But nonetheless, the effect of the book is fractured and disorientating: contrasting strongly with other works written at a comparable speed such as, say, Ben Jonson's tightly structured *Volpone* from an earlier century, or Samuel Johnson's *Rasselas* from his own.

Walpole, on the other hand, was more consciously disjunctive. He was, after all, an antiquarian, actively promoting and publicizing his interests in the arts of the Gothic Middle Ages. Accordingly, he was also a passionate reader of manuscripts which by definition were often fragmentary at the time of reception. Because of his unashamed dilettantism in the subject, he tended to use such sources as imaginative springboards for a dreaming of the past rather than for any more systematic project. It is a tendency which can also be seen in his collection of architectural ornaments and fragments from the same period, which were arranged around his Gothic home at Strawberry Hill to create a maximum of impact, but with almost no regard for their original structural function.

Hence it is hardly surprising that, as well as sporting a hopelessly convoluted plot full of rapid transitions, *The Castle of Otranto* should have been foisted on its audience as the translation of an anonymous Italian work, printed in Gothic black letter at Naples in 1529 and discovered at a Catholic home in the north of England. Such a provenance was all, of course, a fabrication on Walpole's part, yet it ensured that before having read a word of the story, the reader had been disorientated by the implied distances of transmission between an original (non-existent) manuscript, the printed (non-existent) book, a (non-existent) act of translation and stylistic smoothing, and the final artifact.[15]

Outside the text itself, in other words, the Gothic novel (like the artificial ruins of the same period), already gestured towards the aesthetics of incompleteness and imperfection. Nor does it seem — on this level — merely coincidental that two of these works were actually inspired by dreams. Walpole, in a celebrated letter of 9 March 1765, reports:

> I waked one morning in the beginning of last June from a dream, of which all I could recover was, that I thought myself in an ancient castle (a very natural dream for a head filled like mine

---

14. MS Townshend, ix [Matthew Lewis. "The Monk"]. MS housed at the Wisbech and Fenland Museum, Wisbech, Cambridgeshire. Louis F. Peck, *A Life of Matthew G. Lewis*, Cambridge: Mass., 1961, 39, 213.

15. *The Castle of Otranto*, 3-6.

with Gothic story) and that on the uppermost bannister of a great staircase I saw a gigantic hand in armour. In the evening I sat down and began to write, without knowing in the least what I wanted to say or relate.[16]

And Mary Shelley, in her 1831 *Preface to Frankenstein*, describes how the main idea of her tale came to her in a late-night "reverie", which she worked into a story in hope that it would "frighten my reader as I myself had been frightened that night!" (10). It was a task for which she was well prepared. We know from her *Journals* that from 1814-16 she was already reading Chatterton's *Works* as well as Richardson's *Clarissa* (1747-48) — with its masterful control of epistolary form, its games with the psychology of perception, its concealment of the novel's central rape scene in the gap between letters, and its enactment of Clarissa's mental agony through a sequence of "torn" notes and papers.[17] At the same time she was immersing herself in the Gothic influences of Byron, Coleridge, Lewis, and early Maturin; and we could add that on the 9th, 22nd, and 23rd January 1817 — when she was well into the writing of *Frankenstein* — she was developing her knowledge of ancient dream theory by reading Macrobius's *Somnium Scipionis*.[18] In themselves, dreams — with their natural condensation, displacement, and re-dramatization of materials — tend anyway to fall into fragmented, discontinuous forms.[19] But what is interesting for us about the novelists' accounts of the creation of their works is that, in both cases, they seem to pander to the possibilities offered by the oneiric mode. Walpole writes on, unaware of what he is to say next, while Mary Shelley concentrates on the affective qualities of her tale. The first rends the newly established mores of novelistic verisimilitude through the density and number of his dream-based intrusions; the second coolly plays out a dream form through the intensified and disjunct moments afforded by the epistolary medium.

---

16. Quoted in Mario Praz, "Introductory Essay", in *Three Gothic Novels*, ed. P. Fairclough, Penguin, 1983, 17.

17. Samuel Richardson, *Clarissa, or the History of a Young Lady* (1747-48), ed. Angus Ross, Penguin, 1985, 890-93.

18. *The Journals of Mary Shelley: 1814-1844*, 2 vols, eds P. R. Feldman and D. Scott-Kilvert, Oxford, 1987, II, 641-42, 669-70.

19. Sigmund Freud, *On Dreams* (1901), ed. Ernest Jones, trans. James Strachey, London, 1952, 26.

If, then, these devices — the fragment, manuscript, letter, ruin, dream — are badges of Gothic from Walpole to Borges, it is worth pausing to consider their meaning in more detail. Where do they stand, for instance, in relation to the literature of the generation preceding Walpole's? What is it about this inherently gapped structure that appealed to the Gothic writer?

At the risk of oversimplifying, an answer to the first question might be to see these features as both a reaction to, and an extension of, the gesture of Augustan certainty. By this, I do not mean that the Augustans were any less uncertain than any other generation, but rather that their art tended to embody the clearly defined — and often obsessively symmetrical — results of adherence to prescriptive rules based on a desire for completeness which, even then, could not be easily grounded in a coherent philosophy. Hence Ralph Allen, Postmaster General (and model for Fielding's Squire Allworthy in Tom Jones), liked to reside in his neo-classical house at Prior Park, Widecombe, near Bath: a beautifully symmetrical home complete with a Palladian Bridge.[20] It was ordered by modular proportions, and these in turn were for the most part based on the simple integral number relationships which — from the time of Augustus to Palladio — had been thought to reflect the harmonic construction of the real known universe. Since, however, the discoveries of Kepler and Newton, the absolute correctness of such numbers for describing the universe had been called into question so that, instead of acting as metonyms of religiously inscribed truth, these proportions could only act for Allen on a pragmatic level as metonyms of political power.

It was to Prior Park that Pope — himself an enthusiast of neo-Palladian architecture — liked to come. And we may feel a certain affinity between the pattern sense informing the aesthetics of neo-Palladianism and that informing the logical balance and precision of the heroic couplet, especially when we remember how, in the *Epistle to Burlington*, Pope had adapted Inigo Jones's own annotations from Palladio's *Quattro libri*, smoothing them into couplet form.[21] Nor is it entirely unexpected that Fielding (staying, interestingly enough, in the Gothic Lodge at Prior Park), should have let the setting inspire him in the writing of *Tom Jones*, with its comic epic form, its neat symmetrical division into eighteen books arranged into three parts, its actions

---

20. Benjamin Boyce, *The Benevolent Man: A Life of Ralph Allen of Bath*, Cambridge: Mass., 1967.

21. Avril Henry and Peter Dixon, "Pope and the Architects: A Note on the *Epistle to Burlington*", *English Studies*, 51 (1970), 437-41.

balancing one another in a carefully ordered eurhythmy which slides into a whole.[22] The point may perhaps be best summed up by a slightly later, but equally telling, example of the paradigm I am invoking: George Stubbs's painting, "Labourers" (1779), where the artfully triangulated group of countryfolk in the foreground was originally balanced in the distance by a symmetrical and pedimented façade which the succeeding Age saw fit to paint over.

An outcome of the Augustan emphasis on product rather than process was that it tended to create works which resonated within their own sureties, rather than outwardly. Correspondingly, as the century progressed, there grew an increasing need to confront the uncertainties that they failed to address. Although, then, in *The Dunciad*, Pope does throw an opponent down an abyss,[23] his most significant poetic utterance on the topic is in the *Essay on Man*, where he envisages Nature teaching people to command the fire, control the flood, or "Draw forth the monsters of th'abyss profound" (*Epistle* III, 221). Likewise we may feel — despite the felicities — a certain tameness in the manner by which, in the 1714 version of *The Rape of the Lock*, he systematically lines up the resonances of his Rosicrucian apparatus to complement even the esoteric meanings of the cards played in Belinda's fateful game of ombre.[24]

Such a working out — indeed, such a tradition of working out — is not, of course, static. There is no end to the possibilities of refinement offered by modular proportion and symmetric form, although it should be added that the very act of refinement changes the implication of the work as a formal statement. Where the system is extended to play in upon itself — as happens in Piranesi's drawings for the *Carceri* (which arose out of his neoclassical concerns) — we enter a nightmarish and labyrinthine world of closed spaces where ungapped logic begins to question itself and the failure to see the meaning of the pattern opens the perceiver to frustration, even to despair. A similar effect is perceivable in Borges's ladder, which offers the security of the predictable only in order to avail us of a richer perception of the unimaginable.

---

22. See Aurélien Digeon, *The Novels of Fielding* (1923), New York, 1970, 172-75; Dorothy Van Ghent, *The English Novel: Form and Function*, New York, 1961, 72.

23. Alexander Pope, *The Poems of Alexander Pope. A One-Volume Edition of the Twickenham Text with Selected Annotations*, ed. John Butt, London, 1963, bk. II, ll. 288.

24. Anthony Johnson, "Om litteratur och tarok", *Finsk Tidskrift*, forthcoming.

Yet equally Piranesian — and equally part of the neoclassical aesthetic of Alberti, Palladio, Jones, and other practitioners of the Vitruvian aesthetic — is the antiquarian interest which concerned itself with ruins. As an aesthetic move it is quite comprehensible that the imaginative reconstruction of the "rules" of ancient architecture should entail a re-evaluation of the remains themselves. Inigo Jones's attempts to reconcile Stonehenge to the requirements of Vitruvian form stand as a testimony of the lengths to which intelligent minds were to go in their over-orchestrated recreation of the harmonies suggested by the classical world.[25] What is interesting for our purposes, however, is the ambivalence that this concern with ruins displayed when it was consciously extended beyond the classical period.

For the most part the manuscripts of the Gothic Middle Ages were not designed to be fragmentary. Similarly, much of the architecture of the period, far from being dark, gloomy, or formless, was based upon a careful rationale of space and light.[26] It was, in fact, mainly after the dissolution that English ecclesiastical buildings were ransacked or left to deteriorate. But the extent of the devastation was such that by the early eighteenth century, no one was far from genuine Gothic ruins, standing as gaunt reminders of the outlawed Catholic culture (a phenomenon, no doubt, which had much to do with the proliferation of the Gothic revival in the Protestant north). In this light it is understandable that ruins should have become included in the developing picturesque sensibility of the time.

Yet it is not so clear why the absence of ruins in some sites should have precipitated the construction of artificial ones. Or why, to put it another way, a country which had a sufficiency of authentic emblems of its past should feel it necessary to re-dream — or, more literally, to re-fabricate — its own history. Plainly the impulse was, at times, similar to that which had led to Chatterton's poetic forgeries (which were only condemned by Walpole, we may note, because the young poet refused, in the face of exposure, to preserve decorum by claiming them as his own). Perhaps, too, as may be seen from contemporary accounts of the period, there was a sense in which the deliberate creation of a particular type of gapped structure could satisfy the Augustan obsession with logical form, affording an opportunity for filling the absences with harmonic

---

25. John Webb, *The Most Notable Antiquity of Great Britain Vulgarly Called Stone-Heng of Salisbury Plain. Restored by Inigo Jones* ...., London, 1655.

26. Nikolaus Pevsner, *An Outline of European Architecture*, Penguin, 1983, 90-91.

solutions which were not possible in natural ruins. This might be one reason why William Gilpin writes of constructing artificial ruins on "as regular, and uniform a plan, as if it had been a real edifice", or that "the several parts should be so traced out, that an eye, skilled in such edifices, may easily investigate the parts, which are lost from the parts which remain".[27] And it would correspond with the use of the manuscript fragment in works of the "explained Gothic" such as Clara Reeve's *The Old English Baron* of 1777 (itself an avowed imitation of *The Castle of Otranto*),[28] where the textual breaks merely serve to hasten on the narrative line without any particular loss of plot material, involving the reader in the imaginative reconstruction of the events themselves and adding (especially through the "editorial" comments about the state of the manuscript) a patina of antiquity to the effect of the whole.

But there is also a deeper effect caused by a contrasting tendency in the ruin itself: that its failure to satisfy a functional meaning endows the perceiver with a sort of overplus of responses which, lacking any logical resolution, grounds itself in emotional vagaries of wistfulness and loss (though it is none the less powerful for that). What were these buildings? Who were its makers? *Ubi sunt qui ante nos fuerunt?* The reaction is common to works as diverse as the Anglo-Saxon poem of "The Ruin", Colonna's Vitruvian romance, the *Hypnerotomachia Poliphili* (1499), or Poggio's description of the ruins of Rome in the early sixteenth century[29] — although it is telling that all three of these confront the lacunae left by the dismembered rationality of Roman constructions. And the sentiment finds a parallel in the "kind of religious melancholy" that writers such as Arthur Young were consciously seeking in eighteenth-century ruins.[30] In a way, then, it seems as though the ruin, disregarding the functional needs of dwelling, throws us back onto the contemplation of Being itself.[31] Its purpose becomes the creation of a space for thought. This, too, would seem to be the effect of Maturin's most finely conceived manuscript gappings: whether in the novel's first

---

27. James Macaulay, *The Gothic Revival 1745-1845*, Glasgow and London, 1975, 19.

28. Clara Reeve, *The Old English Baron: A Gothic Story* (1777), ed. James Trainer, Oxford, 1977.

29. Peter Murray, *The Architecture of the Italian Renaissance*, London, 1981, 10.

30. See Macaulay, 18.

31. Martin Heidegger, *Being and Time* (1927), trans. J. Macquarrie and E. Robinson, Oxford, 1985, 146-48.

negative climax, where Stanton, "plunged in the lowest abyss of human calamity" is visited, in a lunatic asylum, by Melmoth, whose unspeakable condition for his victim's liberation is obscured by multiple fragmentation of the manuscript; or even in its tenderer moments, when the foredoomed courtship of John Sandal and Elinor in a picturesque setting beneath the towers and pinnacles of a great castle is sealed by the eloquence of their silence and a sympathetic breach in the text (45, 58, 467).

If ruins and manuscript fragments could act in this manner as stimuli for the free play of the conscious imagination, then dreams provide an obvious functional correlate from the subconscious. Dreams, as we have noted, occupy an important role within the texts and even in their genesis (possibly influencing their structures accordingly). What is worth stressing here, from a higher perspective, is that in conjunction with the renewed exploration of the psyche initiated by Mesmer and others, mid-eighteenth-century society appeared to be undergoing a constitutive change in its attitude to dreaming. After the Gothic Middle Ages with, paradoxically enough, its own rationale of oneiric interpretation, writers of the late Renaissance, such as Descartes and Kepler, had extended the dream-vision as a vehicle for the propagation of philosophical and scientific ideas which might not otherwise gain social acceptance; and it was this largely rationalistic tradition which was the inheritance of the Augustans. Pope, predictably, serves us explicable dreams in *The Rape of the Lock*. Addison, in his essay on the subject for *The Spectator* (18 September 1712), plays down its darker side (though he does not ignore it altogether) in his attempt to demonstrate how dreams may give us some idea of the excellency of the human soul as well as some intimations as to its dependency on matter. And Smollett, in the opening chapter of *Roderick Random* (1748), presents us with a dream which offers a neat, transparent and instantly explicated emblem of the journeys his hero is to undergo during the course of the novel.[32] What a contrast to the tormented sleeps and nameless dreams of Walpole's, Lewis's, Mary Shelley's, or Maturin's characters. What a contrast is Addison to Monboddo, who attempted, from the 1770s onwards, to demonstrate through dream that the mind is not tied in any way to the body.[33] And what a contrast (to take an example from another sphere) is the "The Nightmare" of Fuseli — one of Mary Shelley's mother's former lovers[34]

---

32. Tobias Smollett, *Roderick Random* (1748), ed. John Barth, New York, 1964, 21.

33. John Grant, *Dreamers: A Geography of Dreamland*, London, 1986, 33-35.

34. Jane Dunn, *Moon in Eclipse: A Life of Mary Shelley*, London, 1978, 8.

— when it is set against art works of the English academicians from the first half of the century. It is as if, on every front, a new sense of interiority was being moulded: and it was one which knew no bounds.

So far, then, we have seen how the particular propriety of gapping was inextricably related to a confluence of socio-historical factors — the cult of the textual fragment, the cult of the ruin, the reappraisal of the value of dream — which manifested themselves with a particular intensity in the years of the mid-eighteenth century. But in so far as they presence themselves structurally or thematically in the novels of the period they are of course little more than symptoms of something (literally) much deeper; and something which gives a curious coherence to the nexus of elements we have been considering: namely, the chasmic or abyssal gap which yawns inchoately from its earliest etymology.

That the concept of the abyss should collocate with the teachings of the Catholic masters of the Gothic Middle Ages is not in itself startling. After all, Catholic contemplation knew the category of *vacatio* — the deliberate meditative emptying of self — and its greatest exponents were the practitioners of the *via negativa*. So, for Meister Eckhart, one has to "penetrate to the abyss of the self",[35] leaving individuality behind in a sinking "from nothingness to nothingness" in the underlying divinity of the soul if one wishes to know the soul itself.[36] So, for John Ruysbroeck, a condition of the spirit coming to God is that it must lose itself in a "Waylessness and in a Darkness, in which all contemplative men wander in fruition and wherein they never again can find themselves in a creaturely way. In the abyss of this darkness, in which the loving spirit has died to itself, there begin the manifestation of God and eternal life".[37] (We could look back further into Origen and Augustine if we wished to find other examples.) For true Gothic theology has the ability to make positivity of negation, to make of the "abysmal Waylessness" a "Divine fruition in the abyss of the Ineffable".[38]

Such concepts appear in the writings of the Christian Alchemists — as we may recall from the declaration in "The All-Wise Doorkeeper" that as we strive to think of God, "we plunge into the Abyss of Silence,

---

35. F.C. Happold, *Mysticism: A Study and an Anthology*, Penguin, 1990, 270.

36. *Ibid.*, 274.

37. *Ibid.*, 290-91.

38. *Ibid.*, 293.

of infinite Glory"[39] — and apart from their monastic flavour, there is no reason why they should not have grounded themselves in Protestant thought either. Certainly, Bunyan, in the mid-seventeenth century, characterizes Christ himself through a dream vision as the "gap" whereby the Christian may reach the church.[40] But a century later — to the mind of the Gothic revivalist such as Walpole, with his aversion to "the foul monkhood";[41] to Lewis, with his deep scepticism of Catholic ritual (evidenced by *The Monk* itself); or to Maturin, whose forbears had suffered active persecution at the hands of the Catholics[42] — such speculations could only lead to the abysm of ignorance and self-delusion. Re-contextualized in the morally fragmented world of Gothic romance, the gap itself tends to become a trivializing emblem of error separated, ironically enough, from its theological ground and losing much through the corresponding reduction in its connotative power.

This helps us comprehend more clearly the weaknesses in the double climax to *The Monk*, which involves, literally, a descent into the abyss at the same time as it exposes the sham mystification underlying Catholicism in the novel. It begins when Lorenzo touches St Clare's Sepulchre (ignoring the superstition that he will die if he does so). He discovers it to be of coloured wood — rather than, as it appears, of stone — with a knob which he turns, to a clanking of chains, revealing a hollow beneath the pedestal:

> A deep abyss now presented itself before them, whose thick obscurity the eye strove in vain to pierce. The rays of the Lamp were too feeble to be of much assistance. Nothing was discernible, save a flight of rough unshapen steps, which sank into the yawning Gulph, and were soon lost in darkness.[43]

The descent is like "walking down the side of a precipice": Lorenzo is obliged to proceed with great caution "lest he should miss the steps, and fall into the Gulph below him" (368). And at their foot he finds the

---

39. Anon., "The All-Wise Doorkeeper", in *"Concerning the Secrets of Alchemy" and Other Tracts from the Hermetic Museum* (1625), Llanerch, 1969, 228.

40. John Bunyan, *Grace Abounding and The Life and Death of Mr. Badman* (1666/ 1680), ed. G.B. Harrison, London and New York, 1953, 21.

41. Austin Dobson, *Horace Walpole: A Memoir* (1890), London, 1910, 42.

42. Niilo Idman, *Charles Robert Maturin: His Life and Works*, Helsinki, 1923, 4-5.

43. *The Monk*, 367.

clearest evidence of the Domina's deepest infamy: the emaciated Agnes de Medina (long since supposed dead) clutching the putrescent body of her child; beside her a rosary, before her a crucifix (369). But this is not all. Having freed the victim he and Don Ramirez "penetrate into the further vaults" (376). There they complete their exposure of Catholic corruption by discovering Antonia — recently raped and stabbed by Ambrosio — and she dies in Lorenzo's arms as Don Ramirez apprehends the Monk himself (393).

The limit to the vault is thus a "bottoming out" to the abyss of uncertainty in the novel itself: the shallow exposure of a trickery by male and female Catholic figureheads which differs little in effect from the "explained Gothic" of Radcliffe and Reeve. For here — after an initial, fruitful ambiguity — Ambrosio's accomplice, Matilda, turns out to be a succubus rather than a human being. And Ambrosio, at the end of the novel, is dropped down a precipice by a real demon. In this sense the novel grounds itself in eschatological "certainties" which align it with the theatrical worlds of Marlowe's *Faustus* and the medieval Mystery tradition. Nor should we forget that spirits such as Matilda technically had no place in Protestant theology. Lewis has affirmed the iconography of the very faith he aimed to debunk, and the result is twofold. On one hand he flattens the resonance and subtlety of the novel through the limited view of the Catholicism he seeks to employ. On the other, he shirks the glowering epistemological consequence that a rejection of the Catholic machinery would have entailed.

> *Above all, let me fearlessly descend*
> *into the remotest caverns of my mind*
> *carry the torch of self-knowledge*
> *into its deepest recesses.*[44]

What happens if you don't "bottom out"? Edward Young — battling with the problems of factionalized Christianity, paganism and atheism in the 1740s — had already begun to see the problem, articulating it most clearly in his consideration of those who reject the significance of the crucifixion:

> Draw the dire steel — ah, no! the dreadful blessing
> What heart or can sustain or dares forego?
> There hangs all hope: that nail supports
> The falling universe: that gone, we drop;

---

44. *The Journals of Mary Shelley: 1814-1844*, entry for 25 February 1822.

Horror receives us ....[45]

Without a theology the possibility of a new and more terrifying abysm had manifested itself. For where there was no ground, either for good or for evil, there loomed an endlessness which was seemingly void of meaning. Saint Augustine appears to have teetered on the brink of this realization in his assertion that one should not look for an efficient cause of the evil will, since it is not efficient but deficient, as the will itself is not an effecting of something but a defect (although he extricated himself from the implications of his observation by special plea: "Let no one, then, seek to know from me what I know I do not know, unless he perhaps wishes to be ignorant of that of which all we know is, that it cannot be known"[46]). More mundanely, we find a reflection of Young's crisis in Samuel Johnson's dread of nothingness. And though the novels of Walpole, Lewis, and Maturin (not to mention those of Radcliffe or Reeve) significantly resolve into the lemmas of traditional morality and theology, there are hints, elsewhere, of a movement towards less complacent rationalizations.

In the cancelled ending to *Caleb Williams* (1794), for example, Mary Shelley's father, William Godwin, toyed with the possibility of his narrator failing to expose the villainies of Falkland and languishing beneath the continued wrath of the English legal system. "I should like to recollect something", writes Caleb from his prison cell, "... but it is all a BLANK! — Sometimes it is day and sometimes it is night — but nobody does anything and nobody says anything."[47] He cannot even find a respite in sleep:

> I have dreams — they are strange dreams — I never know what they are about — No, not while I am dreaming — they are about nothing at all — and yet there is one thing first, and then another thing, and there is so much of them, and it is all nothing — when I am awake it is just the same (334).

Godwin was dissatisfied with his original ending, feeling, perhaps, that the implicit nihilism of Caleb's outlook (as he dwindles in the final lines

---

45. Edward Young, *Young's Night Thoughts* (1742), ed. George Gilfillan, Edinburgh, 1853, Bk. IV, ll. 172-76.

46. Augustine of Hippo, *The City of God* (c. 413-26), trans. M. Dods, New York, 1950, 387.

47. William Godwin, *Caleb Williams* (1794), ed. David McCracken, London, 1970, 333.

to a living tombstone) was at odds with the aesthetics of closure. For whatever reason, he softened the final vision, damning Falkland at the same time as he exculpated Caleb — granting the latter the grace and clarity of mind to present his narrative to the world, at last, as the true and unmangled version of the events it described (326).

His daughter, on the other hand, did not back down. In *Frankenstein* she unblinkingly envisioned a creature whose adult mind was without memory, who was without race or family, and who could conceive of his past life as nothing more than "a blot, a blind vacancy in which I distinguished nothing" (121). It is a Godless vision, and it may well be significant that in the novel Christian theology gives way to alchemical science, in which descent — through the putrefaction of body and mind — into the abyss of the *prima materia* leads to a reconstitution of being which is clearly paralleled in the monster's creation.[48] Here, in the monster's despair, we see reflected the then unacceptable face of a philosophy towards which the eighteenth-century strategists of gapping were unwittingly reaching. It resounds over subsequent decades in the meaningless roar of Poe's "A Descent into the Maelström". It clarifies itself in his story of "The Masque of the Red Death", where the mysterious figure bringing death to a castle in time of plague is climactically unmasked, revealing the spectre of nothingness — pure absence — beneath the clothes.[49] And it becomes explicit in Nietzsche's description of the abyss of the Will to Power which — like Lacanian desire — is literally groundless ("Abgrund"), undermining the whole order of essences, revealing caves behind other caves, "an abysmally deep ground behind every ground, under every attempt to furnish 'grounds'" (*Beyond Good and Evil* § 289).[50] For when it is realized that Being — the only presence on which we can ground meaning — is, itself, "the Abyss of meaninglessness",[51] then we have little left other than the choice between a tentative affirmation of the provisional, or an acceptance of the unfillable gap: that horrific void which opens at the centre of *Heart of Darkness* and which glimmers behind the unimaginable worlds of Borges.

---

48. *Frankenstein*, 38-42, 47-49, 54; and Johannes Fabricius, *Alchemy: The Medieval Alchemists and their Royal Art*, Wellingborough, 1989, 20-21.

49. Edgar Allan Poe, *The Fall of the House of Usher and Other Tales*, ed. R.P. Blackmur, New York, 1960, 152.

50. Alphonso Lingis, "The Will to Power", in *The New Nietzsche*, ed. D.B. Allison, Cambridge: Mass. and London, 1988, 38.

51. Martin Heidegger, "Building Dwelling Thinking" (1954), in *Poetry, Language, Thought*, trans. A. Hofstadter, New York, 1971, 143-61.

OSSIAN, BLAKE AND THE QUESTIONABLE SOURCE

DAVID PUNTER

I first wrote on the issue of Blake and James Macpherson's "Ossian" poems in 1982 in an article called "Blake: Social Relations of Poetic Form".[1] The arguments of that essay are still relevant to our present concerns, and this, incidentally, has proved an interestingly problematic process, because I could not decide whether I was writing this paper in the past or present tense; but precisely this problem of the complexity of writerly and psychic time is one to which I shall return.

My argument develops in four stages: first, through some further attention to the Ossian poetry; second, by considering Blake in relation to Ossian; third, by thinking a little about the whole issue of the "questionable source" in Gothic; and finally by trying to develop, very briefly, an argument about the problem of literary sources. I hope the implied connections in my title will become obvious. They are twofold: first, how are we to treat the relationship between Blake and the Ossian poetry; but second, and to my mind more important, what are we to make of a "source" like Macpherson, who on closer inspection turns out to be no simple source at all but rather a kind of collage, or rather an indicator of doubt which calls the whole issue of the source into question?

The essential thrust of my earlier article was about versification, and particularly about the metrical structures, norms and ideals of Blake's longer Prophetic Books, and where, if anywhere, we might find models for them. This is a question which has been elided in Blake criticism with other arguments which belong to different realms. For example, critics of Blake who are obsessed with the parallels between Blake and Milton — immense as these are — incline to ignore the obvious fact that

---

1. David Punter, "Blake: Social Relations of Poetic Form", *New Literary History*, 18 (1982), 182-205.

metrically Blake and Milton have nothing in common whatever.[2] Blake,
throughout the works he considered as major, uses an essentially
septenary line; rhymeless like much of Milton but otherwise rigidly
eschewing the pentameter which is the ground of poetry in English.

That septenary, as Blake uses it, is of course a metrical ideal and he
varies upwards and downwards — for example, *The French Revolution*
is written mostly in eight-foot lines — but the question nevertheless arises
as to where we can find a poetry in English with a central septenary
structure; rhymeless; highly rhetorical and thus frequently variable in
length and stress; and organized largely according to the dictates of the
verse paragraph. My major answer was Ossian, by which of course I
mean the English purported translations, published by Macpherson. In
my article I provided several examples of similarity; here is an example
from Blake's *America*:

> Solemn heave the Atlantic waves between the gloomy nations,
> Swelling, belching from its deeps red clouds & raging Fires!
> Albion is sick! America faints! enrag'd the Zenith grew.
> As human blood shooting its veins all round the orbed heaven
> Red rose the clouds from the Atlantic in vast wheels of
>   blood
> And in the red clouds rose a Wonder o'er the Atlantic sea;
> Intense! naked! a Human fire fierce glowing, as the wedge
> Of iron heated in the furnace; his terrible limbs were fire
> With myriads of cloudy terrors banners dark & towers
> Surrounded; heat but not light went thro' the murky
>   atmosphere[3]

And this is from the First Duan of Macpherson's *Cath-loda* (the line
arrangement is my own):

> U-thorno, that risest in waters! on whose side are the
>   meteors of the night!
> I behold the dark moon descending, behind thy resounding
>   woods.
> On thy top dwells the misty Loda: the house of the spirits
>   of men!
> In the end of his cloudy hall bends forward Cruth-loda of

---

2. See, for example, J. Middleton Murry, *William Blake*, London, 1933, and
Mark Schorer, *William Blake: The Politics of Vision*, New York, 1946.

3. William Blake, *The Poetry and Prose of William Blake*, ed. D.V. Erdman,
New York, 1965, 51-52.

swords.
His form is dimly seen, amid his wavy mist.
His right hand is on his shield. In his left is the half-
   viewless shell.
The roof of his dreadful hall is marked with nightly fires![4]

In pursuing this argument, I wanted to proceed to a further stage and discuss what might be called the "ideology of metre". In other words, it would be perfectly simple to talk about a general ideological connection between Macpherson and Blake, and the crucial term would be to do with national liberation, the overturning of what Blake refers to as "the sleep of Albion". But I was more interested in the specific rejection of the pentameter, with all the regularity, order, convention this stood for: above all, the association of the pentameter, through the heroic couplet, with the form of eighteenth-century English cultural domination from which both Macpherson and Blake were trying to assert difference on what might be called, simplifying radically, national and class grounds respectively.

This "ideology of metre" seemed important also in another sense, because the attempt in both Blake and the Ossian poetry is to restrict the sphere of "poeticization", and to give over the control of voice to a form of rhetoric. In many of the examples which I quoted, as in much of the poetry generally, this is a martial rhetoric; and thus the irregularity of metre, the insistence on the rambling verse paragraph at the expense of the neatly honed couplet, figures as an implicit call to arms, as a series of re-enactments of the heat of battle, as a way of infusing a specific and bloody past into the drawing-rooms of London and Edinburgh.

Central to my argument was, and is, that a great deal of Blake's poetry can be considered as Gothic in important respects, and, further, that in Blake we see a very clear choice as to what type of Gothic interests him. When writing of Gothic fiction, it is very tempting to begin with *The Castle of Otranto*; but this implicitly means that one is beginning with a notion of medievalism. Never mind whether Walpole, or other Gothic novelists, got the Middle Ages right, in any respect at all; the essential context of an assumed medieval Britain remains.

I want to refer to this form of the Gothic as the "chivalric Gothic", and I would like to claim that the immediate fount and origin of this "chivalric Gothic" (problematic as I intend later to make those terms

---

4. "Ossian", *The Poems of Ossian*, trans. James Macpherson, 2 vols, London, 1807, I, 236.

seem) is Bishop Hurd.[5] Ossian, I would suggest, represents something
quite different, something which might be called "heroic Gothic"; I
would like finally to claim — and I hope I demonstrated this in my
earlier article — that Blake made a series of choices, dubiously deliberate
but at all events reflected in at least his metrical decisions. These
privileged the "heroic Gothic", the Dark Ages, the forgotten corners of
Britain, the shadows, over the bright daylight colours, the trysts and
troubadours, the jousts and joyings, of Hurd's chivalric medievalism.

I said earlier that there were two major parallels to Blake's
versification. The other one is the ballad tradition, for of course the
septenary, written out in a different form as alternating tetrameters and
trimeters, is also a ballad staple. Perhaps you can set this alongside the
Blake and Ossian passages which I quoted above:

> O, then began the bloody fray, with bayonets and broad
>   swords champing,
> Through bones and bellies we made our way, and dying men
>   under us trampling;
> Of seven hundred Spaniards here, scarce left alive was
>   eighty,
> Velasco by his standard fell, whose deeds were counted
>   mighty.[6]

Or compare this celebrated passage of Blake:

> With what sense is it that the chicken shuns the ravenous
>   hawk?
> With what sense does the tame pigeon measure out the
>   expanse?
> With what sense does the bee form cells? have not the mouse
>   & frog
> Eyes and ears and sense of touch? yet are their habitations
> And their pursuits, as different as their forms and as their
>   joys:[7]

with

---

5. Richard Hurd, *Letters on Chivalry and Romance* (1762), ed. H. Trowbridge,
Los Angeles, 1963.

6. *Naval Songs and Ballads*, ed. C.H. Firth, London, 1908, 224.

7. *The Poetry and Prose of William Blake*, 46.

What makes the rich, without all feare,
    disdain the lowly mind?
What causes the sonne his father dere
    denye against all kind?
What causes whordome now prevayle,
    of theft so muche to raigne?
This filthy pride, for why, some steale
    their mynions to maintaine.[8]

Reduced to essentials, the point is a twofold one: first, about the way in which it is precisely rhyme which prevents these ballads from attaining to the metaphorical richness of Blake's writing, although equally it confers on them certain obvious virtues which Blake's septenary poetry often does not have — instant memorability, for one thing. Secondly about the way in which the relationship between metre and content here underscores the arguments about the ideology of metre I have been trying to make above.

Ideally I would wish to consider the role of Hugh Blair in the description and definition of the "heroic Gothic", as I understand it, but it may suffice to give one example of the difference between Hurd and Blair, the great expositor and defender of the Ossian poetry. Where Hurd cites Tasso, and does not scruple to elide his notions of medieval chivalry with writing which properly belongs to the Renaissance, Blair instead digs out a "genuine" Gothic poem, written by the Danish king Lodbrog and recalled to life by the scholar Olaus Wormius, and says of it, admiringly, that it is

> such poetry as we might expect from a barbarous nation. It breathes a most ferocious spirit. It is wild, harsh, and irregular; but at the same time animated and strong; the style, in the original, full of inversions, and, as we learn from some of Olaus's notes, highly metaphorical and figured.[9]

Blair hastens on to assert that Ossian's poetry is far superior to Lodbrog's, but this is not the main point, which is that the search for the source in Blair is clearly taking a different turn from what is apparently a similar search in Hurd and Walpole. We can put this very crudely as follows: the chivalric search of Hurd is for evidence of continuity, whereas the heroic search of Blair is for evidence of difference. This

---

8. *Old English Ballads*, ed. H.E. Rollins, Cambridge, 1920, 249.

9. *The Poems of Ossian*, I, 95.

may seem historically very bland, although I would suggest that a comparison of Walpole and Macpherson would reveal further depths to the comparison: but it is of much greater importance if we think about it in terms of cultural psychology. For both of these searches for sources, these attempts at genealogy are attempts at inspecting the basis of the contemporary society: *one* looks, however, to *underpin*, to validate through historical experience the values of civilization, while the other searches precisely for the opposite, for the evidence of barbarism which may explain how it is that the passions maintain their disruptive existence despite the veneering of civilized norms.

Thus far I have followed my previous essay, but now I would like to press on to some further thoughts about the Ossian poems. It is necessary, of course, first to allude to the complexities of their actual position; for the debate initially raised about their authenticity turned into a veritable Hydra. This debate as first mooted, concerned as it was with whether Macpherson translated them from extant, discovered originals of some antiquity, or wrote them himself — soon turned up a quite different set of problems which touched, and still touch, on the whole question of the individuality of authorship.[10] To put the conundrum at its simplest: if it could be shown that the accounts we find in Macpherson's texts had been handed down through folk tradition from distant ages, did that contribute to their authenticity, as antique poems, or their inauthenticity, in the terms which Macpherson had offered for their provenance? The paradox developed further, for what Macpherson had done, perhaps partly unwittingly, was to confront us with a question insoluble in the then current critical terms about the relationship between source and judgement: for what was supposed to be judged? The parallel with Blake is perhaps, at least, suggestive, for Blake sometimes said that his poems had been directly offered to him by divine spirits: is he therefore to be accused of infringing an Olympian Copyright Act? Perhaps this is the reason why the Chinese have never understood the notion of copyright and still, as far as I know, resist signing any such international agreements, for the relationship between manifestation and source, considered interculturally, probably has a strong metaphorical relationship to familial and generational relationships; and if your ancestors are still alive within you, what need have you of apologizing to their spirits if you speak in their tongues?

Let me return to Ossian, and take a fairly typical passage, from *Temora* (again in my line arrangement):

---

10. Bailey Saunders, *The Life and Letters of James Macpherson*, London, 1895; J.S. Smart, *James Macpherson: An Episode in Literary History*, London, 1905.

They came forth, like the streams of the desert, with the
    roar of their hundred tribes.
Conar was a rock before them: broken they rolled on every
    side.
But often they returned, and the sons of Selma fell.
The king stood, among the tombs of his warriors.
Darkly he bent his mournful face. His soul was rolled into
    itself:
and he had marked the place where he was to fall:
when Trathal came, in his strength, his brother from cloudy
    Morven.
Nor did he come alone. Colgar was at his side;
Colgar the son of the king and of white-bosomed Solin-corma.

As Trenmor, clothed with meteors, descends from the halls
    of thunder,
pouring the dark storm before him over the troubled sea:
so Colgar descended to battle and wasted the echoing field.
His father rejoiced over the hero: but an arrow came.
His tomb was raised, without a tear. The king was to revenge
    his son.
He lightened forward in battle, till Bolga yielded at her
    streams.[11]

There are obvious Blakean parallels here: the biblical "streams of the
desert", the notion of the earth rolling into itself, the image of being
"clothed with meteors", the "echoing field"; but it is not these which I
want to discuss. Rather, it is the reader-relations established in this
passage. For it seems to me crucial that what is happening here is that
the reader is being exposed to a story already told, a tale he is supposed
to know already. It is there in the phrase "the place where he was to
fall"; in the important alternation between past and present tenses, which
is designed to return us to the scene of battle but also to hint at the way
in which, for example, the descent of Trenmor is not just a simple past
action but, first, an action which is repeated every time the oft-told tale
is brought out, and second, and vestigially, an event which recurs
throughout human history in the manner of Blake's quasi-myths; it is
there in the tense structure of "The king was to revenge his son".

    Although it is true that these features could be readily paralleled in the
Greek epics and indeed in other poetry in Britain, it does still seem that
the conjunction between these sourcing devices and the uncertainty of

---

11. "Ossian", *The Poems of Ossian*, trans. James Macpherson, ed. William
Sharp, Edinburgh, 1896, 243-44.

source represented by the Ossian poetry itself forms a historically unusual conjuncture: we may go so far as to say that all constructions of national histories are based on fraud, but still be left with a wider problem of authenticity of tone.

Let me try to clarify this by contrasting Macpherson here with the Gothic in its more obvious formulations, in Radcliffe, Lewis and Maturin, for example. Essentially the key Gothic fictions are dramas of individual activity and passivity: the Gothic here is focused into a psychology and although this psychology is suggestive, instructive and cumulatively insightful, it acts as an individualized concentrator of heroism, whereas the quality of the Ossianic is as a *diffuser* of the heroic, so that it is possible immediately to characterize an age, a phase in human development, a totalizing *mise-en-scène* in which no individual survives independently but all become incarnations of a myth.[12]

I do not think I need to point out that this is what Blake does too; nor perhaps to indicate the obvious ways in which this heroic Gothic stands over against the induced forms of eighteenth-century individualism. But it is perhaps worth saying that this impulse towards the incarnating of the gods is precisely the discursive shape assigned to dream in the writings of the neo-Jungian psychoanalysts, principally James Hillman.[13] The gods, for Hillman and others, are only regarded by us as remote avatars because we come across them nightly (rather, indeed, than "knightly", which would signify the alternative form of the chivalric) and their power, their flat rejection of attribution to persons whom we know, love and hate, is frightening to us; in a reversal of the loop of time, it is thus we who relegate the gods to the remote historical and topographical depths — because it is their contemporaneity we cannot stand or understand — rather than the other way around.

And this too I think Blake knew, and I think it has to do with the various forms of the Gothic: so let me again try to take up the question of Blake and his intentions. What Blake really wanted to find in the Gothic as he understood it was an antiquity in which the whole issue of "source", in the straightforward sense of historical antecedence, could be relativized. His most obvious concern in this area was with the relationship between the history of Britain and the histories recounted in the Old Testament. It is too easy to say that, when he was constructing his scenarios of bloodshed and revolution, he was looking for biblical

---

12. David Punter, *The Literature of Terror: A History of Gothic Fictions from 1765 to the Present Day*, London, 1980, 402-27.

13. See James Hillman, *The Dream and the Underworld*, New York, 1979.

analogues to the history of his own times: rather, he was looking to evolve a form of discourse in which such notions of analogy were themselves swept away and replaced by a vision of history in which successive waves were re-perceived as mutual avatars. The connection with the topography of the unconscious as elaborated by Freud and Jung need not be laboured. What does need to be mentioned is the threat that this process, as promulgated by Blake but also as we think about it in wider theoretic terms, poses to historicism and even to the new concept, historicism, which presupposes a concept — certainly an elaborated concept, but nonetheless a unitary one — of source, such that events can still be strung along a single thread.[14] The new historicism, it seems to me, follows the logic of the clue, and thus the motif of the thread gains added resonance from the topos of Ariadne;[15] but this topos still bears the marks of its own limitations, and the labyrinth still rises to re-critique the wish-fulfilling notion of the thin clear line of success and survival. Blake's own dealings with Ariadne and the web, we may recall, were negative and fearful; a fear all the more resonant because it is conveyed through the burgeoning anxieties of Urizen, the master web-maker himself, who finds himself imprisoned by his own sticky and endless productions.

In Blake this attempt to relativize historical succession evidences an engagement with some key motifs of the Gothic, and has also to do with the suppression of "character", as he understood it. If the "source" itself is at best imperceptible and at worst a delusion, then any attempt to account for action or state of affairs in terms of individuated psychology is foredoomed, and here the most revealing figure in Blake, a figure which has been frequently misrepresented and misinterpreted, is Los. The misinterpretation has usually followed from the habits of schematization which beset students of Blake; I do not want to denigrate the efforts of those critics, Northrop Frye first and magisterially foremost among them, who have tried to provide us with a working chart of Blake's figures — while conscious that this chart-making is limited — but it still seems to me important to dwell for a moment on the most obvious and most

14. Richard Lehan, "The Theoretical Limits of the New Historicism", *New Literary History*, 21 (1990), 533-53.

15. Chris Downing, "Dionysos in Jung's Writings", in *Facing the Gods*, ed. James Hillman, Irving: Tex., 1980, 135-49.

ignored of Los's connotations; for he figures loss, and psychic loss cannot be properly figured in any system.[16]

This loss is multiple and endless; certainly it is that factor which inspires vision and which enables vision to work continually, and under the most impossible of circumstances, against the spectrous tendencies of the history of the surface; but it is also that factor which always and everywhere subverts its own likelihood of success, for Los's malleation of hard substances, his activity at the forge, is precisely connected, and not in the manner of a cause and effect, with his agonized sense of his own malleability. As part of a human typology he stands precisely for the impossibility, the threatened loss of all typology, the point at which the human characteristic as such has to recognize its ceaseless flinching under the impress of something which is stronger than itself, and in the face of which it has only two choices; to act as the agent of, or to subvert the agency of, "that which is already going on". The connection here is with the heroic Gothic, in which the limits of agency are under ceaseless questioning.

For Blake, one of the crucial critical terms which can be mobilized here is "expressionism". It is interesting, and explicable, that this is not a term which tends to be used of the literary arts, although there are two uses, both flawed but of relevance, at which we may look. The first, of course, is as a description of a kind of mainly German twentieth-century drama, of which Brecht is the best remembered but by no means the most typical exponent, and I would say that the Brechtian notion of the "gestus" represents the most important theoretic elaboration of literary expressionism.[17] The second usage occurs in recent anthologies of British poetry where writers including Ted Hughes and Sylvia Plath have been gathered together under this dubious heading.[18]

But the connection I want to make can be drawn most tightly, I think, if we are to put alongside a Blake poem like "The Smile" a painting by Edward Munch like *The Scream*. In both of these cases, we sense primarily a phased recession of individual will and its replacement by the

---

16. Northrop Frye, *Fearful Symmetry: A Study of William Blake*, Princeton: NJ, 1947; see also Morton D. Paley, *Energy and the Imagination: A Study of the Development of Blake's Thought*, Oxford, 1970.

17. Renate Benson, *German Expressionist Drama: Ernst Toller and Georg Kaiser*, New York, 1984; J.M. Ritchie, *German Expressionist Drama*, Boston: Mass., 1976; Bertold Brecht, *Brecht on Theatre*, ed. and trans. John Willett, New York, 1964, 198-201.

18. *British Poetry since 1945*, ed. Edward Lucie-Smith, Penguin, 1985, 141-66.

presence and enormous pressure of the "gestus", the gesture, the expression mustered to meet a variety of cases, the tendency towards demonstrating the persistence of the phase as emblem of the whole of the irreducible "phenomenal", despite and through the pressures of evolution and history. The gesture in this sense, the expression as such, represents a culmination of an attempt to get at the survival of the passions, and here again we see the relevance of the attempts of the Gothic to tell us that these expressions, the phenomena as it might be of the yell of terror, the scream of ambiguous recognition, the sob of relief, themselves outdate as they antedate historical shaping and comforting.

Behind all this in Blake lies a realm of sexual fear, for the condition of his "male" figures as conduits of the passions is achievable only at the cost of the exile of the feminine in the form of the "emanation", and indeed the origin and fate of this exile, considered supra-historically, *is* the narrative of the major Prophetic Books. There is an appalling mutual gender violence in Blake, usually depicted in several stages: it occurs in various forms, at its greatest condensation although not entirely typically in "The Mental Traveller", and it is hard to describe because different poems enter us upon the scene of violence at different points, but one way to put it is like this: the male divides from the female, casting the female into the outer darkness; the female grows bitter and twisted and becomes the superego, the nanny, the figure which thwarts desire in the growing male; the male, divided from his emanation, enters upon a state of lamentation and indeed figures this as the only available form of adulthood; both genders pass their lives away in the separated wilderness, while their mysteriously conceived children receive no instruction as to how to avoid this fate for the coming generation. It needs perhaps only to be added that in some of Blake's versions of this myth it is the sin of the woman which is placed foremost as she, the "Woman Old", performs her initiating violence on the young male, cutting out his heart and genitals before he can escape her; although perhaps this should be considered as in itself beneficent as it is at least a projected way of avoiding the fatal repetition of the ages. David Black's poem, "Song for a Player King", provides a recapitulation of the entire process, informed by Jungian ideas and an awareness of the "anima" dimension suffusing this arena of thought:

> What did my Mother sing to me,
> bouncing upon her sunlit knee?
> "Of all the creatures in God's mind,

fairest by far is womankind."[19]

Thus the poem begins, but we see by the end that this teaching produces nothing but rage and carnage:

Comrades, what can I do but roam
the wastes and deserts far from home,
and with my kingly rage and greed
eat out my heart, spreading my seed?

The fact that this poem ends on a question is not irrelevant to my theme.

This is all about a set of problems about nurturing, upbringing and vulnerability, which we can also find in the mainstream of the Gothic, both heroic and chivalric, and it is here, perhaps, that we can begin to see how these versions of the past, which I have been characterizing as different, join together at a common root; for of course heroism, the wish to go it alone, the need to embark on the journey, the exile, to do things one's own way, to labour at the forge or to fight the ogre despite everything, all these occur in the Gothic as manifestations of the narcissistic ego-ideal, the implicit rejection of communitarian possibilities which is, above all, Blake's agon as it is the Gothic's own. That it is also Ossian's is, again, obvious and was indeed obvious to those nationalist Scottish idealists who immediately saw in the Ossian poetry — sometimes despite their own well-founded rational doubts as to its authenticity — a route directly towards the reinstatement of a general national spirit which was radically different in kind from that which might be provided — and was, in the shape of Burns, shortly to be provided in terms of a single genius on whom the culture could vicariously, or indeed prosthetically, batten; that there might be a contradiction hidden within this projected reinstatement of a communitarian hero was indeed a bedevilling thought, but one necessarily suppressed in the urgencies of the search for national self-renewal.[20]

These reflections bring me back to the general issue of the "questionable source", a phrase which has by now, I hope, begun to reveal its duplicity of meaning: on the one hand, we have the source which can stand as an authority to which we might address our questions and which might stand towards us as parents are suppose to stand towards their children; on the other, the source which is inherently

---

19. David Black, *Gravitations*, Edinburgh, 1979, 10.

20. *James Macpherson: An Episode in Literary History*, 129-62.

suspect, which sets itself up as holding a notion of "antecedence" which is spurious, which only serves to foreshorten and forestall our interrogation of the past or, perhaps better, of the multiple flow of the present.

The Gothic is structured around this notion of the questionable source in a variety of ways. There is, for example, the motif of the lost manuscript, symbolizing ambivalence about lost authority and the vanishing of the past; if this putative manuscript were to be recovered, then indeed we might discover some secret of our "origins" but at the same time we might be laid under a parental injunction, perhaps not unlike that delivered to Hamlet, which would reduce our previously well-planned and ordered lives to ruin.

In much Gothic fiction there is a wish and a need to interrogate the parents, if only to discover who they actually are and to rid oneself of nagging fears and doubts. But the nature of acceptable evidence remains confused, especially over the question of whether the written document is to be regarded as superior or inferior to the "text of the senses", or indeed of the sensual; what, we might ask, permits the greater forgery, the birth certificate (or more frequently the written signature on the will), or the stamp of heredity on the countenance? Of course, it is relevant that the scientisms of physiognomy and phrenology were strongly alive in the heyday of Gothic, and perhaps here we might glimpse from a new angle one of Gothic's own deep secrets — that it is a mode of fiction, or perhaps better a mode of apprehension in both senses of that term, which is precisely about writing and about the validity that writing might be seen to have as constituting the most we can attain to in terms of a quasi-legal history; all this at a time of formalization of the law and of debate around the issue of a written constitution.[21] What, Gothic might be seen as asking, better enshrines the people's rights, or at least the rights of heredity which, especially in the context of the debates about primogeniture which inform so much of the writing, might be considered as ensuring every citizen's place within society: the written contract or the gestural guarantee of assurance? And what, to continue the image for a further moment, constitutes the greater threat to safety of life, limb and reputation: the betrayed gesture, or the purloined letter?

This fascination with secrets, the locked aspects of the wish to know and the wish not to know, plays itself out through Gothic like Ariadne's thread, leading us into byways of fraud and orphanage. In the labyrinths of the darkened castle we sense corridors down whose twisting length

---

21. G.S. Veitch, *The Genesis of Parliamentary Reform*, London, 1965, and R.J. White, *The Age of George III*, London, 1968, 42 ff.

questions unravel which have no beginning and no end but are bound within the eternal present of the enclosed family — the eternal return of Oedipus and Electra, the doubt otherwise imaged in Narcissus' lack of conviction when faced with an Other to rejoin whom would mean accepting the inevitability of his own death, his own return to a sphere where the breath of change is no more possible than the recognition of fixity, where the crypt would close over his head before the possibility of decrypting could become more than vestigial..

Nunneries, of course, inscribe these doubts with unparalleled richness, for Gothic writers and as seen in the "holy places" of Blake. In Gothic fiction they are places of safety and enclosure which might at any moment turn the other cheek and reveal themselves as sites of original infection, an infection which is not stopped by their athwartness to the overt genealogical line. That they are female is, of course, part of the systematic attribution of sexual disease to women which we find throughout the eighteenth and nineteenth centuries, and from which Blake is by no means exempt: the various figures of his Whore of Babylon, the feminine scarlet with blood, are precisely elements in this further "web" spread to catch women while at the same time its manipulation and even its weaving are attributed, through the cover-story of the three Fates, to women themselves.[22]

We may also see this issue of the questionable source in another way, as arising in the presentation of the sublime. For at least at one level the sublime is that quality, or perhaps better that psychic constellation, which prevents the asking of questions: human interrogation is reduced to pettiness and incivility when faced with the gigantic inexorable forces of nature. We can see this mechanism all too clearly in Coleridge and in Wordsworth when at various points they give up the world of questioning and make us aware as they claim themselves to have been made aware instead of the wildness of the external storm. We can perhaps sense a similar mechanism in John Martin's paintings: how, when reduced to thunderstruck or avalanched amazement on the sheer high precipice, can we be bothered to pursue the doubts and uncertainties about God and destiny which we might entertain and which might even obsess us under more civilized circumstances, questions in particular about our own source and destination?

And as a final thought about sources in the Gothic, we might want to return to the issue of passion. Gothic is a gallery of passions; the early theorists were in no doubt that this was its contribution to an age where

---

22. *Women in the Eighteenth Century: Constructions of Femininity*, ed. Vivien Jones, London, 1990, 61-97.

the passions were held in check, locked away themselves as secrets beneath the public rooms of the castle, the country house, or exiled in the line which was to find culmination in Dickens's variant of expressionism to the seething incomprehensibility of the city, where nothing was ever or could ever be written because the very power of the word itself was threatened by anonymity and the pressure of the nameless and the mass. But Gothic is also a constant questioning of the source of these passions, a constant placing of doubt as to whether what exists in the outer world is an adequate objective correlative for feelings, or whether feelings are in constant excess, as irony or as tragedy, over the occasions of the external.

All of this leads naturally to some closing reflections on the theory of sources. It is tempting to say that we would need to look first at a lengthy prehistory during which no such theory existed or was deemed necessary, and that only recent theoretic twists have altered this situation, but I believe that this is not so, and have brought forward the Ossian instance precisely as a way of showing that these contortions and complications are not new; and we could certainly trace them as far back as Rome and discern the shapes of the questionable source in the relations between Roman and Greek culture.[23]

However, it is certainly true that the radically renovated scepticism which we know as deconstruction has given a new inflection to the theory of sources, if only by insisting that there is no such thing as a source and that all our searches in this area are in fact motivated attempts at stopping or unpicking the seamless flow of history, although deconstruction itself, being a theory without a psychology, hazards no guesses as to why we should pursue this course of action, preferring to read it as some kind of hypostatized inevitability flowing from the persisting nature of textuality.

The notion of the source is perhaps better addressed than in classic deconstruction by Harold Bloom's developing train of reflections about the anxiety of influence, where it is quite clear that the need for a source is precisely bound up with anger and vengeance, and where we see laid out for us clearly the necessity for *surpassing* the past which paradoxically provides an "origin" for our search for the "source".[24]

---

23. Gordon Williams, *Tradition and Originality in Roman Poetry*, Oxford, 1968, 250-357.

24. Harold Bloom, *The Anxiety of Influence*, New Haven, 1973; and Harold Bloom, "The Breaking of Form", in *Deconstruction and Criticism*, eds Bloom *et al.*, London, 1979, 1-37.

The giants of the past which are the projected forms of preceding "writers" — a term which needs to be interpreted liberally to include those heroes who "inscribe" themselves on memory and the scene of action — are omnipresent in Blake as they are in the Ossian poetry, in the latter case pre-eminently in the form of "Ossian" himself, and indeed in the significantly doubled and divided relationship between Ossian and Fingal, in which the perennial dilemma of time in writing is writ large, in the sense that there is an unhealed gap in Ossian's perception which relates to his presence and yet simultaneous absence from the scene of battle, a frequently asserted physical presence inevitably accompanied by the kind of implied "absence of mind" necessary if one is to adopt the mediated, writerly or bardic role in relation to events — a problem, precisely also one of sourcing, which also inflects Los's multifarious activities as blacksmith, builder of cities, writer himself and, indeed, writer *of* himself.

This question of the "writerly scene" and of the gaps in time necessary to the process of mediation, those absences so evident in, for example, Yeats's "Long-legged Fly",[25] is one which could be explored further, and especially so since it is possible to detect in contemporary writing a renewed attention to the temporal loops which render a unilinear theory of sourcing so problematic: for example, D.M. Thomas's *The White Hotel* and its scandalous assumption of violent prefiguration, and Peter Ackroyd's more recent *Hawksmoor*, with its multiple twistings of history and personality. What all this hinges on for me — and Thomas, at least, makes this evident even if in a manner designed to stir up direst doubts — is the problem of "time in the mind" and the ways in which the time of the unconscious differs from and resists the timescale superimposed on it through the regular patrolling of the ego. At the end of the day, as it were, I suspect that the Ur-"differance" at stake in deconstruction may be precisely this discrepancy in time, which threatens to rob us of *all* assurances which might be given, through written contract or even through the apparently organic assumption of the singleness and uniqueness of a life, the adequacy of a single lifetime to a single physical presence.

Behind this lie shades of the realms inhabited during what many cultures refer to and marvel about as the "period of excarnation"; I say this not to suggest or validate mystical perceptions but rather to point to the unavoidable possibility that the reason why the notion of the "source"

---

25. W.B. Yeats, *The Poems*, ed. R.J. Finneran, London, 1983, 339.

refuses to settle down — why, one might alternatively say with Macpherson, Blair and others, antiquity resists becoming civilized — is that it always refers us to "another scene", a scene of stillness, certainty, the immoveable; which we know only as the unconscious, but with which we are perennially prevented from remaining constantly in touch. Which, then, is the absence, as we spend our lives oscillating between two planes neither of which is capable of retaining, or willing to retain, the mnemonic impress of the other?

It is these questions, I believe, which are opened up by the mysteries of the "time" of writing in Gothic and also in the Ossian poetry. Where and when was the original text? It needs perhaps to be added that this is a problem bounded by cultural psychology, or at the very least one susceptible of numerous different cultural refractions; and that, for example, the Chinese concept of existence in incarnated form, even when we think of it in terms of buildings or natural scenes rather than of the more problematic category of human life, is not the same as the Western one, and that it therefore follows that excarnation must occupy a similarly different space.[26] And behind this again, and inescapably if we are to take seriously speculations about the theory of the source, lies the whole problematic of reincarnation; although perhaps this is not to put it in the best way. For reincarnation itself, suggesting as it does no particular implications for consciousness or even for the unconscious, is not perhaps the problem; the problem is memory, and what it is that seeps through the walls between conscious and unconscious, between the linear and the non-linear, between the single life and the many lives; and these are all, it seems to me, problems of the Gothic and ones which gleam, at least fitfully, through the literary-historical complexities of Ossian and Blake and the curious bearing their relationship has on the formulation of the source which is not — at least yet — a source.

---

26. Lucien W. Pye, *The Spirit of Chinese Politics*, Cambridge: Mass., 1968, 85-163.

THE GOTHIC REVIVAL AND THE THEORY OF KNOWLEDGE IN THE FIRST PHASE OF THE ENLIGHTENMENT

MICHEL BARIDON

The title of this paper may be long but it has the merit of stating the nature of its content as clearly as a label. Had we appeared here in tie-wigs, it would have been called *A Philosophical Enquiry into the Origins of the Gothic Revival*; but we now prefer more direct methods. By Gothic revival I mean the return to, or the renewed interest in, pre-Renaissance literature and architecture as it began to develop in the eighteenth century. There are well-known examples of these new tendencies: Chatterton's pseudo-Chaucerian English; Bishop Percy's interest in folk literature; Diderot's use of medieval superstitions in *Jacques le Fataliste*, Wright of Derby's use of Gothic architecture in some of his pictures and, most famous of them all, Vanbrugh's and Horace Walpole's surprising decision in favour of the Gothic for their own houses. The mention of Strawberry Hill and of Vanbrugh Castle will help us to clarify one further point.

When we enquire into the origins of an architectural Gothic revival let it be understood that we speak of the Gothic revival in civil architecture. It is only too easy to deny that there ever was a Gothic revival, and to speak of a Gothic survival instead.[1] A clear distinction has to be made between civil and ecclesiastical architecture, since Gothic survives in ecclesiastical architecture, but is revived in a civil context. Wren restored Gothic buildings in Oxford and Cambridge, but he would never have built himself a Gothic house as Vanbrugh did as early as 1717. And Vanbrugh built Vanbrugh Castle at the same time as critics such as Addison and Hughes were reviving an interest in the literature and the manners of medieval times. It is this early interest in the Gothic

---

1. On the Gothic "survival", see Kenneth Clark's first chapter in his *Gothic Revival* (1928), London, 1974, and B. Sprague Allen, *Tides in English Taste* (1932), New York, 1969, II, 79: "Walpole's achievement was the product of historic sympathies which had continued from the days of Dugdale and Anthony à Wood in the seventeenth century."

that I would like to analyse, hoping to show that it is connected with the general evolution of ideas and with the scientific movement of the turn of the seventeenth century, the time when Locke and Newton stood like the Pillars of Hercules on the threshold of the Enlightenment.

In these decades, great changes were taking place. Among many others, there was a spectacular development of the press and of the book trade when the Licensing Act was permitted to lapse in 1695. The treaty of Ryswick made England the leader of the Protestant powers in Europe. Low-Church circles gained steadily in importance. Dryden died quite fittingly in 1700, the same year as Le Nôtre, and just as *The Way of the World*, the swan song of the Restoration comedy, was produced on the stage. *The Spectator* soon appeared as the mouthpiece of the consensual majority which supported the Revolution settlement, a majority which extended from the "presbyterians turned latitudinarians" of the Defoe type to the great Lords of the Junto whose "brains trust" met at the Kit-Cat Club. It was this majority which spread the new climate of sensibility and which launched new ideas.

As early as 1711, in *The Spectator* No. 70, Addison wrote in praise of "the old song of Chevy chase the favourite ballad of the common people of England". He argued from history to account for the beauty of the poem:

> At the time when the Poem we are now treating of was being written, the Dissentions of the Barons who were then so many petty princes ran very high and whether they quarrelled among themselves or with their neighbours they produced unspeakable calamities to the country.

This enabled him to equate the old ballads with the masterpieces of antiquity because:

> the greatest Modern Critics have laid it down as a Rule that an Heroick Poem should be founded upon some important precept of morality, adapted to the constitution of the country in which the poet writes.

This sets the anonymous author of "Chevy Chase" beside the greatest classics on the grounds that he had caught the true spirit of the feudal age. Yet Addison, while he argued from history to praise old ballads, condemned "the Gothic style of writing" for being heavy and over-ornamented. Making a female reader speak in defence of the hats then in fashion he wrote:

We make a regular figure but I defy your Mathematicks to give Name to the Form You appear in. Your Architecture is mere Gothick and betrays a worse genius than ours.[2]

In other words, Addison equated Mathematics with regularity, and the Gothic with irregularity. This is a very penetrating anticipation of Blake's famous dictum: "Grecian is mathematical form; Gothick is living form."[3] Even if Addison remained a neo-classicist at heart, as his *Cato* proved, he was ready to make room for new critical standards, among which must be noted the possibility of choosing a medieval subject (as Aaron Hill was to do with his Anglo-Saxon tragedy *Athelwold*), using poetic forms which shook the supremacy of the heroic couplet, and stating clearly the relation between mathematics and regularity at the end of the baroque period.

Another interesting rediscovery of Gothic literature implying a reappraisal of critical standards was John Hughes's *Remarks on the Faërie Queene* (his *Works* were published by Tonson in 1715) in which he made the point that Spenser's own standards were influenced by the love for "old Gothick chivalry" and by the imitation of models such as Ariosto. Hughes made another point which concerns the Gothic directly. He paid tribute to the "noble and antient kind of writing" which he connected with the East and more particularly with the Jewish prophets in whom was to be found, he said, "a Spirit of Poetry surprisingly sublime and majestic".[4]

Such remarks prove that the authority of critics like Rapin, Boileau, Racine and Le Bossu in France or Rymer and Dryden in England was now being questioned. If one argued from the historical conditions prevailing when a given work was written, there was an end to the axiomatic, a priori, mathematical method of the neo-classicists whose standards were conceived in the abstract.

The same evolution was taking place in art criticism. There is evidence of this in the letter sent by Vanbrugh to the Duchess of Marlborough to prevent the demolition of Woodstock Manor in the grounds of her new palace at Blenheim:

---

2. *The Spectator*, No. 145.

3. "On Homer's Poetry and on Virgil", in William Blake, *Complete Writings*, ed. Geoffrey Keynes, Oxford, 1969, 778.

4. John Hughes, *Works*, 6 vols, London 1715, I, xlvi.

I hope I may be forgiven, if I make some faint Application of what I say of Blenheim, to the Small Remains of ancient Woodstock Manour.

It can't indeed be said, it was Erected on so Noble nor So justifiable an Occasion, But it was rais'd by One of the Bravest and most Warlike of the English Kings; And tho' it has not been Fam'd, as a Monument of his Arms, *it has been tenderly regarded as* the Scene of his Affections. Nor amongst the *Multitude of People who come daily to see what is raising to the Memory of the Great Battle of Blenheim; Are there any that do not run eagerly to See* what Ancient Remains are to be found of Rosamonds Bower .... But if the Historical Argument Stands in need of Assistance; there is Still much to be said on Other considerations .... were the inclosure filld with Trees, (principally Fine Yews and Hollys) Promiscuously Set to grow up in a Wild Thicket. So that all the Building left, (which is only the habitable part) and the Chappel might Appear in Two Risings amongst 'em, it wou'd make One of the Most Agreable Objects that the best of Landskip Painters can invent.[5]

In English art history, this is, to my knowledge, the earliest association of the national past, the landscape garden and the poetry of Gothic ruins, an association which, as we shall see, proved exceptionally fruitful.

But there were other forces contributing to the same evolution. When the Society of Antiquaries was founded in 1719 it laid stress not so much on churches (as Dugdale had done) as on all the remains of the past, Stonehenge included. The Preface to Stukeley's *Itinerarium curiosum* (1724) is of particular interest because it stated quite clearly that antiquities must be studied "taking things in the natural order and manner they presented themselves", so that "our country" he said, should no longer "lie like a neglected province". When he spoke in defence of Dour Castle which was threatened with demolition, Stukeley said "let it stand a monument of antiquity or sink slowly by its own ruin".[6]

The same early interest in the Gothic past of the country took many different artistic forms: sometimes medieval vestiges were landscaped and turned into a picturesque object (Aislabie at Fountains Abbey), sometimes sham ruins were erected to achieve the same effect (Bathurst and Alfred's Castle), sometimes the Gothic style was copied to give distinction to

---

5. Quoted in John Dixon Hunt and Peter Willis, *The Genius of the Place*, London, 1975, 120-21.

6. William Stukeley, *Itinerarium curiosum*, London, 1724, 121.

small villas on the banks of the Thames where "cits" turned gentlemen erected battlements with money made behind the counter.

We may smile at this naive *engouement* for the Gothic, but snobs are good indicators of the popularity of a movement and the very fact that the Gothic was used in the country proves that the old style and the landscape were inseparably linked. Two fine examples could be given here. Vanbrugh's house towering over the Thames Valley at Greenwich Park and Kent's work at Rousham where he planted battlements on top of the walls while he transformed an old farm into a Gothic eye catcher, making it quite clear that it was from the country that echoes of the old Gothic past reverberated to the house.

Now that we have seen some of the major aspects of the early Gothic revival we may perhaps enquire into its causes and study its relations to the scientific movement.

The first question we are confronted with is: why did the so-called old style appear as the style which stood for the modernity of the age? The answer could be because it was a good conductor of new ideas, or because it was responsive to the questionings of artists and writers anxious to produce something new. The modernity of an age can be defined as the consciousness men have of adding new elements to what was known before. When Flaubert and Baudelaire coined the word *modernité* they were aware of the fact that nothing like the age of machines and the advent of democracy, nothing like art for art's sake, had been known before. Of course, this concept has proved very useful in our world with planes getting bigger and bigger, trains faster and faster and the colossal mushrooms of thermo-nuclear bombs looming higher and higher over the horizon. But even in the days of Vanbrugh and Pope, modernity existed under another name — think of Pope's *The Year One Thousand Seven Hundred and Thirty Eight* — and snobs brought the good news to the rest of the world. Even Boileau, while he protested that he was merely repeating what the Ancients had found long before him, was in fact conscious of the modernity of his own school. When he wrote *"Enfin Malherbe vint"*, he clearly implied that the critical standards of the Renaissance were at last superseded by sounder views. In the same way, the English gothicists of the eighteenth century could have said "At last Vanbrugh came, At last Kent came". They did in fact. We all remember Horace Walpole's famous: "Kent leapt the fence and found that all nature was a garden." But why was the modernity of the time so conscious of a mysterious reconciliation of the Gothic with the landscape? And why was the movement away from neo-classicism conducive to the Gothic revival?

A movement of this kind is so important in the history of taste that it can only have resulted from a combination of factors, all interacting. Some concern large groups of men, others small minorities of creative artists. As we have very little time for socio-cultural history, I shall only mention the fact that the world of politics played a part in the Gothic revival because the myth of Gothic liberty was one of the moving forces behind the mixed constitution on which eighteenth-century Englishmen often prided themselves. Whigs and Tories alike developed the idea that the seeds of British liberty had been sown on English ground by the Saxons who came from the forests of Germany and that, in spite of the encroachments of the Norman kings, the mixed constitution had been revived by Magna Carta, enforced by the Tudors, threatened by the tyranny of the Stuarts and saved by the Glorious Revolution. Swift, a Tory, said, "As to Parliaments, I adore the wisdom of that Gothick institution",[7] while Molesworth, a Whig, proclaimed "My notion of a Whig .... is one who is exactly for keeping the strictness of the old Gothick constitution".[8] Montesquieu, when he praised the English constitution in the *Esprit des Lois*, described it as a "fine system found in the woods".[9] And he explained this somewhat cryptic assertion in a footnote referring the reader to Tacitus's *Germania*, the book in which the Roman historian praises the Germans for having set up, in the woods of their native land, a type of government which might serve as an example to his countrymen. The baronial style or castle style could provide an image of Gothic liberty because Magna Carta had limited the absolute power of kings. This enhanced its beauty in Vanbrugh's imagination, and the mental attitude perceptible in his defence of Woodstock Manor is also to be found in Fielding's description of Allworthy's house in *Tom Jones*, in Kent's illustrations to the *Fairy Queen* and in Gibbs's Temple of Gothic Liberty at Stowe.

But a creative artist does not thrive on the reviving of old ideas for antiquity's sake. His concern is with the modernity of his time and, even when he uses the past, he copies it in such a way as to make the old and the very old modern. Witness Picasso's use of pre-Columbian art or Matisse's borrowings from the art of Islam. What Vanbrugh and Kent

---

7. Swift to Pope, in *The Correspondence of Jonathan Swift*, ed. H. Williams, London, 1963, II, 372.

8. Quoted in H.T. Dickinson, *Politics and Literature in the Eighteenth Century*, London, 1974, 24.

9. Montesquieu, *L'Esprit des Lois*, ed. G. Truc, Paris, 1956, I, 174 (my own translation).

were after was a resurrection of the Gothic likely to express new climates of sensibility and the structure of the new world view.

This is where the scientific imagination comes into play. In the sixteenth and seventeenth centuries, artists and scientists alike celebrated the triumph of geometry. Ever since the early days of the Renaissance, the development of the new physics, the physics of the impetus, had made it evident that the world was to be understood by new methods and by the application of new paradigms (I use Kuhn's sense of the term in his *The Structure of Scientific Revolutions*; I could alternatively have used Piaget's term "cognitive scheme"). To adopt a working definition of these philosophical terms let us say that they stand for definite processes of experimentation as well as for the conception of intellectual structures which make the world intelligible. We know from the works of historians of science such as Duhem, Crombie and Dijksterhuis that already in the thirteenth century and throughout the fourteenth century there was a gradual downfall of Aristotelian physics accompanied by what Kuhn calls "a paradigm shift". The physics of motion evolved its own paradigms which implied an extensive use of optics and geometry. It was by using telescopes that men were able to construct the new geometrical world picture. Artists eagerly seized upon the modernity of this mode of representation, and perspective became the basic way of representing the position of objects in relation to an observer and in relation to one another. Dürer, Piero della Francesca, Alberti and many others wrote treatises on perspective. Space was perceived and constructed geometrically by all the painters of the Renaissance.

The omnipotence of geometry was well established when Kepler introduced the idea of infinity in scientific discussions. This concept shows clearly the connection between the sciences, literature and the arts. It became one of the great subjects of meditation for the philosophers as we can see from Descartes' discussion of the infinite and the indefinite or Pascal's almost obsessive preoccupation with the actual size of man in the universe.

Perspective, the infinite, the nature of light and the nature of air, the gas which had to be taken into account to calculate the velocity of falling bodies, were central to the research work of seventeenth-century scientists. Their discoveries were turned into concepts by the philosophers and they percolated into the scientific imagination of the age. The writers and the critics conceived literature *more geometrico*. The artists represented the heroes of these great intellectual discoveries — see for example Vermeer's "Astronomer", and the statue of Geometry at Vaux le Vicomte — but they also changed the representation of space either by dramatizing it with light or by making the vanishing point part of the image of the infinite in the world as we see it. While so doing they also revealed that the air stood between the observer and the horizon. Part of the modernity of Cuyp and Lorrain can be explained by the discoveries of Galileo, Torricelli and Pascal.

If we keep in mind this short presentation of the scientific imagination in the age of the baroque we can now turn to the end of the seventeenth century in order to see what new paradigms, what new type of scientific imagination appeared when Newton emerged as a key figure among the scientists of Europe.

The very first lines of the *Principia Mathematica* are worth quoting here:

> I wish we could derive the rest of the phenomena of nature by the same kind of reasoning from mechanical principles, for I am induced by many reasons to suspect that they may all depend upon certain forces by which the particles of bodies by some causes hitherto unknown, are either mutually impelled towards one another and cohere in regular figures or are repelled and recede from one another.[10]

If, according to Newton, nature cannot be explained by reasoning "from mechanical principles", the Cartesian paradigm which represents the world as a *plenum* and motion as resulting from the direct interaction of bodies is no longer valid. The universe is not a windmill or a clock, because attraction cannot be given a concrete shape. It acts unseen according to laws discoverable by the physicist, but that does not make it part of matter. Matter is to be found under the form of particles over all the universe and these particles are in endless motion because they attract or repel one another.

This had far-reaching consequences on the perception of time. In the mechanistic world view, motion was communicated by instant propagation. The universe being a *plenum*, the motion of the smallest body implied the motion of the whole world and there could not be any time-lag in the process. The universe always recomposed itself by successive reshufflings. Things were completely different in the Newtonian world picture since particles took their time to go from one place to another and spent some of their energy on the way. Descartes' world looked like a huge kaleidoscope, Newton's like a billiard-table.

---

10. *Sir Isaac Newton's Mathematical Principles of Natural Philosophy and His System of the World Turned into English by Andrew Motte (London 1719)*, ed. F. Cajori, Berkeley, 1946, xvii.

It was not only the structure of the Newtonian world picture which was new. It was also the disposition of its elements. When Newton's *Opticks* was published in 1704, it became evident that chemistry and physiology, the sciences of the living world, would henceforward be among the chief preoccupations of the scientists. In a passage which has not always received sufficient attention Newton said:

> Seeing therefore the variety of motion which we find in the World is always decreasing, there is a necessity of conserving and recruiting it by active Principles such as are the cause of Gravity, by which Planets and Comets keep their Motion on their Orbs, and Bodies acquire great Motion in falling; and the cause of Fermentation by which the Heart and the Blood of Animals are kept in perpetual Motion and Heat; the inwards parts of the Earth are constantly warmed, and in some Places grow very hot; Bodies burn and shine, Mountains take fire, the Caverns of the Earth are blown up, and the Sun continues violently hot and lucid and warms all things by Light.[11]

A text such as this was likely to be read by a wider public than the *Principia* because it was written in English, not Latin, and because it appeared at a time when the elements of the Newtonian world picture had been made familiar to many readers by the controversies raised by Whiston's hypothesis concerning the solar system and by the great success of Thomas Burnet's *Sacred Theory of the Earth*, a book which made great use of the geological history of our planet to explain its present appearance. Burnet had been in contact with Newton who found nothing wrong with the basic thesis of his book.[12]

To conceive the world picture in modern terms was to reject the "old mechanical physicks" with its emphasis on the direct action of forces made visible by geometrical figures. The new paradigms implied not only a more mysterious universe but a universe of plastic forces, of gases and of fluids developing by almost imperceptible motions (hence the importance of infinitesimal calculus) and none of them reducible to the paradigms of the mechanistic world view.

The omnipotence of geometry was shaken. Henceforward, the leading sciences were to be chemistry, physiology and analytical calculus, all stressing the importance of the living world, a world of concatenation,

---

11. *Opticks* (1704), 3rd edition, London, 1720, 375.

12. Marjorie Hope Nicolson, *Mountain Gloom and Mountain Glory*, New York, 1959, rpt. 1963, 235.

a world of combined elements in which the life impulse became the active power giving shape to matter. Leibniz comes to mind here with the strong emphasis he put on the individual character of all beings, a view which was incompatible with their reduction to abstract geometrical models. The clarity, the preconceived regularity of geometrical systems no longer offered a plausible structure for the world view of the "new science". Irregularity and asymmetry looked far more appropriate to suggest the mysteries of Newtonian science and the deformities of the new world-picture.

Side by side with this new paradigm, and far less metaphysical, a theory of knowledge was increasing its influence in scientific circles. It was prevalent in the Royal Society and began to gain ground in proportion as the Cartesians were losing influence. It proposed a new model for the strategy to be adopted by scientists. It was called the "new philosophy" or the "new science" among the members of the Royal Society and was directly derived from Baconian empiricism. While the geometricians had thought in terms of system (blood circulation, watches which measured time by a geometrical mechanism), the Baconians thought in terms of histories. The histories were collections of data recorded with extensive indications concerning the time and the place in which the observations were made. These indications were known as the particulars of an experiment. These particulars testified to the thoroughness of the observer's method at the same time as they gave substance to the theory which might be framed from the experiment.

Boyle, one of the great scientists of the age, repeatedly advised the correspondents of the Royal Society on the best way to compile such histories. The great Locke himself wrote a history of the weather for the year 1692, indicating the temperature, the atmospheric pressure, and the state of the sky four times a day and every day. This implied two things: first, that clear indications of time and place should be provided whenever an experiment was described; second, that the validity of a theory depended on concurring indications which could never be discovered all at the same time. Hence the place of time in the new strategies of knowledge.

The role of this method is apparent in Thomas Burnet's *A Sacred Theory of the Earth*, a book which generated a new vision of the landscape by impressing on the minds of its readers vivid representations of cosmic irregularity. Burnet's explanation of the form of continents enjoyed a great superiority over all other cosmogonies: it was in the form of a history and accounted for things as they were by things as they had been. One is immediately reminded of Defoe's sentence "The fate of things gives a new face to things". The full title of Burnet's book runs:

The Sacred Theory of the Earth: Containing an Account of the Original of the Earth and of all the General Changes Which It Hath Already Undergone or is to Undergo, till the Consummation of All Things.

By the historical method, Burnet reached the conclusion that:

We justly admire its [the Earth's] greatness though we cannot admire its Beauty and Elegancy, for 'tis deformed and irregular as it is great.[13]

The Earth reflected the terrible effects of God's wrath after the Fall of Man; it had lost its former glory because it had been reduced to ruins:

there appearing nothing of Order or any regular design in its parts it seems reasonable to believe that it was not the work of nature, according to her first Intention, or according to the first Model that was drawn in Measure and Proportion by the line and by the Plummet but a secondary Work, and the best that could be made of broken Materials.[14]

The modern reader cannot help thinking that, if he is to follow Burnet, the Earth was meant by God to resemble a French garden, but through Adam's fault, it was turned into an English one. But it was a splendid garden; full of the cosmic poetry that true Bible readers could infuse into it. Recent research has gone into the problem of the connection between Newtonian science and Jewish theology.[15] Addison again was not slow in detecting this new covenant of Newtonian science, religion and cosmic poetry. He wrote in *The Spectator* No. 565:

The noblest and most exalted way of considering this infinite Space is that of Sir Isaac Newton who calls it the Sensorium of the Godhead.

The use of the term *sensorium* is of great importance here for it was already to be found in Boyle and the idea that matter is what acts on our

---

13. Thomas Burnet, *The Sacred Theory of the Earth*, London, 1684, 215.

14. *Ibid.*, 196.

15. Brian P. Copenhaver, "Jewish Theologies of Space in the Scientific Revolution: More, Raphson, Newton and Their Predecessors", *Annals of Science*, XXXVII/5 (1980), 489-548.

senses was central to Locke's psychology which must also be taken into account to explain the Gothic revival.

The question of Locke's debt to Newton cannot be fully discussed here, but it is beyond doubt that he described sensation as a process which had its origin in what he called "the operation of insensible particles on our senses".[16] This makes it clear that he had adopted the corpuscular physics used by Boyle, Sydenham and Newton. But he acknowledged other debts to the Royal Society. According to him, it was the combination of sense impressions which enabled the mind to compare and to judge, but the whole process would have come to nothing had not memory preserved impressions as they occurred accompanied by pain and pleasure. Sensations were the warp and woof of mental life, but memory was the loom, endlessly increasing the range of knowledge as a human being passed from childhood to adolescence and from adolescence to adulthood. Time was so essential to this theory of mental life that Locke explained how a blind man could acquire the sense of time by mere olfactory sensations changing with the seasons. Since Locke had explained the formation of man's ideas by a process derived from the observation of nature in the successive ages of man, he could state, as he did in the preface to the *Essay Concerning Human Understanding* that it was written by "the historical plain method", the method of histories.

If the structure of the world view had changed, if the methods of observations had changed, if the very way man went discovering the nature of his own thought had changed, aesthetic standards could not but change too. Irregularity was felt to be the true image of the world, asymmetry the basic structure of nature. Gone were the *a priori* conceptions of the Cartesians deciding axiomatically that there was a hierarchy of beautiful forms and all of them geometrical. God had willed the world otherwise. Truth imposed a new image of reality.

The English garden soon made this image visible. It was the very representation of the empirical way of knowing nature. The observer gradually acquired this knowledge by following winding alleys and chancing upon unexpected prospects. He discovered one particular after another exactly as the experimentalist noted things as they took place and when they took place. Besides, the English garden was the garden of the new way of ideas. It was a provider of sensations following in close succession and yet always unforeseeable. The visitor's impressions changed continually as he followed a winding alley with the sun now on

---

16. Locke, *Essay Concerning Human Understanding*, ed. Peter Nidditch, London, 1975, 136.

side now on the other, the noise of a river now quite close now almost gone and the sound of birds now overhead and now far away. This could never have happened in a French garden where the best way to know nature was to climb stairs and discover the whole geometrical pattern at a glance. The new form of gardening was an exercise in experimental psychology at the same time as it produced a true image of nature, irregular, pregnant with sensations, alive and free.

Such a conception of nature called for a reconsideration of architecture. And here ruins played a central role. They became a success in the English garden, a thing utterly unthinkable in the aesthetics of Le Nôtre. They had every reason to succeed because they were the embodiment of the empirical paradigm of histories at the same time as they proved efficient sensation providers. Ruins actually proved that "the fate of things gives a new face to things". The scars they could show were as many signs of their former splendour; they constituted as many particulars of their long destiny. The names of battles came to mind as you looked at them, together with a wealth of sensations. They provided visual impressions generated by their irregular contour (with the added attraction of holes sometimes) and the play of endless nuances of colours, light and shade on their irregular surfaces; they also provided tactile sensations due to their rugged appearance which contrasted with the smooth surface of the surrounding grass; and then there were also auditory sensations provided by the wind, the birds and the occasional fall of stones from their nodding tops. Eighteenth-century poets never fail to mention "the moping owl", "the clamorous crow" and "the weak-eyed bat" in their descriptions. But the poets, for whom we have little time here, used the Gothic for purposes other than descriptive: their experiments with old forms or with the Pindaric ode shows to what extent they were breaking the fetters of the couplet and rejecting the rhyme which Dryden had praised because "it circumscribed the fancy". Gray and Macpherson's Ossian are fitting examples here.

Lockean psychology made ruins part of the landscape in a way unknown before and different from that of the Renaissance. This point was underlined vigorously by William Mason when he declared in *The English Garden* that only Gothic ruins should be seen in an English landscape since all others "mocked historical credence".[17] The strangest thing is that ruins which were supposed to result from the decay of old buildings gradually assumed the opposite function and they gave life to

---

17. William Mason, *The English Garden* (1771-81), *Works*, London, 1811, 353.

a numerous progeny of houses loudly proclaiming their ancestry. Vanbrugh, as we have seen, was a precursor.

To a large extent Palladianism brought welcome changes. It revived the spirit of the Renaissance, more open to the life of nature and less given to the pomposity of cosmic geometrization than the baroque. Besides, Renaissance architects had always played with the idea that art and nature had to offer strong contrasts. Kent and Vanbrugh concurred on this point. Gothic architecture when embosomed in trees and seen from a distance was the nicest object that a landscape painter could find. The early manifestations of the Gothic revival thus linked quite naturally the forest, the landscape and the pointed arch. Since, as Stukeley and later Warburton said, the Gothic suggested trees and since the forest was the image of Gothic times it was natural that they should go together.

But the great difference between the true Gothicists — Vanbrugh and, later, Sanderson Miller and Walpole — and the occasional Gothicists — Kent, Batty Langley and their imitators — was that the former understood that irregularity lay at the core of the Gothic.[18] This enabled them to assert the truly English character of the Gothic at the same time as they used it under both its civil and ecclesiastical form probably because the association of ideas gave churches an advantage over castles: they generated more sublime impressions by being associated with death and they were directly linked with the anonymous masses which were preparing more democratic times. But this concerns the second half of the century and need not detain us here.

Some concluding remarks can be offered. The first is to express the hope that the present essay has shown that the scientific movement has played a part in the process by which the creative imagination of the architects and of the poets of the eighteenth century gradually warmed to Gothic shapes. The second remark proceeds from the first: the theory of knowledge seems to be the field on which the arts and the sciences find grounds common to their seemingly different pursuits. This provides critical approaches which have a threefold advantage: they take the historical context into account and rule out all attempts to reduce criticism to intellectual levitation; they give a precise meaning to what is often loosely called the spirit of the age and they show creation not as the passive transmission of influences but as a passionate, sometimes desperate, quest for coherence and intelligibility.

---

18. For a stimulating discussion of the problem, see Sir Nikolaus Pevsner, "Richard Payne Knight", in *Studies in Art, Architecture and Design*, 2 vols, New York, 1968, I, 111-13.

THE ROOTS OF THE SYMBOLIC ROLE OF WOMAN
IN GOTHIC LITERATURE

MANUEL AGUIRRE

Gothic Fiction constitutes a *genre* (or *sub-genre*) traditionally looked
upon with a certain contempt by the Western intelligentsia, and nowadays
included under the somewhat redeeming label "marginal literature"
(Dutch and German critics, with perhaps less compassion, use the term
Trivialliteratur; the French, possibly more neutral, include the genre
under the terse label of *Le Fantastique*). All too often, however,
"marginality" comes to be used as a category which, purposely or not,
tends to isolate the genre from other literary ventures. For a text to be
"on the margin of" usually means either "it is not worth talking about"
or "by all means let us discuss it, to the exclusion of everything else".
And rarely do we see genuine bridges established between core and
margin without an apology for dealing with such things as Gothic or
Science-Fiction in the context of mainstream literature.

I shall not enter the debate concerning the interrelation between Canon
and Non-Canon and the mutual dependence between literary systems, but
there is a point which I would like to make: whereas we tend to think of
Gothic as if at all *indebted* by way of influence to the mainstream, we
should consider the serious possibility that the debt is only secondary,
and that the real "influence" is not exerted so much by mainstream
literature as by the myths which, whether or not we are aware of it,
condition both mainstream and marginal writing in fundamental ways.
My objective in this article is to emphasize a specific area where Gothic
fiction is indebted to developments in the field of mainstream literature,
only to the extent that the mainstream has been able to codify and
transmit essentially mythic values.

The area in question is that of the function and behaviour of female
figures in Gothic Fiction. We are all aware of the clichés in this field:
beautiful, weak, sublime, helpless females crouching on floors, hiding
behind doors, dominated by brutal lascivious males, kidnapped, murdered
or worse, their virtue always at stake, their beauty their great misfortune

— the stuff sentimental romances are made of. The thing which infuriated Mary Wollstonecraft even more than the treatment women received at the hands of a patriarchal society was woman's own ridiculous helplessness:

> Fragile in every sense of the word, they are obliged to look up to man for every comfort. In the most trifling danger they cling to their support, with parasitical tenacity, piteously demanding succour; and their *natural* protector extends his arm, or lifts up his voice, to guard the lovely trembler — from what? Perhaps the frown of an old cow, or the jump of a mouse; a rat would be a serious danger. In the name of reason, and even common sense, what can save such beings from contempt, even though they be soft and fair?[1]

The cliché of the sublime fragility of women is at its best, or worst, in the three main female figures that drag their tearful selves through the pages of the very first Gothic novel, *The Castle of Otranto*. Hippolita, a helpless wife and mother, ever submissive, ever weeping, ever cringing before her sullen, despotic husband Manfred; Matilda, tremulous daughter of the tyrant and fated to become his victim; Isabella, ever pursued by Manfred with ignoble purposes. All three display a considerable gift for attracting oppression, and an immense capacity for suffering. But the sources of the cliché are not to be overlooked, for these women are endowed with an uncommon degree of "fine feeling" which alone explains their proneness to victimization and the intensity of their suffering. They are victims, but they are such in an archetypal way. The concept of *Sensibility* dominated the second half of the eighteenth century as evinced in the poetry of the Graveyard School, in the Gothic Novel, in Burke's philosophy of "the sublime and the beautiful". Mary Wollstonecraft denounced the follies of sensibility in her *Vindication*, and Jane Austen poked fun at it in her *Sense and Sensibility*. But the concept is rich in meaning: as Ann Radcliffe put it in *The Mysteries of Udolpho*, sensibility "is a dangerous quality, which is continually extracting the excess of misery, or delight, from every surrounding circumstance".[2] It is this very excess — of joy or, much more usually according to Radcliffe and the other Gothic writers, of misery — which takes the

---

1. Mary Wollstonecraft, *Vindication of the Rights of Woman*, London, 1792, 153.

2. Ann Radcliffe, *The Mysteries of Udolpho*, ed. Bonamy Dobrée, Oxford, 1970, 79.

person of feeling out of the mundane round of things and places him or her in touch with the Numinous, with the Otherworldly in nature, with the unearthly, be it divine or (much more usually) infernal.

Another term favoured by the eighteenth century was "passion", central (negatively) to the literature of the Modernity as that force which, if unchecked, might upset the fragile dominion of Reason. Since the sixteenth century, Reason held a much challenged stronghold on Western culture as the organizational principle ruling thought, science, law, and social structure. Passion appeared more and more as the great danger and threat to this faculty. Thus Horatio begged Hamlet not to approach the ghost, lest it "deprive your sovereignty of reason/And draw you into madness" (*Hamlet*, I.iv.73-74). In *Paradise Lost* Milton wrote of "sensual Appetite, who from beneath/Usurping over sovran Reason claim'd/Superior sway" (*Paradise Lost*, IX, 1129-1131). Pope bemoaned man's insufficient self-control, that "when his own great work is but begun,/What Reason weaves, by Passion is undone" (*An Essay on Man*, II, 41-42). In November of 1793, at the height of the French Revolution, the cathedral of Notre-Dame of Paris was consecrated to Reason, and two years later, Thomas Paine was able to look back over the eighteenth century and proclaim the triumph of Reason in a title which gives its name to a whole period: *The Age of Reason*. Reason had indeed become sovereign. Even so, as late as the 1830s Edgar Allan Poe could introduce the poem "The Haunted Palace" into his "The Fall of the House of Usher" to stress the terrors which the downfall of that sovereign faculty has always threatened upon the Modern age.

In the Gothic, all female protagonists are either victims or pursuers, extreme sufferers or equally extreme villains. The contrast is perfectly established by Radcliffe in the figure of suffering Emily:

> Hers was a silent anguish, weeping, yet enduring; not the wild energy of passion, inflaming imagination, bearing down the barriers of reason and living in a world of its own (329).

The innocence of Ellena in Radcliffe's *The Italian* is the perfect foil for the relentless evil of the Marchesa; virtuous Antonia in Lewis's *The Monk* faces the stern cruelty of the Abbess; if Immalee embodies a more-than-human innocence in Maturin's *Melmoth*, Matilda is literally a more-than-human fiend in *The Monk*; to the ignorance of Christabel, Coleridge opposed the wise malignity of Geraldine. The villainesses are, like their male counterparts (Manfred, Schedoni, Montoni, Ambrosio) guided by that "ruling passion" so fashionable in the literature of the late eighteenth century, a passion which, indeed, "bears down the barriers of reason".

The victims, on the other hand, find their greatest source of suffering in their own heightened sensibility, yet their dignity is also at its highest in their silent *endurance* and, along with it, in their *faith*.

For every persecution of woman has as its object to change her from her steadfast adherence to principles of virtue and loyalty; this is in total contrast with the unruly, unprincipled passion of her pursuers, whose goal is precisely to go beyond the control, "the barriers" of reason. *Faithlessness* is an attribute of the passionate individual as much as *faithfulness* is of the man or woman of feeling. This concept of faith must be seen not only in its matrimonial but also in its political, religious, even metaphysical implications. Geraldine the vampire is faithless to human nature and seeks to pervert Christabel's; Lewis's arch-cruel Abbess is unfaithful to her profession of the Christian faith, and Matilda first appears as a young male novice who turns out to be a pious girl who is really a passion-ruled woman who then reveals herself as an imperious witch who finally turns out to be a demon: there is faithlessness for you. And of course, as faithlessness is associated with both passion and evil in the genre, so faithfulness and its accompanying suffering are identified with truth, feeling and goodness.

Nevertheless, when all is said and done there remains the fact that the majority of Gothic males are guided by that "ruling passion" so fashionable in the late eighteenth century, while the women are, typically, "women of feeling". Both this kind of extremeness and such a pat distribution of roles are far from being a matter of clichés: they reveal archetypal figures placed in contrast so as to convey the grand conflict of the age, the struggle for the supremacy of the new *Weltanschauung*. Passion in the man is condoned, because it is not thought to be truly disruptive: like the Faustian pact, it liberates a diabolic energy which, it is hoped, will be harnessed to the accomplishment of the grand dream of Faustus and Frankenstein — the overcoming of death. By contrast, if sentiment is to remain in woman in the Age of Reason, then it is better it should remain as feeling under the aegis of Reason and inspired by faith and steadfastness, rather than as flooding passion, disrupting patterns of control without which the new political and industrial world would not be able to exist. And this discrimination as to the propriety of passion in men and women hangs together precisely with that numinous quality particularly ascribed to woman.

The conflict long predates the Gothic novel, since the placing of woman in such peculiar roles goes back to, first of all, Elizabethan drama. The revival of interest in and respect for Shakespeare's work, usually credited to Coleridge, begins, in a humble manner, decades before Coleridge, with Gothic writers ransacking Shakespeare's plays for themes, images, situations, even language. For example, Walpole acknowledged his considerable debt to the Shakespearian model in the foreword to his *Otranto*; Clara Reeve imitated *Hamlet* servilely in *The Old English Baron*; Lewis took up much from Marlowe's *Doctor Faustus* in *The Monk*. Faustus-like and Macbeth-like characters abound in Gothic literature; Radcliffe's very definition of passion as a force "bearing down the barriers of reason" is indebted to Hamlet's complaint about the "o'ergrowth of some complexion,/Oft breaking down the pales and forts of reason" (*Hamlet*, I.iv.27-28). If in this context we look at some Elizabethan female characters we shall at once recognize the essential traits that were later to define Gothic women. The witches, together with Lady Macbeth, manage to corrupt Macbeth's allegiance to his king. Goneril and Regan monstrously betray their father Lear, even as Cordelia remains a tower of misunderstood loyalty. Sycorax is the villainous figure who sets the stage for Prospero's exile from humanity, even as innocent Miranda is the instrument of his return to the human world. In Kyd's *The Spanish Tragedy*, Bellimperia is both helpless victim and relentless executioner. Gertrude's "unfaithfulness" is the source of Hamlet's mistrust of women — a mistrust which will cost naive Ophelia her sanity. In the anonymous *Arden of Feversham*, Alice Arden will undertake about ten separate attempts on her husband's life. And possibly the text which best defines the trend whereby the unruly "woman of passion" is vilified and the meek, constant "woman of feeling" praised is *The Taming of the Shrew*. These are the models which inspire the roles woman is to play in Gothic literature, with the difference that, in the Gothic genre, the woman of passion is in a minority: the shrew has been generally tamed.

But there is more. Through her husband's death, Alice Arden seeks to wed Mosbie, who covets Arden's lands; Old Hamlet's death results in Gertrude wedding Claudius and passing the crown to him; Lear's destruction will allow his erstwhile power to be effectively passed on, via Goneril and Regan, to their husbands; Duncan's death, engineered by Lady Macbeth, will bring the crown to her husband. Something beside faithlessness on the part of woman lies at the root of these texts: the transmission of power is at stake, and woman is the key figure, without whose intervention or consent Mosbie, Claudius or Macbeth will never occupy their masters' place; essentially, woman is here an agent of (unwanted) change.

At this point, one further historical dimension opens up, linking Elizabethan types to certain protagonists in medieval romance. Who is Gertrude but a reduced, subdued manifestation of that figure exemplified by Guinevere? As Arthur's queen takes a new paramour, Lancelot, Gertrude takes a new consort, Claudius. In the first case, this act will result in the death of the old king at Camlan; in the second, it is preceded by the death of the old king; in both tales, catastrophe ensues from the queen's wilful choice. Or take Bellimperia, ever befriended by men doomed to die, often at the hands of her next paramour (a similar pattern is found in Webster's *The White Devil*): who is she but a version of Gudrun, the sinister queen of several Germanic sagas, ever dooming her husbands to die at the hands of some new suitor? The same pattern reappears in Saxo Grammaticus's version of the Hamlet-myth, where the warrior-queen Hermutrude kills all her wooers until she meets Amleth, but eventually will betray even him and wed his slayer. The capricious queen is called Thryth in *Beowulf* and, like Hermutrude, she kills her suitors. Needless to say, these women all resemble Circe, forever welcoming new men into her palace only to turn them into beasts.

And below the romances, the lays, the sagas, we will find a still deeper layer of texts in which the Lady emerges in all her mythical status as Queen or Goddess, her prerogative being to dispense Sovereignty on her chosen suitor — and to dispense it again to another after a certain time. Celtic and Germanic mythology abound in versions of what has been called the "Theme of King and Goddess", and one peculiarity of the theme is the transformation which the Lady undergoes in the course of the story. In the Irish tale "The Adventure of the Sons of Eochaid", young Niall meets a loathsome hag who demands a kiss in exchange for water; having acquiesced, he finds her transformed into a beautiful girl who identifies herself as "The Sovereignty of Ireland" and proclaims him High King of Tara. In the English-speaking world, this ambiguous woman is known as "the Loathly Lady" of several narratives, Chaucer's "Wife of Bath's Tale" amongst them. Essentially, she symbolizes Earth, the cycle of the seasons, the process of life and death; winter yields to spring as the Loathly Lady turns into a fair maiden, or as Hermutrude, Saxo's hateful warrior-queen, turns into a loving wife.

But, also loving Hermutrude betrays Amleth, and fair Brynhild Sigurd, and Gudrun her husbands when, in the fullness of time, Earth comes to the end of her cycle and seeks to renew herself. The myths do not make moral judgments, they merely offer metaphors for the cycle of existence. But slowly the medieval mentality develops a disparaging concept of woman as fickle, as variable, as subject to irrational moods and changes — as faithless to the grand rational enterprise the West is engaged in. Her symbolic Sovereignty is questioned, challenged, literalized as sovereignty-in-marriage, mocked, or dismissed. Her double role as maiden-and-hag, as *puella senilis*, as imperious queen and meek lover, cruel and peaceful, giver of life and death, is rationalized into two female stereotypes: the beauty and the hag of *Sir Gawain and the Green Knight*, the Good Woman and the Wanton, Shrew or Witch. In so far as she is still credited with a certain power or sovereignty, she is rejected as evil, unreasonable, or silly.

Reason must rule. As the concept of the "Sovereignty of Reason" gains ground in a more and more patriarchal culture, woman's "proper" role more and more becomes that of submissive lover, faithful wife, unassuming servant. And if she does not comply with this injunction, she will be typecast as the shrewish, malevolent woman whose purpose seems to be to wreak havoc in an otherwise well-ordered society.

Of her shrewish role, little is left in the Gothic: it mostly emerges as a potential threat in the danger of virtue-lost, in the possibility, hardly ever realized, of revolt. Mostly she appears in her over-sensitive role; and yet, even here something of her former importance lingers in the helpless heroines of the Gothic genre. She may have lost her Sovereignty to man and his all too rational world, but perhaps for this very reason she retains, enhanced, her link with the Other. Moved by feeling, the Gothic woman still reveals that numinous touch which, as a symbol of Earth itself, she enjoyed in traditional myth. One may go even further: she has come down to the late twentieth century and, in her very helplessness, she has been granted a transcendental quality in much modern horror literature. She is Rosemary, destined to birth the Antichrist, the great agent of a revolution that will signal the passing of the Age of Reason. And so, in a way, the Woman of horror literature remains sovereign, numinous, a symbol for the ever-turning Earth, the Mother of Change.

LAYING THE GROUND FOR GOTHIC: THE PASSAGE OF THE SUPERNATURAL FROM TRUTH TO SPECTACLE

E.J. CLERY

The town it long has been in pain
About the phantom in Cock-Lane[1]

"Scratching Fanny", the Cock Lane Ghost, was the sensation of London in 1762. Crowds flocked to the haunted house day and night in the hope of witnessing her performances, queues of carriages coming from the West End blocked the Strand, the taverns and alehouses in the neighbourhood overflowed with thirsty tourists, and the Methodists, who had adopted the spirit as their own, laid on emergency food supplies. Fanny never in fact appeared, but she would tap out answers to questions put to her, "One knock signifying yes, and two knocks, no". She said she was a young woman who had once lived in the house in Cock Lane and had been cruelly murdered by her lover; she had returned to the world as an invisible spirit to seek justice.

Fanny was a spectre perfectly adapted to modern urban living. Not for her the retirement of a crumbling mansion or country churchyard. She chose to manifest herself in the very heart of commercial London, was willing to regulate her visitations for the benefit of sightseers, and seemed to actively solicit the attentions of the press. With a ghost so open to public scrutiny, there would inevitably be more at stake than the criminal indictment of one man. Here at last, after years of inconclusive debate, was a chance to settle once and for all the question of the possibility or impossibility of spirits. There was a flurry of serious treatises for and against.

But there were also pantomimes, ballads, prints, which took a more light-hearted view, whether celebrating or ridiculing the haunting. There was a revival of Addison's comedy *The Drummer: or, The Haunted House* (1715) in which the line "'Tis the solitude of the Country that creates these Whimsies; there was never such a thing as a Ghost heard

---

1. Cited in Douglas Grant, *The Cock Lane Ghost*, London, 1965, 96.

of at *London*" regularly brought the house down. Above all, there was Garrick's hugely popular interlude *The Farmer's Return*, in which the level-headed Farmer, played by Garrick himself, teases his family with an account of his meeting with the famous ghost in the capital.

The success of *The Farmer's Return* was due to the comic disruption of expectations, its reversal of the standard mapping of superstition in the countryside and scepticism in the town. Here, instead, a sceptical rustic mocks the credulity of city-folk; a straightforward enough device. But if we extend the frame of the theatrical spectacle to include the spectators, the city-folk themselves, their laughter, ironically self-directed, could be taken to relate to a more complex perception, something exceeding the simple defeat of expectations; a new object, a new joke, beyond the county/city opposition. It is not that the city has regressed into superstition: there is nothing to distinguish the crowds who squeeze into the small room at Cock Lane from the crowds who congregate at Drury Lane Theatre to mock the haunting. It is as though the urban relocation of the supernatural has effected a change in the very nature of superstition. The audience's laughter seems to mark a transition, a displacement of the old antinomy of belief and scepticism, truth and error. It celebrates the wresting of the invisible world from the sphere of religious doctrine, and its incongruous, hilarious embrace by the fashion system of the city. Freed from the service of doctrinal proof, the ghost was to be caught up in the machine of the economy; it was available to be processed, reproduced, packaged, marketed and circulated by the engines of cultural production. All spirits, whether spuriously real or genuinely fictional, will from this time be levelled to the status of spectacle. The supernatural, deregulated, was going laissez-faire.

It is difficult for us, the legatees of this event, to appreciate the impact of Garrick's joke. But a rapid circuit of the first half of the century will help to establish the significance of Cock Lane as a point of confrontation and reordering for rival techniques of ghost-seeing which had originated long before. To help in this endeavour, I will pick out of the crowd two familiar figures, Samuel Johnson and Horace Walpole. Their differing responses to the Cock Lane ghost identify them, on this question, as the subjects of alternative mental paradigms, distinct epistemological fields, positing two discrete objects: a "real supernatural" and an "aesthetic supernatural".

The difference between the aesthetic and the real supernatural in this period is not the same as the division between the sceptics, and the believers who engage them in debate. Believers and sceptics are equally locked into a problematic of truth: both seek to establish by rational proof the essential nature of the spectral thing-in-itself, both reject

CREDULITY, SUPERSTITION, and FANATICISM.
A MEDLEY.

Believe not every Spirit, but try the Spirits whether they are of God, because many false Prophets are gone out into the World.

1. John. c.64. V1.

Design'd and Engrav'd by W.ᵐ Hogarth.

Publish'd as the Act directs March y.ᵉ 15.ᵗʰ 1762.

popular superstition as the mindless gossip of the low and uneducated. Their presuppositions are almost identical, because the terms of their dialogue are set by natural reason; perhaps all that differs is the will of the believer to overcome the sceptic in himself. Boswell described Dr Johnson's avid interest in ghosts as that of a "candid enquirer after truth"; in fact his situation seems to have been that of a would-be believer tormented by a model of truth that effectively undermined belief. The demands of empirical reason would not allow him to accept customary or second-hand evidence of the existence of spirits, and thus of the reality of immortal souls; but the dread that after death came nothingness would not allow him to finally reject them. The Cock Lane affair seemed a heaven-sent opportunity to put an end to uncertainty, and he agreed to serve as a member of an unofficial investigating committee which resolved to put to the test "the existence or veracity of the supposed spirit." His report of the proceedings, presented in the mode of a controlled experiment, was published in the *Public Ledger*: "The supposed spirit ... publicly promised, by an affirmative knock, that it would attend one of the gentlemen into the vault ... where the body is deposited, and give a token of her presence there by a knock upon her coffin."[2] The knock never came, the ghost was eventually exposed as a fraud, and Johnson resigned himself once again to doubt.

The testing of spectres was one consequence of empiricism's constitutive role in the ghost debate; what is most interesting for our purposes is the type of ghost story it gave rise to. Although marvels and miracles were disqualified from the realm of natural law precisely because they tended to exist only in the testimony, or narratives, of others, apologists for the supernatural were constantly on the lookout for new, better, more convincing ghost stories: for the ghost story so transparently referential that it would bring the most obstinate Deist, the most hardened atheist, back to the orthodox fold. In a rationalist ghost story the mode of discourse must make up for the gap in sense-perception. Only the self-effacing rhetoric of objectivity will be countenanced. Tales of the marvellous were sifted for reliability, and republished in anthologies like *Saducismus Triumphatus* (1681) by Joseph Glanvill (who was, appropriately enough, a member of the Royal Society) and *The Certainty of the World of Spirits* (1691) by Richard Baxter. These documentary narratives of the supernatural, as Michael McKeon has remarked, "speak to skepticism and atheism in the only

---

2. *Ibid.*, 71.

Fielding. Foote. English Credulity, or the Invisible Ghost in Cock Lane. Feb. 1762

language they will understand".[3] Apparition narratives such as Defoe's
A True Relation of the Apparition of One Mrs Veal (1706) were intended
to overturn disbelief by the patient, methodical and exhaustive display of
facts: proper names of objects and people, exact measurement of
distances of time and place, precise recollection of speech and actions.
Here, monotony became a virtue; disinterestedness a requisite. There
must be no hint of exchange-value, of a desire to entertain or cash in on
idle curiosity or blind faith.

But sceptics were disappointingly slow to acknowledge the distinction
between a rational and an irrational ghost story. For Hume, any narrative
of the marvellous threatened to seduce and corrupt the faculty of reason:

> The passion of *surprize* or *wonder*, arising from miracles, being
> an agreeable emotion, gives a sensible tendency towards the belief
> of those events, from which it is derived. And this goes so far,
> that even those who cannot enjoy this pleasure immediately, *nor
> can believe these miraculous events*, of which they are informed,
> yet love to partake of the satisfaction at second-hand and by
> rebound, and place a pride and delight in exciting the admiration
> of others.[4]

The "passion of *surprize* or *wonder*" is inimical to common sense, let
alone rational judgment. Hume's backward glance at a regressive feature
of human nature and human society emphasizes that narratives of the
supernatural, the least of any narrative type, can escape their exchange-
value, their rhetorical dimension. Their effect is such that "even those
who cannot enjoy this pleasure immediately" (the pleasure of communal
belief) can "partake of the satisfaction at second-hand and by rebound",
delighting in the performance alone, and the power of discourse to move,
irresistibly, the emotions. In making this observation Hume unknowingly
foresees the rise to authority of a hedonistic and aestheticized version of
the supernatural which will render the problem of belief indifferent, and
restore the ghost story to universal currency — only this time in the form
of a consumer commodity, a fiction to be bought and sold. The social
body will then be able to draw its coherence, not from metaphysics as
traditionally conceived, but from the totalizing operations of the market-

---

3. Michael McKeon, *The Origins of the English Novel 1600-1740*, London,
1988, 87.

4. David Hume, "Of Miracles", *Essays Moral, Political, and Literary*, 2 vols,
London, 1875, II, 95 (in the quotation, my italics).

Fig. 3: "David Garrick as the Farmer"

place. If collective truth is no longer attainable, let there be collective phantasy, a phantom collectivity.

The truth-problematic of the real supernatural was founded on the forgetting of the religious doctrine of the Protestant Reformation, which had rejected the idea of purgatory, and therefore of spirits of the dead who return to earth, as nothing more than a Popish imposition.[5] The aesthetic supernatural was in turn based on the forgetting of the exigencies that drove Johnson, Addison, Glanvill and Defoe to attempt the resurrection of the spirit world in the realm of the humanly knowable. With Horace Walpole's visit to the house in Cock Lane, Johnson's tragic failure is replayed as farce.

> We set out from the Opera, changed our clothes at Northumberland House, the Duke of York, Lady Northumberland, Lady Mary Coke, Lord Hertford, and I, all in one hackney coach, and drove to the spot; it rained torrents; yet the lane was full of mob, and the house so full we could not get in — at last they discovered it was the Duke of York, and the company squeezed themselves into one another's pockets to make room for us. The house, which is borrowed, is wretchedly small and miserable; when we opened the chamber in which were fifty people, with no light but one tallow candle at the end, we tumbled over the bed of the child to whom the ghost comes, and whom they are murdering there by inches in such insufferable heat and stench. At the top of the room are ropes to dry clothes — I asked, if we were to have rope dancing between the acts? — we had nothing; they told us, as they would at a puppet-show, that it would not come that night till seven in the morning — that is, when there are only prentices and old women. We stayed, however, till half an hour after one.[6]

There are two basic reasons for comparing a haunting or any other fantastic phenomenon to theatre. In the first place, because like a stage-play it is based on illusion; this is a metaphorical attribution, belonging to satire and demystification. In the second place, because, whether genuine or false, it appeals to audiences like a stage-play; this is a literal identification, which hedonistically accepts the marvellous as a spectacle like any other, as a fiction with an immanent, self-sufficient standard of believability. Walpole is indifferent to the question of truth; he and his fashionable friends come to Cock Lane because it is a novelty, an

---

5. Keith Thomas, *Religion and the Decline of Magic*, Penguin, 1971, 702-705.

6. *The Yale Edition of Horace Walpole's Correspondence*, ed. W.S. Lewis, 48 vols, New Haven and London, X, 5-7.

entertainment on a par with rope-dancing or a puppet-show. "The most diverting part", Walpole writes at the conclusion of his account, "is to hear people wondering *when it will be found out* — as if there was anything to find out; as if the actors would make their noises where they can be discovered". There is no truth detached from the representation, the only truth is that of illusion itself.

A number of earlier fabulous frauds, including Mary Tofts who gave birth to a litter of rabbits and the conjuror who claimed to be able to put himself inside a bottle, had prepared the way for the representation of the Cock Lane ghost as theatre in the metaphorical, demystifying sense. In each of these cases figures in public authority had become embarrassingly involved, the Lord Mayor, or a member of the Royal household, provoking ridicule or rioting among the populace. The social hierarchy implicit in the enlightenment binary high/reason, low/superstition was dramatically inverted, provoking demonstrations of the carnivalesque. But as the literal sense of "theatre" overtakes the metaphorical, social tensions diminish. Once the paradigm of truth and error is abandoned, divisions of rank within the audience are no longer meaningful. The spectacle guarantees democracy at the level of epistemology: the élite are not expected to "know better". All are cultural consumers drawn together by a common appetite for novelty and the marvellous.

Parallel to this series of representations of the supernatural *as* theatre, ran developments in the role of the supernatural *in* the theatre. In spite of Dryden's defence of apparitions as a dramatic device, post-Restoration playwrights generally adhered to the rulings of the "real supernatural"; that is to say, the insistence that the supernatural be represented only in terms of truth, not as fiction or entertainment. Thus the only allowable ghost in modern drama was a pretended ghost, a ghost that was unmistakably *un*real, as in Addison's *The Drummer*, where the audience is alerted to the ruse in the Prologue, forestalling any danger of awakening superstitious passions. Yet at the same time Addison, among others, was evolving a theory of the sublime which would ultimately subvert the framework of the "real supernatural" and remake the spectral object in terms of aesthetics. In an essay in *The Spectator* concerning sources of the terrible in tragic drama, Addison adopts a mocking tone to describe the conventional English stage ghost in his "bloody shirt", but he cites classical precedent to support the claim that objects of terror, "when they come in as aids and assistances to the poet ... are not only to be excused, but to be applauded".[7] The tragic ghost is not simply an

---

7. Joseph Addison, *The Spectator*, ed. Donald F. Bond, 5 vols, Oxford, 1965, I, 185.

object of terror, as a real ghost would be. Nor is it a source of the pure delight to be derived from a mock ghost. The effect it produces is pleasurable in so far as the object is known to be fictional and enjoyed as part of the dramatic artifice, but terrible in that, simultaneously, disbelief is suspended far enough for the passions to operate *as if* the object were a reality. The vacillation, the doubt, becomes part of the pleasure. We find here the outlines of an autonomous realm of the aesthetic, the awakening of a sensibility detached from truth. But it was not until the arrival of Garrick's Hamlet that this vision was actualized in stage practice, by means of the audience's sympathetic identification with the actor's virtuoso depiction of fear. You will remember that Tom Jones's superstitious companion Partridge did not believe that the man "in that strange dress" was meant to be a ghost until he saw the testimony of Garrick's reaction "and fell into so violent a trembling, that his knees knocked against each other".[8] For Fielding the sympathetic act of transference is merely ludicrous, but others described the performance as a revelation: "he preserved Shakespear's fire undiminished, faithful as the electric, and sent the animated shock of nature's flame home to the heart."[9] The spirit world is here reconceived as the catalyst for sublime emotion. Garrick taught the new aesthetically reified fear of the supernatural by example.

I should perhaps insert two disclaimers. It has not been my intention to suggest that there is a straight path leading from Cock Lane and Drury Lane to the enthusiastic reception of *The Castle of Otranto* and *The Monk*. In fact, as we know, their reception was stormy; plenty of injunctions and prohibitions remained to trouble the writing and reading of modern fictions of the supernatural until well into the following century. Neither would I want to pretend that ghost belief suddenly vanished in the year 1762; but what *was* lost in the debâcle was a viable public discourse in which to express that belief — it would not be recovered until the renaissance of spiritualism in the mid-nineteenth century. Summing up, the Cock Lane incident marks, in the form of an exemplary parable, a shift in paradigms of thought, an enabling condition for the literary exploitation of supernatural terror, and thus for the fictional genre we call Gothic.

---

8. Henry Fielding, *Tom Jones*, Penguin, 1966, 757.

9. Anonymous, *An Essay on the Character of Hamlet as Performed by Mr. Henderson at the Theatre-Royal in the Hay-Market*, 2nd edn, London, 1777, n.p.

SENTIMENTAL HORRORS: FEELING IN THE GOTHIC NOVEL

PETER DE VOOGD

The most one can hope to do in a short article like this is to introduce an argument, or throw up some ideas that might be fruitfully picked up in a much longer discussion. So my title is not only pretentious but also somewhat misleading: it sounds like the title of a book. But it is a book that might be written.

Let me begin by whetting your appetite with two short Gothic passages, one from a highly dramatic speech, the other from a more narrative section, both taken from novels discussed here. This is the first passage:

> The prisons of the inquisition .... Hark! — What a piteous groan!
> — See the melancholy wretch who utter'd it, just brought forth to
> undergo the anguish of a mock trial, and endure the utmost pains
> that a studied system of *religious cruelty* has been able to invent.
> Behold this helpless victim delivered up to his tormentors. His
> body so wasted with sorrow and long confinement, you'll see
> every nerve and muscle as it suffers. — Observe the last
> movement of that horrid engine! — What convulsions it has
> thrown him into! — Consider the nature of the posture in which
> he now lies stretch'd, — What exquisite tortures he endures by it!

How very typical this is: the groans are as "piteous" as the wretch is "melancholy", and of course the pains are not only "utmost", but finally "exquisite" as well. And here is the second passage, in which the names are just right, and in which the customary exhortation for the reader to visualize ("Observe!") is coupled with emotive punctuation marks:

> Alas! Don Alfonso, said the Friar, raising himself up a little, I
> have nothing to bequeathe which will pay the expence of
> bequeathing, except the history of myself, which, I could not die
> in peace unless I left it as a legacy to the world ... it is a story so
> uncommon, it must be read by all mankind .... Almighty director
> of every event in my life! he continued, looking up earnestly and

raising his hands towards heaven — thou whose hand has led me on through such a labyrinth of strange passages down into this scene of desolation, assist the decaying memory of an old, infirm, and broken-hearted man — direct my tongue, by the spirit of thy eternal truth, that this gentleman may set down naught but what is written in that Book, from whose records, said he, clasping his hands together, I am to be condemn'd or acquitted!

And then, at long last (since a number of parenthetic phrases that further delay the beginning of the story proper have been left out) the passage ends with these words: "and the old gentleman turning a little more towards the notary, began to dictate his story in these words — And where's the rest of it, La Fleur? said I, as he just enter'd the room."

Because, in fact, that was a page from *A Sentimental Journey* — but Sterne's notary public was changed into Don Alfonso, and his old gentleman into a Friar, for the right sort of *frisson*. The first fragment was taken from Laurence Sterne's famous sermon on "The Abuses of Conscience" (first published in 1750), which is read by Corporal Trim in volume 2 of *Tristram Shandy* (1760), with comical interruptions by Uncle Toby, Walter Shandy and Doctor Slop.[1]

The Gothic genre derived nearly all of its techniques and mannerisms from the Sentimental novel, and only gradually (and unevenly at that) changed its themes, turning away from the sentimentalist belief in an innate Moral Sense, towards the much grimmer view that ours is the realm of an amoral sublime. It may be useful to give a general characteristics of Sentimentalism, in which (I think) the "Gothicist" will find much that sounds familiar.

Sentimentalism, which is often said to have had its hey-day in the Fifties, Sixties and Seventies of the eighteenth century, cannot be characterized simply as a passing and slightly embarrassing vogue for the portrayal of virtuously distressed men and women much given to sympathetic tearfulness and a strange propensity for staring at the moon, turning pale, and swooning. The vehement debate and emotion which the sentimental vogue caused at the time, as well as its influence, which lasted well beyond the middle of the nineteenth century (Thackeray still parodies it in *Vanity Fair* and Dickens used it to full effect) indicate that it cannot have been as marginal a phenomenon as it is often taken for.

---

1. Laurence Sterne, *The Life and Opinions of Tristram Shandy*, London, 1760, II, 143-45; *A Sentimental Journey*, London, 1768, II, 139-43.

Sentimentalism finds its origins in certain developments in eighteenth-century philosophy. As a reaction to the ideas of Hobbes and Mandeville, who regarded egoism and self-interest as man's most important mainsprings, more "optimistic" theories were developed which presented the world as the best of all possible worlds, God as desirous of man's happiness, and man as "good" by nature, key concepts being sympathy, described as "our fellow-feeling with any passion whatsoever" by James Sambrook, and its nearly-synonymous partner, benevolence.[2] Shaftesbury's philosophy emphasized man's Moral Sense: an innate conscience which is the source of our moral distinctions and which enables us to distinguish *perfectly* between good and evil, thus also being a means of achieving happiness. In the Moral Sense view, ethics and aesthetics are closely linked: "what is at once both *beautiful* and *true*, is, of consequence, *agreeable* and GOOD."[3] In the literary works that this philosophy influenced, an unusually strong connection is assumed between life and literature, which leads to a central characteristic of sentimentalism: its purpose is not so much to analyse feelings as to moralize on them so as to teach the reader certain values that at the time were still regarded as absolute.

Since vice is unnatural, and man is by nature good and endowed with an intuitive Moral Sense which only needs to be activated and developed, sentimental literature strongly concentrates on the good, the virtuous and the pious, and it does so with characters that are on the whole simplified and exemplary, and situations that are mostly conventional (probably in order not to distract the reader from the moral message). Elizabeth Napier, one of the best recent critics of the Gothic genre, points out that in Gothic fiction the "more elaborate the plot, the more disposable [are] the characters".[4] This equally applies to Sentimental fiction. Thus few readers notice that in *A Sentimental Journey* Yorick's manservant La Fleur disappears without leaving a trace the moment he is no longer necessary to further what little plot the novel has. For that matter, very few people are fully aware of the extent to which Sentimental characters are as inconsistent as the plots are expansive. After all, these characters merely function as vehicles for the more important purpose: by learning

---

2. James Sambrook, *The Eighteenth Century: The Intellectual and Cultural Context of English Literature, 1700-1789*, London, 1986, 55.

3. Shaftesbury, *Characteristicks ...*, Vol. III, "Miscellaneous Reflections", London, 1714, 183.

4. Elizabeth Napier, *The Failure of Gothic: Problems of Disjunction in an Eighteenth-Century Literary Form*, Oxford, 1987, 36.

about "good feelings" in fictional characters, the reader's sympathy is aroused as his Moral Sense is appealed to, and he is educated through the identification with the sensitive and virtuous people he reads about. It is this centrality of the moral *sententia* (and it is useful here to remember the original sense of the word "sentiment") which is Sentimentalism's most distinguishing element.

Form and style of the sentimental novel also illustrate the prominence of emotion over psychological development and plot. Rather than presenting longer lines of narration in a logical order, it tends to concentrate on scattered moments of intense feeling. These are more often than not described in identical terms, so that the well-read reader is, as it were, pre-programmed to respond in the appropriate manner. The convention of the lost manuscript of which only bits and pieces remain, and the epistolary form in which many novels of sentiment were written are means of achieving a certain fragmentariness of narration, which is often emphasized by an abundant (and much-parodied) use of emotive exclamation-marks, dashes, capitals and italics which break the flow of a sentence.

As an illustration of the sentimental style, here follows a passage from Samuel Richardson's *Pamela* (in the text of the original 1741 edition). Pamela's circumstances have just changed for the better: from a servant-girl, harassed by her master Mr B., she has become his bride-to-be and future mistress of the house. Her father, whom she has not seen for a long time, has been invited by Mr B. who, for the amusement of his guests, has organized their first meeting to take place with everyone present. Pamela (who has not been told a thing) now enters the room where her father is sitting in a corner. The passage is part of a letter from Pamela to her mother:

> Miss *Darnford* rose, and met me at the Door, and said, Well, Miss we long'd for your Company. I did not see my dear Father; and it seems his Heart was too full to speak; and he got up, and sat down three or four times successively, unable to come to me, or to say any thing ....
>
> Said my Master, Did you send your Letter away to the Post-house, my good Girl, for your Father? To be sure, Sir, said I, I did not forget that: I took the Liberty to desire Mr. *Thomas* to carry it. — What, said he, I wonder, will the good old Couple say to it? O Sir, said I, your Goodness will be a Cordial to their dear honest Hearts! At that, my dear Father, not able to contain himself, nor yet to stir from the Place, gush'd out into a Flood of Tears, which he, good soul! had been struggling with, it seems; and cry'd out, O my dear Child!

I knew the Voice, and lifting up my Eyes, and seeing my Father, gave a Spring, overturn'd the Table, without Regard to the Company, and threw myself at his Feet, O my Father! my Father! said I, can it be! — Is it you? Yes, it is! It is! — O bless your happy — Daughter! I would have said, and down I sunk.

My Master seem'd concern'd. — I fear'd, said he, that the Surprize would be too much for her Spirits; and all the Ladies ran to me, and made me drink a Glass of Water; and I found myself incircled in the arms of my dearest Father. — O tell me, said I, every thing. How long have you been here? When did you come? How does my honour'd Mother? And half a dozen Questions more, before he could answer one.

They permitted me to retire, with my Father; and then I pour'd forth all my Vows, and Thanksgivings to God for this additional Blessing; and confirm'd all my Master's Goodness to his scarce-believing Amazement. And we kneeled together, blessing God, and one another, for several ecstatick Minutes; and my Master coming in soon after, my dear Father said, O Sir, what a Change is this! May God reward and bless you in this world and the next![5]

Several characteristic sentimental features can be pointed out in this passage. The reunion of Pamela and her father arouses vehement emotions in them both, and their gestures and postures leave the reader in little doubt about this. When the old man sees his daughter again, whose "Virtue" he has been so worried about ("If she be but virtuous, 'tis all in all"), his heart is at first "too full to speak". He remains in his chair, unable to stir or say anything, until a remark by Pamela causes him to gush out in a flood of tears and cry out. Pamela, when she spots her "dear father", runs to him, knocking down a table in the process, and throws herself at his feet, after which she manages to sink down even further in a swoon, like a true sentimental heroine. Mr B. apparently regards her as such too, for he now expresses his concern about her delicate spirits.

Pamela's eye-witness account to her mother records all the particularities of speech that indicate highly exciting moments. Her normally rather formal diction ("I took the Liberty to desire Mr Thomas to carry it"; "your Goodness will be a Cordial to their dear honest Hearts") changes into a rapid succession of questions, exclamations, and unfinished sentences at the supreme moment ("O my father! my father!

---

5. Samuel Richardson, *Pamela*, London, 1741, II, 105-106.

can it be? Is it you? Yes, it is! it is! O bless your happy — "). Needless
to say, when Pamela and her father are at long last "permitted ... to
retire", they do not forget their religious duty and spend "several
ecstatick Minutes" on their knees thanking God, their fervour
underscoring the moral end of such writing.

None of this will be very unfamiliar to the Gothicist, and it may be
instructive, for a closer comparison of the Sentimental and the Gothic,
to look at another reunion of daughter and father, that of Isabella and
Frederic in Walpole's *The Castle of Otranto*. Theodore, the hero, tall,
dark and handsome and covertly admired by both the princesses Isabella
and Matilda, has by accident wounded a knight in battle whom he
thought was a retainer of the tyrant Manfred. The error is soon cleared
up but the knight seems to think he is dying, which conveniently makes
for the following emotional scene, just before the surgeon tells him that
none of his wounds is dangerous:

> The Knight recovering his speech, said in a faint and faultering
> voice, generous foe, we have both been in an error: I took thee for
> an instrument of the tyrant; I perceive thou hast made the like
> mistake — It is too late for excuses — I faint — if *Isabella* is at
> hand — call her — I have important secrets to — He is dying! said
> one of the attendants; has nobody a crucifix about them? *Andrea*,
> do thou pray over him — Fetch some water, said *Theodore*, and
> pour it down his throat, while I hasten to the princess — saying
> this, he flew to *Isabella*, and in a few words told her modestly,
> that he had been so unfortunate by mistake as to wound a
> gentleman from her father's court, who wished e'er he died to
> impart something of consequence to her. The princess, who had
> been transported at hearing the voice of *Theodore* as he called her
> to come forth, was astonished at what she heard. Suffering herself
> to be conducted by *Theodore* the new proof of whose valour
> recalled her dispersed spirits, she came where the bleeding Knight
> lay speechless on the ground — but her fears returned when she
> beheld the domestics of *Manfred*. She would again have fled, if
> *Theodore* had not made her observe that they were unarmed, and
> had not threatened them with instant death, if they should dare to
> seize the princess. The stranger, opening his eyes, and beholding
> a woman, said — art thou — pray tell me truly — art thou *Isabella*
> of *Vicenza*? I am; said she; good heaven restore thee! — Then
> thou — then thou — said the Knight, struggling for utterance —
> seest — thy father — give me one — oh! amazement! horror! what
> do I hear! what do I see! cried *Isabella*. My father! you my father!
> how come you here, Sir, for heaven's sake speak! — oh! run for
> help, or he will expire! — 'Tis most true, said the wounded

Knight, exerting all his force; I am *Frederic* thy father — yes, I
came to deliver thee — It will not be — give me a parting kiss,
and take — Sir, said *Theodore*, do not exhaust yourself: suffer us
to convey you to the castle —[6]

The similarities with the aims of Sentimentalist authors are obvious, and
so are the methods. Here, as in *Pamela*, the punctuation is used to full
effect to express the characters' vehement emotions. The dashes of
varying length, the idiosyncratic use of full stops, colons and semi-colons
as well as the abundance of exclamation-marks make for jerky sentences
with abrupt transitions, and this syntax is meant to evoke in the reader
the appropriate emotional responses. Not only the violence but also the
variety of the emotions which the characters undergo is impressive.
Within split seconds Isabella feels "transported" and "astonished", her
spirits are "dispersed" and almost immediately "recalled", her fears
return as soon as they are allayed, she wants to flee, yet stays.

The purpose of all this was clearly stated by Walpole (or should one
say, the finder of the novel, which according to one of the conventions
of sentimental novel-writing is allegedly a manuscript "found in the
library of an ancient Catholic family in the north of *England*" and
"printed at *Naples* in 1529") in the prefatory Sonnet to Lady Mary Coke,
which was added in the second edition:

> The gentle Maid, whose hapless tale
> These melancholy pages speak;
> Say, gracious Lady, shall she fail
> To draw the tear adown thy cheek?
>
> No; never was thy pitying breast
> Insensible to human woes;
> Tender, tho' firm, it melts distrest
> For weaknesses it never knows.

And so on. The main purpose of early Gothicism was to move the heart
rather than frighten it, and it would have recognised Richardson's
explicitly stated moral end: "My Story is designed to strengthen the
tender Mind, and to enable the worthy Heart to bear up against the
Calamities of Life" (letter to Lady Bradshaigh, 15 December 1748).
Contemporary book illustrations bear this out. A closer look at **Figs 4-6**

---

6. Horace Walpole, *The Castle of Otranto*, 4th edn, London, 1782, 125-27.

Fig. 4: "Affecting interview between Pamela and her father in
the presence of the Squire and his guests" — *Pamela; or,
Virtue Rewarded*, London, 1801-03, II, facing page 50,
engraving by A. Warren after R. Corbould.

"Art thou—pray tell me truly—art thou Isabella of Vicenza!"
p. 123.

Fig. 5: "Art thou — pray tell me truly — art thou Isabella of Vicenza!" — woodcut facing page 123, *The Castle of Otranto: A Gothic Story*, London, 1809.

"I am going where sorrow never dwells." *p.* 189

Fig. 6: "I am going where sorrow never dwells." — woodcut
facing page 189, *The Castle of Otranto: A Gothic Story*,
London, 1809.

will yield very little to distinguish the Sentimental from the Gothic *tableau*.

As a final example of the largely similar techniques of Gothic and Sentimental fiction, here are two descriptions of the deaths of the protagonists of *The Castle of Otranto* and Mackenzie's *The Man of Feeling* respectively. Matilda has been stabbed by her father; in the ensuing commotion Theodore suggests he marry her ("at least she shall be mine in death"), but

> — *Isabella* made signs to him to be silent, apprehending the Princess was near her end. What is she dead? cried *Theodore*; is it possible? The violence of his exclamations brought *Matilda* to herself. Lifting up her eyes, she looked round for her mother — Life of my soul! I am here; cried *Hippolita*; think not I will quit thee! Oh! you are too good; said *Matilda* — but weep not for me, my mother! I am going where sorrow never dwells — *Isabella*, thou hast loved me; wot thou not supply my fondness to this dear, dear woman? — indeed I am faint! Oh! my child! my child! said *Hippolita* in a flood of tears, can I not withhold thee a moment! — It will not be; said *Matilda* — commend me to heaven — where is my father? forgive him, dearest mother — forgive him my death; it was an error — Oh! I had forgotten — dearest mother, I vowed never to see *Theodore* more — perhaps that has drawn down this calamity — but it was not intentional — can you pardon me? — Oh! wound not my agonizing soul! said *Hippolita*; thou never couldst offend me — alas! she faints! help! help! — I would say something more, said *Matilda* struggling, but it wonnot be — *Isabella* — *Theodore* — for my sake — Oh! — she expired. *Isabella* and her women tore *Hippolita* from the corse; but *Theodore* threatened destruction to all who attempted to remove him from it (192-94).

Harley, the man of feeling, is ill and visited by Miss Walton. He has silently been in love with her for a long time but has never dared to express his feelings to her.

> He paused some moments — "I am in such a state as calls for sincerity, let that also excuse it — It is perhaps the last time we shall ever meet. I feel something particularly solemn in the acknowledgement, yet my heart swells to make it, awed as it is by a sense of my presumption, by a sense of your perfections" — He paused again — "Let it not offend you to know their power over one so unworthy — It will, I believe, soon cease to beat, even with that feeling which it shall lose the latest. — To love Miss

Walton could not be a crime; — if to declare it is one — the expiation will be made." — Her tears were now flowing without controul. — "Let me intreat you, said she, to have better hopes — Let not life be so indifferent to you; if my wishes can put any value on it — I will not pretend to misunderstand you — I know your worth — I have known it long — I have esteemed it — What would you have me say! — I have loved it as it deserved." — He seized her hand — a languid colour reddened his cheek — a smile brightened faintly in his eye. As he gazed on her, it grew dim, it fixed, it closed — He sighed, and fell back on his seat — Miss Walton screamed at the sight — His aunt and the servants rushed into the room — They found them lying motionless together. — His physician happened to call at that instant. Every art was tried to recover them — With Miss Walton they succeeded — But Harley was gone forever![7]

These passages contain 497 words, 48 dashes and 18 exclamation marks. This abundance of emotive markers is not the only link with Sterne's texts, which were for that very reason so eminently adaptable in the beginning of this article.

My thesis can be summarized as follows: the Gothic genre arose from the Sentimental, and its early history should be written in terms of that continuation. This does, of course, raise the issue of dates. Boldly put, Sentimentalism begins with Samuel Richardson's novels, as summarized in his amazing and mammoth *Collection of the Moral and Instructive Sentiments, Maxims, Cautions, and Reflexions to be derived from* Pamela, Clarissa, *and* Sir Charles Grandison (published in 1755); it culminates in the works of Laurence Sterne in the 1760s and Mackenzie's *The Man of Feeling* (published in 1771 but begun earlier), after which it unavoidably tapers off. Gothicism has a later start, with a curiously long interval between Walpole's trend-setting 1764 *The Castle of Otranto* and the much later Gothic 1790s. What happened in the nineteenth century does not concern us here. Which means that I cannot, in the short space allotted to me, work out precisely how Sentimentalism, in due course, led to Maturin's *Melmoth the Wanderer*, that marvellous collection of Gothic and Sentimental tales, the main interest of which lies not in the mostly unfinished action, but in emotions and their effects upon personality — as Maturin himself put it in the preface to *The Milesian Chief* (1811).

---

7. Henry Mackenzie, *The Man of Feeling*, London, 1787, 272-74.

When Elizabeth MacAndrew states that the purpose of Gothic fiction was "closely allied" to that of the Sentimental novel, this is not enough.[8] Nor does the commonplace that Gothic and Sentimental share methods of characterization, structural and narrative systems, devices and images, and the recurrent theme of imprisonment and fragmentariness, in itself explain very much. I would like to stress that such general descriptions tend to lose sight of the historical order of things. Thus it is slightly weird to read in Coral Ann Howells's otherwise excellent *Love, Mystery, and Misery* that the Gothic writers "made the first experimental attempts to write a new kind of fiction which dealt primarily with emotional and imaginative awareness, something that had been regarded as the domain of poetry and drama, not of the novel" — this is an unhistorical overstatement contradicted by her own observation elsewhere that "Gothic fiction represents the extreme development of the eighteenth-century cult of Sensibility, as if Richardson's heroines had finally lost all sense of objective reality".[9] Indeed, the extent to which Horace Walpole was indebted to the Sterne he so despised (a social upstart, and a Northerner to boot) must still be traced. Close analysis of Sterne's rhetorical effects will demonstrate the masterly way in which he described the subtlest of external details of emotional display of his characters' emotive behaviour so that the reader can deduce the highly complex inner psychological movements that lead to his characters' behaviour.

I obviously cannot entirely agree when Elizabeth Napier comments in her stimulating *The Failure of Gothic*:

> The link, indeed, between Gothic and sentimental fiction is strong: both modes assume the primacy of feeling, and the pleasure of exercising it vicariously, and gain their effect by encouraging particularly strong emotional responses from their readers. The forms can overlap because it is the intensity of the response and not the type of experience eliciting the response (pleasurable, terrifying) that is in question. Gothic novels are, thus, replete with sentimental episodes.[10]

I have argued that, in the second half of the eighteenth century, the Sentimental, which had contained "Gothic" elements from the start, was

---

8. Elizabeth MacAndrew, *The Gothic Tradition in Fiction*, New York, 1979, 3.

9. Coral Ann Howells, *Love, Mystery, and Misery: Feeling in Gothic Fiction*, London, 1978, 8.

10. *Ibid.*, 26-27.

replaced partly by the Gothic, which was to contain "Sentimental" elements until its end. The two modes (rather than "forms"), which in Napier's account are regarded as separate if similar, in my view are coexistential parts of the same continuum, in which, historically, the Sentimental came first.

STURM UND DRANG IN RADCLIFFE AND LEWIS

HELGA HUSHAHN

On 21 April 1788, having procured two collections of *Theatre
Allemande*, French translations of the latest German plays, one by Friedel
and De Bonville, the other by Junker and Liebault, Henry Mackenzie
read an *Account of the German Theatre* to the Royal Society of
Edinburgh. On the whole, his criticism was enthusiastic, commenting
upon the irregularity of Goethe's *Sturm und Drang* play *Götz von
Berlichingen*, and at the same time noticing beauties in "the simple
manners, the fidelity, the valour and the generosity of a German knight
… portrayed in a variety of natural scenes".[1] He devoted twelve of the
37 pages of his account to *The Robbers*, and introducing Schiller to
Britain, he claimed that "the most remarkable, and the most strongly
impressive of all pieces contained in these volumes, is that by which the
collection of Mr Friedel is closed, *Les Voleurs*, a tragedy by Mr Schiller,
a young man, who at the time of writing it was only twenty three". Here
again he mentioned the "total disregard of regularity", but otherwise
spoke in glowing terms: "[Schiller] has endowed [his] characters with a
language in the highest degree eloquent, impassioned and sublime …. it
appears to me one of the most uncommon productions of untutored
genius that modern times can boast" (180-81, 191). Mackenzie cannot
refrain from translating three scenes from what is already a translation,
and one of the scenes he chooses (it is his second sample) is from the
fourth Act: a scene in which Charles discovers his father, whom he
believes to be dead, imprisoned in a ruined tower, and which contains the
most striking Gothic features. Mackenzie ends his account of *The
Robbers* in words that without hesitation lead me to conclude that he
understood it as a Gothic play:

---

1. Henry Mackenzie, "Account of the German Theatre", in *Transactions of the
Royal Society of Edinburgh*, Edinburgh, 1790, 178.

If [Schiller's] genius can accommodate itself to better subjects, and to a more regular conduct of the drama, no modern poet seems to possess powers so capable of bending the mind before him, of rousing its feelings by the elevation of his sentiments, or of thrilling them with the terrors of his imaginations (192).

In the first phase of his reception in Britain, a part of Schiller's *oeuvre* seems to have been destined to provide motifs of terror for a generation of writers of Romance. The first English translation of *Die Räuber*, Schiller's most exalted piece from his *Sturm und Drang* period, was made by Alexander Fraser Tytler in 1792.[2] Exponents of *Sturm und Drang* (which one normally thinks of as covering the period 1760-1790) "painted life in the extremes", probed mysteries, exposed horrors and blended Gothic properties into their literary output, in a fashion which appealed to the whole of Europe. Therefore, it is not surprising that those who wished to write Romances in the Gothic mode, such as Matthew Gregory Lewis and Ann Radcliffe, made use of Schiller's writings. Radcliffe was to draw upon his unfinished novel *Der Geisterseher* (1788), rather than upon *The Robbers*, and it is with this relationship that I will deal in the first part of this essay. Lewis also used the *Sturm and Drang* writers in *The Monk*, Schiller amongst them, and an indication of the variety of his sources will be given in the second.

Ann Radcliffe and *Der Geisterseher*

From the evidence of passages in her *Journal through Holland and Germany* (1796) it has been claimed that Ann Radcliffe possibly knew some German,[3] and this is supported by her use of *Der Geisterseher*, Schiller's final contribution to his youthful *Sturm und Drang* output, in *The Mysteries of Udolpho*, which appeared before Schiller's work was translated into English. *The Ghostseer; or the Apparitionist* (as Schiller's work was called when it was translated into English in 1795) is set in Venice and its immediate environment, but the setting does not have quite the same function in Schiller's work as it does in Ann Radcliffe's Romance. In Schiller's tale an incidental description of the banks of the

---

2. As far as I know Douglas Milburn was the first person to demonstrate by virtue of a letter of Tytler's that he was the translator: see, Douglas Milburn, "The First English Translation of 'Die Räuber': French Bards and Scottish Translations", *Monatshefte*, 59 (1967), 41-63.

3. L.F. Thompson, "Ann Radcliffe's Knowledge of German", *Modern Language Review*, 12 (1925), 190-91.

Brenta serves as the backdrop for his characters — a party of young nobles on a "Bildungsreise" — and furthers the plot.

In Schiller's work this episode remains only a short section, but in Ann Radcliffe's tale a description of the journey to Venice on the Brenta, evidently derived from Schiller,[4] is returned to on three different occasions. The first occasion, the approach of Emily St Aubert and Montoni's travelling party towards Venice on the Brenta has a great deal in common with Schiller's text in its depiction of the rich natural beauty of the banks of the river.[5] The motivation for the second occurrence of the Brenta motif — when Montoni and his family embark on an excursion in order to "avoid the heats, and catch the cool breezes of night" (206) — is very like that in *Der Geisterseher*, when the Prince, who has been ill, is advised by his physician "to make an excursion on the Brenta for a change of air".[6] In *The Mysteries of Udolpho* the barge steers towards the Adriatic, and through a minutely detailed description of the surroundings in the fading light accompanied by calm sounds, Emily's mood is temporarily soothed into composure (206-209). The motif is used for the third time when Emily takes "the *fresco* along the bank of the Brenta in Madame Quesnel's carriage" (214). What is conveyed is Emily's melancholy in contrast to the charming gaiety of the natives.

In *The Mysteries of Udolpho* Ann Radcliffe reproduces a puzzling inconsistency derived from Schiller when she has the Montoni party arrive at Venice while the Carnival is in progress. In *Der Geisterseher*, the Count of O**, who tells the tale in his Memoires, writes that "It was on my return to Kurland that I visited the Prince of ** at Venice in the year 17** at the time of carnival".[7] It seems strange that in both works the characters need to seek refuge from the heat and air of the city just before the beginning of Lent, in late winter. Perhaps the mistake occurs because Schiller, like Ann Radcliffe, needed to consult secondary sources

4. See Frederic Ewen, *The Prestige of Schiller in England 1788-1859*, New York, 1932, 35 ff.

5. Ann Radcliffe, *The Mysteries of Udolpho*, ed. Bonamy Dobrée, Oxford, 1970, 174-75.

6. Friedrich Schiller, *Der Geisterseher*, with an Introduction by Emil Staiger, Frankfurt am Main, 1976, 85: "eine Spazierfahrt auf der Brenta zu machen, um die Luft zu verändern."

7. *Ibid.*, 77: "Es war auf meiner Zurückreise nach Kurland, im Jahre 17** um die Karnevalszeit, als ich den Prinzen von ** in Venedig besuchte."

for his description of Italy, since he had never travelled outside Germany.

In Ann Radcliffe's *The Italian, or the Confessional of the Black Penitents* the borrowings from *Der Geisterseher* are not restricted to one or two motifs. Both works make use of the "Black Legend", Northern European imaginations of the darker side of Catholicism. The starting point for Schiller's story is the fact that the Prince at the onset of the story is a Protestant, who by the death of a cousin has moved up the line of succession to the throne. For the Catholic church it is of paramount importance to undermine the stability of Protestantism and to promote the establishment of another Catholic state; the Jesuits therefore conspire to persuade the Prince to convert to Catholicism, which he ultimately does. They recruit an Armenian (or a Jesuit posing as an Armenian), one of the *Geisterseher* of the novel. Ann Radcliffe likewise exploits the black legend which associates the Catholic church with sinister intrigue, by placing her protagonists in a mysterious Catholic environment. The story concerns the tribulations of a young couple, who are entangled in the snares of a religious system in which an obscure confessor and his helpers try to thwart their union by criminal means.

In *The Italian*, the affections of Ellena Rosalba and Vincentio di Vivaldi, at first frustrated, but eventually successful, are of central interest, while the Prince's love story in *Der Geisterseher* plays only a secondary role. The Prince in *Der Geisterseher* is introduced as a man "at the age of thirty-five [who] up to now ... has remained indifferent to the fair sex" ("in einem Alter von fünfunddreißig Jahren ... Das schöne Geschlecht war ihm bis jetzt gleichgültig gewesen"[8]); later in the second volume of the "interessante Geschichte", after he has changed his attitude towards his faith, he visits a church on La Giudecca. There, like Vivaldi in *The Italian*, Schiller's Prince similarly sees a beautiful woman of mysterious antecedents. The Prince's investigations suggest, at first, that she is of noble Greek origin, and a Catholic.[9] Later it is established that she is actually a German of noble extraction, the illegitimate child of an aristocratic mother. While, like all her mysteries, the origin of Ann Radcliffe's heroine is finally explained, the enigmatic veil surrounding Schiller's mysterious young woman is never entirely lifted.

---

8. *Der Geisterseher*, 78.

9. "Eine Griechin also, und von Stande, wie es scheint, von Vermögen wenigstens, und wohltätig .... Aber eine Griechin und in einer katholischen Kirche!" (*Ibid.*, 179).

The most striking evidence of Ann Radcliffe's exploitation of *Der Geisterseher* is found in the figure of the prophetic monk of Paluzzi. When Schiller wrote his story, the theme of necromancy was in the air and in the news, partly because of the current fame of Cagliostro, alias Guiseppe Balsamo, a charlatan who wandered throughout Europe claiming supernatural powers and preternatural longevity. In *Der Geisterseher*, while the Carnival is in progress in Venice, a figure masked as an Armenian proclaims to the Prince: "At nine o'clock .... Wish yourself happiness, Prince. At nine o'clock he died."[10] A week later, the Prince receives news of the death of his cousin, the Crown Prince, which means that between him and his accession to the throne there now stands only an uncle without issue. Sinister and mysterious allusions still remain hidden, but from this moment on unaccountable occurrences as well as fraudulent incidents succeed each other.

In *The Italian* a comparable kind of figure has the similar task of initiating the mysterious intrigue in which the main protagonists are ensnared. A seemingly superhuman creature with knowledge of Vivaldi's concerns at first glides past him as a warning, and later more menacingly as a creature in a monk's habit bids him, "Go not to the villa Altieri ... for death is in the house!".[11] These prophecies by a stranger or a monk or an Armenian, unaccountably turning up with knowledge about the hero's affairs, in both cases are the means by which a higher power attempts to win him for its own purpose. In the case of Schiller's tale the Protestant Prince is lured into what the Protestant court terms apostasy, while in *The Italian*, the prophetic monk is the agent of the schemer Schedoni, who is acting for the powerful Marchesa di Vivaldi who has ambitious plans for her son.

The scene in *The Italian* when Vivaldi is summoned by the Inquisition echoes the episode in *Der Geisterseher* when the Prince is summoned to witness its swift justice. The terror of conspiracy prevails in *Der Geisterseher* as it was to do in *The Italian*. Both Schiller and Radcliffe in their elaborate and contrasting stories transmit comparable messages: Schiller's message is rationalist, the writer being concerned with the Catholic takeover of the State of Württemberg; Ann Radcliffe is concerned that superstition should be properly restrained.

---

10. "Neun Uhr .... Wünschen Sie sich Glück Prince .... Um neun Uhr ist er gestorben" (*Ibid.*, 79).

11. Ann Radcliffe, *The Italian, or the Confessional of the Black Penitents*, ed. Frederick Garber, London, 1968, rpt. 1970, 41.

Matthew Gregory Lewis and *Sturm und Drang*

Some have contended that Matthew Gregory Lewis's *The Monk* stands entirely in the tradition of the English Gothic. Others have maintained that it is an amalgam of at least two French sources — J. Cazotte's *Le Diable amoureux* (1772) and Jaques Marie Boutet Monvel's play *Les Victimes cloitrés* (1791). A third group of scholars and critics is convinced that *The Monk* derives entirely from German sources, and have demonstrated Lewis's central concern with *Sturm und Drang* literature and its fringes.[12]

As far as Lewis's borrowings from Schiller are concerned, *The Robbers* was to become particularly important in his later works, especially in *The Castle Spectre* (1798). In *The Monk*, it is echoes of *Der Geisterseher* that are to be found. It is Schiller's Armenian that provides Lewis with the physiognomy of the Stranger in the story of Agnes and Raymond in *The Monk*. Like the Armenian, this figure has knowledge of the protagonist's secrets, and when he offers his help in exorcizing the ghostly nun, he addresses Raymond's page in a manner very like that of Schiller's Armenian:

> "Youth!" said He in a solemn voice, "He whom you seek, has found that, in which He would fain lose. My hand alone can dry up the blood: Bid your Master wish for me, when the Clock strikes, 'One.'"[13]

Anticipating Ann Radcliffe's summoning of her monk, Schedoni, to appear before an ecclesiastical tribunal, Lewis brings Ambrosio together with his temptress and partner in crime to trial by the Inquisition. Lewis subjects his protagonist and the reader to prolonged apprehension in following the processes of the Inquisition. When he is forced to witness a summary execution,[14] Schiller's Prince faints in the arms of his attendants; Ambrosio, in a similar fashion, "turned pale, and with difficulty prevented himself from sinking upon the ground" when he "perceived" the instruments of torture.

---

12. See, for example, Karl S. Guthke, *Englische Vorromantik und Deutscher Sturm und Drang: M.G. Lewis' Stellung in der Geschichte der deutsch-englischen Literatur-beziehungen*, Göttingen, 1958, esp. 31-35.

13. Matthew Lewis, *The Monk: A Romance*, ed. Howard Anderson, London, 1973, 167.

14. *Der Geisterseher*, 83-84.

Other German sources Lewis seems to have drawn on include Johann Karl August Musäus' story "Die Entführung" ("The Elopement"), derived from his *Volksmährchen der Deutschen* collected and adapted between 1782 and 1786, which is used in *The Monk* as the basis of the parallel story in the subplot of Raymond and Agnes;[15] and Christian Friedrich Daniel Schubart's lyrical ballad, "Der ewige Jude" ("The Wandering Jew"), written in 1783, which contributes a version of the symbolic figure of the Wandering Jew or the Wanderer to *The Monk*.[16] To these works one should add "Die Teufelsbeschwörung" ("Evocation of the Devil"), contained in the fourth volume of *Sagen der Vorzeit* (*Legends of Ancient Times*), by Georg Philip Ludwig Leonhard Wächter, alias Veit Weber, published in Berlin between 1787 and 1798, on which

---

15. It is not clear whether Lewis, who spent nearly nine months in Germany in 1792-1793 (seven months of his stay in Weimar) in order to learn German, drew on the German original or the English translation which had been available from 1791 under the title *Popular Tales of the Germans*. In a short note, "The Monk and Musäus 'Die Entführung'", in *Philological Quarterly*, 32 (1953), 346-48, Louis F. Peck argues that it is not certain that Lewis had drawn upon Musäus's story, despite Sir Walter Scott's accusation in 1830 of plagiarism. Peck bases his argument on Lewis's letter of 2 October 1807 to Sir Walter Scott where he refers to reading "Musäus's five volumes (in which by the bye, I found the same tradition employed under the name of 'Die Entführung' which furnished me with the Bleeding Nun)". The implication seems to be that he had only recently been reading Musäus, and had come on the story of "Die Entführung" by chance (an implication which Scott seems to have forgotten or ignores in his comment of 1830). The parenthesis in the letter echoes what Lewis said in his Advertisement to the first edition of *The Monk*. However, despite Peck's case, even if Lewis seems to be claiming that he had not read "Die Entführung" before 1807, by comparing the text of his Advertisement to *The Monk* with the first sentence of Musäus's tale the similarities seem too strong to allow one to believe anything other than Lewis's understandable desire to be economical with the truth. Defending himself against the anticipated charge of plagiarism in his Advertisement, Lewis writes: "The *Bleeding Nun* is a tradition still credited in many parts of Germany; and I have been told, that the ruins of the Castle of *Lauenstein*, which she is supposed to haunt, may yet be seen upon the borders of *Thuringia.*" Compare this with the beginning of "Die Entführung" (J.K.A. Musäus, *Volksmährchen der Deutschen*, Leipzig, 1847, 481): "Am Wässerlein Lockwitz im Voigtlande, auf der thüringischen Grenze, ist gelegen das Schloß Lauenstein, welches vor Zeiten ein Nonnenkloster war, das im Hussittenkriege zerstört wurde" ("Near the Lockwitz brook in Voigtland on the borders of Thuringia the Castle of Lauenstein is situated, which a long time ago had been a convent and was destroyed during the Hussite war"). The evidence of the verses exchanged between the "lovers" in Musäus's story (quoted below pp. 96-97), and Lewis's version of them, would seem to be conclusive evidence against Peck's argument.

16. Eino Railo, *The Haunted Castle*, New York, 1927, repr. 1964, 197.

Lewis modelled the demolition of his hero-villain in *The Monk*.[17] Each of these I will consider in turn.

We can appreciate the depth and complexity of Lewis's borrowings in *The Monk* when we consider the way in which he mixes and blends the account of the elopement of Agnes and Raymond appropriated from Musäus with the even more sensational story of a bleeding nun;[18] to which he adds Schubart's Wandering Jew, to some extent identical with the Armenian or Franciscan monk in *Der Geisterseher*, and now used by Lewis to expand Musäus's humorously ironic story even further and in a wholly different direction.

The prompting for the first sequence of borrowings seems to be the request in "Die Entführung" that the hero makes to a friend, to rid him of the torment of a nun's ghost. This seems to lead Lewis to Schubart's Wandering Jew, Ahasver,[19] a man compelled to wander the earth for at least two thousand years because of his refusal to allow Christ, on his way to Golgotha, to rest in front of his door.[20] Lewis succeeds in combining the supernatural attributes of an eternal Wanderer, who conveys information about the protagonist at a crucial moment, with the figure of the necromancer.

The two short verses in Musäus's tale, one of which is quoted by the lover to the nun's spectre under the delusion that he is speaking to his mistress in disguise, and the second of which is recited by the spectre to the lover, are simply taken over by Lewis:

[Der schöne Fritz] "faßte sie herzig in die Arme und sprach:

Ich habe dich, ich halte Dich,

---

17. In general the availability of German works in English is no problem as far as Lewis is concerned: very soon after his arrival in Weimar he had himself embarked on a translation of some verses from Wieland's *Oberon* (see Louis F. Peck, *A Life of Matthew G. Lewis*, Cambridge: Mass., 1961, 12; and Karl S. Guthke, 49).

18. See Railo, 345-46 n.97 for the controversy involving Georg Herzfeld, Otto Ritter and August Sauer about the claim that Lewis had plagiarized an anonymous novel *Die blutende Gestalt mit Dolch und Lampe oder die Beschwöhrung im Schlosse Stern bei Prag* for *The Monk*; from which it emerges that the Prague book must indeed have been derived from *Ambrosio*, the German translation of *The Monk*.

19. Railo, 195.

20. Schubart's own suffering, when he was incarcerated arbitrarily by his Prince, Karl Eugen of Württemberg, for ten years in the fort of Hohenasperg, no doubt played a part in the creation of this poem.

nie laß ich dich;
fein Liebchen du bist mein,
fein Liebchen ich bin dein,
du mein ich dein, mit Leib und Seel![21]

In Lewis's version Raymond relates his experiences to Agnes's brother Lorenzo:

"Agnes!" said I while I pressed her to my bosom,

Agnes! Agnes! Thou art mine!
Agnes! Agnes! I am thine!
In my veins while blood shall roll,
Thou art mine!
I am thine!
Thine my body! Thine my soul![22]

Ambrosio's final overthrow and destruction appears to derive from Veit Weber's "Die Teufelsbeschwörung".[23] Here the protagonist, Francesco, climbs to the highest point of the cliff and plunges onto a shelf of rock in the sea. Like Ambrosio when he is dropped by the devil on to a rock, Francesco is not dead. His limbs are broken and his skin is torn from the left side of his face, but his mind and his body are not damaged. Both Francesco and Ambrosio have to suffer the physical and mental agony of "Tagelang [zu] sterben" ("a protracted agony") before they are both swept to their watery graves.[24] Similarly both men have their eyes gouged out by a bird of prey, Francesco by a vulture and Ambrosio by an eagle.

By the time Lewis wrote *The Monk*, Schiller and his contemporaries had outgrown *Sturm und Drang*. Schiller had studied Kant and had concerned himself with the ideal of aesthetic determinability — the identification of inclination with duty. Schubart and Musäus were already

21. *Volksmährchen der Deutschen*, 490 (although this is obviously intended as a rhymed verse, it is printed as prose in the mid-nineteenth-century edition that I have used: I have not been able yet to consult any earlier edition).

22. *The Monk*, 155 ff.

23. See Peck, 22. Guthke lists alphabetically those German authors whose works Lewis knew, distinguishing between works for which there is secure evidence and those which one can assume that he may have read (214-16).

24. Cf. Veit Weber, "Die Teufelsbeschwörung", in *Sagen der Vorzeit*, Leipzig, 1840, 67 and *The Monk*, 441-42.

dead, while Weber (Wächter) continued to write for some time on the margins of the movement.[25] The generation of Romantics to come were to pick up the thread that the *Sturm und Drang* writers had dropped. Lewis selected what he needed in order to delve into the recesses of the human mind which shocked his contemporaries as much as it secretely enthralled them. As Lewis's first biographer was to say in respect to his interest in German literature:

> Lewis's predilection for German literature is conspicuous in all his after productions; a propensity little to be wondered at, considering the store of materials which it afforded for his romantic imagination to work upon; and, with the exception of the talented authoress of Frankenstein, we know no English writer who has so successfully adopted both in prose and verse, the wild and bizarre character of that singular school.[26]

---

25. In fact, independently of Schiller, Weber wrote a play, *Wilhelm Tell* (1804).

26. Margaret Baron-Wilson, *The Life and Correspondence of M.G. Lewis*, London, 1839, 73.

NATURE AND PSYCHOLOGY
IN *MELMOTH THE WANDERER* AND *WUTHERING HEIGHTS*

THOMAS KULLMANN

One of the outstanding features of Gothic novels is the frequent descriptions of landscape and weather, including depictions of grand and violent nature, of huge mountains, and thunderstorms. A common feature of these descriptions is that they seem never to be indulged in for their own sake. Nature constantly "means" something beyond itself. Sunsets and moonshine, as well as rain and storms, can either refer to the transcendental order of the universe or serve as a sign system to reflect the psychology of the characters.[1] This sign system was to become one of the main features of Victorian novel-writing. I should like to argue that its origins are to be found in the Gothic novel.

The idea that natural phenomena can be interpreted as signs of something beyond the visible world is also found in Romantic poetry, and can be traced back to the moral philosophy and the pantheistic concepts of the Earl of Shaftesbury, given poetic utterance in Thomson's *The Seasons*.[2] In Shaftesbury and Thomson, natural phenomena form an ill-defined substitute for a personal God, who, in an age of scientific objectivity, is no longer "visible".[3] While scriptural doctrines cease to be accepted as eternal truths, it is in God's works that we become aware of God and the excellence of his creation. A similar approach to Nature

---

1. For a more detailed account of this sign system, see my book *Vermenschlichte Natur: Zur Bedeutung von Landschaft und Wetter im englishen Roman von Ann Radcliffe bis Thomas Hardy*, Tübingen, 1994.

2. Amy Louise Reed, *The Background of Gray's Elegy: A Study in the Taste for Melancholy Poetry 1700-1751*, New York, 1962, 135-37; Wolfgang Herrlinger, *Sentimentalismus und Postsentimentalismus: Studien zum englischen Roman bis zur Mitte des 19. Jahrhunderts*, Tübingen, 1987, 156-58.

3. Joachim Ritter, *Landschaft: Zur Funktion des Ästhetischen in der modernen Gesellschaft*, Münster, 1963, 21-25.

is found in the works of Jean-Jacques Rousseau.[4] Both Thomson and Rousseau emphasize the improving effects of contemplating nature. In this respect Ann Radcliffe is certainly a close follower of Rousseau.[5]

While Radcliffe favours picturesque views which mirror a moral and transcendental ideal, Charles Maturin's landscapes are mostly gloomy and portentous, referring the protagonists and the reader to the evil side of Nature's workings. In Thomson's poem, all varieties of the natural scene are interpreted as signs of the harmony of creation. Maturin's universe, by contrast, seems to be characterized by disorder; and this disorder is paralleled by disorder in nature. As there is no longer any cosmic certainty, there is no certainty about the "meaning" of creation either. As a consequence of this uncertainty, the scope of meanings attributable to Nature is considerably enlarged.

As an example of a description of dark and disorderly nature, I should like to quote a passage from the first part of *Melmoth the Wanderer*. Young John Melmoth, who has just witnessed the death of his uncle on a lonely farm near the east coast of Ireland, has found a mysterious manuscript, which he proposes to read at night-time. His anticipation of reading the manuscript is paralleled by the weather:

> The remainder of the day was passed in gloomy and anxious deliberation, — in traversing his late uncle's room, — approaching the door of the closet, and then retreating from it, — in watching the clouds, and listening to the wind, as if the gloom of the one, or the murmurs of the other, relieved instead of increasing the weight that pressed on his mind.[6]

As far as the plot is concerned, the description of nature appears to be superfluous, as the weather has nothing to do with John Melmoth's anxiety about his uncle's papers. The sentence structure, however, indicates a parallel between the weather and the mental state of the hero: both the clouds and Melmoth's thoughts are "gloomy". There is no evidence of any causal connection between the weather and the mind. We

---

4. Daniel Mornet, *Le sentiment de la nature en France de J.-J. Rousseau à Bernardin de Saint-Pierre: Essai sur les rapports de la littérature et des moeurs*, Paris, 1907, 183-85.

5. Marlis Lemberg-Welfonder, *Ann Radcliffes Beitrag zur englischen Rousseau- -Rezeption im Zeitalter der Französischen Revolution*, Diss. Heidelberg 1989, and see also my book on *Vermenschlichte Natur*.

6. Charles Maturin, *Melmoth the Wanderer*, ed. Douglas Grant, Oxford and New York, 1989, 22.

only get a vague idea that some cosmic upheaval is taking place, which might have a certain influence on the mind of Melmoth. Another narrative function, however, seems to be more important: John Melmoth's mental gloom is given visibility in natural phenomena.

Sometimes, a causal explanation for this parallelism of mind and nature is conveyed through the concept of affinity: characters feel at home in natural scenes which provide analogies for their psychological plight. Immalee, who grows up on a paradisiacal island in the Indian Ocean, experiences nature as harmonious and joyful until she falls in love with Melmoth, the agent of Evil. Her appreciation of nature then undergoes a profound change:

> ... she no longer loved all that is beautiful in nature; she seemed, by an anticipation of her destiny, to make alliance with all that is awful and ominous. She had begun to love the rocks and the ocean, the thunder of the wave, and the sterility of the sand, — awful objects, the incessant recurrence of whose very sound seems intended to remind us of grief and of eternity. Their restless monotony of repetition, corresponds with the beatings of a heart which asks its destiny from the phenomena of nature, and feels the answer is — "Misery".
> Those who love may seek the luxuries of the garden, and inhale added intoxication from its perfumes, which seem the offerings of nature on that altar which is already erected and burning in the heart of the worshipper; — but let those who *have* loved seek the shores of the ocean, and they shall have their answer too (312).

It is obvious that the nature of the island remains the same after Immalee meets Melmoth. The only change is that Immalee now chooses a different set of phenomena as her "habitat". As in the first example, the meaning of nature is determined by the mental state of the onlooker.

This function of the description of nature becomes particularly obvious when the same set of natural phenomena means different things to different persons. When Immalee and Melmoth look at the ocean, they interpret it in opposite ways:

> The ocean, that lay calm and bright before them as a sea of jasper, never reflected two more different countenances, or sent more opposite feelings to two hearts. Over Immalee's, it breathed that deep and delicious reverie, which those forms of nature that unite tranquillity and profundity diffuse over souls whose innocence gives them a right to an unmingled and exclusive enjoyment of nature. None but crimeless and unimpassioned minds ever truly

enjoyed earth, ocean, and heaven. At our first transgression, nature expels us, as it did our first parents, from her paradise for ever.

To the stranger the view was fraught with far different visions. He viewed it as a tiger views a forest abounding with prey; there might be the storm and the wreck; or, if the elements were obstinately calm, there might be the gaudy and gilded pleasure barge, in which a Rajah and the beautiful women of his harem were inhaling the sea breeze under canopies of silk and gold, overturned by the unskillfulness of their rowers, and their plunge, and struggle, and dying agony, amid the smile and beauty of the calm ocean, produce one of those contrasts in which his fierce spirit delighted (299-300).

Immalee's enjoyment of nature corresponds to the view of a benevolent universe; as in Radcliffe's novels, the observation of nature ennobles the virtuous observer. Immalee's appreciation of nature, however, is solely due to her own qualities and her own state of mind, not to any universal order. Melmoth, on the other hand, perceives tranquillity in nature as deceptive.

Sets of natural phenomena, therefore, not only correspond to universal moral concepts such as good and evil, but also, and to a greater extent, to states of mind such a happiness and unhappiness or tranquillity and agitation. Description of nature thus provide an outward correlative to the inner life of the onlooker. With the help of this technique Maturin reaches a new dimension of psychological awareness.

Victorian authors, such as the Brontës, took up this technique of using nature to further their narrative purposes. While little or no reference to cosmic or transcendental conditions are discernible, descriptions of nature become, essentially, a narrative device for presenting the mental state of a novel's characters and of accentuating the development of the plot. Sometimes natural phenomena were given human emotions, as in "raging waves" or "melancholy clouds", but it was understood by the readers that these personifications should not be taken literally, a technique which Ruskin was to define as "pathetic fallacy".

In *Wuthering Heights*, there is no explicit commentary on the meaning of Nature, which is mainly described as a physical presence. But implicit parallels between nature and human life are present whenever nature is described:

> Wuthering Heights is the name of Mr Heathcliff's dwelling. "Wuthering" being a significant provincial adjective, descriptive

of the atmospheric tumult to which its station is exposed in stormy weather. Pure, bracing ventilation they must have up there at all times, indeed: one may guess the power of the north wind, blowing over the edge, by the excessive slant of a few stunted firs at the end of the house; and by a range of gaunt thorns all stretching their limbs one way, as if craving alms of the sun. Happily, the architect had foresight to build it strong: the narrow windows are deeply set in the wall, and the corners defended with large jutting stones.[7]

This passage may remind us of the frequent descriptions of an active and violent nature found in *Melmoth the Wanderer*. A striking element of the Brontë text, however, is its factuality. The reader is informed about the physical effects of the weather peculiar to a certain place. This factual description of the weather of an English region seems to be much more realistic than Maturin's account of exotic places such as India or Spain. Moreover, there are no observers who are in any way inspired by, or experience an affinity to nature. The relationship between nature and humans appears to be on a purely physical level. The only anthropomorphic phrase ("as if craving alms of the sun") obviously does not refer to human beings. On the contrary: if the gaunt thorns are craving alms of the sun, the inhabitants of Wuthering Heights are not.

Nevertheless, the reader is struck by the resemblance between the site of the house and the character of its inhabitant, Heathcliff, who, on the previous page, has been described by Lockwood as "a capital fellow" and a misanthropist. For all its factual realism, the semiotic function of nature description as psychological analogy is immediately evident to the reader. The author obviously arranges correspondences at her own discretion, making the sun shine, rain fall, winds blow whenever this seems appropriate to the story line, as with the thunderstorm on the occasion of Heathcliff's disappearance:

About midnight, while we still sat up, the storm came rattling over the Heights in full fury. There was a violent wind, as well as thunder, and either one or the other split a tree off at the corner of the building; a huge bough fell across the roof, and knocked down a portion of the east chimney-stack, sending a clatter of stone and soot into the kitchen fire.
We thought a bolt had fallen in the middle of us, and Joseph swung onto his knees, beseeching the Lord to remember the patriarchs Noah and Lot; and, as in former times, spare the

---

7. Emily Brontë, *Wuthering Heights*, ed. David Daiches, Penguin, 1985, 46.

righteous, though he smote the ungodly. I felt some sentiment that it must be a judgment on us also. The Jonah, in my mind, was Mr Earnshaw, and I shook the handle of his den that I might ascertain if he were yet living. He replied audibly enough, in a fashion which made my companion vociferate more clamorously than before that a wide distinction might be drawn between saints like himself, and sinners like his master. But the uproar passed away in twenty minutes, leaving us all unharmed, excepting Cathy, who got thoroughly drenched for her obstinacy in refusing to take shelter, and standing bonnetless and shawlless to catch as much water as she could with her hair and clothes (124-25).

In this passage Joseph's "interpretation" of nature is quite openly ridiculed. His assumption that the storm has a meaning, does, however, induce the reader to look for a meaning. As Catherine is the person who suffers most from the physical effects of the storm, we come to realize that this physical suffering in some way mirrors her inner turmoil after Heathcliff's departure.

The regularity of these parallels enables the author to present a character's feelings to the reader without any elaborate verbal analysis. Nature description alone, as the appropriate accompaniment of mental processes, can convey the relevant information. Psychological phenomena acquire the same immediacy as the sensual experiences provided by landscape and weather.

The "meaning" of nature in this novel, however, goes beyond mere mirroring of human emotions. As has often been observed, the two houses of the novel, Wuthering Heights and Thrushcross Grange, form a pair of symbolic opposites representing fundamental states of being.[8] The meaning of these symbols is expressed in terms of landscape and nature. As elsewhere, the physical effects of natural phenomena are prominent in the following description of Thrushcross Grange:

... the full mellow flow of the beck in the valley came soothingly on the ear. It was a sweet substitute for the yet absent murmur of the summer foliage, which drowned that music about the Grange, when the trees were in leaf. At Wuthering Heights it always

---

8. C.P. Sanger, "The Structure of *Wuthering Heights*", in *The Brontës: A Collection of Critical Essays*, ed. Ian Gregor, Englewood Cliffs: NJ, 1970, 7-18 (first published in *Hogarth Essays*, 19 [1926], 193-208); David Cecil, "Emily Brontë and *Wuthering Heights*", in *Early Victorian Novelists: Essays in Revaluation*, London, 1934, 147-93; Jay Appleton, *The Experience of Landscape*, London, 1975, 168.

sounded on quiet days, following a great thaw or a season of
steady rain — and, of Wuthering Heights, Catherine was thinking
... (193).

For all its factuality, we realize that Nelly Dean's description represents
a peaceful state of mind, where Catherine obviously does not feel at
home. Her preference is with the activity and violence of Wuthering
Heights. This "affinity" is emphasized when Catherine compares her love
to Edgar with the "foliage in the woods", while her love to Heathcliff
resembles "the eternal rocks beneath" (122). The two elements of nature
adduced by Catherine can easily be related to Thrushcross Grange and
Wuthering Heights, respectively. The two houses with their respective
attributes of landscape and nature form an analogy to the universe of the
mind. This universe is given a visible shape, "a local habitation and a
name".

Like Charles Maturin in *Melmoth the Wanderer*, Emily Brontë
contrives to explore certain limits of experience with the help of the
analogy of violent or peaceful forms of nature. Maturin, however, still
retains the concept of nature mirroring moral forces in the universe,
although he replaces the idea of universal benevolence with the
dichotomy of good and bad, of heaven and hell. In *Wuthering Heights*,
heaven and hell are still present, ironically represented by the two
farmhouses, but they are situated within the human mind. The
transcendental sphere, as well a the question of good and evil in the
manifestations of nature, have given way to a system of defining specific
moods and characters.

Like other novels of the early Victorian age, *Wuthering Heights* is
often associated with the concept of realism. A point which is often
overlooked by critics is the simultaneity of detailed, factual realism with
narrative techniques which are to the highest degree metaphorical or
symbolic. The landscape and the weather described may be correct
representations of the author's own experiences of nature. Nevertheless,
the novel is clearly not about Yorkshire but about the human soul.

While Victorian novels achieved a much greater factual as well as
psychological "realism", Victorian techniques of psychological analysis
could not have been developed without the influence of the Gothic
novels.[9] It was authors such as Maturin who first explored the human

---

9. R.B. Heilman makes a similar point concerning "Gothic" elements in *Jane
Eyre*; see Robert B. Heilman, "Charlotte Brontë's 'New' Gothic", in *From Jane
Austen to Joseph Conrad: Essays Collected in Memory of James T. Hillhouse*, eds
Robert C. Rathburn and Martin Steinmann Jr., Minneapolis, 1958, 123.

psyche through the metaphor of natural phenomena, while it was left to Victorian authors such as Emily Brontë to establish the means of detailed psychological analysis on this basis.

JANE AUSTEN'S GOTHIC ARCHITECTURE

CLAIRE LAMONT

When Catherine Morland is invited to visit the Tilneys at Northanger Abbey these are her reflections:

> She was to be their chosen visitor, she was to be for weeks under the same roof with the person whose society she mostly prized — and, in addition to all the rest, this roof was to be the roof of an abbey! — Her passion for ancient edifices was next in degree to her passion for Henry Tilney — and castles and abbies made usually the charm of those reveries which his image did not fill. To see and explore either the ramparts and keep of the one, or the cloisters of the other, had been for many weeks a darling wish, though to be more than the visitor of an hour, had seemed too nearly impossible for desire. And yet, this was to happen. With all the chances against her of house, hall, place, park, court, and cottage, Northanger turned up an abbey, and she was to be its inhabitant. Its long, damp passages, its narrow cells and ruined chapel, were to be within her daily reach, and she could not entirely subdue the hope of some traditional legends, some awful memorials of an injured and ill-fated nun.[1]

This paper is about Jane Austen's Gothic architecture. I have started with a quotation which expresses Catherine Morland's view of Gothic architecture, that it is a matter of "castles and abbies". The Gothic novels of the late-eighteenth century make frequent use of these two types of medieval building, the castle and the monastery, both of which had a domestic function but were not primarily defined by that function. As these two settings figure repeatedly in Gothic novels they come to take on features of two opposing signifying systems. The castle is associated with aggression, extroversion and the male; it dominates its landscape. The monastery is associated with repression, introversion and the female,

---

1. Jane Austen, *Northanger Abbey* (1818), ed. Anne Henry Ehrenpreis, Penguin, 1972, 149-50.

and lies half-hidden in a valley. It is typical of early Gothic novels to be set in remote parts of continental Europe, and in an earlier century. However vestigial the historical sense of the novelists they set their novels in some sort of medieval world. In *Northanger Abbey*, however, the setting is in the south-west of England in Jane Austen's present, the late eighteenth and early nineteenth centuries. Medieval castles and monasteries were visible in her world but both would have lost their *raison d'être*, military or spiritual. They would be visible as ruined, restored or imitated.

In *Northanger Abbey* the heroine makes her first visit from home to Bath, apparently one of the least Gothic of settings. Having been originally a Roman settlement, it was rebuilt in the eighteenth century with neo-classical architecture as the medicinal properties of its waters were exploited. From Bath Catherine Morland makes two Gothic excursions. The first is the abortive trip to Blaize Castle; the second is the visit to Northanger Abbey. Catherine imagines Blaize Castle to be "an edifice like Udolpho" (102), and before agreeing to go on the trip asks "may we go all over it? may we go up every staircase, and into every suite of rooms?" (102) She anticipates "the happiness of a progress through a long suite of lofty rooms" or "along narrow, winding vaults" (104). The party never reaches Blaize Castle, and it is never actually pointed out in the novel that it was it was not, as John Thorpe had asserted, an old castle, "the oldest in the kingdom" (101), but an eighteenth-century Gothic imitation.[2]

There is no doubt about the age of Northanger Abbey. Catherine learns its history from Eleanor Tilney:

> Many were the inquiries she was eager to make of Miss Tilney; but so active were her thoughts, that when these inquiries were answered, she was hardly more assured than before, of Northanger Abbey having been a richly-endowed convent at the time of the Reformation, of its having fallen into the hands of an ancestor of the Tilneys on its dissolution, of a large portion of the ancient building still making a part of the present dwelling although the rest was decayed, or of its standing low in a valley, sheltered from the north and east by rising woods of oak.

Critics of the Gothic motif of the monastery usually stress imprisonment rather than the spiritual role of such a building. A monastic building in

---

2. Andor Gomme, Michael Jenner and Bryan Little, *Bristol: An Architectural History*, London, 1979, 174-75.

the Gothic novel is a place where someone is kept either against their will or at least in denial of the full range of their passions. Catherine Morland shares this view; she expects to find evidence of "an injured and ill-fated nun" (150). Eleanor Tilney's account of the history of Northanger Abbey, however, does not appear to invite that interpretation. Northanger had been "a well-endowed convent at the Reformation" which had "fallen into the hands of an ancestor of the Tilneys on its dissolution" ("fallen" implies either coming down, or chance). The word "convent" was in the late eighteenth century just acquiring its specific modern meaning of a religious house for women.[3] We may read the convent as a safe and spiritual retreat for women, which has now become the personal property of one man. What was endowed as a convent has become a private house where women are oppressed by one man, and a man significantly called *General* Tilney. His name indicates that he would be more at home in a castle. Catherine Morland, who is not interested in history, and particularly not the "quarrels of popes and kings" (123), does not meditate on this paradox. For her a castle or an abbey would do. She does not detect that although castles may have lost their original purpose with the cessation of fighting, it is a question whether the same can be said of a convent. One thing that the English Reformation has achieved is to give the powerful male, whose attributes are reflected in the castle, ownership also of the convent.

General Tilney exercises his ownership of Northanger Abbey in a way that no other man does in Jane Austen's novels. In her other novels a woman is mistress of the house and is in charge of the domestic arrangements. This is still the case when the mistress is not a wife but an unmarried daughter. Even Sir Walter Elliot in *Persuasion* does not deny his daughter her rights as mistress of the house. General Tilney issues invitations on behalf of his daughter and orders meals, overriding his daughter in each case (148, 171, 186). Catherine expects the domestic arrangements at Northanger to be in Eleanor's hands: after Henry Tilney's frightening account of a Gothic bedroom she takes comfort from the belief that "Miss Tilney, she was sure, would never put her into such a chamber as he had described!" (167) (She does not say that the Abbey would not have such a chamber.)

Jane Austen's norm of village Anglicanism does not imply that society is any the better for the dissolution of a convent. Catherine Morland's progress in the novel is from her parsonage home at Fullerton to the vicarage she will share with Henry Tilney at Woodston. Between these

---

3. *The Oxford English Dictionary*, 2nd edn, 1989, convent, sb., 6.

two havens of integrity she visits Bath and Northanger. Both of these, built as places of healing, have lost their proper function and are now given over to fashion and materialism.

Catherine's Gothic reveries are filled with "castles and abbies": "To see and explore either the ramparts and keep of the one, or the cloisters of the other, had been for many weeks a darling wish ..." (150). For Catherine a Gothic castle should contain, besides its defining architectural features of ramparts and keep, towers and long galleries, suites of lofty rooms, many staircases, and narrow, winding vaults (101-102, 104). An abbey should have cloisters, long, damp passages, narrow cells and a ruined chapel (150). That much she has gathered from her reading of Gothic novels, before her conversation with Henry Tilney in the curricle on the way to Northanger. He confirms her view that a Gothic house has staircases, gloomy passages and lofty rooms, not to mention "a secret subterraneous communication between your apartment and the chapel of St Anthony, scarcely two miles off" (164, 166).

How are these expectations fulfilled at Northanger Abbey? Jane Austen does not usually spend much time describing a house from the outside. She is more interested in a house as a living space, and with its interior dynamics. However, the approach to a Gothic building is an important descriptive moment in the Gothic novel, and Catherine's first sight of Northanger Abbey cannot be passed over:

> every bend in the road was expected with solemn awe to afford a glimpse of its massy walls of grey stone, rising amidst a grove of ancient oaks, with the last beams of the sun playing in beautiful splendour on its high Gothic windows. But so low did the building stand, that she found herself passing through the great gates of the lodge into the very grounds of Northanger, without having discerned even an antique chimney (167).

In the Gothic that draws on architecture the façade is frequently presented as the face in front of the labyrinthine brain behind (Poe's House of Usher is perhaps the most famous example). Northanger Abbey will not be read from the outside, and the heroine enters with no guidance.[4]

---

4. In contrast, Emma remarks of the other abbey in Jane Austen's novels, Donwell Abbey, home of Mr Knightley, "It was just what it ought to be, and it looked what it was" (*Emma* [1816], ed. Ronald Blythe, Penguin, 1966, 353).

Once inside, Catherine is first shown into "the common drawing-room". The architectural feature mentioned in that room is the Gothic window:

> The windows, to which she looked with peculiar dependence, from having heard the General talk of his preserving them in their Gothic form with reverential care, were yet less what her fancy had portrayed. To be sure the pointed arch was preserved — the form of them was Gothic — they might be even casements — but every pane was so large, so clear, so light! To an imagination which had hoped for the smallest divisions, and the heaviest stone-work, for painted glass, dirt and cobwebs, the difference was very distressing (168).

Catherine is obviously in a house which has undergone modern restoration. The General has preserved the pointed arches of the windows, but has made a compromise with history in not restoring painted glass, small divisions in the panes, dirt, and cobwebs. He has picked on a characteristic feature, the pointed arch, for preservation and discreetly modernized the rest. The Gothic here appears to be optional; it is not structurally necessary. Catherine may criticize this compromise, but then she has no clear sense of the implications of what she is asking for. She wants not only the original windows, but also the dirt derived, presumably, from many years of subsequent neglect. As her mother was to remark of her, "Catherine would make a sad heedless young house-keeper to be sure ..." (245).

Of all Jane Austen's novels, *Northanger Abbey* gives the most detailed description of a domestic interior. It is the only one of her novels to make serious use of architecture in its plot. The Gothic house with its complicated interior, its subterranean vaults, or, especially in later novels, its attics, lends itself to interpretation which sees these architectural features as representing aspects of life which have been frustrated or repressed. For all Henry Tilney's terrifying description of the subterranean passage that leads from the heroine's bedroom to the ruined chapel of St Anthony (166) Northanger Abbey is not described as having any subterranean passages, not even a decent cellar. Nor is it described as having an attic. The architecture, and any psychological reading of it, is not based on a vertical view of the house with "normal life" on one or two floors and the suppressed abnormal in basement or attic below or above. The important architectural feature of Northanger Abbey is not its vertical dimensions, but its horizontal ones. Catherine expected an abbey to have cloisters; Northanger Abbey does; it is based on a quadrangle.

On her first evening Catherine sees that the house is built on a quadrangle (168). The next day she is given a tour. The house surrounds a court (181), and it has two floors. On the ground floor are the public rooms and offices, and on the upper floor the bedrooms. The rooms on the ground floor are tall, which is why the "broad staircase of shining oak" required "many flights and many landing-places" to reach the upper floor (168). Catherine is first taken round the building on the ground floor. She is taken through a suite of rooms: the "common drawing-room", which led into "a useless anti-chamber" which led in turn into "the real-drawing-room" which led into the library (186). Catherine had expected a Gothic building to offer "suites of rooms", that is rooms leading off each other, rather than each going off a hall or corridor. Northanger Abbey offers such a suite, though not quite up to Catherine's wishes (186). As she is taken round the quadrangle she is told that three sides retain the original Gothic architecture, and that of these one was more Gothic than the other two in that it retained elements of its convent origin in the remains of a cloister and cells (187). The fourth side of the building was modern. After being shown round the ground floor, Catherine is taken upstairs. There, the organization of the rooms was different. The rooms did not open off one another in a suite, but there was on the inner side of the quadrangle a corridor or gallery, whose windows looked across the quadrangle, and off this gallery were the bedrooms whose windows therefore looked outwards (168). Eleanor Tilney shows Catherine round the upper floor, but she is twice interrupted by an imperious request from her father before they can get right round. On both occasions they are stopped at a folding door, on the far side of which is the room which Eleanor's mother had occupied (189, 194). The consequence is that Catherine has been taken round the house on the ground floor; but only round part of it on the upper floor.

Catherine had glimpsed beyond the folding door on the upper floor "a narrower passage, more numerous openings, and symptoms of a winding stair-case" (189). She deduced that this was the side of the house where the remains of the original abbey were most preserved (191). She had seen that it had a staircase, and her Gothic imagination had speculated that Mrs Tilney could have been taken down it "in a state of well-prepared insensibility" (191). On the third attempt to see Mrs Tilney's room Catherine goes alone.[5] She walks round the gallery, through the folding door, and enters Mrs Tilney's room (196). She is

---

5. Catherine's solitary exploration of Northanger may draw on Blanche's exploration of Chateau-le-Blanc in Ann Radcliffe, *The Mysteries of Udolpho* (1794), ed. Bonamy Dobrée, Oxford, 1966, 479-80.

disappointed. It is a pleasant modern room, with sash windows, through which the western sun was shining. Gothic rooms, as had been established earlier, have casement windows (168). It was usually the east wing in a Gothic novel that was the most ruinous.[6] Catherine had wanted to visit a Gothic house; she has done so, and has been muddled by its architecture. She realizes her mistake in interpreting the upper floor of Northanger Abbey in terms of her Gothic expectations rather than in the light of her knowledge of the ground floor. She knew that the fourth side of the quadrangle was modern; but she had not supposed Mrs Tilney's room to be at one end of that side (196).

I have suggested that an important feature of the Gothic interior is the suite of rooms, one room leading off another. In the Gothic building the room does not have have certain bounds. This is true on the ground floor of Northanger Abbey, where one room leads off another in wealthy show. It is of more threatening significance in the Gothic bedroom. As Henry Tilney points out, a Gothic heroine hoping to have safety at last in a bedroom finds that the room has no lock, or that some hidden door opens off it (165-66). The Gothic bedroom is not a place of security because its bounds are not secure; there might be a hidden opening within it leading to a succession of vaulted chambers containing who knows what horrors, most of which are not at first noticed.[7] This is the parodic version of the splendid suite of rooms. The two versions of the suite of rooms may be thought of as representing public show and private neurosis. At Northanger Abbey Catherine was relieved to find that her room was decorated with wallpaper (169). The Gothic bedroom would be hung with tapestry, and there would be no knowing, until some storm of wind revealed an irregularity in the wall behind, what sort of hidden entrance it might conceal. It is an indication of the all-revealing nature of modern architecture, and the speedy collapse of her Gothic fantasies, that Catherine was so sure that the doors that she observed in Mrs Tilney's modern room led only to dressing-closets that she did not even bother to check that that was so: "she had no inclination to open either" (196).

---

6. For instance in *The Mysteries of Udolpho*, 377. This detail was picked up by Walter Scott in a humorous account of the types of novel popular in his day, "... must not every novel-reader have anticipated a castle scarce less than that of Udolpho, of which the eastern wing had long been uninhabited ..." (*Waverley* [1814], ed. Claire Lamont, Oxford, 1981, 3).

7. This is true of Emily's bedroom at Udolpho (*The Mysteries of Udolpho*, 235) and Adeline's in Ann Radcliffe's *The Romance of the Forest* (1791), ed. Chloe Chard, Oxford, 1986, 144.

It is a feature of recent criticism of *Northanger Abbey* to acknowledge but not stress Catherine's Gothic disappointments. Feminist critics in particular have drawn attention to the fact that while Catherine may have been mistaken in thinking that Mrs Tilney had been either murdered or imprisoned, no one believes that she had been a happy woman. The patriarchal power of General Tilney over the women in his household is the modern equivalent of the authoritarian power of the Gothic hero.[8] The fact that Catherine's three disappointments (over the chest, the ebony cabinet and Mrs Tilney's room) all involve her expectations of Gothic evidence being followed by an extremely domestic reality (the folded counterpane, the laundry list, and the well-kept bedroom) can be read as a reproof to Catherine for her failure to realize the progress of society which has allowed a comfortable home to supersede the discomforts of the Gothic. Or, following Katherine Ferguson Ellis, her discoveries can be read as representing the tyranny of the home-as-haven ideal on the woman who inhabits it.[9] In such readings *Northanger Abbey* is a Gothic novel in spite of itself.

Northanger Abbey is a Gothic novel which uses architecture as a way of exploring unacknowledged areas of human psychology. If one such area is patriarchal power, another is the nature of the attraction which Catherine feels for Henry Tilney. Repeatedly, Catherine's interest in Gothic architecture is matched by her interest in Henry Tilney: "Her passion for ancient edifices was next in degree to her passion for Henry Tilney" (149). On the way to Blaize Castle she had "meditated, by turns, on broken promises and broken arches, phaetons and false hangings, Tilneys and trap-doors" (103). On the road to Northanger she had "an abbey before, and a curricle behind" (162). In deciding to explore Mrs Tilney's room on her own she chooses a day when Henry Tilney is away. But he returns before he is expected. Catherine has just let herself out of the bedroom and closed the door:

> At that instant a door underneath was hastily opened; some one seemed with swift steps to ascend the stairs, by the head of which she had yet to pass before she could gain the gallery. She had no power to move. With a feeling of terror not very definable, she fixed her eyes on the staircase, and in a few moments it gave Henry to her view.

---

8. Sandra M. Gilbert and Susan Gubar, *The Madwoman in the Attic*, New Haven and London, 1979, 135.

9. Kate Ferguson Ellis, *The Contested Castle: Gothic Novels and the Subversion of Domestic Ideology*, 1989, x-xii.

"Mr Tilney!" she exclaimed in a voice of more than common astonishment. He looked astonished too. "Good God!" she continued, not attending to his address, "how came you here? — how came you up that staircase?"

"How came I up that staircase!" he replied, greatly surprised. "Because it is my nearest way from the stable-yard to my own chamber; and why should I not come up it?" (196-97)

Catherine had not experienced Gothic terror in the bedroom; she was feeling it now. Catherine knew that Gothic buildings had staircases, and she knew of the existence of this one. She is surprised because the only function she had had for that staircase was for Mrs Tilney to be brought down it "in a state of well-prepared insensibility". The staircase had not delivered an unconscious woman, however, but a lover come back before he was expected.

Northanger Abbey is the only novel by Jane Austen in which the heroine goes to stay in the hero's home, and there is sexual tension in her use of its architecture. Catherine's love of Henry Tilney and her love of the Gothic had always been confused. In her search for Mrs Tilney's room she manages to put herself in the direct route between the stables and Henry's bedroom. As Henry points out where she stands is in his space rather than in hers:

"This passage is at least as extraordinary a road from the breakfast-parlour to your apartment, as that staircase can be from the stables to mine" (197).

There seems to be sexual adventure in Catherine's Gothic enquiries. Her conscious mind is exploring a Gothic bedroom; but in so doing she is suppressing knowledge she had about the house. Henry Tilney rushing up the staircase while she is frozen at the top of it is a powerful image. Her astonished question, "how came you here?" is a statement of her failure to understand the architecture which had so engrossed her imagination.

Fig. 7: Prince Vladimir Fyodorovich Odoevsky (1804-69).

GOTHIC AND ITS ORIGINS IN EAST AND WEST: VLADIMIR ODOEVSKY AND FITZ-JAMES O'BRIEN

NEIL CORNWELL

We have become familiar, thanks to various studies, with the origins of Gothic fiction in generic terms, rising with Horace Walpole and shaped by motifs from graveyard poetry and Jacobean melodrama. We are aware too of the double-edged Germanic feeling of the term "Gothic" and its impact on English culture; of the labyrinthine influences (metaphorically speaking) of theology and the law and (more literally) in the grandiose mania of the etched emanations of, for instance, Piranesi. As Gothic interfaces with Romanticism, however, particularly on the European side of its development, further philosophical and pseudo-philosophical and scientific traditions come into play. Joyce Tompkins wrote in 1932 that "a fantastic element enriched the confusion in the stories of occult powers ... on the confines of magic and science, of moral idealism and charlatanry", going on to mention Rosicrucianism, freemasonry and Illuminism as sources of such activity;[1] we could of course add Mesmerism, Galvanism and other burgeoning pseudo-scientific teachings. Leslie Fiedler remarks on "the convention of treating magic as science and thus reclaiming it for respectability in the Age of Reason".[2] This brings us precisely to the Gothic use of one tradition relevant to this paper, that of alchemy as used by romantic or fantastical writers on the eastern and western peripheries of the European Gothic scene: Russia and Ireland (or Ireland pushed further west to America). Another, older, tradition of relevance will emerge later.

---

1. *The Gothick Novel: A Casebook*, ed. V. Sage, London, 1990, 96. On Protestant theology in this context, see V. Sage, *Horror Fiction in the Protestant Tradition*, London, 1988; on Piranesi, see Neil Cornwell, *The Literary Fantastic: From Gothic to Postmodernism*, New York and London, 1990.

2. Leslie Fiedler, *Love and Death in the American Novel*, London, 1967, 139.

Prince Vladimir Fyodorovich Odoevsky (1804-69) was one of the most extraordinarily versatile figures of nineteenth-century Russia. As well as being a public servant from 1826 until his death, he enjoyed fame as a writer of romantic fiction and as a children's writer, thinker, musicologist, educationalist, philanthropist, amateur scientist and general *uomo universale*.[3] He has been called "the Russian Hoffmann" and "the Russian Faust"; "the Russian Goethe" would be nearer the mark, although the comparison flatters and although Odoevsky did not write poetry. A reputation for eccentricity, "encyclopaedism" and dilettantism led to his being taken less seriously for much of his lifetime than was his due. Following decades of neglect, his reputation enjoyed minor revivals early this century and again in the 1950s, when important collections of his literary, musical, and educational writings were published. A few of his children's stories remain highly popular, but it is as a leading representative of high Russian romanticism — and indeed of Russian Gothic — that he now finds his niche: a 1988 Moscow paperback edition of his *Tales and Stories* enjoyed a print-run of no less than 2,700,000 copies.

An aristocratic "prince" (as a *knyaz* he traced his lineage back to Rurik) and later officially Russia's "premier nobleman" Odoevsky nevertheless always had to work for a living, because the family fortune had been dissipated during the eighteenth century and Odoevsky's father had married beneath him into the lower levels of the landowning class. These factors made Odoevsky something of an upper-class outsider who, despite years of loyal government service, enjoyed little political trust following his tenuous links with the Decembrist revolt which, at the end of 1825, inaugurated and determined the reactionary reign of Nicholas I.

Odoevsky's first literary success occurred in the first half of the 1820s, when he presided over "The Society of Wisdom Lovers", a philosophical circle influenced mainly by Schelling, which included among its adherents some of the principal originators both of Westernizing and of Slavophile thought. He also co-edited the almanac *Mnemosyne* (1824-25) which, in its four issues was as culturally vital as it was financially nonviable. Following the Decembrist upheaval, Odoevsky married, entered government service, moved to St Petersburg and immersed himself ever deeper in the esoteric and occult philosophy which lay at the roots of that strand of European romanticism to which

---

3. See Neil Cornwell, *V.F. Odoyevsky: His Life, Times and Milieu*, London and Athens: Ohio, 1986.

he was most inclined. This channelling of his thoughts into creative activity was to reach fruition in the 1830s.

Odoevsky is perhaps best known for his unusual creation of cycles of stories. The "cycle" as opposed to the mere collection, requires thematic and stylistic connections, albeit oblique: "threads" which connect the individual stories. Several of these attempts remain uncompleted, others were scarcely begun. Two which did reach completion are now counted among the fundamental works of Russian romantic prose. *Variegated Tales* (1833), the first real fruit of Odoevsky's mature literary period, is a delicate collection of parodies of Russian and European romantic themes. The remarkable *Russian Nights* (1844) which contains some fine individual stories (ranging from the Gothic to the musical-artistic to the anti-Utopian) is set in a substantial philosophical, largely Schellingian, frame-tale, addressing many of the preoccupations of Russian intellectual circles of the 1830s.

The decade and a half from about 1829 until the appearance of his three-volume *Compositions* in 1844 and his subsequent virtual retirement from literature, saw the flowering of Odoevsky's literary achievement in society, philosophical and anti-Utopian tales, as well as in works in the Gothic mode. One of the best known of these romantic-Gothic compositions is the tale "The Sylph" ("Sil'fida") of 1837.[4]

"The Sylph" is subtitled "from the notes of a reasonable man" (Odoevsky was ever suspicious of reliance on reason *per se*) and begins with seven letters from one Mikhail Platonovich to his friend and eventual editor, the "reasonable man" who fails wholly to understand his artistic spirit. Ironically, the "authorial" confession with which the tale ends, displays great rationality, both by purporting to understand "nothing in this story" and by mangling the protagonist's name as "Platon Mikhailovich". Bored with provincial life, the protagonist discovers the cabbalistic books and folios of his dead uncle's secret library and immerses himself in the pursuit of sylphs. The "reasonable man"'s account of the "saving" of his friend for marriage and a conventional provincial lifestyle frames the extracts from Mikhail Platonovich's journal, in which the poetic saga of his relationship with a sylph (involving as it does an alternative artistic vision, an alternative reality and the separation of time and space, leading to the "soul of the soul" where "poetry is truth") gradually descends from the sublime to incoherent jottings.

---

4. V.F. Odoevskii, *Sochineniia v dvukh tomakh*, Moscow, 1981. "The Sylph", in *Russian Romantic Prose: An Anthology*, ed. Carl R. Proffer, Ann Arbor: Mich., 1979; *The Salamander and Other Gothic Tales*, trans. Neil Cornwell, Bristol, 1992.

Odoevsky may lack the masterly concision of Pushkin, the stylistic elegance of Lermontov or the sheer linguistic verve of Gogol (although in the 1830s, at the height of his fame, his reputation was not far short of theirs), but his relative verbosity brings him, arguably, closer to the English style of writing of the early nineteenth century. His themes too are close to the romanticism of both European and English literatures. Comparisons can be made not only with Hoffmann, but also with Charles Brocken Brown and, of course, with Poe, Mary Shelley, Maturin and Sheridan Le Fanu. Particularly intriguing, though, is the resemblance between Odoevsky's "The Sylph" (1837) and "The Diamond Lens", a story written some twenty years later (1858) by the Irish-American author Fitz-James O'Brien.

Fitz-James O'Brien was born in Cork in 1828. After occupying himself with poetry and journalism, first in Ireland and then in London, he squandered a substantial family inheritance and left for New York at the end of 1851, where he found immediate success as a prolific contributor to *The Times* (of New York), *Putnam's*, *The Atlantic Monthly*, *Harper's* and other journals.[5] He published poetry, fiction and plays, including a successful two-act piece called *A Gentleman from Ireland*. He supported an extravagantly bohemian lifestyle by his writings and achieved a peak of lionization with his story "The Diamond Lens", published in January 1858.[6] In 1861 the Civil War broke out and O'Brien joined a regiment of the National Guard of New York and was cited for bravery at Bloomery Gap. He was wounded in February 1862 and died in the April of the same year. His stories and poems were collected in 1881. Since the 1880s, collections of his work have been sporadic, but "The Diamond Lens" and one or two other favoured stories have been not infrequently anthologized.

Of his other stories, fleeting mention may be made of "What Was It? A Mystery" (1859), singled out by H.P. Lovecraft as "the first well-shaped short story of a tangible but invisible being, and the prototype of De Maupassant's *Horla*",[7] and "The Wondersmith" (1859) which, with its theme of the infusion of the souls of "demon" children into wooden manikins, bears a superficial and coincidental resemblance to Odoevsky's

---

5. Francis Wolle, *Fitz-James O'Brien: A Literary Bohemian of the Eighteen-Fifties*, Boulder: Colo., 1944.

6. Fitz-James O'Brien, "The Diamond Lens", in *American Short Stories of the Nineteenth Century*, ed. John Cournos, London, 1930, rpt. 1982, 109-29 (see also O'Brien's *Fantastic Tales,* London, 1977, and New York, 1988).

7. H.P. Lovecraft, *Supernatural Horror in Literature*, New York, 1973, 66.

tale of girls converted into dolls.[8] One recent commentator picks out four elements of plot found in O'Brien's work which, he claims, have shaped subsequent fantasy: the animated manikin, the lost room, the invisible creature and the microscopic world.[9] While the quality of the microscopic, in Russian literature at least, seems in particular to anticipate the work of Zamiatin in the 1920s, in fact all four of these motifs can be found in stories written in the 1830s by Odoevsky.[10] I shall return to one of these later. For the moment, however, I will concentrate on the better-known tales: Odoevsky's "The Sylph" and O'Brien's "The Diamond Lens".

"The Diamond Lens" is a first-person narrative recounting the protagonist's progress from a boyhood enthusiasm for microscopes to the status of a "constructive microscopist" and on to his final position as "Linley, the mad microscopist". This obsession with microscopy has led Linley to seek the perfect lens, in pursuit of which he consults through a medium the spirit of the Dutch naturalist Anton van Leeuwenhoek (1632-1723), before murdering a French acquaintance in order to steal a 140-carat diamond from which to fashion the required lens. With his now-perfect instrument, Linley is able to discover and observe, within a single drop of water, a sylph of unparalleled beauty and a whole new and poetic world which greatly exceeds the possibilities of his own world, even as embodied in its most graceful ballerina. Linley, however, neglects the laws of evaporation and returns to his vision only to find his sylph dying of suffocation or dehydration. The shock is such that he collapses, thus wrecking his perfect lens, and falls into apparent madness, from which state his account has presumably been written.

In both stories there is ambiguity as to the supposed actuality of what has been observed, in terms of its derivation either from another reality or from the delusions of "crazed imagination". Clareson sees this quality

---

8. V.F. Odoevsky, "A Tale of Why It Is Dangerous for Young Girls to Go Walking in a Group along Nevsky Prospect", in *The Ardis Anthology of Russian Romanticism*, ed. Christine Rydel, Ann Arbor: Mich., 1984.

9. Thomas D. Clareson, "Fitz-James O'Brien 1828-1862", in *Supernatural Fiction Writers: Fantasy and Horror*, ed. E.F. Bleiler, New York, 1985, II, 717-22.

10. The animated manikin is featured in the story just mentioned; the lost room is to be found in "Letter IV" (see *the Salamander and Other Gothic Stories*); the invisible creature occurs in "Igosha" (one of the *Variegated Stories*); a microscopic vision, or something akin thereto, is featured in "The Improvisor" in *Russian Nights* (see note 15).

as crucial in making "The Diamond Lens" O'Brien's finest story.[11] Both stories therefore share a quality of what I have called, in a Todorovian sense, "the literary fantastic".[12] Odoevsky's protagonist arrives in his situation due to the legacy of a deceased uncle; O'Brien's Linley is enabled to pursue his career in microscopy thanks to "a small fortune" bequeathed by his "poor Aunt Agatha". Linley murders to achieve his aims, it might be argued, whereas Mikhail Platonovich does nothing more anti-social than standing up his fiancée. Another Odoevskian protagonist, however (Yakko in "The Salamander") follows the lead of Pushkin's Hermann in *The Queen of Spades* in being willing to kill in pursuit of occult secrets; the example of certain of Poe's characters represents a more probable precedent.

Such structural similarities, or for that matter reversals, are relatively superficial compared to the use in both stories of the figure of a sylph and the proximity of the poetic worlds described as surrounding such a creature. This near-identity of vision between Odoevsky and O'Brien is far more striking than any distinction which can be made between Mikhail Platonovich's naked-eye vision of a sylph in a vase of water, emanating from the action of sunbeams on a turquoise ring, and Linley's more scaled-down and "scientific" vision through a microscope.

Indeed the apparently modern presence of the microscope in "The Diamond Lens" has caused this story to be seen more in terms of early science-fiction than the nature of its vision, deriving rather from the much older occult and Gothic forms, would warrant. The balance has, however, been partially redressed by connections recently made between O'Brien's vision and Poe's aesthetic of beauty. O'Brien's story, it has now been pointed out, "is finally concerned not ... with the ethical ramifications of an obsessive scientific interest, but, rather, with the inevitable failure of man's longing for ideal beauty".[13] In fact, comparisons with Odoevsky help to reinforce the link with Poe, as well as to draw us back to what could be earlier common sources. Odoevsky, like Poe, with whom he later came to recognize a kinship (Cornwell, 313), felt "trapped by a hopelessly inadequate language system and equally trapped by the physical limitations of his own mortality".[14] The

---

11. Clareson, 720.

12. *The Literary Fantastic*, esp. 11-16.

13. Michael Wentworth, "A Matter of Taste: Fitz-James O'Brien's 'The Diamond Lens' and Poe's Aesthetic of Beauty", *American Transcendental Quarterly*, II/4 (1988), 271-84.

14. Wentworth, 274.

possibilities of the true poetic imagination were near enough the same for Odoevsky as for Poe as for O'Brien; however, Odoevsky's sylph, it must be said, is not shown dying (being lost to her admirer merely through the intervention of unsympathetic philistines), whereas the demise of O'Brien's sylph re-enacts Poe's precociously decadent dictum that "the death, then, of a beautiful woman is, unquestionably, the most poetical topic in the world...".

Odoevsky is unlikely to have been familiar with Poe before the end of his own career as a fiction writer, but Hoffmann immediately arises as a possible influence on all three later writers. More interestingly, is there any possibility that O'Brien could have known Odoevsky's work? "The Sylph" had been translated into German as early as 1839 and into French in 1855. Nevertheless, the explanation for the main similarities between the sylphs of Odoevsky and O'Brien could perhaps be much simpler and merely reside quite overtly within the text of each, in the form of references to the pre-romantic and pre-Gothic alchemical tradition.

A comparison between the two texts may be briefly illustrated by quoting the descriptions of the sylph. Here is that of Odoevsky (in my translation):

> But hardly was the water in motion, when once again green and pink threads extended from the rose and flowed together with the water in a variegated stream and my beautiful flower appeared once more at the bottom of the vase. Everything calmed down, but something flashed across the middle of it. The leaves opened little by little and — I couldn't believe my eyes — between the orange stamens there reposed — I wonder whether you'll believe me? — there reposed an amazing, indescribable, unbelievable creature: in short, a woman, barely visible to the eye! How am I to describe to you the joy, tinged with horror, which I felt at that moment! This woman was no child. Imagine the miniature portrait of a beautiful woman in full bloom and you will get a dim notion of the miracle which lay before my eyes. She reposed casually on her soft couch and her russet brown curls, wavering from the rippling of the water, now revealed and now concealed from my eyes her immaculate charms. She appeared to be immersed in a deep sleep and I, my eyes fixed avidly on her, held my breath, so as not to disturb her sweet composure.

Now O'Brien's description of his sylph:

> It was a female human shape. When I say human, I mean it possessed the outlines of humanity; but there the analogy ends. Its

adorable beauty lifted it illimitable heights beyond the loveliest daughter of Adam.

I cannot, I dare not, attempt to inventory the charms of this divine revelation of perfect beauty. Those eyes of mystic violet, dewy and serene, evade my words. Her long, lustrous hair following her head in a golden wake, like the track sown in heaven by a falling star, seems to quench my most burning phrases with its splendours. If all the bees of Hybla nestled upon my lips, they would still sing but hoarsely the wondrous harmonies of outline that inclosed her form.

She swept out from between the rainbow-curtains of the cloud-trees into the broad sea of light that lay beyond. Her motions were those of some graceful naiad, cleaving by a mere effort of her will, the clear, unruffled waters that fill the chambers of the sea. She floated forth with the serene grace of a frail bubble ascending through the still atmosphere of a June day. The perfect roundness of her limbs formed suave and enchanting curves. It was like listening to the most spiritual symphony of Beethoven the divine to watch the harmonious flow of lines. This, indeed, was a pleasure cheaply purchased at any price.

Apart from the obviously voyeuristic quality common to both, and the emphasis in O'Brien's case on the purchase of this delight with another's blood, we should also mention that Odoevsky's protagonist, slightly less hampered by the difference in scale, is purportedly able to communicate with his sylph, following her (mentally at least) into a world of ecstasy beyond time and space, from which he is extracted only through the agency of his rude acquaintances and their merciless rescue operation. Odoevsky's vision of the poetic other world is therefore able to be portrayed in greater depth (as in some of his other works) than is possible for O'Brien.

Odoevsky alludes to alchemical sources in a number of his fictional works. His own scientific activities included alchemical as well as chemical studies, while he frequently referred to the renewed relevance and the lost meaning of the old sciences. In "The Sylph", Mikhail Platonovich discovers in his late uncle's sealed cupboards "the works of Paracelsus, *The Count of Gabalis*, Arnold of Villanova, Raimondo Lulli and other alchemists and cabbalists". In "The Diamond Lens", Linley recalls:

I now comprehended how it was that the Count of Cabalis [*sic*] peopled his mystic world with sylphs —beautiful beings whose breath of life was lambent fire, and who sported for ever in regions of purest ether and purest light. The Rosicrucian had anticipated the wonder that I had practically realised.

Fouqué's *Undine* (1811), another source common certainly to Hoffmann, Odoevsky, Poe and O'Brien, derived, we are told by Lovecraft "from a tale told by Paracelsus" (45). The clearest common ground is, however, *The Count of Gabalis*.

The Count of Gabalis, or Discourses on the Secret Sciences, a book on elemental spirits and their relations with humans, was written and published anonymously in Paris in 1670 by the Abbé Nicolas de Monfaucon de Villars (1635-73). The Abbé de Villars' book, which was reprinted several times, enjoyed a considerable readership and influenced many European writers, including Hoffmann (in such stories as "The Golden Pot" and "The King's Bride"). This passage, quoted from an English translation last printed in 1886, has obvious relevance to the stories of Odoevsky and O'Brien:

> You need but shut up a glass fill'd with Conglobated Air, Water or Earth, and expose it to the sun for a month; Then separate the element according to art, which is very easie to do, if it be Earth or Water. 'Tis a marvellous thing to see, what a virtue every one of these purified Elements have to attract the *Nymphs*, *Sylphs* and *Gnomes*. In taking but never so little, every day, for about a month together, one shall see in the air the volant republic of the *Sylphs* .... Thus venerable Nature teaches her Children how to repair the Elements by the Elements. Thus is Harmony re-established. Thus man recovers his natural Empire, and can do all things in the Elements, without *Daemon*, or unlawful art. Thus you see, my Son, that the *Sages* are more innocent than you thought.[15]

Cognate references may be found in Paracelsus, particularly in the *Liber de nymphis, sylphis, pygmaeis et salamandris, et de caeteris spiritibus*. Odoevsky retains in "The Sylph" the spiritual-magic innocence of such experimentation. In O'Brien's treatment, the magic is more overtly daemonic, although given a scientific veneer. Both writers poeticize or romanticize the vision in the manner of Poe or Hoffmann.

---

15. *Sub-mundanes: or The Elementaries of the Cabala: Being the History of Spirits*, Bath, 1886, 40 (a reprint of *The Count of Gabalis: or the Extravagant Mysteries of the Cabalists Exposed, in Five Pleasant Discourses on the Secret Sciences*. Done into English by P.A. Gent., London, n.d.).

O'Brien may have developed an interest in sylphs either directly from alchemical sources or through a variety of literary intermediaries. He wrote at least one alchemical story "The Gold Ingot" (1858). Odoevsky's sources can be traced back from contemporary romanticism and the philosophical system of Schelling, via the late Hermetic and Cabbalistic traditions, to the original alchemical writings and, via Saint-Martin, John Pordage and Jacob Böhme, as far back as the Neoplatonists.[16] Lovecraft claims that there is a kind of imaginary or Gothic history of the occult, connecting the *magi* of the renaissance directly with the necromancers of the middle ages,[17] and, indeed, the influence of alchemical writings on the fantastic fictions of the nineteenth century cannot be ignored. Perhaps the most celebrated example of this is Mary Shelley's *Frankenstein* in which Victor Frankenstein, in the second chapter, invokes the works of Cornelius Agrippa, Paracelsus and Albertus Magnus. The legacy of the alchemists was felt in Gothic fiction not only upon its eastern and western peripheries, but also at its English and West European centre.

And there we might have been content to leave matters, crediting Fitz-James O'Brien with having created, from his awareness of common sources, an original story called "The Diamond Lens", albeit one showing remarkable similarities to the Russian story "The Sylph". However, there is a detail in O'Brien's literary biography which gives grounds for a reversal of this attitude: in 1857, O'Brien published a story called "Seeing the World" in *Harper's Monthly Magazine*. A synopsis of this story reveals it to be, to all intents and purposes, identical, down to the names of the characters, with Odoevsky's story "The Improvisor" in *Russian Nights*.

Francis Wolle supplies a synopsis of O'Brien's story:

> Cipriano has thought and the creative faculty, but cannot express himself. A physician from India offers him facility in verse-making, with the proviso that, if he accepts, the gift shall remain irrevocable, and that it shall be accompanied by a power within him to know and to comprehend everything. Cipriano agrees to the conditions and from that time sees only the material, scientific bases of things. He sees in his loved Charlotte only an anatomical specimen; he sees instead of a picture only canvas and paint; instead of water, he sees molecules, germs and gases. At the same time, he finds that by his astounding performances in feats of poetic improvising, he can make money and live in luxury. His

---

16. *V.F. Odoyevsky: His Life, Times and Milieu*, 104-105.

17. Lovecraft, 18-19.

mind revolts, nevertheless, at his terrible gift, and his reason totters.[18]

This may be compared to the text of "The Improvvisatore"[19] and to my synopsis of it:

> Kipriano, *The Improvisor*, as a young poet composed his verses with immense difficulty and therefore relapsed into the poverty in which he had originated. He turns to Dr Segeliel, a man of diabolical reputation ..., who accords him the ability "to produce without effort" and to "see, know and understand everything". Kipriano's perception and comprehension are immediately transformed: books on the shelves and the letters on their pages assume a state of mobility; everything was reduced to "an arithmetical progression" — the whole of nature lay before Kipriano "like the skeleton of a beautiful woman, whom the dissector has boiled down so skilfully that there did not remain on her a single living vein". His beloved Charlotte is reduced in his eyes to "an anatomical preparation"; his microscopic vision reduces the world to a mechanistic model, dividing him permanently from the rest of its inhabitants .... He composes verses instantly and effortlessly, but to no personal satisfaction; indeed he ends as a wandering jester jabbering verses non-stop in a mixture of all languages.[20]

I have described Odoevsky's story as "Hoffmannesque", Wolle sees O'Brien's tale as "Poesque" (149): "Odoevskian" would be the exact term.

Both "Seeing the World" and "The Diamond Lens" were written in 1857. In 1855 a volume had been published in Paris entitled *Le Décameron Russe: histoires et nouvelles*, translated by Pierre-Paul Douhaire, which included seven stories by Odoevsky, among which were "The Sylph" (under the title "L'Alchimiste") and "The Improvisor" (as "L'Improvisateur").[21] We know from his biographer, Francis Wolle, that O'Brien had an excellent knowledge of French. We are therefore left with the inescapable conclusion that O'Brien's use of the alchemical

---

18. Wolle, 149-50.

19. V.F. Odoevsky, *Russian Nights*, trans. Olga Koshansky-Olienikov and Ralph E. Matlaw, New York, 1965, 132-45.

20. *V.F. Odoyevsky: His Life, Times and Milieu*, 49.

21. *Ibid.*, 384.

tradition masks his use of a further and older tradition and lays him open to a charge (one not unknown in Gothic fiction and one levelled at him here not for the first time) of plagiarism.

ASPECTS OF THE SUPERNATURAL
IN THE SHORTER FICTION OF JAMES HOGG

DOUGLAS S. MACK

This essay focuses on some of the roots of the use of the supernatural in the works of James Hogg; this subject will be approached through an examination of specific examples provided by *The Shepherd's Calendar*, a series of articles contributed by Hogg to *Blackwood's Edinburgh Magazine* between 1819 and 1828.

The Shepherd's Calendar is a title with a long history in the literature of the English language. Hogg, however, had a particular and unusual right to use it: in his youth he had spent many years as a professional shepherd in the remote and mountainous Ettrick district of southern Scotland. Indeed, in parts of his *Shepherd's Calendar* he draws upon the experiences of his own pastoral life in the 1790s; and elsewhere in the series he sets out to re-create on paper something of the manner and the content of the traditional oral story-telling of Ettrick. To describe *The Shepherd's Calendar* in this way seems to suggest that it is a project of a somewhat antiquarian nature, involving an attempt to record and preserve old customs and manners before they finally pass away. That is no doubt part of what Hogg is seeking to achieve; but his "Shepherd's Calendar" articles go far beyond a mere antiquarian interest. Indeed, these contributions to *Blackwood's* make up a sequence of sophisticated and complex narratives in which the supernatural plays a particularly striking role.

Let us begin by looking at "Storms", a largely autobiographical article in which Hogg writes about the trials and dangers encountered by shepherds as a result of severe snow-falls. Much of the article is devoted to an account of Hogg's own experiences during the winter of 1794-95. At this time he was working as a shepherd at Blackhouse in the Yarrow valley, part of the Ettrick district, and he was a member of a local literary society formed by "a few young shepherds". At the society's meetings each of the members "read an essay on a subject previously given out; and after that every essay was minutely investigated, and criticised".[1] In *The Rise of the Historical Novel*, John MacQueen has convincingly argued that the society's agenda probably "included the forbidden subject of radical politics and the need for reform, if not revolution".[2] This was, after all, the 1790s: revolution was in the air.

Be that as it may, Hogg was on his way to a meeting of this society when signs of an approaching storm forced him to turn back. The meeting of the society went ahead in his absence; and as events turned out the shieling at which it was held "was situated in the very vortex of the storm; the devastations made by it extended all around that, to a certain extent; and no farther on any one quarter than another" (16). The storm was universally viewed in the Ettrick community "as a judgement sent by God for the punishment of some heineous offence" (15). Hogg goes on to record a conversation, during which he learned that the blame for the heinous offence was being laid at the door of his literary society:

> "Weel chap" said he to me "we hae fund out what has been the cause of a' this mischief now."
> "What do you mean John?"
> "What do I mean? It seems that a great squad o' birkies that ye are conneckit wi', had met that night at the herds house o' Ever Phaup, an had raised the deil amang them."
> Every countenance in the kitchen changed; the women gazed at John and then at me, and their lips grew white. These kind of feelings are infectious, people may say what they will; fear begets fear as naturally as light springs from reflection. I reasoned stoutly at first against the veracity of the report, observing that it was utter absurdity, and a shame and disgrace for the country to cherish such a rediculous lie.
> "Lie!" said John "It's nae lie; they had him up amang them like a great rough dog at the very time that the tempest began, and were glad to draw cuts, an' gie him ane o' their number to get quit o' him again."
> Lord how every hair of my head, and inch of my frame crept at hearing this sentence; for I had a dearly loved brother who was one of the number, several full cousins, and intimate acquaintances; indeed I looked on the whole fraternity as my brethern, and considered myself involved in all their transactions. I could say no more in defence of the society's proceedings, for

---

1. James Hogg, *Selected Stories and Sketches*, ed. Douglas S. Mack, Edinburgh, 1982, 5.

2. John MacQueen, *The Rise of the Historical Novel*, Edinburgh, 1989, 208.

to tell the truth, though I am ashamed to acknowledge it, I
suspected that the allegation might be too true (16-17).

"For to tell the truth, though I am ashamed to acknowledge it, I
suspected that the allegation might be too true." These are highly
significant words. They show the young Hogg wholly at home with a
system of assumptions in which a blizzard can be explained as the
judgement of God, and in which it can seem natural to encounter the
physical and active presence of the Devil, here and now, among one's
relations and intimate acquaintances. On the other hand, he says "I am
ashamed to acknowledge it". The mature Hogg is by no means contained
by a naive acceptance of the old beliefs: he is fully aware that times have
changed, and that in a post-Enlightenment world the old ideas have come
to be seen as childishly absurd. All this points to a crucial feature of
Hogg's intellectual and cultural position: he is situated between two
worlds — or rather, he is fully part of two very different worlds. One of
these worlds is the Ettrick of his pastoral youth, a district where he
continued to spend much of his time throughout his life, and where he
died. His other world is Edinburgh, which he graced for more than a
quarter of a century as a professional author.

It would not be extravagant to say that in Hogg's lifetime each of
these two worlds was in its own way a key site in the intellectual life of
Europe. From Edinburgh, Walter Scott was enthralling an international
audience with his poetry and his novels; and the Scottish capital was still
basking in the afterglow of the great days of David Hume and Adam
Smith, of Hutton the geologist and Black the chemist, and of all the other
major figures of the Scottish Enlightenment. Ettrick also had its
importance, at any rate for those sensitive to the living significance of the
great traditional ballads. It was from Ettrick that Scott (with Hogg's help)
obtained some of the material for *Minstrelsy of the Scottish Border*; and
it was Yarrow (in Ettrick) that Wordsworth famously left Unvisited in
1803 — and later Visited in the autumn of 1814, with Hogg as his guide.
The mature Hogg was the heir of the Edinburgh of the Enlightenment,
and he was also the heir, and even the embodiment, of Wordsworth's
unvisited Yarrow, with its "treasured dreams of times long past".

Hogg's place within these two worlds is important for his fiction;
indeed much of his writing can be seen as an assertion, aimed at a
sceptical Edinburgh audience, of the validity of traditional Ettrick beliefs
and values. An excellent example of this process is provided by "Mr
Adamson of Laverhope", a story from *The Shepherd's Calendar* in which
a narrator, who clearly shares the assumptions of Enlightenment
Edinburgh, offers for our contemplation an account of what peasant

superstition has made of a natural calamity — a man being killed by lightning during a thunderstorm.

How does the story of Mr Adamson appear if we accept the supernatural interpretation of the superstitious inhabitants of Ettrick? In this view, we are not dealing with a natural event in which a man is struck by lightning; we are dealing rather with a divine judgment. God's lightning strikes down an evildoer; and the Devil, who has been present in disguise, carries Mr Adamson's soul off to Hell in the last thunderclap of the storm. What has Adamson done to deserve this condign punishment? His first offence is that, while seeking to collect debts, he has evicted a poor family and caused their goods to be sold by public auction. Thereafter, the community comes together to shear Mr Adamson's sheep, "it being customary for the farmers to assist one another reciprocally on these occasions"; but Adamson, dissatisfied with himself over the eviction, sours the usual hilarity of the communal shearing by irritably and violently attacking first a sheep-dog, and then a boy who comes to the dog's defence. Finally, Adamson refuses the customary alms to a beggar who visits the shearing. It is made clear that all these actions are contrary to Adamson's duty as a professing Christian; and we are also made to see that his actions outrage the shared values of an agricultural community which must depend upon mutual support for survival in a harsh environment.

The values of Ettrick are celebrated within the story by means of a detailed and affectionate account of the shared pleasures of the communal sheep-shearing, and these values are given explicit expression through the words and actions of the shepherd Rob Johnson. The Good Shepherd is always a resonant figure in Hogg. Behind fictional characters like Rob Johnson and Daniel Bell of *The Three Perils of Woman* there lies, of course, the figure of James Hogg the Ettrick Shepherd; but we are also reminded of the biblical King David, once a shepherd boy — and of Jesus, the supreme Good Shepherd.

In the supernatural interpretation of "Mr Adamson of Laverhope", then, evil deeds provoke divine vengeance. This view is powerfully backed up by Hogg's detailed rendering of the convulsion of the thunderstorm, a notable feature of which is a description of a flood which sweeps down on Adamson's sheepfolds "with a cataract front more than twenty feet deep" (33). This is an apt image in a story of divine anger; but surprisingly enough it is also true to weather conditions in southern Scotland, where flash floods of this kind are by no means unknown. For example, a report on the front page of *The Scotsman* newspaper for 27 July 1983 describes "a wall of water 20ft high and 200yds wide in places" which earlier in the week had surged across a four-mile area in the valley of the Hermitage Water, causing widespread damage to property and considerable danger to life and limb.

The flood, then, however extraordinary, nevertheless remains firmly within the boundaries of the possible; and this may serve as a reminder that Hogg's Enlightenment narrator does not share the Ettrick community's supernatural interpretation of Mr Adamson's death. For the narrator, Adamson is simply the unfortunate victim of a natural event, and this interpretation is reinforced by the narrator's concluding anecdote concerning the death by lightning of Mr Adam Copland of Minnigess. In this anecdote there is not a hint of the supernatural; instead we have cool, detached and rational comments on the operation of "the electric matter that slew Mr Copland". The story of the death of Mr Copland is, as it were, an Enlightenment version of the story erected by peasant superstition around the death of Mr Adamson; but Hogg so manages matters that the peasant superstition becomes much more coherent, impressive and convincing than the views of his Enlightened narrator. Hogg, that is to say, subverts his own narrator — just as the Editor is subverted in *The Private Memoirs and Confessions of a Justified Sinner*.

It seems, then, that in "Mr Adamson of Laverhope" Hogg employs a devious narrative strategy in order to question the Enlightened assumptions of his readers; indeed, the thrust of the story is that the traditional Christian world-view, dismissed by the narrator as peasant superstition, is in fact the source of an enlightenment which is genuine and real. Such a view sits comfortably with opinions expressed by Hogg in other contexts, for example in the sermon on Deism in the *Lay Sermons* of 1834, and in the poem "Superstition", which dates from 1815. "Superstition" looks back with regret to the old Ettrick belief in the supernatural, which has faded under the advance of modern rationalism.

> Those were the times for holiness of frame;
> Those were the days when fancy wandered free;
> That kindled in the soul the mystic flame,
> And the rapt breathings of high poesy;
> Sole empress of the twilight — Woe is me!
> That thou and all thy spectres are outworn;
> For true devotion wanes away with thee.
> All thy delirious dreams are laughed to scorn,
> While o'er our hills has dawned a cold saturnine morn.[3]

---

3. James Hogg, *Selected Poems*, ed. Douglas S. Mack, Oxford, 1970, 75; ll. 91-99.

The Ettrick tradition was a Christian one, but it contained elements surviving from pre-Christian times. This is reflected in a number of Hogg's works, in which a young woman is taken from Scotland to a heavenly land, from which she returns transformed in one way or another. Most of Hogg's variations on this theme have certain things in common: the story is usually set in pre-Reformation Scotland; the young woman is usually linked in some way to the Blessed Virgin Mary — indeed, she is usually called Mary; the question of whether she does, or does not, remain a virgin is always an issue of some importance; and the heaven to which she is taken always has strong hints of pre-Christian or non-Christian traditions about Fairyland. This group of Hogg texts includes such works as "Kilmeny", *The Pilgrims of the Sun*, "A Genuine Border Story", and "Mary Burnet".

The last-named, from *The Shepherd's Calendar*, is a story quite different in tone from "Mr Adamson of Laverhope". The central character, Mary Burnet, is subjected by her lover John Allanson to something between a seduction and a rape. Supernatural forces, both good and evil, are brought into play by this outrage; and Mary, apparently under the protection of the Blessed Virgin, disappears from earth to become a part-heavenly, part-fairy creature. In her fairy guise, Mary returns to earth to lure her seducer to his destruction, and seven years after her disappearance she returns again, in heavenly and fairy glory, to give comfort to her grieving parents. The word "glamour" came into use in the Scots language before becoming established in English usage; and this word, in its traditional Scots sense of "magic, enchantment, witchcraft", exactly captures the spirit of "Mary Burnet".

Another aspect of Hogg's use of the supernatural in *The Shepherd's Calendar* comes to the fore in the story "The Brownie of the Black Haggs", a work which explores deep and disturbing recesses of the human mind. Lady Wheelhope becomes obsessed by Merodach, a servant thought by the country people to be a brownie sent to haunt her as a punishment for her wickedness. Her obsession deepens and becomes more complex as, again and again, she tries unsuccessfully to harm him only to suffer herself from the results of her own actions. We are told that the lady "fixed her eyes on Merodach. But such a look! ... It was not a look of love nor of hatred exclusively; neither was it of desire or disgust, but it was a combination of them all. It was such a look as one fiend would cast on another, in whose everlasting destruction he rejoiced" (105). The author of *The Private Memoirs and Confessions of a Justified Sinner* is very much on his home ground here.

I have been attempting to suggest that Hogg's short stories are richly complex works which draw on deep wells of tradition in their resonant use of the supernatural; and it would be fair to say that his shorter fiction is beginning to achieve a high reputation, especially in Scotland and North America. If this emerging reputation is deserved, why has it taken so long for the worth of these stories to be recognized? A clue is provided by "Tibby Hyslop's Dream", another of the *Shepherd's Calendar* pieces. This is in effect a story of sexual harassment and attempted seduction; but in the numerous nineteenth-century collected editions of Hogg's works the text is so heavily bowdlerized as to be almost entirely innocent of sexual implication. The story is thus emptied of its significant content.

The posthumous nineteenth-century collected editions of Hogg are all deplorably inadequate; and, as was to be expected in the circumstances, his reputation — high in his lifetime — declined rapidly thereafter. There has been a substantial revival over the past forty years or so, as good modern editions of some of his works have become available. A complete and accurate edition of *The Shepherd's Calendar* has still to appear, however: and the same could be said of many other major Hogg texts and collections. It is therefore pleasant to be able to record that a new and complete edition of Hogg is at present in active preparation, under the auspices of the University of Stirling's Centre for Scottish Literature and Culture.

THE SUPERNATURAL IN THE STORIES OF ELIZABETH GASKELL

ALAN SHELSTON

For many readers *Mary Barton* (1848) is Elizabeth Gaskell's representative novel: it is one of the classic texts of socio-documentary realism. "I have tried to write truthfully", Gaskell said in her Preface, of "the lives of some of those who elbowed me in the busy streets of the town where I resided".[1] But in a letter written in response to the reception of the novel she justifies its "truth" rather differently:

> I told the story according to a fancy of my own; to really SEE the scenes I tried to describe, (and they WERE as real as my own life at the time) and then to tell them as nearly as I could, as if I were speaking to a friend over the fire on a winter's night and describing real occurrences.[2]

Here Gaskell refers not to the conventions of social documentation but to those of oral narrative. The telling of stories "over the fire on a winter's night" is a process which traditionally allows for a freer play of the fancy (note Gaskell's own use of the term) than social documentation might be expected to allow for. Winter's tales are usually romances rather than realities — or rather they allow for the crossing of the boundaries between realism and romance in a way which Gaskell's comment in fact acknowledges ("They WERE as real as my own life"; "... as if I were ... describing real occurrences"). At the same time they carry the full weight of an authenticity born of the narrator's own experience. I shall approach my stated topic of the supernatural in Gaskell's fiction by way of her interest in oral narrative.

---

1. Elizabeth Gaskell, *Mary Barton* (1848), ed. Edgar Wright, Oxford, 1987, xxxv-xxxvi.

2. *The Letters of Mrs Gaskell*, ed. J.A.V. Chapple and Arthur Pollard, Manchester, 1966, no. 48, 82.

Gaskell was an instinctive and natural story-teller — unlike perhaps George Eliot, of whom Trollope remarked that "the nature of her intellect is very far removed indeed from that which is common to the tellers of stories".[3] We find evidence of her enthusiasm for oral narrative constantly in her letters, as well as in the novels themselves. "I know a man who has seen the Fairies and tells the story in the prettiest possible way", she writes in an early letter in which she records her own interest in "old halls and family traditions". On the same occasion she goes on to tell a story of her own:

> I should like nothing better than to roam through the old nooks of Lancashire, exploring more fully a place near Rivington which I just glimpsed at lately; a country hall with the odd name of Street, looking down a beautiful valley. It is falling to ruins now, but in the reign of Queen Anne belonged to a Lord Willoughby, the President of the Royal Society, and author of some book on natural history. He left two daughters, and the estates were disputed and passed to the male heir by some law chicanery; his descendants are cotters in a neighbouring village. Some friends of mine walked to the Hall one evening; part of it was occupied by little farmers, but they peeped into large wainscoted rooms and wandered about fine, old-fashioned gardens, when one of the party bethought himself of asking for admittance into the house to explore the deserted rooms. The woman of the place looked aghast at this proposal, for it was twilight, and said: "They dare not go to that part of the house; for Lord Willoughby walked, and every evening was heard seeking for law-papers in the rooms where all the tattered and torn writings were kept."[4]

"For Lord Willoughby walked" — here we have, in essence, a Gaskell ghost-story — in fact, as we shall see, the anecdote is very close to the material of her first published supernatural story, "The Old Nurse's Story". Gaskell's letters are full of such narrated incidents — few of them perhaps supernatural, but many of them, to take the ambiguously worded title of a fairy story she wrote, "Curious if True". One of the most famous narratives within her letters is her extended account of her first meeting with Charlotte Brontë, which was later to be expanded into the *Life of Charlotte Brontë*, and it is in the *Life* itself that she records an occasion when she restrained herself on the point of

---

3. Anthony Trollope, *An Autobiography*, 2 vols, 1883, II, 66.

4. *Letters*, no. 12, 32.

telling "some dismal ghost-story, just before bed-time" on account of the effect she might have on Charlotte Brontë's nervous sensibilities.[5]

If Charlotte Brontë's sensibility had to be protected, Dickens's did not. In another of the letters Gaskell accuses him of stealing "my story of the lady haunted by the face".[6] This story, which Dickens published as "To Be Read at Dusk" in *The Keepsake* of 1852, concerns a woman who is troubled by her repeated dream of a face she does not recognize. The face turns out to be that of a mysterious stranger who later enters her life with terrible consequences. Dickens admitted his debt in terms which testify to Gaskell's own story-telling powers:

> It came into my mind (you remember that it struck me very much when you told it) as a remarkable instance of a class of mental phenomena at which I have glanced in my little sketch.[7]

Gaskell's facility with oral narrative reveals itself throughout her published fiction. She took full advantage of the flexibility of publishing conventions; as well as her full-length novels she exploited the opportunities provided for more occasional and often pseudo-fictional pieces by the popular journals, like Dickens's *Household Words*. She wrote Christmas stories — although for her one Christmas book, *The Moorland Cottage* (1850), she explicitly avoided the supernatural — and she collected her stories for volume publication. Most of her novels contain tales within tales, like old Alice's account of her past in *Mary Barton*, or Job Legh's account of his mission of mercy in the same novel. *Cranford* (1853), another work which might fairly be described as representative, is in effect a series of stories told by an openly communicative narrator; many of these stories she in her turn has received from the various old ladies who form the principal characters of the novel. A somewhat similar process takes place in the stories that go to make up the volume entitled *Round the Sofa* (1859): the framework for the volume is provided by a group of narrators who form a story-telling circle to entertain a bed-ridden invalid: the stories form a more disparate collection than those that make up *Cranford*, although the most

---

5. Elizabeth Gaskell, *The Life of Charlotte Brontë* (1857), ed. Alan Shelston, Penguin, 1975, 501.

6. *Letters*, 172.

7. *The Letters of Charles Dickens*, eds Graham Storey, Kathleen Tillotson and Nina Burgis, VI (1850-52), Oxford, 1988, 546.

important of them, "My Lady Ludlow", covers somewhat similar ground.

I shall come shortly to Gaskell's explicitly supernatural stories, and in particular to "The Old Nurse's Story" (1852), and to "The Poor Clare" (1856), the only two of her more substantial stories whose action depends exclusively upon supernatural agency. But in larger terms these two stories have more in common with her anecdotal narratives generally than difference from them. In the first place the processes of oral narration, particularly when they involve a second, and receding narrator, establish contact with the immediate, but irrecoverably receding past: this is as true of *Cranford*, where the narration of what has been received as narration takes us back into the latter years of the preceding century, as it is of "The Old Nurse's Story", where the narrator is an old family retainer, now nurse to a third generation who form the audience for her account of the horrors that afflicted the first. Gaskell's ways of establishing contact with a past at once so immediate and so irreclaimable must have had obvious attractions for a generation whose favourite poet was Tennyson, and whose favourite poem *In Memoriam* — "What hope of answer or redress/Behind the veil, behind the veil!" (Gaskell was later to use these lines as a motto for *Sylvia's Lovers* [1863]). Secondly, the feeling for history is accompanied by a feeling for region. As we have seen, Gaskell was particularly intrigued by the remoteness of northern England, that area stretching beyond and away from the modern Manchester which she knew from day to day. But the precise definition of location and region is a feature of all of her fiction whatever its setting: just as she passes through the barriers of time, so she does those of place. Furthermore all of these stories must be in her term "curious": the curiosity value may not always be as extreme as that of "Curious if True" (1860), where a traveller in France finds himself in a chateau in which a ball is taking place made up entirely of figures from a different age acting out the roles of fairy-story, but it must always be the element that provokes the narrator's — and thus the reader's — fancy. From the curious it is only a short step to the macabre, and another to the violent, and thus it is that many of Gaskell's stories — "The Crooked Branch" (1859), for example, a story of a crime perpetrated upon his parents by an errant son, and most notably "Lois the Witch" (1859), her outstanding story of the Salem witch-hysteria — deal with the darker and more irrational sides of human nature, invariably within the context of the family. Along with the transgression of the boundaries of time and place, then, goes a transgression of the boundaries that social norms place upon human behaviour. Finally the stories must project themselves as being "true". The precisely defined narrator, with his or her own relationship with the reader, is of course the primary guarantor, but Gaskell frequently reinforces the process by narrative devices with which we are all familiar: the reading of a manuscript, for example, as in her Gothic tale, "The Grey Woman" (1861), or the use of a lawyer as narrator, as in "The Poor Clare".

I come now to the two stories which I have identified as depending exclusively on the supernatural as the agent of the action, "The Old Nurse's Story", first published in the extra Christmas number of *Household Words* in 1852, under the heading "A Round of Stories by the Christmas Fire",[8] and "The Poor Clare", a longer three-part story appearing in instalments, first published in *Household Words* over the Christmas period in 1856.[9] In that they may not be familiar, I will offer a brief outline of the plot in each case.

"The Old Nurse's Story" is, as its title indicates, told by an old family retainer to the children currently in her charge. It concerns a period in the childhood of their mother who, having been orphaned, has been taken, in the care of the nurse herself, to her mother's ancestral home, deep in the Cumberland fell-country. Apart from the servants, the house is occupied only by an old unmarried lady, Miss Furnivall, and her companion. The nurse and the child are exposed to a sequence of supernatural experiences: mysterious music is heard to come from an old and broken-down organ in the hall of the house, an instrument which we are told was installed and played upon by the long-dead Lord Furnivall. More threateningly the child is seduced onto the open moorland in the height of winter by a phantom child who, somewhat in the manner of the young Catherine in *Wuthering Heights*, appears at the windows and pleads to be let in. The nurse is determined to protect her charge, and the climax of the story comes when, to the sound of the organ's music, the ghost of the old Lord Furnivall is seen to drive from the house the phantom figures of a mother and child — in effect his eldest daughter and a child she had kept secretly from him. In this he is encouraged by a further phantom manifestation, that of the surviving Miss Furnivall, who had been her sister's rival for the love of the father of the child. The story concludes with her dying words: "Alas! Alas! What is done in youth can never be undone in age! What is done in youth can never be undone in age!" (56).

---

8. Page references to "The Old Nurse's Story" are to the World's Classics edition of *Cousin Phillis and Other Tales*, ed. Angus Easson, Oxford, 1981.

9. Page references to "The Poor Clare" are to the World's Classics edition of *My Lady Ludlow and Other Stories*, ed. Edgar Wright, Oxford, 1989.

"The Poor Clare" is a rather more complex affair. This time the narrator is an old lawyer, telling of an experience in his youth, when he was required to investigate the affairs of an old Catholic family living in the north-west of England. In the first of the three instalments of the story we are given the pre-history of the situation he discovers. An old Catholic family have retired into their family estate after the collapse of the Stuart cause and the accession of King William in 1688. They have an Irish servant, Bridget Fitzgerald, whose beautiful daughter leaves home for the continent, leaving only her pet dog for her mother to remember her by. The dog is carelessly destroyed by a member of a hunting-party, and the instalment closes with Bridget placing a terrible curse on the guilty party: he will see the creature he loves best become "a terror and a loathing to all, for this blood's sake" (283). The two remaining instalments deal with the increasingly predictable working-out of the curse. This is somewhat complicated, but basically the curse, in the form of a malevolent double, falls upon a beautiful young woman, Lucy Clarke, who turns out to be not only the daughter of the man whom Bridget Fitzgerald has cursed, but also her own granddaughter. The curse is lifted when Bridget — by now a member of the religious order of the Poor Clares in Antwerp — forgives Lucy's father on her deathbed. Bridget, now "Sister Magdalene", dies with the words "She is freed from the curse!" on her lips (333).

Of the two stories "The Poor Clare" is the more ambitious, "The Old Nurse's Story" in its own terms the more successful. Whereas "The Poor Clare" increasingly strains for its effect, relying on elements of coincidence and melodrama that undermine the force of its genuinely paranormal effects, "The Old Nurse's Story" allows the supernatural to grow naturally out of its command of place and situation. Like other Gaskell stories in a similar setting, it has strongly Wordsworthian overtones: the story of the rejected mother and her child, cast out onto the fells to die is a latter-day Lyrical Ballad. At the same time its horrific effects — and in particular the threat to the child who has to be protected by its nurse — can be justifiably said to anticipate those of Henry James. There is a simple moral coherence to the shorter and more unified story: the wickedness of the past cannot be escaped by its agent, while the innocence of the child is protected by the steadfastness of its protector. In "The Poor Clare", by contrast, a number of discrete factors seem uneasily related. There is a central division between the English setting, skilfully and accurately handled by Gaskell, and the much more stagey introduction of both an Irish and a Continental context. Catholicism lies at the core of the story, and here again there is a contrast between Gaskell's understanding — again very accurate — of the situation of an

English Catholic family in the north-west of England, and her recourse to mid-Victorian sensationalism on the subject of Catholic practice. Irish Catholics are irrational, continentals are devious; only the English aristocratic variety can be trusted not to proselytize. Like her friend Charlotte Brontë, Gaskell was deeply suspicious of Romanism in most of its forms. Nevertheless the divisions of "The Poor Clare" perhaps suggest a rather deeper complexity than anything we are offered in "The Old Nurse's Story". The optimistic morality of the earlier work recurs in the later: hatred is redeemed by self-sacrifice and the innocent heroine is released into love. At the same time, however, "The Poor Clare" confronts us with emotions more passionate, more arbitrary, more wilful and less controllable than its resolution allows for, most notably in the situation of Bridget Fitzgerald herself, defined in the early part of the story as a woman with far more potential — and with a far greater capacity for suffering — than her situation can allow her to express, and in the introduction of the double, not so much as an alternative personality for Lucy Clarke (as Enid Duthie points out, "Instead of being ... evidence of a divided personality this 'ghastly resemblance' is totally alien to the real character of the innocent victim"[10]) but as an alternative emblem of womanhood generally.

Gothic fiction, supernatural fiction, is devised to threaten the reader's sense of the normal. Both "The Old Nurse's Story" and "The Poor Clare" assume this sense of a normal here and now, against which to project the disturbing experiences of another time, another place. What is suggested by the strategies of such fiction is the vulnerability of the reader's sense of the normal — of what may be taken for granted. Gaskell's stories focus in particular on assumptions about women, and about the family, which lie at the heart of her own fiction, and of Victorian realist fiction generally.

The ideal, in both stories, is the self-enclosed family unit. This is reflected most obviously in the assumed audience of oral narrative: stories told around the fire are stories for domestic consumption. Within "The Old Nurse's Story" itself, the assumed audience are the children of the current generation, whose security in the present — Gaskell intimates that they have prosperous Manchester connections — is the measure against which to set the trauma of the past. In the case of "The Poor Clare" Gaskell is more elusive about the circumstances of the narration. The story opens with the date from which the narrator looks back over his own career — December 12th 1747 — and only slowly comes to the

10. Enid Duthie, *The Themes of Elizabeth Gaskell*, Basingstoke, 1980, 141.

revelation that his professional involvement led to his love for "poor Lucy", on whom the curse of the double had fallen. Her release from the curse would have left them free to marry, but there is no indication that this has ever happened: the horrors of the past may therefore have been compounded by domestic unhappiness in the life of the narrator himself. Gaskell was famous, even in her own day, for the deaths in her fiction, but in each story the family is revealed as the site not simply of the kind of sadness and loss inevitably associated with family life, but of conflict and violence. The tableau at the end of "The Old Nurse's Story" presents a mother and child expelled from the family by the contrivance of her sister and the violence of her own father. The sisters themselves have quarrelled over the love of the child's father: driven by jealousy they have lived separate lives in the opposite wings of the house. In "The Poor Clare" family structures are similarly damaged. The old Starkey family has degenerated: in the family of Bridget Fitzgerald passionate women are paired with dissolute husbands and lovers, while mothers are separated from their daughters in a family history that, in a parody of the norm, descends through the female line. These stories thus allow for two projections of the family: the ideal, in the form of the assumed audience, and an anti-type, reflected in both the circumstances of the stories, and their action. It is worth reminding ourselves that while Gaskell was the only major Victorian woman novelist with a conventional family of her own, her childhood experience of family was one of disruption, separation and loss.

Of particular significance in the family context of the stories is the emphasis which they each place upon inheritance; in "The Old Nurse's Story" we work back through the generations; in "The Poor Clare" Bridget's curse has unforeseen consequences for the generations of the future. Gaskell based several stories on this theme: for example "Morton Hall" (1853) and "The Doom of the Griffiths" (1858). The idea of the family curse is, of course, a mainline myth in Victorian fiction. It is readily associated on the moral level with the theme of nemesis, on the economic with property rights, and on the anthropological with evolutionary and genetic theory. If a diachronic as well as a synchronic view of the family is adopted the ideal must be one of moral, economic and genetic development: the issue was an important one for a new middle-class, establishing its own dynasties against those of the traditional past. Gaskell's declared fascination with "old halls and family fortunes", if at one level a reflection on the natural wastage of time, carries this deeper significance. Within this context, however, is set the evil of family violence, sowing seeds of destruction that foredoom the

future. The greatest threat to the ideal of family is the violence inherent
in its own structures.

I come finally to the portrayal of the women in the stories. I have
already referred to the conventionality of Gaskell's own family
circumstances. This needs qualification: she was in fact the mother of
four daughters, while her two (as we now know) sons had died in
infancy. It was therefore a very feminine household. As her novels show,
she was more than usually concerned with mothers — extant or absent
— and daughters, and this we have seen reflected in the matriarchal line
of succession that forms the basis of "The Poor Clare". Ideals of
motherhood are shown in "The Old Nurse's Story", in the combination
of the surrogate figure of the nurse herself, the young mother, and her
young mother, "my pretty young mistress". Against these are shown the
"unnatural" women — the spinster Miss Furnivall, and her sister, whose
furtive marriage had ended in her disgrace. In "The Poor Clare" the
images are more challenging. Bridget Fitzgerald, if a deserted mother,
has a strength issuing from her own independence which allows her both
to release her child and to grieve for her loss: she is driven to the curse
that she utters and her perversity is inherent in her strength. We first see
her walking towards the old family mansion "with a strong and firm
step" by the side of a cart carrying her belongings on which sits her
daughter, "a girl of dazzling beauty, perched lightly on the topmost
trunk, and swaying herself fearlessly to and fro" (274). Mother and
daughter thus present images of womanhood which are at the same time
positive and unconventional: the effect is intensified by the
ineffectiveness of the family whom they serve. "Lucy", the last of the
line, will be a rather different figure — a Victorian heroine of the
preceding century, threatened, like Laura Fairlie, or Lucy Manette, by
an evil over which she has no control. But she too is resolute — she
endures her fate, and is brave enough to warn her lover against becoming
involved with her. By contrast the men in the story, where they are not
villainous, are only marginally adequate: if, in the time-sequence of the
story, the lawyer-narrator is resolute in his determination to free Lucy
from the curse, he nevertheless writes from a position of implied
retirement. Rosemary Jackson has written of Gaskell's supernatural
stories as expressing "disillusionment with ideals of historical progress",
and "revealing a profound dissatisfaction with cultural possibilities".[11]
This, I think, is to oversimplify both the reading of the stories, and the
contrast with the novels. In historical terms, at least, the mid-nineteenth

---

11. Rosemary Jackson, *Fantasy: The Literature of Subversion*, London, 1986,
126.

century *is* invariably represented by Gaskell as a time of enlightenment, while the projection of gender roles and of the family as an institution is more complex than Jackson's comment allows for. Neither the novels nor the stories take these things for granted. Gaskell's supernatural stories allow her to explore the possibilities inherent in her accepted structures: in doing so they draw our attention to similar possibilities in her more substantial fiction.

THE END OF THE LINE:
THE FAMILY CURSE IN SHORTER GOTHIC FICTION

CHRIS BALDICK

My purpose in this article is to examine briefly the fate of shorter Gothic fiction in nineteenth-century Britain, with particular reference to the degree of coherence it manages to sustain by resort to the theme of dynastic extinction.

The shorter Gothic tale is a form little studied outside the works of Poe. There are some good reasons for this neglect, principally the fact that it is largely parasitic upon the more substantial and complex tradition of the Gothic novel or romance proper. Whereas the line of novels from Walpole to Maturin at least forms a recognizably coherent phase of generic development (even if the story becomes more complicated later on), no such distinct tradition of short stories stands out either as an episode or as a clearly recognized line of development in nineteenth-century British fiction. What can be reconstructed, at best, is a succession of attempts to adapt and sustain Gothic effects in the shorter form; a succession which does not impose itself upon the attention of literary history with the force of a self-sustaining tradition, so comparatively enfeebled and pallid is this lineage.

By contrast, the vitality of the Gothic tale, and indeed of the short story form in general, is more impressive in the United States from the time of Hawthorne and Poe onward. In what follows I am implicitly adopting Poe's "The Fall of the House of Usher" as a model of the Gothic tale fully achieved and concentrated, so that the hesitant career of shorter Gothic Britain can be conceived as a sequence of attempts to catch up with the more happily inaugurated American tradition.

The problem of reproducing the Gothic within the short story form can best be highlighted by recalling some of the notable features of the longer Gothic novel. The use of extended lingering suspense in the works of Radcliffe and Lewis is closely connected to the rambling exfoliation of subplots and digressive or diversionary narrative excursions, so that typically a leading character will be left under the tortures of the inquisition for several chapters while we follow the adventures of some other personage. More is involved than a simple tormenting of the reader's expectations, though. The formal asymmetries and meandering complications of the full-length Gothic novel provide at the level of structure an apt reduplication of the central symbolic setting: the labyrinthine building. Protagonist and reader alike, then, lose themselves in blind alleys and in obscure passages that lead nowhere; and in the most extravagant case of this narrative over-elaboration — Maturin's *Melmoth the Wanderer* — the novelist himself appears to have got lost in his own digressive maze. The fully Gothic effect, then, would appear to be tied to modes of narrative extension and complication foreign to the disciplines of the short tale.

The early history — we may as well call it a prehistory — of shorter Gothic fiction offers no satisfactory answers to this difficulty. Instead we have two different intertextual strategies whereby some aspect of the Gothic novel may be recaptured and presented in shorter compass. The first is that of the Gothic "fragment", a short-lived form which made its appearance in some of the magazines of the late eighteenth century, the best known and earliest example being Anna L. Aikin's "Sir Bertrand". As its name suggests, the fragment presents itself as an inconclusive episode from some larger lost work. In its brief description of, say, a knight encountering a ghost and a distressed maiden in a castle, it can reproduce without preliminaries the intense atmosphere and familiar iconography of some exciting chapter in a Gothic novel, but without real narrative momentum or resolution. On the other hand, the second shorter form attempted in this early phase — the shilling shocker or bluebook tale — approaches the problem from the other side. The shilling shocker, which flourished in the popular market in the first two decades of the nineteenth century, was parasitic upon the Gothic novel in the more obvious mode of plagiarism. What one finds in these works (some of which have been reprinted in Peter Haining's *The Shilling Shockers*, 1978) are hastily summarized plots bearing close resemblances to those of Radcliffe and Lewis, but this time of course without the atmospheric development of setting or the lingering exploitation of suspense found in the full-length form; all that remains is a breakneck resumé of one sensational scene after another.

In these two abortive early forms of shorter Gothic, then, we have either atmosphere without plot, or plot without atmosphere. The breakthrough by which shorter Gothic fiction was to achieve any degree of formal coherence would need to combine narrative momentum with symbolic resonance, somehow focusing and centring the notoriously decentred and ramshackle constructions of the Gothic novel within the discipline of a new formula. And in the successful case of Poe, something like this was achieved: by a process of rigorously economical distillation, Poe purified from the disparate materials and effects of the inherited Gothic tradition a radically streamlined reformulation of its conventions. The dismantling of the cumbersome conventional machinery and its disorderly multiplication of incidents made way for a clarification and foregrounding of a narrative and thematic model hitherto lying dormant and imperfectly realized in Gothic writing (and in the surrounding culture of Romantic sensationalism): the decline and extinction of the old family line. The exemplary fiction of the House of Usher famously harmonizes the terminal involution of the Usher family with the physical crumbling of its mansion: of house as dynasty with house as habitation. In doing so it selects from the properties of earlier Gothic writing a characteristic symbolic location (the threatening old building), and derives from it a clear focus of narrative direction, the vanishing point being that of the old family's imminent extinction.

The slower development of shorter Gothic fiction in Britain, as I want to show, follows a faltering trajectory in the same direction, shifting from the accumulation of sensational scenes of arbitrary persecution, imprisonment, and cruelty to a more selective and pronounced interest in processes of degeneration, so that the centre of interest is less the claustrophobia of incarceration within the old house as building than the claustrophobia of heredity within the old house as dynasty. As an awesomely poetical subject, the extinction of the family line has of course respectable precedents in both ancient and early modern tragedy, the full tragic effect being accomplished by the destruction not of the protagonist alone, but of the wider family group, innocent and guilty alike: some families may be cursed over several generations, like the house of Atreus in Greek legend, while others may be torn apart by brief outbreaks of hubris, as with the royal houses of Macbeth, Lear, and Hamlet. Tragic nemesis is a blaster of whole houses rather than of individual miscreants: a point well understood by the pioneers of British Gothic fiction and embodied in the pseudotragic ambitions of their works. Walpole's *Castle of Otranto* notably concerns the efforts of a usurper, Manfred, to continue his family line, against the evident wishes (as in *Hamlet* and *Macbeth*) of the rightful owner's restless ghost; and the accepted pattern of tragic self-destruction dictates that these efforts should ironically only bring about the premature end of his dynasty, here through the inadvertent murder of his own daughter Matilda. Likewise, although through a sensationalist twist rather than by strict tragic logic, Ambrosio in *The Monk* succeeds in eliminating the womenfolk of the family he had not realized he still had.

As a theme, however, or as a self-sustaining narrative pattern, this catastrophic implosion of the old family line never separated itself out from the surrounding mayhem of horrors and cruelties until the discipline of the shorter form summoned it forth as the most promising dominant or foregrounded element in later nineteenth-century Gothic: overnight in the case of Poe, but by a more tentative and hesitant process in the British short-story tradition, to which we may now turn.

In this context it will be profitable to review four more or less Gothic works: the anonymous tale "The Astrologer's Prediction; or The Maniac's Fate", published in London in 1826 in a shilling-shocker collection entitled *Legends of Terror*, and recently reprinted in two modern anthologies; Elizabeth Gaskell's tale "The Old Nurse's Story", published in the Christmas number of Dickens's *Household Words* in 1852, and since reprinted in many modern ghost-story collections; Arthur Conan Doyle's Sherlock Holmes story "The Adventure of the Speckled Band", which appeared in February 1892 in the *Strand* magazine before being collected the same year in *The Adventures of Sherlock Holmes*; and finally, slightly out of chronological order, a longer short story by Robert Louis Stevenson entitled "Olalla", first published in 1885 and collected in *The Merry Men* (1887). Oddly, this last story, the most intriguing and most subtly crafted of the four, is rarely reprinted in modern selections of Stevenson's fiction.

"The Astrologer's Prediction; or The Maniac's Fate" is a clumsily over-excited production, remarkable at least for springing upon its readers the motif of the hereditary curse within its first two sentences:

> Reginald, sole heir of the illustrious family of Di Venoni, was remarkable, from his earliest infancy, for a wild enthusiastic disposition. His father, it was currently reported, had died of an hereditary insanity; and his friends, when they marked the wild mysterious intelligency of his eye, and the determined energy of his aspect, would often assert that the dreadful malady still lingered in the veins of young Reginald.[1]

The fall of the young Reginald and of his family is both predicted and hastened by a wizened old astrologer who takes up residence in a ruined tower near to the Venoni family seat in the Black Forest. Pointing out the star of Reginald's nativity in the heavens, he forecasts that when it begins to plummet like a meteor, Reginald will commit a deed of blood in this very tower. Thrown into a nervous fever by this prediction, Reginald is

---

1. *The Oxford Book of Gothic Tales*, ed. Chris Baldick, Oxford, 1992, 63.

sent by his mother to Italy to recover his spirits. In Venice, he falls in love with and marries the Doge's daughter Marcelia, but a few months later is called back to attend the deathbed of his mother. Her death plunges him into melancholy delirium, and he proposes a suicide pact with his wife, so that they may join her. His mother's ghost appears to him in a dream, encouraging him to pursue this plan. Marcelia, to calm his spirits, takes Reginald (now described by the narrator simply as "the maniac") for a restorative walk — unfortunately in the direction of the fateful ruined tower; at the sight of which he drags Marcelia to the top and, after noticing the now "sickly lustre" of his star in the sky, strangles her. A moment of rational calm intervenes before he finally hurls himself, with a fiend-like laugh, from the summit of the tower.

Although this tale manages to summon a more satisfying Gothic "atmosphere" of doom and foreboding than many shilling-shocker works, it suffers from severe confusion in its presentation of causality. Reginald's fatal star is seen to dim at the story's end, as the astrologer has foretold, but its predicted meteoric fall never occurs. Instead it is the maniac, as he then is, who himself plummets deathward — a catastrophe caused either by his hereditary insanity, or by the star, or by the astrologer (whose instruction to bury him after his death Reginald has ignored), or by his mother's ghost, or by his own unwillingness to be divided from his dead mother. Any one of these elements could be read as the symbol or portent indicating any one of the others as prime cause, but which is which cannot be determined amid the hectic overproduction of motivations for the maniac's fall. This typically Gothic overloading of the tale pays a certain price in clarity of effect, but it retains the distinction of having adopted, some years before Poe, the snuffing of the family line as the "vanishing point" at which its multiple lines of causality converge. 1826, the year of this tale's publication, was, incidentally, something of a bumper year for racial and dynastic extinctions, being the year also of Fenimore Cooper's *Last of the Mohicans*, John Galt's *Last of the Lairds*, and Mary Shelley's *The Last Man*. Two years after Byron's death, the god Terminus was in the ascendant.

Elizabeth Gaskell's "The Old Nurse's Story" represents, at least within the terms of the teleology I am adopting here, something of a relapse: a dilution of Gothic possibilities under the conventional pressures of the moralizing Christmas ghost story, for which Dickens had provided the most popular model, with its cheery sentimentalities of familial

forgiveness.[2] The first thing we learn in the tale is the reassuring fact
that the line of the story's family is not extinct, since the narratees are
evidently a group of bonny children listening to their aged nurse's
account of an episode of their mother's infancy which leads to events
three and four generations behind them. The mother, Rosamond,
orphaned at the age of five, is accompanied by the then teenage nurse,
Hester, to Furnivall Manor, once the ancestral home of her mother's
family but long abandoned by the Furnivall clan, with the exception of
an ancient great-aunt, Miss Grace Furnivall. The manor house has a
dilapidated and apparently uninhabited east wing and, in the great hall,
a broken-down organ which nevertheless emits strange musical sounds
when stormy weather impends. As Hester eventually learns from the
other servants (who include the almost obligatory Radcliffean Dorothy),
the phantom organist is deemed to be the restless ghost of the old Lord
Furnivall, Miss Grace's father. After an alarm in which little Rosamond
is summoned out into a blizzard by a ghostly child and almost dies of
exposure, the full story is revealed: in her youth Miss Grace had been
the rival of her sister Maude for the love of a foreign music teacher, by
whom the more favoured Maude had secretly had a child. Eventually
discovering her sister's secret, Miss Grace had betrayed it to their angry
father and joined him in driving Maude and the child from the house in
a snow-storm which killed them both.

The story's climax comes on a stormy night when the door to the east
wing crashes open to admit a ghostly ensemble in choreographed
formation: the old lord, the two young ladies, and the spirit-child are all
gathered there to re-enact in the form of a tableau or charade the family
trauma of Maude's expulsion. The old Miss Grace now looks on in
horror as her father strikes his repudiated grandchild with his crutch, and
she pleads unavailingly for the child to be spared; but the ghostly image
of her younger self is revealed as callously abetting the cruel deed. Miss
Grace is carried to her deathbed that night, muttering "Alas! alas! what
is done in youth can never be undone in age!" And there the story ends,
wrapped up with an evident warning against acts of hard-heartedness that
we will later come to regret. It has its evident strengths as a crafted tale,
in its handling of narrative voice and of setting, but we do not have here
the fully achieved Gothic impetus of the family curse at work. At least
one branch of the family, of course, survives in little Rosamond, for her
children to hear the tale. More importantly, the true subject of "The Old
Nurse's Story" is not a family's terminal degeneration but the exposure

2. Elizabeth Gaskell, *Cousin Phillis and Other Tales*, ed. Angus Easson,
Oxford, 1981.

of a concealed family crime. In this it shows itself to belong with the classic ghost story, in which typically a single ancestral misdeed awaits expiation, rather than with the Gothic tale proper with its far more grimly deterministic logic of inherited and vertiginous decay.

Of Conan Doyle's shorter Sherlock Holmes stories, there are several which glisten with a slight Gothic colouring: "The Adventure of the Copper Beeches", for instance, with its use of the incarcerated daughter; or "The Five Orange Pips", with its pattern of vengeance inflicted on succeeding generations of a family. The topos of the family curse, however, is displayed more openly in "The Adventure of the Speckled Band", in which a flamboyantly wicked stepfather, Dr Grimesby Roylott of Stoke Moran, attempts to kill both of his stepdaughters rather than allow their deceased mother's fortune to pass to them as it must as soon as they marry. The first stepdaughter, upon becoming betrothed, has already died in mysterious circumstances, in her locked bedchamber adjacent to Dr Roylott's, when the second, Helen Stoner, is obliged, after contracting an engagement of marriage, to move into the same room. Wisely, she consults Holmes, who discovers that Roylott has been slipping a poisonous viper into the room through a ventilator. Given a sound thrashing by the hermit of Baker Street, the viper wriggles back through the ventilator and bites its evil master, who dies within a few seconds.

Although the story is set in the very recent past — April 1883, to be precise — Doyle is at pains to establish the archaic quality of Roylott's patriarchal malevolence. This he attempts by sketching a family history behind the villain's murderous character. As Helen Stoner explains upon her arrival at Baker Street:

> I am living with my stepfather, who is the last survivor of one of the oldest Saxon families in England, the Roylotts of Stoke Moran, on the western border of Surrey .... The family was at one time among the richest in England, and the estate extended over the borders into Berkshire in the north, and Hampshire in the west. In the last century, however, four successive heirs were of a dissolute and wasteful disposition, and the family ruin was eventually completed by a gambler, in the days of the Regency. Nothing was left save a few acres of ground and the two-hundred-year-old house, which is itself crushed under a heavy mortgage. The last squire dragged out his existence there, living the horrible life of an aristocratic pauper ....[3]

---

3. Arthur Conan Doyle, *The Adventures of Sherlock Holmes*, Penguin, 1981, 168.

This man's son, Grimesby, the last of the Roylotts, has sought his fortune as a doctor in India, where he married a rich military widow, Mrs Stoner. But having beaten his native butler to death in a fit of anger, and served a term of imprisonment for the offence, he has returned to England. Following his wife's death in a railway accident, he has established himself in the half-ruined and lichen-blotched ancestral mansion, only one wing of which is still habitable. Helen Stoner continues her account to Holmes:

> Instead of making friends and exchanging visits with our neighbours, who had at first been overjoyed to see a Roylott of Stoke Moran back in the old family seat, he shut himself up in his house, and seldom came out save to indulge in ferocious quarrels with whoever might cross his path. Violence of temper approaching to mania has been hereditary in the men of the family, and in my stepfather's case it had, I believe, been intensified by his long residence in the tropics (160).

Roylott's dangerous disposition, then, is presented as the culmination of a prolonged degeneration of the family's character, his forebears having passed down to him their lack of self-control. Under the midday sun of India, he has become an English mad dog; and the exotic animals with which he surrounds himself — a cheetah, a baboon, and the fatal snake — serve as emblems of this terminal decline into sub-human ferocity. His temporary status as a member of Dr Watson's own respectable profession has been only a failed effort to avoid his inevitable reversion to type, the type itself being quite clearly the Gothic figure of the Manfredian aristocrat, for whom barbarity and lust of conquest are in the blood. In this tale the family curse runs its full Gothic course, the lucky survivor being of course not a blood relative but a victim of misalliance between the healthy professional and administrative classes favoured in the Sherlock Holmes cycle (doctors, soldiers, stenographers, clerks, and the like) and the doomed predators of the feudal past.

Stevenson's "Olalla" employs a somewhat similar Gothic contrast between a modern professional (in this case a British officer convalescing from injury in the Peninsular War in Spain) and the last generation of a declining aristocratic family. The unnamed officer, who narrates the tale, is advised by his doctor that he needs the pure air of the sierra to complete his recovery, and is given this account of an impoverished noble family willing to accommodate him in their isolated mountain home:

The mother was the last representative of a princely stock, degenerate both in parts and fortune. Her father was not only poor, he was mad: and the girl ran wild about the residencia till his death. Then, much of the fortune having died with him, and the family being quite extinct, the girl ran wilder than ever, until at last she married, Heaven knows whom; a muleteer some say, others a smuggler; while there are some who upheld there was no marriage at all, and that Felipe and Olalla are bastards.[4]

Of these dubious adolescent children, it is Felipe whom the narrator first encounters: he is a strong but lazily idiotic lad with a streak of furtive cruelty but with an evident reverential obedience to his mysterious sister. The mother, clearly degenerate in the imbecilic blankness of her expression, lolls and basks in the sun in sensual slothfulness all day. Having seen a two-hundred-year-old portrait of one of his hostess's beautiful ancestors, and ominously understood "that to love such a woman were to sign and seal one's own sentence of degeneration" (69), the narrator sums up his impressions of the family's decline:

> The family blood had been impoverished, perhaps by long inbreeding, which I knew to be a common error among the proud and the exclusive. No decline, indeed, was to be traced in the body, which had been handed down unimpaired in shapeliness and strength .... But the intelligence (that more precious heirloom) was degenerate; the treasure of ancestral memory ran low; and it had required the potent, plebeian crossing of a muleteer or mountain contrabandista to raise, what approached hebetude in the mother, into the active oddity of the son (76).

When the mountain wind starts to blow fiercely, the officer is kept awake at nights by the blood-curdling yells, apparently of some lunatic or tortured animal. Not having yet met the daughter of the house, he guesses that she must be insane, and possibly mistreated as well. But when he stumbles upon Olalla's room in her absence, he finds books of religious devotion in Latin, and even pious poems written in her hand. She would appear to be a saintly ascetic, quite at odds with the sensuality of her family. Only half way through the tale does he come face to face with Olalla herself, and the two instantly fall in love at first sight, although they cannot bring themselves to speak for several days. The officer cannot understand why, after their first embrace, Olalla flees and

---

4. R.L. Stevenson, *The Supernatural Stories of Robert Louis Stevenson*, ed. M. Hayes, London, 1976, 64.

leaves him a letter imploring him to go away and forget her. But the same day, he accidentally cuts his wrist and appeals to Olalla's mother for first aid. Instead she stares strangely at the wound and bites it to the bone, in an uncontrollable animal frenzy only subdued when Felipe drags her away.

The word "vampire" is never used in the tale, and indeed the conventional trappings of vampire lore are carefully avoided by Stevenson. His interest here is in heredity alone, unaccompanied by supernatural effects or suggestions, and his cleverly misleading sunlit location precludes the use of more familiar northern Gothic machinery. It is not the precise nature of the mother's affliction that matters, but only the gravity of its bestiality and therefore of Olalla's now evident predicament: she is a pure soul trapped within a beautiful but (we must assume) secretly blighted body which will in time betray her to the curse of her mother's blood. As the officer goes through a second convalescence, this time tended by Olalla herself, he realizes that his love for her has still not been dispelled by the revelation of the family curse. Against his continued pleadings, she now unfolds her understanding of her fate, and her resolve in facing it:

> The race exists; it is old, it is very young, it carries its eternal destiny in its bosom; upon it, like waves upon the sea, individual succeeds to individual, mocked with a semblance of self-control, but they are nothing. We speak of the soul, but the soul is in the race ... you have seen for yourself how the wheel has gone backward with my doomed race. I stand, as it were, upon a little rising ground in this desperate descent, and see both before and behind, both what we have lost and to what we are condemned, to go farther downward. And shall I — I that dwell apart in the house of the dead, my body, loathing its ways — shall I repeat the spell? Shall I bind another spirit, reluctant as my own, into this bewitched and tempest-broken tenement that I now suffer in? Shall I hand down this cursed vessel of humanity, charge it with fresh life as with fresh poison, and dash it, like a fire, in the faces of posterity? But my vow has been given; the race shall cease from off the earth (97-99).

Olalla finally sends the reluctant officer away through the neighbouring village, where the peasants cross themselves at his approach.

This story by Stevenson deserves to be more widely recognized as the most impressive of shorter British Gothic tales in the nineteenth century, and certainly as the "purest" type of the family curse fiction, emancipated as it is both from ghost-lore and from the accumulated trappings of graveyard sensationalism. We have passed beyond the confused multicausality of "The Astrologer's Prediction" to a monocausal narrative logic founded on genetic determinism; and we can see this tale to be unencumbered likewise with the distracting supernaturalism and moralizing alike of Gaskell's "Old Nurse's Story", just as it is free of the minutiae of deductive ingenuity that push the Gothic family curse into a subordinate position in Doyle's "The Speckled Band".

Far from being serenely at ease with itself, though, Stevenson's tale is of course seething with powerful undercurrents of anxiety and dread, among them a Calvinist fear of the body, a more general Protestant suspicion of Catholics, a northern revulsion at southern sensuality, and of course a scarcely concealed chivalrous misogyny which frames female sexuality as witchcraft. The surprise of this story is how successfully all this phobic tumult is subdued into a consistent tone of melancholy resignation, far from the hysterical pitch of Poe's tales. It is likely that the disciplined unity of effect in "Olalla" owes something to the example of Poe's "House of Usher"; but it would be misleading to suggest that after a delay of forty years the Gothic short story in Britain had arrived at the same point as its earlier American counterpart. For the meanings of heredity, degeneration and atavism had in the meantime acquired a new resonance with the impact of Darwin's work upon the intellectual and imaginative world of the later nineteenth century: a fact evident in the longer Gothic works of Stevenson's contemporaries, Wilde's *The Picture of Dorian Gray* being a case in point. With "Olalla", then, Stevenson may be said to have stabilized in convincing form the unstable materials of Gothic, but around a governing principle antithetical to that employed by Poe. Whereas Poe had distilled an essentially psychological form of Gothic, claiming in the language of Romantic idealism that his terrors were those of "the soul", Stevenson, in bringing the British Gothic tale to its maturity, announces through the doomed family of Olalla the defeat of the soul, which is now powerless to overcome the advancing tide of tainted blood.

THE GIST OF THE GOTHIC IN ENGLISH FICTION; OR, GOTHIC AND THE INVASION OF BOUNDARIES

C.C. BARFOOT

"Gist", of course, is a play on words, an allusion to all those "ghosts" which are one of the ways that the Gothic element manifests itself in non-Gothic novels. Some of these "ghosts" may be real (if one can properly talk of *real* "ghosts"). More frequently they are hallucinations, nightmares or waking dreams experienced by one or more of the characters. Most often they are suppositious ghosts, or shocking unexpected encounters — with a convict leaping up from among the gravestones or Miss Havisham in her "withered bridal dress" amidst the decay of the uneaten bridal breakfast in her darkened rooms in a wrecked mansion with the stopped clocks:

> So she sat, corpse-like .... I knew nothing then of the discoveries that are occasionally made of bodies buried in ancient times, which fall to powder in the moment of being distinctly seen; but, I have often thought since, that she must have looked as if the admission of the natural light of day would have struck her to dust.[1]

Or such an hypothetical or assumed ghost may be someone, long thought lost or dead, and almost forgotten, who returns to plague and haunt, to generally stir up trouble among old friends, relations and acquaintances — an example that easily comes to mind being the return of the convict, Magwitch or Provis in the same novel, *Great Expectations*.

From such phonetic resemblances as "gist" and "ghost", the verbal ghosts of folk-etymologies, a string of other verbal apparitions unwinds

---

1. Charles Dickens, *Great Expectations* (1860-61), ch. 8, Penguin, 1965, 90. In the case of all quotations from the familiar much reprinted nineteenth-century novels to which I will be referring, chapter numbers will be given as well as page numbers.

itself — "guest", "jest", "gesture" and, even, "yeast" (especially since in Dutch "yeast" is indeed "gist"). At a purely factitious level "ghosts" are always something of a jest — even Hamlet after his interview with the ghost of his father is both hysterical and exhilarated, jesting and hilarious by turns: for indeed ghosts do jest with us, teasing us over the boundaries of life, and the frontier between the living and the dead. And this notion of the ghost as a tease is universal, I believe: poltergeists being the clowns of the spook world. So the gist of the Gothic is a jest, and also a gesture, made by the dead to the living. More literally, ghosts are frequently described as gesturing, beckoning the observer on, making it incumbent upon the ghostseer to make a gesture back, consciously or unconsciously, by displaying the usual symptoms of a cold sweat, goose-pimples, the hair standing on end, screeching and screaming, fainting; above all, by recording the presence of the ghost, like Hamlet with his tablets, by signalling the intervention of the unknown, the unknowable in the known, knowable, visible and touchable world.

Ghosts and Vampires (for we should not neglect the latter, since Heathcliff for one is a very obvious vampire), as figures of the walking and the living dead, are embodiments of boundary invaders (just as clairvoyants or ghostseers cross the threshold the other way). Even the yet living who erupt into our lives — "Oh it's you, you gave me such a start!", we say — disturb our mental self-possession by materializing physically in such a way that temporally we are shocked and stunned: they too may be considered a sort of ghost.

Therefore the gist of Gothic may be regarded principally as an element of mystery designed to upset our everyday lives and move us in new creative directions. Uninvited, intrusive and probably unannounced, these Gothic guests compel us to fathom their identities and their origins, as well as our own identities and origins. Their destinies, their probably misshapen and misdirected fates, "doomed for a certain term to walk the night" or confined to a living tomb, force us to query our own past roots, our present route, and future destination. The guesses engendered and stirred in us by the ghastly guest, like a new leaven in our lives, a yeast (that Dutch "gist"), help to stimulate the imagination. We are compelled by the rising imaginings, the ghostly summonings, to travel mentally, just as the heroes and heroines of Gothic fictions are frequently drawn to journeys, quests, of a physical as well as of a spiritual kind; which is natural to a genre allied to or descended from the Romance "gest" — "notable deeds or exploits, actions ... a story or romance in verses ... the various stages of a journey" (*OED*) — not quite a Gothic fiction, although a fiction of the Gothic era, anticipating the Gothic tale of the modern period. Ghosts, guests, gestures, jests, gests, quests — all are gists of Gothic, all pointing to the Gothic as an invasion of the known present by the hidden past, an encroachment of the closed past onto the open present, a disturbance of the apparent daylight of today by the dark of yesterday.

The Gothic highlights cultural encroachment and the invasion of boundaries, and dramatizes the disturbances caused by geographical dislocation, as well as by the rift between the secular and the sacred, innocence and guilt, the beautiful and the ugly, surface and depth. In early Gothic novels (from Walpole's *The Castle of Otranto* [1765] to Ann Radcliffe's *The Mysteries of Udolpho* [1794] and *The Italian* [1797] and M.G. Lewis's *The Monk* [1796]) this clash of cultures was marked by their southern settings. In later novels where the gist of Gothic is to be found, these southern settings are not necessarily evident at all, but still in one way or another the encounter between distinctive and opposed cultures, social or ethnic are crucial to the Gothic. In the original novels it could be said that the Gothic represents a troubled northern dream of the south,[2] an actual or latent Protestant nightmare of the horrors of Catholicism, with all the secrets and mysteries of its covering vestments, its rituals and doctrines, the dark hidden corners and covert depths of its associated architecture. This sectarian sense, this inherent belief that other cultures and habits are more perverse, more corrupt, full of disturbing and shocking difference (perhaps signified most characteristically by references to the Inquisition and to the Jesuits) inspires Gothic fiction, and in turn is fed by Gothic fiction.

Gothic novels and novels with a gist of the Gothic are full of prejudice and distrust, guilt and fearful anticipation; full of bias in favour of the usual, the everyday, the ordinary, which is habitually frustrated and denied by the threat of uninvited guests, the ghosts, the phantoms and fantasies that confirm the suspected instability of the normal, cast doubt on the daylight and undermine the present with

---

2. Cf. speculations about the origins of Gothic architecture: "Wren thought they [Gothic buildings] came from the Saracens via the Crusades, Warton from the Moors and Stukely from the Saracens (and Druids)" (Terence Davis, *The Gothick Taste*, Newton Abbot, 1974, 21); "When the Goths had conquered Spain and the genial warmth of the climate, and the religion of the old inhabitants had ripened their wits and inflamed their mistaken piety, *they struck out a new species of architecture*, unknown to Greece or Rome, upon original principles, and *ideas much nobler* than what had given birth even to classical magnificence" (Bishop Warburton, quoted in Kenneth Clark, *The Gothic Revival*, London, 1928, rpt 1974, 36-37).

charges from an atavistic unreformed past. The Gothic represents the wilful incursion of the irrational into the literature of the Age of Reason, of reasonable analysis, of the calm consideration of passion. Gothic fiction resurrects satanic figures dressed as gaudily as you would expect fine ladies and gentlemen to be, or in dark or resplendent ecclesiastical robes, depending on the status of the character concerned, often with the power of entrée (granted by their rank, their social position or some diabolic tool), and reveals what erotic and destructive passions are gathering underneath, and what dangers to discreet, guarded selves they represent. Hence the importance in Gothic fiction of locks, keys, doors, chains, and other means of holding danger at bay or expelling encroaching menace. The Gothic therefore exploits the discordant and incompatible aspects of outer and inner men and women; the irreconcilable clash between what the outer form claims and proclaims and what the inner self knows and desires. Hence the exploitation in Gothic fiction of the lurking evil in monks and nuns, and in handsome men and beautiful women since in these figures the inconsistency and incongruity is felt most sensitively.

The most famous reflection on some of these juxtapositions is, of course, that put into the mind of Catherine Morland while staying at Northanger Abbey by her sceptical creator, Jane Austen:

> Charming as were all Mrs Radcliffe's works, and charming even as were the works of all her imitators, it was not in them perhaps that human nature, at least in the midland counties of England, was to be looked for. Of the Alps and the Pyrenees, with their pine forests and their vices, they might give a faithful delineation; and Italy, Switzerland, and the South of France, might be as fruitful in horrors as they were represented .... But in the central part of England ....[3]

But even in Jane Austen, in novels which seek to still and keep at bay the Gothic vices and horrors of the south, by reminding the narrators, the protagonists, the readers alike that "in the midland counties of England" human nature was free to flourish in stable uncriminal behaviour, figments of the Gothic are not entirely banished. A father returns to spook and spike a dangerous amateur dramatic performance, a lover returns to disturb the stoic self-denial of an abandoned fiancée, while the ghosts of philanderers have to be accommodated, and the moral transgressions and faults of good taste continue to haunt their

---

3. Jane Austen, *Northanger Abbey* (1818), ch. 25, Penguin, 1972, 202.

perpetrators until absolved by the recognition of error and the resolution
not to err again. These are not real ghosts, of course, not even unreal
ghosts — I realize that I am stretching a metaphor, possibly to breaking
point — but it is worth stretching in order to suggest that Gothic
hauntings may have wider and more moral significance in Gothic novels
than we might have supposed, and that novels dealing with
representations of the everyday world of courtship and marriage,
gaining and retaining fortunes, making one's way in a material world
where cash and class mainly count, emotional and moral decisions may
assume a glimmer of the anxiety, the hysteria, the shock, the agitation
(a favourite word in the period, especially for Gothic writers), the
mortifications and commotions that the more sensational writers seek to
portray as a consequence of their dark mysteries. The cultural clashes in
Jane Austen may be smaller and more delicate than those in classic
Gothic novels or in the Brontës, but nevertheless they are telling enough
to be registered on the Richter scale of the society she is so carefully
scrutinizing.

In a novel like *Villette* the greater shock-waves of cultural clash are
graphically signalled in Gothic elements: superficially in the form of the
legend of the ghost of the "black and white nun" that is said to haunt
Mme Beck's house (see ch. 12); more deeply in the personal
disorientation that the heroine, Lucy Snowe, suffers in Catholic
Brussels, which for her represents the threatening, hallucinatory, exotic
south. So many of Lucy's experiences in Villette (the place, as well as
the novel) are nightmarish, and constantly threatening to drive her
across that other boundary into nervous breakdown, which is indeed
what eventually happens. In this novel Catholicism seems particularly
tempting and threatening, attractive and frightening, as does so much to
Lucy Snowe, the heroine with the exposed bright chilly name (the
question we need to ask on occasions is whether Lucy is the ghost or
the ghosted, the haunting or the haunted?) drawn to comforting darkness
with its hidden fires, struggling with an alluringly strange environment
and language — it is a significant aspect of the text of *Villette* that so
much of the dialogue is in French in order to stress the foreignness of
the experience not only for Lucy but also for the reader. Agonized and
antagonized by a sense of difference and division without and within,
Lucy begins the painful process of self-questioning to find out who she
herself is, beset both by unbidden and unconsciously bidden ghosts.
Villette (again the city and the novel) is full of ghosts, figures who
disappear and then turn up again unexpectedly, like Dr John. This
pattern of strange reappearance gives particular poignancy to the end of
the novel, where, in some famously ambiguous and haunting phrases,

the possible return of the man Lucy is supposed to marry, M. Emanuel, the very embodiment of allure and menace in the novel, is left hovering in the air after the storm:

> And now the three years are past: M. Emanuel's return is fixed. It is Autumn; he is to be with me ere the mists of November come ....
>
> The wind shifts to the west. Peace, peace, Banshee — "keening" at every window! It will rise — it will swell — it shrieks out long: wander as I may through the house this night, I cannot lull the blast. The advancing hours make it strong: by midnight, all sleepless watchers hear and fear a wild south-west storm.
>
> That storm roared frenzied for seven days. It did not cease till the Atlantic was strewn with wrecks ....
>
> Peace, be still! Oh! a thousand weepers, praying in agony on waiting shores, listened for that voice, but it was not uttered — not uttered till, when the hush came, some could not feel it: till, when the sun returned, his light was night to some!
>
> Here pause: pause at once. There is enough said. Trouble no quiet, kind heart; leave sunny imaginations hope .... Let them picture union and a happy succeeding life ....[4]

One may compare Lucy Snowe's disconcerting experiences when she goes south to Brussels with what happens to Mr Lockwood when he goes north to Yorkshire, and finds himself totally at a loss and disorientated in Heathcliff's parlour in Wuthering Heights (as with *Villette* the place name in the title marks the difference and the cause of the confrontation of cultures, the threshold that must be crossed). When Mr Lockwood is forced to stay overnight at Wuthering Heights, he has a nightmare which may be more than a nightmare, and is brutally confronted with the unquiet spirit of the dead Catherine Linton:

> ... I was lying in the oak closet, and I heard distinctly the gusty wind, and the driving of the snow; I heard, also, the fir-bough repeat its teasing sound, and ascribed it to the right cause; but it annoyed me so much, that I resolved to silence it, if possible; and, I thought, I rose and endeavoured to unhasp the casement. The hook was soldered into the staple, a circumstance observed by me when awake, but forgotten.
>
> "I must stop it, nevertheless!" I muttered, knocking my knuckles through the glass, and stretching an arm out to seize the

---

4. Charlotte Brontë, *Villette* (1853), ch. 24, Penguin, 1979, 595-96.

importunate branch; instead of which, my fingers closed on the fingers of a little, ice-cold hand!

The intense horror of nightmare came over me; I tried to draw back my arm, but the hand clung to it, and a most melancholy voice sobbed,

"Let me in — let me in!" ....

... I discerned, obscurely, a child's face looking through the window — terror made me cruel; and, finding it useless to attempt shaking the creature off, I pulled its wrist on to the broken pane, and rubbed it to and fro till the blood ran down and soaked the bedclothes: still it wailed, "let me in!" and maintained its tenacious gripe, almost maddening me with fear.

"How can I!" I said at length. "Let *me* go, if you want me to let you in!"

The fingers relaxed, I snatched mine through the hole, hurriedly piled the books up in a pyramid against it, and stopped my ears to exclude the lamentable prayer ....[5]

Naturally, Lockwood, the rational sophisticated southerner, is the last person to be willing to allow the wild spirit of the first Cathy in, even into his dreams or nightmares, despite the fascination that this other world, mediated mainly through the everyday voice of Nelly Dean, eventually begins to exert on him. The spirit of Cathy is not allowed to cross the casement, and blood runs down the window pane. When Lockwood, after Heathcliff's intervention, is vacating the chamber he observes his host:

[who] got onto the bed, and wrenched open the lattice, bursting as he pulled at it, into an uncontrollable passion of tears.

"Come in! come in!" he sobbed. "Cathy, do come. Oh do — *once* more! Oh! my heart's darling! hear me *this* time — Catherine, at last!"

The spectre showed a spectre's ordinary caprice; it gave no sign of being; but the snow and wind whirled wildly through, even reaching my station, and blowing out the light (70).

Wuthering Heights is full of attempts to cross, and failures to cross, personal, emotional, and social thresholds; and as a babel of languages (from Joseph's at times nearly impenetrable dialect to Lockwood's effete standard English), it is open to constant misunderstanding, even when translation is offered or attempted. It is a novel full of the gulfs and gaps of common and uncommon discernment and comprehension; a

---

5. Emily Brontë, *Wuthering Heights* (1847), ch. 3, Penguin, 1985, 66-67.

novel, therefore, which articulates the chasms and fissures in ourselves and in the world outside ourselves. I would propose that it is the Gothic element in this and other fictions that helps the imagination to come to realize, and begin to come to terms with, those conflicts and divisions which we have to learn to negotiate and the space and breaks in which we have to manoeuvre. Lucy Snowe almost fails to survive; Lockwood, being the coward he is, runs away. Heathcliff and the first Catherine are reduced to haunting spirits by their failure to manage the various intimidating boundaries that encompass them as individuals and as a couple.

I will not go on multiplying examples from this or other novels. But let me summarize before moving on to the next stage of my argument: *Villette* and *Wuthering Heights,* like many other nineteenth-century novels, are full of ghosts and echoes of ghosts in the various forms they may take as boundary invaders, in settings inclining towards the hallucinatory and supernatural, often dark, wild, disturbed, amidst characters threatening and unstable, flourishing amidst secrets and hidden things, with sequences of events and consequences unexpected, violent and shocking, leading to physical breakdowns, suicides, murders and other unnatural deaths. Such novels articulate and dramatize basic oppositions between freedom and control, between the inner and the outer worlds, between the subjective and the objective, between reality and fantasy, between the rational and the irrational, between reason and madness, and between women and men, more importantly between the male and the female genders.

This latter point I realize I have not yet really argued, and will attempt to do so, briefly. Since the development of Gothic literature and the literature of sensibility, the novel of the scream and the novel of the tear, novels of screams *and* tears, took place side by side at the end of the eighteenth century, perhaps it would not be going too far to suggest that each of these are a face of the feminine, the female, in a culture which in the course of the eighteenth century was being transformed from an overwhelmingly masculine culture, dominated by patriarchal reason, reason the bully, the big brother, the demanding father, into a more feminine culture of cries and sobs, of feelings and sensible, and sensitive, fears. The Gothic, and especially the ghosts of Gothic, allowed the novel to escape from the obligation to concentrate on the rational world outside, material reality, masculine doing and busy-bodying, and to concern itself instead with the inner world of the hopes and the fears, the irrational as well as the rational anxieties, the hysterias and the manias of both sexes.

Now this is something the women novelists grasped first, and exploited particularly well in its less pure Gothic form — as in the Brontë masterpieces. In these novels the women are the seismographs of psychic disturbance, themselves crossing the boundaries of the physical world as clairvoyants, as hearers of voices and as ghostseers; often regarding themselves as the commissioned disturbers of the customary material world of men, and of women who, for reasons of convenience and their own comfort, submit to the demands of the patriarchal world by confining their rule to a small enclosed world which they can patrol as night visitors and "rule by espionage" (I am thinking, of course, of Mme Beck). We all know by now of the mad woman in the attic syndrome, and clearly the Brontës, Charlotte and Emily, are amongst the first to dramatize, in more or less sensational Gothic ways, the plight of women who will not submit to the masculine demand that they limit their appetite for control over themselves and their circumstances. There is a natural physical and physiological border between men and women (which possibly results in a psychological frontier too), and sexual congress is the usual way in which the border is breached; but the territory on either side of the border should be equal. If the territory is unequal (as it usually has been and is), if by this means a woman is marginalized, then she can only serve as guest or a ghost in what should be or might have been her own psychic and material terrain. Lady Audley in Mary E. Braddon's novel, with her "smile of fatal beauty, full of lurking significance and mysterious meaning", later described as "staring far beyond the narrow boundary of her chamber wall, into dark distances of visionary horror", before she eventually lapses or wills herself into madness, may be understood as a mature mid-nineteenth-century example of the excluded, marginal woman.[6]

It is not only women writers who are aware of this. I have already named Dickens's Miss Havisham in *Great Expectations*, where Pip is the victim of a whole series of "apparitions", from his first encounter

---

6. *Lady Audley's Secret* (1862), Virago, 1985, 186 and 263. In her Introduction Jennifer Uglow, commenting on Henry James's remark that Lady Audley "successfully maintains a kind of half illusion", suggests that she is "a ghost, zombie or vampire who must be buried alive with a stake through the heart", who "gazes continually 'away into another world' whether it be the twilit Essex marshes or the enveloping mists of Villebrumeuse". Therefore "Lady Audley is at once an 'angel in the house' spreading radiance like a sunbeam; a cold, [*sic*] egoist accumulating a fortune; and a lost, lonely outcast" (xviii). Lady Audley is not the only ghost in the novel as chs 38 and 39, entitled "Buried Alive" and "Ghost-Haunted", make clear.

with the convict to his last with Estella in the ruins of Miss Havisham's estate. This dangerously visionary characteristic of Pip, which is to lead him to all kinds of misunderstandings about his own fate,[7] is described most explicitly towards the end of his first visit to Satis House:

> ... a strange thing happened to my fancy. I thought it a strange thing then, and I thought it a stranger thing long afterwards. I turned my eyes — a little dimmed by looking up at the frosty light — towards a great wooden beam in a low nook of the building near me on my right hand, and I saw a figure hanging there by the neck. A figure all in yellow white, with but one shoe to the feet; and it hung so, that I could that the faded trimmings of the dress were like earthy paper, and that the face was Miss Havisham's, with a movement going over the whole countenance as if she were trying to call me. In the terror of seeing the figure, and in the terror of being certain that it had not been there a moment before, I at first ran from it, and then ran towards it. And my terror was greatest of all when I found no figure there (ch. 8, 93-94).

But think also of Rosa Dartle (one who darts and startles) who haunts Steerforth's home and Steerforth himself in *David Copperfield*:

> a slight, short figure, dark, and not agreeable to look at .... She had black hair and eager black eyes, and was thin, and had a scar upon her lip. It was an old scar .... She was a little dilapidated — like a house — with having been so long to let .... Her thinness seemed to be the effect of some wasting fire within her, which found a vent in her gaunt eyes.[8]

In *Bleak House* there is Lady Dedlock (I hardly need to stress the significance of that name), herself a species of vampire, one of the living dead, haunted by the guilt of desertion represented by "the sound upon the terrace" of the "Ghost's Walk" at Chesney Wold; and eventually dying on the edge of a burial ground in the wet of the thawing snow. *Bleak House* is full of ghosts, because like the house from which it takes its title, it is full of crooks and crannies, hidden corners, secret territories, full of discreditable mysteries preserved by galvanized corpses and barely-bodied spirits. There is no more haunted

---

7. See my "*Great Expectations*: The Perception of Fate", *Dutch Quarterly Review*, VI/1 (1976), 2-33.

8. Charles Dickens, *David Copperfield* (1849-50), ch. 20, Penguin, 1985, 350.

book than *Bleak House* — a horrifying Gothic vision of the penalties that the past enacts upon the present and the difficulty of shaking off those ghosts in order to live sensible lives in the present.

Throughout Dickens, and one could given very many examples, the gist of Gothic represents and articulates difference and division. The females at the centre of his fiction are pale pathetic angels of the hearth — marginal spirits clinging on to household normality, intended to haunt us, if they haunt us at all, with their frailty (rather more complicated, one must admit, in the case of Esther Summerson). But they are surrounded by vampires — the living dead — surviving on the blood of the angels, whose passivity is even created by this blood-drain. These vampires or vamps are tipsy avengers, over-dressed harpies, ridiculously trying to assert that the margin is where the life is — and in a sense it is. The vamps or painted ladies, the frumps, the remnants or reliques often seem to have all the life, and even steal the show.[9] Until they collapse, of course. Life evaporates from this Gothic display with Esther Summerson married to her good doctor and living in the unproblematical second Bleak House; Amy Dorrit and Arthur Clennam walking out into the roaring streets of London; while "Mr and Mrs John Harmon's first delightful occupation was, to set all matters right that had strayed in any way wrong, or that might, could, or should, have strayed in any way wrong, while their name was in abeyance".[10]

I think this kind of pattern is to be found throughout the best nineteenth-century fiction: the gist of the Gothic accumulating at the margins threatening to oust and disturb the centre of apparent common sense reality, normality; the effort to achieve a genuinely deep founded vision of personal and social relationships both prompted and threatened by hysterical hauntings. As the hub of the everyday world fails to sustain human aspiration and interest, especially a young woman's aspiration and interest, there is always that lurking threat of disbelief, breakdown, madness. One could multiply instances, but let me take as a final example George Eliot's last, and greatest, novel, *Daniel Deronda*. Daniel Deronda himself is haunted by his own covered past, and eventually comes face to face with his hitherto unknown mother, whose "worn beauty had a strangeness in it as if she were not quite a human

9. For a consideration of some of these predatory ladies, see my "Swivelling Dick: Dickens as Romantic and Anti-Romantic", *Dutch Quarterly Review*, XIX/4 (1989), esp. 287-91.

10. Charles Dickens, *Our Mutual Friend* (1864-65), Book the Fourth, ch. 16, Penguin, 1971, 874.

mother, but a Melusina, who had ties with some world which is independent of ours".[11] This Princess Halm-Eberstein with whom "it seemed [to Deronda] as if he were in the presence of a mysterious Fate rather than a longed-for mother" (688), confirms his Jewish identity and his Zionist destiny (in contradistinction to his conventional aristocratic English upbringing). So he moves from an apparent centre of Society (with a capital S) to the marginal position of a strongly identifying sympathy with the victims of the diaspora.

The main female figure in the novel, Gwendolen Harleth, through her looks and her talents is given the opportunity to improve the ruined finances of her family by marrying the imposing and demanding Henleigh Mallinger Grandcourt, usually known as Mr Grandcourt, or more imperiously as Grandcourt. To come to terms with what duty demands in the way of personal sacrifice, Gwendolen needs to exert her strong ego in order to suppress her own recognition of the implications of her situation and the decisions it calls for. As a consequence she is frequently brought to the verges of breakdown by glimpses of a ghost of present horror and of horror to come. This struggle is most evidently represented in the novel with her reactions to a "picture of an upturned dead face, from which an obscure figure seemed to be fleeing with outstretched arms" concealed by a panel (56, cf. 91-92), which becomes an emblem of her own struggle to achieve a fulfilled life of her own. She knows that in marrying Grandcourt a "cord ... was now being flung over her neck" (401-402); and she is haunted by the spectre of Grandcourt's former mistress, who is forced to surrender to his new wife "his mother's diamonds, which long ago he had confided to her and wished her to wear" (388). The letter from Lydia Glasher, which Gwendolen receives with the jewel-case on the day of her marriage, is a malediction containing such utterances as "The man you have married has a withered heart. His best young love was mine .... It is dead; but I am the grave in which your chance of happiness is buried as well as mine":

> It seemed at first as if Gwendolen's eyes were spell-bound in reading the horrible words of the letter over and over again as a doom of penance; but suddenly a new spasm of terror made her lean forward and stretch out the paper towards the fire, lest accusation and proof at once should meet all eyes. It flew like a feather from her trembling fingers and was caught up in the great draught of flame. In her movement the casket fell on the

---

11. George Eliot, *Daniel Deronda* (1876), ch. 51, Penguin, 1967, 687-88.

floor and the diamonds rolled out. She took no notice, but fell back in her chair again helpless. She could not see the reflections of herself then: they were like so many women petrified white; but coming near herself you might have seen the tremor in her lips and hands ....

Truly here were poisoned gems, and the poison had entered into this poor young creature.

After that long while, there was a tap at the door and Grandcourt entered, dressed for dinner. The sight of him brought a new nervous shock, and Gwendolen screamed again and again with hysterical violence. He had expected to see her dressed and smiling, ready to be led down. He saw her pallid, shrieking as it seemed with terror, the jewels scattered around her on the floor. Was it a fit of madness?

In some form or other the Furies had crossed his threshold (406-407).[12]

In such a passage as this with its doom-laden collapse; with the implication that each of the "poisoned gems" reflects a ghostly image of the petrified figure of Gwendolen; and with the latent Furies of madness crossing the threshold, the Gothic inheritance has clearly been deployed in a controlled, complex way.

Perhaps the basic orientation of English literature has always been romantic (one hardly needs to invoke the conventional comparison of Shakespeare with Corneille and Racine). However, the Novel as a new genre arose in the Age of Reason, or of Reasonableness, or Calm Passion; and therefore perhaps the natural orientation of the Novel was towards the material conditions and circumstances of life. Amidst this state of affairs the forms of Sentimental fiction and Gothic fiction arose, giving more space and emphasis to fantasy, even to the fantastic, and certainly to tears and screams. On the whole, these particular types of novel in themselves represent a limited, self-limiting, and marginal

---

12. The association of *Daniel Deronda* with the fashionable sensation novels of Wilkie Collins (and one should add Mary E. Braddon) in the 1860s is made by Barbara Hardy in her introduction to the Penguin edition (26-27). Certainly the novel is full of moments (from George Eliot's own epigraph to the novel, beginning "Let thy chief terror be of thine own soul ...", onwards) which link her heroine in particular to such immediate predecessors as Lady Audley. If Gwendolen is haunted on occasions by visions "at which ... her native terror shrank" (337), from another viewpoint she herself is a haunter, as we see in the reflection that "in his freak about this girl [Grandcourt] struck Lush rather newly as something like a man who was *fey* — led on by an ominous fatality ..." (361-62).

achievement. The Novel as a genre primarily concerned with middle-class social norms was consolidated by Jane Austen. But the gist of Gothic, with its hauntings and strange visitors, its quests and its mysteries, was to remain, provoking a sense of difference, waving from the margin to the centre, sometimes even taking charge of the centre for a short while: a Gothic yeast continually erupting in the midst of what was pretending to pass as social normality, thereby suggesting an alternative discourse, an alternative account of life, that deserved to be faced and challenged, and if displaced, then displaced and superseded by a more securely achieved grasp of reality. The importance of the Gothic is that its furies allow us to take nothing for granted and cause us to fight imaginatively for the ultimate richness of an unhaunted existence.

MALE MONSTERS OR MONSTROUS MALES
IN VICTORIAN WOMEN'S FICTION

MARYSA DEMOOR

One of the most notable aspects of the Gothic novel is the use of the monstrous character. Monstrously ugly, or monstrously cruel, the monster has his or her pre-ordained role. The function of the monster in these novels was to act as a foil to the pure, beautiful and innocent heroine or the brave, handsome and self-denying hero. With respect to the female "monsters" (a subject which cannot be treated here) it is clear that a tradition was established long before the Gothic novel's emergence.

According to Sandra Gilbert and Susan Gubar in *The Madwoman in the Attic*, the nineteenth-century male writer also displayed a manifest predilection for the age-old dichotomy of the *woman* as angel versus the *woman* as monster. This view of the female sex, they maintain, influenced women writers in that female authors, consciously or unconsciously, began to deconstruct and reconstruct "the paradigmatic polarities of angel and monster" in their own writings.[1] Mary Shelley's monster, for instance, they argue is a disguised female. They point out that this "apparent" monster, like its creator Victor Frankenstein, has a great many typically feminine characteristics.[2] Both these characters seem to have inherited traits from the creator of the tale, Mary Shelley herself. The female monsters in Victorian women's fiction, therefore, served not only as the antitheses to the good, angel-like protagonists, but they also reflected the hidden selves of their authors.[3]

Nineteenth-century women writers not only incorporated this dichotomy in their own writings but also reacted to it, perhaps

---

1. Sandra M. Gilbert and Susan Gubar, *The Madwoman in the Attic*, New Haven and London, 1979, 76.

2. *Ibid.*, 237-38.

3. *Ibid.*, 78.

unwittingly, by creating monsters (and angels) of the other sex. Elaine Showalter, in her survey of British women's fiction, noticed that by the 1850s "the 'woman's man', impossibly pious and desexed, or impossibly idle and oversexed, had become as familiar a figure in the feminine novel as the governess".[4] She demonstrates that both the "male" angels and the "male" devils are versions of the fashionable feminine *hero*. As such, the two poles which Showalter distinguishes fall outside the limits of my subject, which concerns itself with villains rather than heroes.

Edward Fairfax Rochester, in *Jane Eyre*, is far from being a clear-cut case of "the male monster", although on his first appearance he is wholly monstrous, even supernatural as Jane is reminded of the North-of-England spirit, the "Gytrash", seeing his horse and dog appear through the dusk. Significantly, Jane also makes the association with a goblin while he later refers to himself as a gnome.[5] After that first encounter, Rochester is described as having "a dark face, with stern features and a heavy brow; his eyes and gathered eyebrows looked ireful and thwarted" (162). As we know, Jane and Rochester soon overcome any initial antagonism and Jane succeeds in convincing the reader of the human qualities of her future husband, one of her more subtle arguments being based on phrenological ascertainments.[6] But it remains an irrefutable fact that this heroic figure has for years imprisoned his wife on the third floor of his house, and has failed to inform Jane of the fact, in the hope of marrying her before she finds out. The punishment of this ambiguous character at the end of the book is a lenient one, as befits his mixed nature. He is maimed and partially blinded, but he has got rid of his importunate first wife (without losing

---

4. Elaine Showalter, *A Literature of Their Own*, London, 1978, 133. Showalter, in her turn, quotes Eliza Lynn Linton's remark in *The Girl of the Period* that "They are goody men of such exalted morality that Sir Galahad himself might take a lesson from them. Or they are brutes with the well-worn square jaw and beetling brow, who translate into the milder action of modern life the savage's method of wooing a woman by first knocking her senseless and then carrying her off" (134).

5. Charlotte Brontë, *Jane Eyre* (1847), eds Jane Jack and Margaret Smith, Oxford, 1983, 172.

6. Although his mouth, chin and jaw are pronounced to be very grim, and his nostrils are said to denote choler (146), his eyes compensate for this, "for he had great, dark eyes and very fine eyes too" (160); and in spite of the obvious absence of any inclination towards benevolence or philanthropy, his head showed those protuberances which were believed to indicate a prominent conscience (161).

her dowry) and can now wed the younger woman (who, again, is financially independent). That ugliness and unattractiveness did not go hand in hand in women's fiction is clearly illustrated by Jane Eyre's short digression on the matter:

> I had a theoretical reverence and homage for beauty, elegance, gallantry, fascination; but had I met those qualities incarnate in masculine shape, I should have known instinctively that they neither had nor could have sympathy with anything in me, and I should have shunned them as one would fire, lightning, or anything else that is bright but antipathetic (138).

Rochester is not a real monster, and Brontë clearly did not intend him to remain unredeemed, despite his physical (and, intermittently, moral) "monstrousness". The role of true monster Brontë reserved for the young John Reed and the clergyman Brocklehurst. Both of them display a cruel animality; John Reed was

> large and stout for his age, with a dingy and unwholesome skin; thick lineaments in a spacious visage, heavy limbs and large extremities. He gorged himself habitually at table, which made him bilious, and gave him a dim and bleared eye and flabby cheeks (6).

Brocklehurst's monstrous first appearance (inanimate rather than supernatural or animal) is never modified by the emergence of redeeming features:

> I looked up at — a black pillar! — such, at least, appeared to me, at first sight, the straight, narrow, sable-clad shape standing erect on the rug: the grim face at the top was like a carved mask, placed above the shaft by way of capital (33).

Jane clearly has some difficulties in realizing that this is truly a human being and not some monstrous artefact: "He, for it was a man, turned his head slowly towards where I stood, and having examined me with two inquisitive-looking eyes which twinkled under a pair of bushy brows, said solemnly, and in a bass voice: 'Her size is small: what is her age?'" This close encounter reproduces a fairy-tale fright, comparable to Little Red Riding Hood's when she begins to recognize the wolf in the clothes of her grandmother: "What a face he had ...! what a great nose! and what a mouth! and what large prominent teeth!" (33-34).

Charlotte Brontë, then, introduces three conspicuous categories of men. There is the masculine, passionate but ugly brute who despite his roughness and weakness is capable of amelioration. As his foil there is a superficially perfect being, typified by the cold beauty of St John Rivers with his Greek face, blue eyes and fair hair. The harmonious beauty of St John — who is compared to Apollo — cannot compete with the passion of Rochester — who is compared to Vulcan. The third category consists of the pure male monsters: Brocklehurst and John Reed.

Critics have often tried to explain women authors' fascination with such outlandish lovers as Rochester. Mrs Oliphant believed that the creation of such characters expressed woman's sincere wish not to be pampered and sheltered any longer as the weaker sex but to be considered man's equal. Showalter argues that those heroes are projections of the authors' own hidden sexuality and power.[7] It could be argued that they reflect their authors' natures in so far as they represent both a craving for passionate sexual expression as well a revulsion from the carnal side of love.[8]

If the label "male monster" fits such characters as Brocklehurst and Reed because their inhuman or animal-like qualities are reflected in their physical appearance, it is unsurprising that there are also what might be called "monstrous males". These seem to be more numerous than the first kind. They also display the cruelty and wickedness which are prerequisites of a monstrous nature; but the monstrous male is in fact potentially more dangerous than the male monster if only because his genuine nature is hidden behind a handsome, sometimes even an angelic, countenance. To the female characters in the novel the monstrous male will usually first appear in the guise of the seducer. Charlotte Brontë came very close to this when she created the handsome

---

7. Showalter, 143.

8. In terms of Jungian terminology, one might think of Rochester as Brontë's animus; In her analysis of demon lovers and their victims, Toni Reed has pointed out the convenience of Jung's concept of the anima, the animus and the shadow to a discussion of the conflict. Reed, however, seems to unhesitatingly equate the demon-lover with both the animus and the shadow, whereas Jung never fails to stress that the shadow shares the sex of the subject. In novels written by women, therefore, one can hardly claim the shadow to be reflected in the demon-lover (Toni Reed, *Demon Lovers and Their Victims in British Fiction*, Lexington: KE, 1988, 96-98; Carl Gustav Jung, *Aion* [1959], in *The Collected Works of Carl Gustav Jung*, eds Sir Herbert Read, Michael Fordham, Gerhard Adler, William McGuire, London, 1968, 10).

and literally enthralling St John Rivers. In spite of Jane's perceptiveness in gauging Rivers's character, she falls under his "freezing spell" soon enough (508). But she escapes unharmed, when she realizes that marriage to St John would be a "monstrous" martyrdom (517).

In Mrs Gaskell's story *Ruth*, it takes the innocent heroine a long time to discover the true nature of the man she loves. Like a younger version of Rochester, Henry Bellingham first confronts Ruth Hilton while riding. Bellingham's rescue of the drowning boy at once wins Ruth's admiration and her love. From then on she remains blind to the man's egoism and meanness even though old Thomas tries to warn her by quoting from the Bible: "My dear, remember the devil goeth about as a roaring lion, seeking whom he may devour."[9] The horse and the lion, then, are introduced from the very beginning as a powerful set of symbols for dangerous male seduction. It should be noted that Carl Gustav Jung argued that the horse is a "symbol of the animal component in man ... it represents the sexual instinct" and it has "numerous connections with the devil".[10] Bellingham, now living under the alias of Mr Donne, reminds another character in the novel, Jemima Bradshaw, most of all of a horse. Her mother, obviously shocked by the comparison, retorts that she should not compare Mr Donne to a "brute", but Jemima's reply is richly ambiguous: "Brutes are sometimes very beautiful, mamma" (261).

Ruth herself finds it uncommonly hard to recognize Bellingham's cruelty towards her. Torn between love and her awareness of the suffering which Bellingham has inflicted upon her, she decides to resist him: "Oh, my God! I do believe Leonard's father is a bad man, and yet, oh! pitiful God, I love him; I cannot forget — I cannot!" (271). Bellingham's past conduct is again and again described as "cruel" and "merciless". Ruth feels haunted by Bellingham's passionate glance, "those eyes of evil meaning", even in church (279). Her deliverance comes from a visual intuition when, in the darkness of the church, she notices the striking face of a gargoyle. This beautiful face, placed significantly next to that of a grinning monkey, expresses intense suffering but also a state of being at peace with oneself and with God. It is this notion of peace with God expressed by a carving in a church which strengthens her to confront Bellingham once more, nursing him as he is literally "burning" with fever. It is she who smoothes "the

9. Elizabeth Gaskell, *Ruth* (1848), London, 1925, 50.

10. *Aion*, 277 and 280.

wild, raging figure", hushes "his mad talk" (439) and buys his life with her own.

The monstrous male might be said to reach an acme in the person of Grandcourt in George Eliot's *Daniel Deronda*. Grandcourt's marriage to Gwendolen Harleth is motivated by ambitions of domination: "[H]e meant to be master of a woman who would have liked to master him, and who perhaps would have been capable of mastering another man."[11]

Grandcourt's physique is said to be "decidedly handsome", in every sense that of the correct Englishman, yet he is characterized throughout by the "monstrous" animal images. His companion, Mr Lush, compares him to an alligator (195); Gwendolen initially thinks of him as "a handsome lizard of a hitherto unknown species, not of the lively, darting kind ...". Quite erroneously she conjectures that this "splendid specimen was probably gentle, suitable as a boudoir pet" (173-74). Gwendolen's realization of the true nature of her marriage explodes in a torrent of animal imagery:

> Already, in seven short weeks, which seemed half her life her husband had gained a mastery which she could no more resist than she could have resisted the benumbing effect of the touch of a torpedo ... she had found a will like that of a crab or a boa-constrictor which goes on pinching or crushing without alarm at thunder (477).

The harmless lizard has turned into a man-killing snake, the snake which destroys women, the snake which caused Eve to be expelled from Paradise:

> Quarrelling with Grandcourt was impossible: she might as well have made angry remarks to a dangerous serpent ornamentally coiled in her cabin without invitation (735).

This image will never leave Gwendolen; she watches Grandcourt's every move with horror:

> That white hand of his which was touching his whisker was capable, she fancied, of clinging round her neck and threatening to throttle her (481).

---

11. George Eliot, *Daniel Deronda* (1876), Penguin, 1967, 365.

Out of self-defence, this fear for her life, or her sanity, turns into an ardent wish for him to die:

> The thought that his death was the only possible deliverance for her was one with the thought that deliverance would never come — the double deliverance from the injury with which other beings might reproach her and from the yoke she had brought on her own neck .... The thought of his dying would not subsist: it turned as with a dream-change into terror that she should die with his throttling fingers on her neck avenging that thought (669).

Next to the obvious associations of the serpent with the devil and evil, there are equally patent phallic undertones.

Like most Victorian girls, Gwendolen was probably brought up in total ignorance of the physical side of a marriage. Her intuition tells her that there is such a thing, and since society keeps it closely hidden she concludes that it must be unpleasant rather than otherwise. Certainly the text makes it quite clear that physical contact with men, the idea of making love in itself is abhorrent to her:

> she objected, with a sort of physical repulsion, to being directly made love to. With all her imaginative delight in being adored, there was a certain fierceness of maidenhood about her (101-102).

When the spirited and dedicated Rex Gascoigne falls desperately in love with Gwendolen only absolute disgust fills her. This reaction should prepare the reader for those constant associations of Grandcourt with the animal and reptile image-cluster which Jung saw as pre-eminent symbols of the sexual urge. Gwendolen's physical antipathies seem to be very strong indeed. At the dance after the archery contest, she refuses to dance anything but the quadrille, openly acknowledging that she "can't bear having ugly people so near" (151). Mr Lush inspires her with such a revulsion that she prefers to avoid his company altogether and she makes his dismissal one of the conditions of her marriage (350). But the most patent manifestation of Gwendolen's frigidity occurs upon her acceptance of Grandcourt's proposal: he is merely allowed to kiss her hand (373). The conflict between Gwendolen and Grandcourt, then, might well fictionalize and symbolize the confrontation of the conscious mind (represented by Gwendolen) with the unacknowledged, repressed feelings of the unconscious (represented by Grandcourt).

Grandcourt's cunning wielding of power and tyranny without actually physically abusing his wife has been compared to the mature Heathcliff's mental cruelty towards his infirm son in Emily Brontë's *Wuthering Heights*.[12] Yet Heathcliff's treatment of his wife, Isabella Linton, is a clearer example of "male monstrosity". His persistent mental torture of his wife knows no bounds and turns the devotion of this infatuated young woman into a feeling of absolute hatred.

Isabella's "degradation" is not only the result of her blind passion for the very male and handsome person of Heathcliff but also of society's partiality towards money and appearance. Indeed, one cannot imagine the delicate Isabella falling in love with Heathcliff in his former guise when his character was written all over his countenance, when, in other words, "personal appearance sympathised with mental deterioration" and he had acquired "a slouching gait", "an ignoble look" and an "idiotic excess of unsociable moroseness".[13] But who can doubt the respectability of the man who presents himself at the Grange a few years later in this guise:

> He had grown a tall, athletic, well-formed man .... His countenance ... looked intelligent, and retained no marks of former degradation. His manner was even dignified, quite divested of roughness though too stern for grace (135).

Isabella is again, classically, deceived by an altered appearance; Cathy, however, knowing her "second self" best of all, feels that she has to warn her sister-in-law against the true nature of the "fierce, pitiless, *wolfish* man" (141; my italics).

Isabella, like Gwendolen Harleth, realizes her mistake within the first twenty-four hours of her marriage. Her letter to Nelly Dean shows her to be in doubt as to the very nature of the creature she has married:

> "Is Mr Heathcliff a man? If so, is he mad? And if not, is he a devil?" (173)

During a subsequent encounter with Nelly, she calls her husband "a lying fiend, a monster, and not a human being!" (188). Heathcliff's monstrosity, the cruelty and wildness of his nature, is highlighted

---

12. Merryn Williams, *Women in the English Novel 1800-1900*, London, 1984, 151.

13. Emily Brontë, *Wuthering Heights* (1847), Penguin, 1973, 108.

repeatedly throughout the tale. Again, the darkness of his appearance, his constant association with night and the inscrutability of his nature remind one of the murky depths of the unconscious.

Though preponderantly belonging to the physically attractive "monstrous males"-class, Heathcliff's shifting appearance does, at times, take him towards the "male monster"-category. Similarly, Mr Casaubon in Eliot's *Middlemarch* is not so easily allocated to either category. It is clear that Celia Brooke considers his outward appearance — his "moles and sallowness"[14] — distasteful, although Dorothea has no such thought. Casaubon is a pitiable monstrous male. Of all the examples mentioned here, he is the only one who does not realize that his behaviour towards his young wife is not appropriate. Worse, he had never envisaged that a young wife could be so "troublesome" and could even possess some ideas of her own. The realization that Dorothea does not continue to worship him unconditionally and does not believe him to be "unmixedly adorable" (456) leads him to feel grievously betrayed. Casaubon nurses this total failure of communication in private, as the air between them grows chiller: "he distrusted her affection; and what loneliness is more lonely than distrust" (480). Thus, slowly, Casaubon's initial egotism and self-deification fosters an all-consuming jealousy whose sole aim is to crush another being's happiness. Eventually, the special clause in his will, stipulating that Dorothea be disinherited if she marries Will Ladislaw displays the cruelty of the monstrous male at its worst.

In fact, the other characters in the book show far less sympathy with Casaubon's lofty objectives in life than his wife, and his appearance is described by some in metaphors more suitable to a monster than a hero. Upon hearing about Dorothea's view of her prospective husband as a "great soul" whom she is willing to serve, Mrs Cadwallader claims the comparison to "a great bladder for dried peas to rattle in" to be far more suitable (82). His blood she declared to consist of "semicolons and parentheses" while his dreams are footnotes that "run away with all his brains" (96). In short, she thinks "he looks like a death's head skinned over for the occasion" and feels sure Dorothea will hate him before a year has elapsed (117).

Will Ladislaw's metaphorical language is on a par with Mrs Cadwallader, showing a preference for the adjective "dry" in combination with some unflattering noun. Nevertheless, the fragile person of his uncle is made to appear more formidable than a dragon

---

14. George Eliot, *Middlemarch* (1871-72), Penguin, 1985, 46.

solely because his position has society's sanction (see 237, 241 and 253).

Paradoxically, then, Casaubon can be viewed as either the anti-climactic conclusion to this list of male characters — since "the victim", Dorothea, continues to respect him until his death — or as its climactic end, since the proposal of a withered and selfish old man to an attractive and idealistic young woman might be considered the acme of cruelty.

These figures whom I have called "monstrous males" share more than just a capacity for cruelty. Bellingham, Grandcourt, Casaubon, Tito in *Romola* and Donnithorne in *Adam Bede* all present a thin layer of culture and refinement whose superficiality is all too quickly perceived by their victims. Only Heathcliff stands somewhat apart from the rest. He passionately loves Cathy Earnshaw; prevented fom marrying her, he directs his cruel behaviour towards the other women in the story, Isabella, the second Cathy and, one might add, the feminine Linton Heathcliff. Be that as it may, each of these men serves as a warning against appearances and arranged marriages. They are late, strange projections of the old tale of woman tempted by the devil in disguise who lures her to her own destruction by means of false riches.[15] On a deeper level, these monstrous males give voice to Victorian women writers' fear of dominating male sexuality and of woman's own unconscious drives.

---

15. Reed, 27, 98.

MYTHS OF ENCLOSURE AND MYTHS OF THE OPEN IN *THE MONK* AND *WUTHERING HEIGHTS*

GUDRUN KAUHL

The Monk

In an article published in 1981 Ronald Paulson, particularly instancing *The Monk* (1796), wrote that "the popularity of Gothic fiction in the 1790s and well into the nineteenth century was due in part to the widespread anxieties and fears in Europe aroused by the turmoil in France".[1] Arnold Kettle's comment on a novel written fifty years later, in 1847, is differently accented, but in its basic concept it is almost identical. "*Wuthering Heights*", he said, "is an expression in the imaginative terms of art of the stresses and tensions and conflicts, personal and spiritual, of nineteenth-century capitalist society".[2] Thus, Paulson and Kettle see both novels as expressive of social and political change. However, both novels have also been objects of intense psychological research, the results of which support Tzvetan Todorov's statement that much of the energy which flows into explicit psychoanalysis today went in the nineteenth century into the symbolic discoveries of the Gothic novel.[3] Both novels in question are indeed obsessed by their explorations into "character", not in the sense of a fixity of personal traits but in its developments and transformations, as if the consciousness of the historicity of the social and political situation led to a corresponding awareness of the instability of personality.

The extent of the political tensions that are to be found in *The Monk* can already be exemplified by a reference to its beginning and ending.

---

1. Ronald Paulson, "Gothic Fiction and the French Revolution", *ELH*, XLVIII (1981), 536.

2. Arnold Kettle, "Emily Brontë: *Wuthering Heights*" (1951), in *Twentieth-Century Interpretations of* Wuthering Heights, ed. Thomas A. Vogler, Englewood Cliffs: NJ, 1968, 42.

3. Tzvetan Todorov, *Introduction à la littérature fantastique*, Paris, 1970, 168.

The beginning is marked by a distanced perspective. The Madrid it leads into is "a city where superstition reigns with ... despotic sway".[4] The ending, however, shows a monk who in trying to escape from this rigid structure of belief sold himself to the devil and perdition. In between there are two stories in which both the oppression through existing institutions and attempts at liberation and self-liberation prove equally disastrous. The monk Ambrosio follows the deceitful shades of "philosophy" and discards all the rules of his past in the interests of self-gratification and self-preservation. In the murder of his mother and the rape and murder of his sister he destroys his soul. That his character has been formed by the institutions in which he grew up is critically noticed. "His Instructors", so we are told, "carefully repressed those virtues, whose grandeur and disinterestedness were ill-suited to the Cloister" (237). Still the alternative of self-liberation — "your freedom is bred and deformed in the shadow of your oppression"[5] — proves equally disastrous, and the same oscillations of attitude can be observed in the parallel story of Agnes. Brought to a convent against her will, punished by the head of the convent for her secret sexual contacts with a young man, she is finally rediscovered in a hidden dungeon, a half-emaciated woman with a dead child in her arms. Although this echoes Christian iconography in a perverted form and thereby points to the perversions of religiosity in these institutions, the description of her release again leads to a counter-emphasis. The chapter is headed by a quotation from Cowper's "Charity" which celebrates the "altar" of "sacred Liberty" (343), but it pictures a scene of frenzied mob-riot.

Still, the political story is not dominant. The question of socio-political change rather activates a process of exploration into the acquisition of all grammar of behaviour. That this is primarily a story of an initiation into life is made clear in the very first chapter which introduces us to Ambrosio: a monk of unknown origin (he has been found as a little child at the monastery door), who has passed all of his life "in study, total seclusion from the world, and mortification of the flesh"; who had, until he was chosen superior of his society, "never been on the outside of the Abbey-walls" (17); who has even made a vow "never to leave his own precincts" (30). The suggestiveness of the architecture, the circle described by the strong walls of the abbey, strengthens the sense of inner spaces which are known to the person and

---

4. Matthew Lewis, *The Monk* (1796), ed. Howard Anderson, London, 1973, 7.

5. Terry Eagleton, *Myths of Power; A Marxist Study of the Brontës*, London, 1975, 104.

of "outside" possibilities. This situation at the beginning of life is shared by two further young people who come to the church in order to hear Ambrosio's sermon, Lorenzo and Antonia. Lorenzo falls in love with Antonia at first sight. After the sermon he remains in the church and dreams of marrying her, but the dream turns into nightmare as an "Unknown", a "Monster", rushes into the ceremony and rapes and destroys the bride (28). On re-awakening Lorenzo observes how a stranger hides a letter under the statue of the patron saint, and how this letter is taken up by a nun. He discovers that she is his sister Agnes, the stranger is his close friend Raymond.

The sequence questions the sharp dividing line between "inside" and "outside" which was originally established. Ambrosio, we were first told, had never been outside the abbey walls; similarly, he had no knowledge not belonging to the monastic tradition. With Lorenzo's story, however, the "unknown" already appears within the church in the shape of a dream and in a letter hidden under the statue of the saint. That "outside" is "inside" is underlined by the incidents of the second chapter. Agnes loses the secret letter, significantly during confession, which reveals that she is pregnant. Ambrosio goes to his monastic cell and his sensuous adoration of the picture of the Madonna reveals that in spite of all "mortification of the flesh" passion is not unknown to him.

The fact, however, that this new experience cannot be contained within the accepted frame of knowledge changes its character and the first two chapters already illustrate some of the basic modes of transformation which desire will take in the text. The first is given in Lorenzo's dream, precisely because it turns into nightmare: in this novel sexuality will repeatedly be presented as a frenzied violence, causing the destruction of purity. The second mode of transformation is given in Ambrosio's encounter with Rosario, a young novice close to Ambrosio who, mirroring Ambrosio's own situation, is without known origin, even without a known face. Developing the feminine implications of the name Rosario[6] she identifies herself as a woman (Matilda) in love with the monk, thereby also establishing Ambrosio's own sexual identity. Her face is that of the Madonna. The significance of this encounter is given in an episode in which Rosario, ostensibly ready to leave the monastery, asks for a rose as a farewell-present: touching the rose-bush, Ambrosio is stung by a serpent. The opposition

---

6. The rose is symbolic of sensual love, as well as of the Catholic rosary, dedicated to the Madonna. *Rosario* is a name given to Spanish girls, not boys (Lewis may not have known this), an abbreviation of *Madonna del Rosario*, "our Lady of the Rosary".

between bridegroom and monster upon which Lorenzo's dream was based is here repeated in the opposition between rose and serpent. Sexuality is the circulation of poison.

The first two chapters create a frame from which the stories of Ambrosio and Antonia and Lorenzo, of Lorenzo's friend Raymond and of Agnes receive a distinct flavour. Agnes was from her birth destined for a monastic life. Her mother, we are told, almost died during her pregnancy and dedicated the child, should she survive, to a saint. Was she dying because she was pregnant? Was the daughter dedicated to a saint in order to spare her a similar fate? During her youth the girl is kept in a castle, watched by a powerful aunt. It is here that she comes to know Raymond, and they both plan to elope together using the disguise of a "Bleeding Nun", the spectre of a nun with a deep wound on her breast that appears in the castle every five years. Their elopement seems at first to have succeeded; but Raymond discovers that the woman to whom he has sworn to be "thine" forever actually is the Bleeding Nun herself. He looks into the face of death:

> She lifted up her veil slowly. What a sight presented itself to my startled eyes! I beheld before me an animated Corse. Her countenance was long and haggard; her cheeks and lips were bloodless; The paleness of death was spread over her features, and her eye-balls fixed stedfastly upon me were lustreless and hollow (160).

In his dreams following upon this apparition the distinction between Agnes and the nun is blurred. "Agnes and the Bleeding Nun", Raymond narrates, "presented themselves by turns to my fancy, and combined to harass and torment me" (161). Agnes is thus in Raymond's experience assimilated to the spectre of death, and this spectre itself is again characterized by the same oppositions which were contained in the composite image of Agnes and the Bleeding Nun: promise of life and warning of death, the nun's purity and her bloody dress, her piety and the execrations which she howls in the castle.

In his *Interpretation of Dreams* Freud wrote about "the psychological pressure caused by constricted thinking" in order to explain how shapes of a different logic can assert themselves against the surface shapes of the text in an urge to find expression.[7] The image of the "Bleeding Nun" is a shape of this kind. Its basic logic is repeated twice more in this novel, in the sequels to Agnes's and Ambrosio's

---

7. Sigmund Freud, *Die Traumdeutung* (1900), Frankfurt a. M., 1972, II, 339.

stories. After the failed elopement Agnes enters a convent; Raymond finds her there; she becomes pregnant. The head of the convent punishes her with incarceration. The convent is destroyed by a frenzied mob and the abbess is lynched. Agnes is rediscovered almost dead, with a dead child in her arms. Ambrosio, after tiring of Matilda, begins to be attracted to Antonia. Matilda provides him with secret means so that he can approach Antonia at night during her sleep. He is, however, surprised by her mother. He kills the mother, manages to get Antonia into his power, and rapes and kills her. The sequence of incidents in both cases is identical in spite of all surface differences; and it is the pattern of Raymond's first adventure. In trying to reach the object of their desire, the young men are confronted by a commanding guardian-figure and then experience desire itself transfigured by death (the appearance of Agnes on rediscovery), or as a simultaneous attraction and repulsion (Ambrosio's reaction as he sees Antonia, 387) which double-binds them. In *The Monk*, the desire to reach beyond the walls of the monastery, to transcend the limitations of an established tradition in all its sociopolitical implications, appears bound to this specific shape of a primal desire which is experienced as tabooed. The political ambivalences on the surface of the text, the stalemate between a suffocating oppression and an inhuman liberation, derive from this.

Wuthering Heights

Wuthering Heights, which is the more complex novel of the two, shares much of the same ground; its symbolic world, however, is more hidden and the problems it deals with are to a higher degree internalized. In this case, too, we start with the idea of "unknown spaces" in order to explore the topography of a person's mind. The unknown space is the house of his "solitary neighbour" in the north of England into which Mr Lockwood, the narrator, twice leads us in the first three chapters of the novel.[8]

Lockwood's first visit is stylized as the mock-heroic invasion of a foreign territory. The date "1500" over the principal entrance characterizes the enclosed space of the Heights (a house with narrow windows and defended corners, a closed gate against the barrier of which Lockwood's horse has to push) as belonging to another "age", another "civilization". Although this different civilization comes to attack Lockwood in the shape of some "grim, shaggy sheep dogs" (4), their assault on the first visit can still be warded off by "a lusty dame",

---

8. Emily Brontë, *Wuthering Heights* (1847), ed. Ian Jack, Oxford, 1982, 1.

"flourishing a frying-pan" (5). During the second visit, however, which leads him into the inner circle of the family living at the Heights (Ch. 2), the stylized conventionality of Lockwood's speech and manners collapses before a reality which disrupts all accepted rules of social grammar: the owner of the place, Heathcliff, is (3) a "dark-skinned gipsy in aspect, in dress and manners a gentleman" (that is, a "gypsy-gentleman"), and the young man of the house, who bears the name Hareton Earnshaw inscribed over its entrance, is (8) "like ... a common labourer: still his bearing was free, almost haughty" (that is, a "free servant"). As Lockwood tries to establish their relationship to the young woman of the family by enquiring whose "amiable lady" (9) or "beneficent fairy" (10) she is, he nearly causes open violence. The end of the scene sees Lockwood, the society-weary young man of the world, reduced to a "poor lad" who is "fair choking": he is "hatless and trembling with wrath" (14).

It is in the context of this development where a person through collision with an unknown reality is transformed into a headless/hatless human being (and "hatless" would refer to his lost social status), that the question of personal identity is raised. Immediately afterwards (Ch. 3) Lockwood will find, scratched on the window-ledge of his bedroom on the Heights, "a name repeated in all kinds of *characters*, large and small — *Catherine Earnshaw*, here and there varied to *Catherine Heathcliff*, and again to *Catherine Linton*" (15, Brontë's italics). The central thematic concerns of the novel are presented here in a condensed form: the question how a character is formed through social biography (paradigmatically rendered in the story of Catherine Earnshaw Linton Heathcliff) and through psychological biography. How is a person constituted out of the original fluidity of impulses? The diary which Lockwood then opens ("Catherine Earnshaw, her book", 15) answers that this occurs through a painful process in which part of this fluidity is ruled out as "not belonging" to the person, as constituting its dark underside. The diary in a childish hand leads into the centre of this process: written on the blank spaces (16) of a Testament, it emphasizes that part of our behaviour which is not governed by "Thou shalt". Lockwood's subsequent dreams continue the same theme: the first dramatizes a playful, mock-heroic rebellion against a religious instruction which in banishing transgressions kept the idea of transgression alive, "odd transgressions that I never imagined previously" (19). This playful dream is then, paralleling the development of Lockwood's visits to the Heights, transformed into nightmare as Lockwood finds himself confronted by a ghostchild that begs to be readmitted into the house: it had lost its way on the moors.

How are the incidents of these first three chapters connected? First of all by the two parallel developments which Lockwood, their central figure and the reader's substitute in entering (the structure of) *Wuthering Heights*, undergoes. They lead him from an initial playfulness to a serious recognition of human realities which destroys his original pose/composure. Secondly, they are connected by two parallel movements which are movements towards an exploration of alien/unknown spaces, first geographically (the house on the Heights) and then temporally (the pre-history of the house). More important than this mere parallelism, the two sequences share a community of symbols, so much so that both sequences appear as different transcriptions of an identical situation, as explorations of the same psychological "place" in a passage from another place/time to the Other (in its psychological significance).[9] Thus there is — above the principal door to the house — "a quantity of grotesque carving", and particularly "among a wilderness of crumbling griffins and shameless little boys ... the date '1500', and the name 'Hareton Earnshaw'" (2). This in itself suggests the writing of another time and thereby foreshadows the "faded hieroglyphics" (16) of Catherine Earnshaw's childish hand. The carving with its "crumbling griffins" and "shameless little boys", signs of authority and signs of disobedience, emblematically renders the contents of Catherine's rebellion. The idea dominating the dream sequence, the idea of "odd transgressions", is finally enciphered into the human relationships of this house which imply a destruction of established categories, a "transgression" ("stepping over") from one category to another, incompatible category: the free servant, the gypsy gentleman. These, finally, are not the characteristics of a structure principally unknown to Lockwood. Whereas he first meant to invade this place with impunity, his "horse's breast fairly pushing the barrier" (1), in an inversion of this original situation this place then comes to "haunt" him, to "grip" him in the shape of the ghost-child. Whereas he first thought to read the writing of another, he then experiences the same conflicts rising within himself when, on closing his eyes, "a glare of white letters started from the dark" (15).

It is in this context that the idea of being "in the moors" accumulates significance. Already during the evening of Lockwood's second visit Heathcliff's statement, "Do you know that you run a risk of being lost in the marshes?" (9) and Lockwood's own request, "Do point out some landmarks by which I may know my way home" (12) begin

9. Jacques Lacan, "Das Drängen des Buchstabens im Unbewußten oder die Vernunft seit freud", *Schriften*, 1975, II, 50-55.

metaphorically to echo his growing entanglement in a grammar of human behaviour which he does not understand. But it is the apparition of the ghostchild that suggests the possibility of getting "lost" so radically that it amounts to an exclusion from one's "home", again metaphorically heightened to imply the exclusion from the human (20). This changed awareness is inscribed into the description of the landscape — originally welcomed by him as a "perfect misanthropist's heaven" (1) — which Lockwood gives after leaving the Heights:

> ... the whole hill-back was one billowy, white ocean; the swells and falls not indicating corresponding rises and depressions in the ground ... I had remarked on one side of the road, at intervals of six or seven yards, a line of upright stones, continued through the whole length of the barren: these were erected, and daubed with lime on purpose to serve as guides in the dark ... : but, excepting a dirty dot pointing up here and there, all traces of their existence had vanished ... (25).

The Dark Child and the Fair Child
The history of the children of Wuthering Heights, which Nelly Dean narrates to Lockwood (from Ch 4 onwards), slowly explores the reality of the place into which Lockwood intruded. Using the insights offered by Bruno Bettelheim's understanding of fairy tales as the secret writings of the soul, the account of the children's early infancy has been analysed by Sandra Gilbert and Susan Gubar in their *Madwoman in the Attic*. Restating the core of Lockwood's experience in the introductory chapters, the children's growth into maturity is again (in their interpretation) essentially a conflict between different grammars of behaviour, or, rather, between "language" and "ungrammaticalness".[10] "Ungrammaticalness" is represented by Heathcliff, the gypsy-boy who was adopted into the family, since he at first only speaks "some gibberish" (30). "Ungrammaticalness", however, is also present in young Catherine, who is at first "wild" and "wicked" (34), but who has to learn how to walk with measured steps. In the eyes of the world, what is finally against the rules is the close relationship between a gypsy-boy and a farmer's daughter. Learning the rules in this novel means the introduction to a complex code in which behavioural instruction (forbidding wild, un-measured movements), religious

---

10. Sandra M. Gilbert and Susan Gubar, *The Madwoman in the Attic: The Woman Writer and the Nineteenth-Century Literary Imagination*, New Haven and London, 1979, rpt. 1984, 294.

instruction (the tracts on "The Helmet of Salvation" and "The Broad Way to Destruction" which the children have to read) mingle with a narrower social code so that, for example, "scouring the country with a gipsy" can become equivalent to growing up "in absolute heathenism" (41). The essential step, however, which the novel takes is in showing how this conflict between original impulse and the demands of the world becomes internalized in the children themselves. In his interpretation of "Cinderella" Bettelheim wrote that children secretly "know" why they have to live "in ashes": they secretly believe that from the point of view of the language of the world some of their desires must be "guilty", condemning them to a life in abjectness.[11] This consciousness comes to the surface when Heathcliff says of himself, "I shall be as dirty as I please: and I like to be dirty, and I will be dirty" (44). It is also there in Catherine's brother Hindley who, admonished to take mercy on his soul, shouts, "Not I! On the contrary, I shall have great pleasure in sending it to perdition to punish its Maker ..." (63). But it is in Catherine that the drama is staged most fully: after the narration of early infancy there come the three great decision scenes in which she is the centre.

On the surface, her decision concerns the choice between two men, Heathcliff, the gypsy, and Edgar Linton, son of the manor house. Moving in the world of Thrushcross Grange has already, as we are told,

> led [Catherine] to adopt a double character without exactly intending to deceive anyone. In the place where she heard Heathcliff termed a "vulgar young ruffian", and "worse than a brute", she took care not to act like him; but at home she had small inclination to practice politeness that would only be laughed at ..." (56).

But hers is not only a social decision against childhood loyalties: "It would degrade me to marry Heathcliff now", "if I marry Linton, I can aid Heathcliff to rise" (68 and 69). The relevance of the decision rather reveals itself when we follow an intuition of Dorothy Van Ghent's concerning the "two children"-figure in Emily Brontë's novel and poetry: one child dark and brooding, the other fair and blissful, they represent a visualization of psychological states, or metamorphoses of

---

11. Bruno Bettelheim, *Kinder brauchen Märchen* (*The Uses of Enchantment*, 1975), Munich, 1980, 291.

the soul.[12] Casting doubt on her decision for Edgar Linton (and, at the same time, through the very choice of her words, casting suspicion upon her loyalty for Heathcliff), Catherine herself tells a "queer dream" in which she had found herself in heaven:

> ... heaven did not seem to be my home; and I broke my heart with weeping to come back to earth; and the angels were so angry that they flung me out into the middle of the heath on the top of Wuthering Heights; where I woke sobbing for joy .... I've no more business to marry Edgar Linton than I have to be in heaven ....

Still there is the emphatic rejection of the dark child: "It would degrade me to marry Heathcliff now ..." (67).

Following upon this speech, which in part he overheard, Heathcliff disappears. Catherine finds the gate open; there is her anguished question, "What did I say, Nelly?" (71). A thunderstorm develops and Catherine exposes herself to the tumult of the elements during the whole night. In the morning she crouches back to "the almost extinguished embers" (73) and asks the servant to shut the window. Delirium follows; she is brought to Thrushcross Grange for convalescence where both the elder Lintons catch the fever and die.

This sequence is not accidental. It rather "opens the gate" to an understanding of what it means not to belong "to heaven": an agony of guilt (the elder Lintons die), fear (of being de/base/d), and unknowing (the pained question, "What did I say?").

The second decision scene, after Catherine's marriage and after Heathcliff's return, wealthy and outwardly transformed, corroborates a reading of this kind. Catherine's renewed collapse and her delirium this time translate her indecision between the two men as an impasse between two modes of existence which are both her own and yet not her own. Twice her memory returns to her childhood. Playing with feathers which she has pulled from her cushion, Catherine remembers:

> ... and this — I should know it among a thousand — it's a lapwing's. Bonny bird; wheeling over our heads in the middle of the moor .... This feather was picked up from the heath, the bird was not shot: we saw its nest in the winter, full of little skeletons. Heathcliff set a trap over it, and the old ones dare not come. I made him promise he'd never shoot a lapwing after that,

---

12. Dorothy Van Ghent, *The English Novel; Form and Function* (1953), New York, 1961, 153-170, 165.

and he didn't .... Did he shoot my lapwings, Nelly? Are they
red, any of them!" (104)

The memory of childhood, of a childhood that was already tainted by
division ("Did he shoot my lapwings?") is followed by an experience of
acute self-alienation. The mirror opposite to Catherine's bed transforms
itself into a black press with an alien face in it which has a life of its
own: it stirs, it may come out. The second time Catherine's memory
goes back in time it is to the sensation of being "enclosed in the
oak-panelled bed at home" and again to an experience of early loss as
she was "laid alone, for the first time" (106). Upon the memory there
follows again recognition of an alien face: "Mrs. Linton, the lady of
Thrushcross Grange", is "the wife of a stranger" (107) and
consequently, as his wife, a stranger to herself.

Gilbert and Gubar argue that this real/ization of her social identity
as alien is the essence of this scene.[13] But the movements described on
these pages point to a more complicated pattern. Memory twice starts
from a recollection of childhood that already contained division (the nest
was destroyed and the bed was empty) in order to lead to a sensation of
existence in which all possibilities of action, all visible "faces", appear
split off from the centre of the person. But only the second time this
visible face is Mrs. Linton's — the first time it materializes out of a
recollection of life in the moors and is accordingly associated with
Heathcliff.

Heathcliff is Catherine's hidden alternative. That he begins to speak
the language of his former enemies has often been commented upon.
Thus Arnold Kettle says of the "revenge" which dominates the second
part of the book, that it

> has a moral force. For what Heathcliff does is use against his
> enemies with complete ruthlessness their own weapons, to turn
> on them (stripped of their romantic veils) their own standards, to
> beat them at their own game. The weapons he uses against the
> Earnshaws and Lintons are their own weapons of money and
> arranged marriages.[14]

This is certainly true but does not go far enough, for Heathcliff speaks
the adversary's language in a far more subtle sense. There is a complex
pattern behind the mechanical reciprocity which the revenge story

13. Gilbert and Gubar, 282.

14. Kettle, 38.

sometimes offers. In part, Heathcliff enacts a parody of his original desire: since he cannot get (the body of) the woman, he makes himself master of the houses to which she belonged, and also master of their offspring. But also, and this is not just a question of adroitly using for his own purposes a social code that was formerly used against him, he begins obsessively to employ the methods under which he himself suffered, passing on "marks of ... degradation" (81) by "painting on [the] white" (91) of another's face. Negating the horror of his life by making it happen all again, he begins to invest into hierarchy: educating his own son, who is significantly called Linton, so as "to preserve the superior and the gentleman in him, above his associates", degrading "their children" so that they "till their father's lands for wages" (178). But the extremity of his state becomes visible in a scene in which he attacks Hindley. As Isabella later narrates: "He trampled on you and kicked you, and dashed you on the ground .... And his mouth watered to tear you with his teeth ... " (155). This is not only a frenzied attack against someone who stood against all his desires; passing on the "marks" it rather appears as an attempt to destroy the wholeness of a person in the same way that his own mind was disintegrated. Adopting the very forms which destroyed his own identity, acting in a way as his own adversary did, Heathcliff in fact becomes comparable to those women whose identification with forms of violence in a climate of social and political oppression Julia Kristeva has described.[15]

There is a muted cry in the description of these developments which is more effective than any more outspoken indictment. Both Kettle and Eagleton have emphasized that by subversively using the enemies' language Heathcliff's career throws into relief the character of their social rules.[16] The same indictment is contained in the description of Catherine's ending. Concerning the social aspects of her behaviour, Nelly Dean had cautiously said of her:

> My heart invariably cleaved to the master's, in preference to Catherine's side: with reason I imagined, for he was kind, and trustful, and honourable; and she — she could not be called the *opposite*, yet she seemed to allow herself such wide latitude ... (91, Brontë's italics).

15. Julia Kristeva, "Women's Time", in *The Kristeva Reader*, ed. Toril Moi, Oxford, 1986, 201-203.

16. Kettle, 38, 41; Eagleton, 104, 108.

Catherine (and Heathcliff) move in a social climate where "allowing oneself such wide latitudes" may easily be interpreted as being "the opposite" of all that is "kind, trustful, and honourable". This knowledge transforms their own attitude to their actions.

Bersani has argued that the novel contains a "passion for otherness", for sheer alterity which even kicks itself free from all "familial patterns of desire".[17] It is true that in Catherine's understanding "Heathcliff" represents a glimpse of freedom, of personal wholeness, and is therefore (in her ambivalent phrasing) "the thing that irks me most in this shattered prison" (137). But as in *The Monk*, so in *Wuthering Heights*, alterity proves an illusion. Catherine's reaching out for "Heathcliff" only serves to reassert her bondage to reality, the reality of her own inner life (she collapses again and "sighed, and moaned, and knew nobody" before her death, 140) and the reality of what Heathcliff has actually turned into. We may therefore say that her quest appears primarily directed at some place of unknowing which is, in Kristeva's words, a-topical, since any attempt to reach it only leads to a deeper entanglement with that consciousness for which "freedom" already is the opposite of all accepted standards and values, and therefore tainted: instead of a promised union and wholeness, "a thing that irks".[18]

As Vogler has said, *Wuthering Heights* is not a novel of "assertion".[19] It is a novel of "articulation, leading to a fuller understanding of a problem's complexities", and the problem which the novel (haunted as it is by Catherine's eyes which are also the eyes of Hindley, of Hareton, and of the younger Catherine to indicate sameness and its possible developments) is concerned with is the formation of "character". This theme is stressed one more time towards the end of the novel when another young one, the younger Catherine, paralleling Lockwood's entrance at the beginning, comes to Wuthering Heights. Re-evoking, too, the situation of *The Monk*, the younger Catherine had spent all of her childhood in complete seclusion in Thrushcross Grange. "Till she reached the age of thirteen, she had not once been beyond the

---

17. Leo Bersani, *A Future for Astyanax: Character and Desire in Literature*, New York, 1984, 214. Oedipal tensions are certainly inscribed into the familial structure of Wuthering Heights as Lockwood — for example — encounters it.

18. Kristeva, 202.

19. Thomas A. Vogler, "Introduction" to *Twentieth-Century Interpretations of Wuthering Heights*, 12.

range of the park by herself" (162). This seclusion was interrupted by
first acquaintance with Heathcliff's house and hearsay of what it
represents, and we are told that Cathy "appeared so deeply impressed
and shocked at this new view of human nature — excluded from all her
studies and all her ideas till now — that Mr Edgar deemed it
unnecessary to pursue the subject" (191). The true meaning of this new
knowledge, however, is rendered in an episode which evokes the story
of "Little Red Riding Hood". During a walk in the park of Thrushcross
Grange, Nelly narrates,

> we neared a door that opened on the road; and my young lady
> ... climbed up and seated herself on the top of the wall, reaching
> over to gather some hips that bloomed scarlet on the summit
> branches of the wild rose trees, shadowing the highway side ....
> In stretching to pull them, her hat fell off; and as the door was
> locked, she proposed scrambling down to recover it (198).

On reaching out for the colour red (and the connotations of the word
"hips" re-emphasize that point), Cathy leaves her former seclusion
behind (and also her former stability, because her hat falls off); on the
other side of the wall she is to meet Heathcliff, the "wicked man"
(199), latter-day representative of all "fierce, pitiless, wolfish men"
(87). Although Nelly Dean pulls her back behind the door, under the
shelter of her umbrella, Catherine will follow him to Wuthering Heights
and begin for herself to read in the book of the world.

GENDER AND ROLE-PLAYING IN *LADY AUDLEY'S SECRET*

ELIZABETH TILLEY

The Gothic novel in England in the 1860s had in many ways almost ceased to be "Gothic" in the traditional sense of the term, probably because the eighteenth-century Gothic novel was not its only parent. The Newgate novel or penny dreadful, stage melodrama, and social novels of the 1840s all had a hand in shaping the form and concerns of what had become by this time a very domestic product.

The novels documented the usual crimes and scandals, but they now occurred at home in an easily understood English landscape rather than in a foreign setting essentially outside time and history. The characters were quintessentially English — middle or upper middle class and comfortable. The only convents, monasteries, or dilapidated castles to appear were Cromwell's ruins — or the successor to the convent — the madhouse. The novels were as much about life among the rich as they were about terror. A privileged glimpse of the rotting core beneath the patina of Victorian respectability was enough to titillate the most discerning readers, and titillation was what these sensation novels, as they were now called, were all about.

Wilkie Collins and M.E. Braddon, hailed as two of the best sensation novelists, were rivals in the 1860s. The fact that Collins is now remembered in a way that Braddon is not may have more to do with Collins's friendship with Dickens than with his creative skill. Collins's masterpieces, *The Woman in White* and *The Moonstone*, outshine all his other more didactic, melodramatic works. Happily, the reprinting of M.E. Braddon's *Lady Audley's Secret*[1] and *Aurora Floyd* by Oxford and Virago have contributed to the current interest in her work. There are other points of comparison: *The Woman in White* was published in 1860 in Dickens's magazine *All The Year Round*. Parts of *Lady Audley's Secret* appeared in 1861 in the journal *Robin Goodfellow*. When the journal folded, the *Sixpenny Magazine* picked up the serial

---

1. M.E. Braddon, *Lady Audley's Secret*, Oxford, 1987.

and ran it from January to December 1862. Braddon has said that she admired Collins's novel, but was not impressed by his choice of heroine. Her own work confirms her admiration. The surface similarities between *The Woman in White* and *Lady Audley's Secret* would probably be grounds for a plagiarism lawsuit in today's courts. Braddon borrows many of Collins's motifs, most importantly perhaps the use of ghostly doubles, loss of identity, heavy Continental atmosphere, threats of murder, and madness. Nevertheless, the differences between the two novels are profound.

Collins's novel is about absolutes: power, justice, goodness, truth, family, and it uses a loose Gothic framework in order to prove the efficacy of these absolutes. Braddon's novel, while appearing to do the same, illustrates, through similar echoes of the Gothic, that they are both gender and class-based. While a thorough comparison of the two novels would show this more clearly, my comments, for the purposes of this paper, will centre on *Lady Audley's Secret*.

Lady Audley's Secret traces the fortunes of one Helen Maldon, daughter to a half-pay naval officer and wife to another officer, George Talboys. Poor and rebellious, Helen believes that marriage to George will improve her prospects, but George's father disapproves of the marriage and cuts his son off. The couple's money soon runs out and George deserts his wife and their young son in order to make his fortune in Australia, hoping to return to England a rich man and reclaim his bride. But Helen is left at home in abject poverty and she assumes, since she hears nothing of George, that he is dead. Accordingly, she leaves her son with her father and hires herself out, first as a teacher, then as a governess, under the name of Lucy Graham. She meets an older, wealthy widower, Sir Michael Audley, who knows nothing of her past and wishes to marry her. Lucy decides to commit bigamy; the rest of the novel concerns Lucy's desperate attempts to hide her past. For example, George returns from Australia and she tries to kill him by pushing him down a well. Robert Audley, a self-styled detective and nephew of Sir Michael, eventually discovers her secret and Lucy tries to murder him by setting fire to the pub in which she believes him to be sleeping. She is of course finally caught, is forced to confess her wrongdoing to Sir Michael, who immediately casts her off, and is ultimately incarcerated in a former convent, turned madhouse, in Belgium. She dies a year later.

Now you will realize that this quick summary does nothing to illuminate the novel's many twists and turns, nor does it do justice to Lady Audley's many attributes: her Pre-Raphaelite beauty, her resourcefulness, her strength of mind. For here is the most interesting fact about this particular sensation novel: the Angel in the House has become the Demon; the golden-haired beauty so praised and protected has become a female vampire.[2] Braddon seems to have accepted the social necessity for a traditional happy ending in which the family expels the offending member (Lady Audley) and once again shows a blank face to the world, but the text itself rebels against this necessity in a way that Collins's *The Woman in White* does not. This idea of a subversive fiction, of what Rosemary Jackson calls a "camouflaged story" lying just underneath the realistic one is theorized by Jackson as part of the fracture of the conventional. She says:

> A fantastic mode had always permitted a society to write out its greatest fears as "demonic" or "devilish": for the Victorian middle class these were the threats of transformation of social and sexual mores. A devil was no longer even equivocally superhuman: it was a working class revolutionary, a desiring female, a social outsider or a "madman".[3]

Lady Audley is all of these things.

I would suggest that Lady Audley, whose consciousness of being placed in an uncongenial Gothic setting and narrative structure is acute, tries to beat down the barrier between the subversive fiction in which she exists and the structure of the realistic fiction above, first by violently discarding the role of Angel in the House, then by appropriating the role of Gothic villain. In final desperation she attempts to destroy the architectural manifestation of the Gothic novel — the Inn, named the Castle, where the detective sleeps — through fire (echoes of *Jane Eyre* are strong at this point) only to be reincarcerated in the far more secure Gothic setting of the madhouse. In this version of the Gothic, the heroine does not emerge unscathed. She is metaphorically buried alive.

Lady Audley's competing roles — angel, demon, Gothic villain, rational woman, Gothic victim — demand the creation of separate identities, and this remarkable profusion of "selves" all seems designed by Braddon to point up the possibility of multiple fictions lying in wait beneath the "true" realistic fiction of an outraged family and the steps it

2. Nina Auerbach, *Woman and the Demon: The Life of a Victorian Myth*, Cambridge: Mass., 1982, 107-108.

3. Rosemary Jackson, *Fantasy: The Literature of Subversion*, London, 1981, 131.

takes to rid itself of a socially undesirable member.[4] In order to function, Helen Maldon manufactures these alternate selves, which take over and act out the romantic archetypes that seem to be demanded of Victorian Gothic heroines. So Helen Maldon creates Helen Talboys, the Angel in the House, then Lucy Graham, the impoverished, pure governess, then Lucy Audley, again acting out the Angel in the House role — for the role fits very well when there is money to be made by it.

Braddon's use of doubles follows Wilkie Collins's more restrained employment of Anne Catherick as the embodiment of Laura Fairlie's troubled self. In *Lady Audley's Secret*, Lucy's maid Phoebe is presented as a pale, passive version of her mistress. Lucy says:

> you *are* like me, and your features are very nice; it is only colour that you want. My hair is pale yellow shot with gold, and yours is drab; my eyebrows and eyelashes are dark brown, and yours are almost — I scarcely like to say it, but they're almost white, my dear Phoebe; your complexion is sallow, and mine is pink and rosy. Why, with a bottle of hair dye, such as we see advertised in the papers, and a pot of rouge, you'd be as good-looking as I any day, Phoebe (58).

Phoebe is never called upon to impersonate Lady Audley as Anne Catherick impersonates Laura Fairlie. Braddon seems more interested here in using Phoebe's fate as a sort of working class parody of the fate of the traditional aristocratic Gothic heroine. She is married unhappily to a drunken brute one cold winter morning, her "eyes, hair, complexion, and dress all melting into such pale and uncertain shades that, in the obscure light of the foggy November morning, a superstitious stranger might have mistaken the bride for the ghost of some other bride, dead and buried in the vaults below the church" (110). Phoebe/Lucy is then trapped in a sort of working-class version of the Gothic tower — the Castle Inn — and there Phoebe acts out another fiction, the tale of poverty and its effects. Lady Audley escapes a possible role through the use of a double, and Braddon demonstrates the multiple possibilities buried in her fiction.

Doing Collins one better, Braddon introduces yet another double for Lady Audley. In an attempt to elude the searches of her husband, Lady Audley tries to stage her own death. The double she employs could scarcely be taken for a double at all. The only points of comparison

---

4. William Patrick Day, *In The Circles of Fear and Desire: A Study of Gothic Fantasy*, Chicago, 1985, 21.

between the vital Lady Audley and the frail, consumptive girl named Matilda are their age and a vague similarity in colour of hair. But this is unimportant, since Matilda is denied a speaking part; she is recruited simply to play the role of Helen as languishing wife, pining after her missing husband (since Helen has herself moved on to another role by this time). Matilda's is a truly dramatic portrayal of the wife's traditionally silent role, played by a self effectively divorced from the whole. She is accepted by George as his wife, because he *expects* to see this sort of degeneration in a woman deprived of his company. Matilda dies, and Braddon borrows another device from Collins for the piece of evidence she calls the "narrative of the tombstone", the seemingly concrete evidence of Lady Audley's death.

The only role that Lady Audley does not choose for herself is the role that is thrust upon her by Robert Audley. Incarcerated at the end of the novel in the madhouse under the name of Mrs Taylor, stripped of identity and dignity, Lady Audley is effectively, as the chapter heading in which this action takes place suggests, buried alive in the Gothic fiction she has tried so hard to avoid.

As Lady Audley's crimes are suspected, her metaphoric removal from the sphere of the Angel in the House role is accomplished in the strenuous efforts made by other characters to ally her nature to the forces of evil. She is called witch, sorceress, mermaid, siren, wild animal, horrible demonic force, beautiful fiend, and finally, most significantly, "no longer a woman" (345). These identities contrast most effectively with the role assigned Lady Audley at the outset of the novel: a babyfied, childish, foolish Madonna. It is only when Lady Audley is forced into action to preserve her hard-won advantages that she employs what the text calls a "newly adopted wisdom" and is transformed from a "frivolous childish beauty into a woman, strong to argue her own cause and plead her own defence" (288).

About half way through the novel, once Robert Audley has decided to pursue Lady Audley in earnest, her role as Gothic villain passes to him, and she is captured, unwillingly, in the role and circumstances of the Gothic heroine. Robert's early references to "overly-imagined German tales" and his cousin's comment that he is beginning to conduct himself "like some ghost-haunted hero in a German story" (262) suggests that his earlier posturing as mild-mannered, slightly eccentric barrister has constituted as complete a mask as that of Lady Audley.

The Gothic setting described at the beginning of the novel is one in which Lady Audley feels at home and in power, but with her realization that Robert is pursuing her, the safe, money-bought haven of Audley Court loses its attractiveness and Lady Audley looks around her gorgeous boudoir "much as if the Sevres and bronze, the buhl and ormolu, had been the mouldering adornments of some ruined castle" (299). Finally, as Robert succeeds in committing Lady Audley to the madhouse (the process takes ten minutes of the Consulting Physician's time and fifteen minutes of the madhouse Director's time) both he and Lady Audley realize that she has been brought to a grave. The last journey to Belgium, back into the heart of the Continental Gothic novel, takes place in the dark, punctuated with stops in mouldering hotels with rats in their cellars. Lady Audley's final resting place is a suite of rooms in the private sanatorium

> which looked dreary enough in the wan light of a single wax candle. This solitary flame, pale and ghostlike in itself, was multiplied by paler phantoms of its ghostliness, which glimmered everywhere about the rooms (389).

That Robert has been her judge, jury, and executioner on behalf of the segment of society he represents is clear. Lady Audley is entreated to resign herself to this life of enforced penitence

> as many a good and holy woman in this Catholic country freely takes upon herself, and happily endures unto the end. The solitude of your existence in this place will be no greater than that of a king's daughter, who, flying from the evil of the time, was glad to take shelter in a house as tranquil as this (391).

Robert acknowledges his role as villain: "He felt as if he had carried off my lady, and had made away with her secretly and darkly" (395). This is, of course, exactly what he has done. The apparent metaphoric confusion between madhouse and convent is not accidental. It is Lady Audley's "uncontrolled" sexuality and her notions of economic and social mobility which so enrage a patriarchal society bent, perversely, on de-sexing and babyfying women, clearly because they are dangerous to the hierarchy in any other form. A male Gothic villain is a known quantity and the rules of the game demand that he be exposed. In *The Woman in White*, for example, Hartright's concept of vengeance against Count Fosco does not include personal execution of the criminal. But in *Lady Audley's Secret*, where the villain is female and therefore an unknown quantity, total obliteration of the threat is apparently the only recourse open to the male detective. First a forceable thrusting of the woman back into her proper role, then a discreet burial. Lady Audley recognizes Robert's tactics and accuses him: "you have used your power basely and cruelly, and have brought me to a living grave" (391).

That Robert's motives are class and gender-based is revealed in his statement that to have acted differently concerning Lady Audley would have branded him a "traitor to society" (391) — by which he means male, upper-class society. For there is one crime of Lady Audley's that remains largely unnoticed, both by Robert, because it is outside the interests of the Audley family, and by twentieth-century critics of the novel, for less discernible reasons. Lady Audley is incarcerated because of her attempted murder of George Talboys. When it appears that George has survived, Lady Audley is not released; her existence remains a moral embarrassment to the family and the possibility of a Chancery suit has Robert worried. Absolutely no mention is made of the fact that Lady Audley has succeeded in burning down the Castle Inn, and in the process has killed the brutish, working-class owner of the pub, Luke Marks. Now it is granted that Luke is really no loss, either to his wife or to the plot, but the fact that Robert — while claiming to be the conscience of society — actually reveals himself to be acting for a very small segment of society, is significant. As I have said, Lady Audley's aggressive roles are a threat to male, upper-class society, and Robert is interested only in "crimes" committed against this segment. The claims of the working-class and of women remain unheeded. Consequently, I would suggest that like Dickens's Dr Manette, Lady Audley becomes a political hostage, the witness to a scandal and a dangerous presence, but not apparently to society as a whole; rather to the men (three of them) who decide that her character is too dangerous and threatening to themselves to acknowledge and to allow to run freely among her sisters. The echoes in the latter part of the novel to Dickens's *A Tale of Two Cities* are therefore meaningful. As I have said, the title of the chapter in which Lady Audley is incarcerated is "Buried Alive". The title of the chapter in which the Audley family seals itself against class and gender outrages is "Restored", an ironic reference to Dr Manette's return to the bosom of his family.

From Gothic villain to Gothic heroine; from Gothic hero to Gothic villain — Lady Audley and Robert battle for position throughout the novel. Lady Audley's bid for freedom from the constraints of class and gender, not the mention genre, ultimately fail. *Lady Audley's Secret* is about apparent violation — of family, class, gender laws, and genre, but the happy picture of restored family security presented at the end of the novel seems hollow: "Mr. Audley's dream of a fairy cottage had been realised between Teddington Lock and Hampton Bridge, where, amid a little forest of foliage, there is a fantastical dwelling-place of rustic woodwork, whose latticed windows look out upon the river" (445). Only here, in a sort of "Wemmick's castle", can the kind of security desired by society be obtained. D.A. Miller notes that the endings of sensation novels are violent wrenchings of the plot back into the realistic mode. About *The Woman in White* he says:

> Herein, one might argue, lies the "morality" of sensation fiction, in its ultimately fulfilled wish to abolish itself: to abandon the grotesque aberrations of character and situation that have typified its representation, which now coincides with the norm of the Victorian household.[5]

In *Lady Audley's Secret*, the outrages performed upon the identity of Lady Audley overwhelm the rather lame attempt to return the world to normalcy, and realism becomes another term for fantasy. I have tried to suggest that Braddon buries (not so deeply) profound clues about how to read her novel. The ambiguity of the text's morality, the confusion of roles and genres point out an ultimate dissatisfaction with the confines of Victorian realism — indeed, of Victorian society as a whole. By the 1860s the Angel in the House/Gothic heroine role was already suspect, but it was not until the 1920s that Virginia Woolf was finally able to kill her off. In this light, Lady Audley's attempts seem valiant, if tragic.

---

5. D.A. Miller, "*Cage Aux Folles*: Sensation and Gender in Wilkie Collins' *The Woman in White*", in *Speaking of Gender*, ed. Elaine Showalter, London, 1989, 198.

OPENING THE TEXT:
THE LOCKED-TRUNK MOTIF IN LATE EIGHTEENTH-
CENTURY BRITISH AND AMERICAN GOTHIC FICTION

W.M. VERHOEVEN

> *"Here has been bloody work*
> *in this closet!"*

The trend in revisionist, theory-oriented criticism that has dominated the arenas of scholarly debate for more than two decades now has contributed significantly to the revaluation of the literary Gothic, to the extent that Gothic fiction has now been effectively de-marginalized and, to some extent, canonized. However, despite the institutionalization of the Gothic as a literary discourse that provides an aesthetically and culturally encoded comment on contemporary society, there is still little agreement amongst critics when it comes to determining the exact significance of the Gothic in terms of ideology. Thus the question whether the tenets of the Gothic are primarily radical or reactionary is still being debated. Arguing in favour of the former, Kenneth W. Graham observes in the afterword to his *Gothic Fictions: Prohibition/Transgression*:

> The Gothic novel springs from fears and uncertainties arising from instabilities in personal, social and political realities during [a] period of revolution. The Gothic novel showed the way to rebellion by daring to ask fundamental questions about the limits of art, social organization, politics, psychology and metaphysics .... Gothic enigmas assault ideological conditionings: they undermine security at many levels of existence.[1]

Revisionist Marxist critics on the whole tend to endorse Graham's assessment of the Gothic. David Punter, for instance, argues that even

---

1. *Gothic Fictions: Prohibition/Transgression*, ed. Kenneth W. Graham, New York, 1989, 262.

in its very form — deliberately "fragmentary, inconsistent, jagged" — the Gothic challenges the dominant eighteenth-century bourgeois ideology based on such principles as rationality, decorum, realism and capitalism: "The most crucial element in the definition of the Gothic is this: that as the realist novel has been the occupier of the 'middle ground' of bourgeois culture, so Gothic defines itself on the borderland of that culture."[2]

However, the view that the Gothic constitutes an inherently revolutionary discourse — that *all* Gothic texts are in effect radical — is not shared by all commentators. Prominent among the dissenting voices is that of Leslie Fiedler, who, in *Love and Death in the American Novel*, argues that while the *European* Gothic tradition indeed reflects a revolutionary ideology, its *American* counterpart is ultimately expressive of a deep-rooted conservatism:

> It should be noted that the shift from the ruined castle of the European prototypes to the forest and cave of Brown involves a shift not just in the manner of saying what the author is after. *The change of myth involves a profound change of meaning.* In the American gothic, that is to say, the heathen, unredeemed wilderness and not the decaying monuments of a dying class, nature and not society becomes the symbol of evil. Similarly not the aristocrat but the Indian, not the dandified courtier, but the savage colored man is postulated as the embodiment of villainy. Our novel of terror, that is to say (even before its founder has consciously shifted his political allegiances), is well on the way to becoming a Calvinist exposé of natural human corruption rather than an enlightened attack on a debased ruling class or entrenched superstition. The European gothic identified blackness with the super-ego and was therefore revolutionary in its implications; the American gothic (at least as it followed the example of Brown) identified evil with the id and was therefore conservative at its deepest level of implication, whatever the intent of its authors.[3]

Cathy N. Davidson, in turn, disagrees with Fiedler's dismissal of the American Gothic as reactionary and inhibitory. In her new historicist project *Revolution and the Word: The Rise of the Novel in America*,

---

2. David Punter, *The Literature of Terror: A History of Gothic Fictions from 1765 to the Present Day*, London, 1980, 409, 417.

3. Leslie A. Fiedler, *Love and Death in the American Novel* (1960), Penguin, 1984, 160-61 (Fiedler's italics).

Davidson develops an argument in support of the subversive, revolutionary quality of the early American Gothic texts: "The Gothic ..., especially as handled by writers such as Rebecca Rush or George Watterson or Charles Brockden Brown, asked precisely those questions that bourgeois ideology labored to suppress."[4]

With critics disagreeing so fundamentally about the true meaning of the Gothic in terms of ideological imput and impact, it is time to start questioning the validity of universal generic classifications for describing the genre: perhaps the Gothic (often referred to as subversive and ambiguous) simply defies classification as part of its discursive singularity. Indeed, in comparison to other fictional genres, Gothic texts appear to be particularly open to contradictory and mutually exclusive readings. Thus it is not difficult to argue (*pace* the Marxist revisionists' reading of the Gothic as anti-bourgeois) that Clara Reeve's popular and in many ways trend-setting Gothic tale *The Old English Baron* is really only a moralistic tale designed to reify the Christian bourgeois value-system of its author and its audience by bringing the world of Gothic horror, as James Trainer puts it, "into the lives of simple men and thereby allowing them a momentary *frisson* which could quickly be banished by appeal to their Christian faith."[5] There is, in other words, every reason to assume that *The Old English Baron* is exactly what the author designed it to be: a tale that will first "excite the [reader's] attention" and then "direct it to some useful, or at least innocent, end."[6] Likewise it seems quite legitimate, despite revisionist claims to the contrary,[7] to regard Mrs Radcliffe's famous discourse of the "explained supernatural" as nothing more than an elaborate verbal game meant to shock the reader into a firmer belief in the convictions which he already held when he first encountered the text. Significantly, both

---

4. Cathy N. Davidson, *Revolution and the Word: The Rise of the Novel in America*, New York, 1986, 237.

5. James Trainer, Introduction to Clara Reeve's *The Old English Baron: A Gothic Story* (1777), ed. James Trainer, Oxford, 1967, xiv.

6. Clara Reeve, from the Preface to the second edition of *The Old English Baron, Ibid.*, 4.

7. Cf., for instance, Kenneth W. Graham's claim that "*The Mysteries of Udolpho* is vitally revolutionary in a manner that the marquis [de Sade] would approve and Dr. Johnson might well protest" ("Emily's Demon Lover: The Gothic Revolution and *The Mysteries of Udolpho*", in *Gothic Fictions: Prohibition/Transgression*, 165).

The Old English Baron and *The Mysteries of Udolpho* end with elaborate accounts of multiple marriages and the restoration of broken genealogies. In the final analysis, harmony, order, continuity and rationality replace conflict, mystery, disruption, and the supernatural.[8]

The recent boom in Gothic criticism appears to have made one thing quite clear: so far we have not been able to set up an analytical model that will provide an adequate generic description of the Gothic. In particular much is still unclear about the origin of Gothic fiction, as well as about the transformation of the European Gothic tradition into a vernacular American Gothic tradition. The present paper aims to make a modest contribution towards a more satisfactory generic description of the Gothic.

I will particularly be concerned with the trans-Atlantic migration of the fictional Gothic, and the obvious starting-point for such an analysis is the work of William Godwin and Charles Brockden Brown.[9] It will be my contention that Godwin's *Caleb Williams* is in many ways a key text, not only for understanding the nature and continuing appeal of the Gothic as such, but also for fathoming the modalities of the indigenous American branch of the Gothic as represented by Brown's novels. I will argue that Brown's work introduces an epistemological element into the discourse of the Gothic that was altogether absent from his British modes. I will do so by means of a comparative analysis of a motif that is central to Gothic fiction — that of the locked trunk — in three closely related, though ultimately quite distinct texts: William Godwin's *Caleb Williams* (1794), George Colman the Younger's *The Iron Chest* (1796), and Charles Brockden Brown's *Edgar Huntly* (1799).

The locked-trunk motif is itself a variation on an even better-known Gothic narrative device: the locked-room mystery.[10] Like the locked-room motif, the locked trunk, chest, or (strong-)box is directly related

---

8. Cf. *The Old English Baron*, 142-53, and Mrs Radcliffe, *The Mysteries of Udolpho* (1794), Oxford, 1980, 670-72.

9. The connection between Godwin and Brown is a well-documented one. See, for instance, Lulu Rumsey Wiley, *The Sources and Influence of the Novels of Charles Brockden Brown,* New York, 1950, notably 243-52, and Jane Townsend Flanders, "Charles Brockden Brown and William Godwin: Parallels and Divergences", unpublished diss., University of Wisconsin, 1965.

10. Cf. Mark S. Madoff: "The locked-room mystery is characteristic of the Gothic. It nearly is the Gothic" ("Inside, Outside, and the Gothic Locked-Room Mystery", in *Gothic Fictions: Prohibition/Transgression*, 49).

to the fundamental Gothic principle of enigma, and it derives its narrative and symbolic potential from the tension that exists between the enigma and the desire to disclose the enigma. The most fundamental difference between the two motifs seems to be the reversal of the inside-outside dichotomy, which in Gothic fiction functions as the dividing-line between the known and the unknown, the conscious and the subconscious, the rational and the irrational. These oppositions can obviously be extended: order and anarchy, conformity and the forbidden; virtue and sin, innocence and guilt.

While the locked-room motif characteristically involves a mysterious crime (particularly a murder) committed in a room that is locked from within and that no longer contains any evidence of the crime or of how the criminal left the room, the locked trunk is expected to contain all the answers to a crime already committed. In other words: while in the case of the locked-room motif the key to the disclosure of the enigma lies somewhere *outside* the enclosed space, in the case of the locked-trunk motif we know (or assume) that the key to the disclosure of the enigma is *inside* the enclosed space — the problem being that it is locked.[11]

Though I would hesitate to identify *Caleb Williams* as a Gothic novel *pur sang*, it is possible, in my view, to read *Caleb Williams* as one of the earliest critical studies of the Gothic genre. It is from his own account of the composition of the novel that we know that Godwin made a careful study of contemporary popular novels, including Gothic tales, in order to master the technique of manipulating his readers'

---

11. The reversal of the inside-outside dichotomy also accounts for the fact that whereas the protagonist of the locked-room mystery most typically belongs to the class of the detective, the protagonist in the locked-trunk mystery is usually associated with the type of the ingenious locksmith. Cf. Caleb's confession early in the novel: "I delighted to read of feats of activity, and was particularly interested by tales in which corporeal ingenuity or strength are the means resorted to for supplying resources and conquering difficulties. I inured myself to mechanical pursuits, and devoted much of my time to an endeavour after mechanical invention" (William Godwin, *Things As They Are; Or, The Adventures of Caleb Williams* [1794], ed. David McCracken, Oxford, 1970, 4). Cf. also Edgar Huntly saying about himself: "I also am a mechanist. I had constructed a writing desk and cabinet, in which I had endeavoured to combine the properties of secrecy, security, and strength, in the highest possible degree" (*Edgar Huntly; Or, Memoirs of a Sleep-Walker* [1799], eds Sydney J. Krause and S.W. Reid, Kent: Ohio, 1984, 115-16).

responses to his story.[12] Given the novel's enormous success with the general public, we may be sure that with *Caleb Williams* Godwin touched the live-wire of Gothic discourse.

Godwin intuitively understood that the tale of pursuit and adventure had potential as a tool in rational dialectics because it tapped directly into the heart of western teleological metaphysics.[13] He realized that at the heart of a successful Gothic text lies an enigma (such as Falkland's crime). He also knew that all he needed to set the narrative going (and to keep it going) was a character who is possessed of a more than average curiosity (Caleb) and a locked trunk which supposedly contains the key to the enigma which (as the experienced reader of Gothic romances had been conditioned to expect) functions as a kind of guarantee that whatever the fate of the inquisitive hero in his battle against the dark unknown, the truth will ultimately be revealed, the guilty will be punished, and order will be restored. It is no coincidence, therefore, that Godwin introduces the trunk in the first chapter, immediately after the introduction of the hero and his adversary:

> One day when I had been about three months in the service of my patron, I went to a closet or small apartment which was separated from the library by a narrow gallery that was lighted by a small window near the roof. I had conceived that there was no person in the room, and intended only to put any thing in order that I might find out of its place. As I opened the door, I heard at the same instant a deep groan expressive of intolerable anguish. The sound of the door in opening seemed to alarm the person within; I heard the lid of a trunk hastily shut, and the noise as of fastening a lock (7).

The sound of the "tabernacle of truth" being closed and locked reverberates through Caleb's inquisitive soul, thereby lending the narrative the "unity of plot" and the "unity of spirit" that Godwin aimed for when he designed the book (337).

---

12. See the preface to the Standard Novels edition of *Fleetwood* (1832), rpt. in *Caleb Williams*, 333-41.

13. For an analysis of Godwin's remarkable conversion from the rhetoric of rational political philosophy to the rhetoric of the Gothic romance, see my "Things As They Seem: *Caleb Williams* and the Art of Deception", in *Tropes of Revolution: Writers' Reactions to Real and Imagined Revolutions, 1798-1989*, eds C.C. Barfoot and Theo D'haen, Amsterdam and Atlanta: Ga., 1991, 72-89.

After its conspicuous introduction in the very first pages of the novel, Falkland's trunk curiously enough drops from sight, until it makes a spectacular come-back in Chapter VI of Volume II. This chapter opens with a remark that is undoubtedly meant to lend more weight to the episode immediately following — Caleb's attempt to open the trunk:

> The period at which my story is now arrived seemed as if it were the very crisis of the fortune of Mr. Falkland ....
> ... [M]y steps by some mysterious fatality were directed to the private apartment at the end of the library. Here, as I looked round, my eye was suddenly caught by the trunk mentioned in the first pages of my narrative.
> My mind was already raised to its utmost pitch. In a window-seat of the room lay a number of chisels and other carpenter's tools. I knew not what infatuation instantaneously seized me. The idea was too powerful to be resisted. I forgot the business upon which I came .... I snatched a tool suitable for the purpose, threw myself upon the ground, and applied with eagerness to a magazine which inclosed all for which my heart panted. After two or three efforts, in which the energy of uncontrollable passion was added to my bodily strength, the fastenings gave way, the trunk opened, and all that I sought was at once within my reach.
> I was in the act of lifting up the lid, when Mr. Falkland entered, wild, breathless, distraction in his looks! (131-32)

This climactic scene of the opening of the trunk is followed by one of the most remarkable narrative gaps in all Gothic fiction: we never learn what those incriminating documents were that Falkland guarded so frantically. Indeed, Godwin never mentions the trunk again in the entire novel. In a less carefully designed novel than *Caleb Williams* the mangling of the trunk motif might be attributed to mere authorial incompetence, but it seems unlikely that such an astute craftsman as Godwin would have mangled the trunk motif if he had not had a clear reason for doing so.

The significance of Godwin's anticlimactic treatment of the trunk motif in *Caleb Williams* becomes apparent when we compare it with the way George Colman the Younger handles the trunk motif in his stage adaptation of Godwin's novel. Colman was quick to respond to the dramatic potential of the trunk motif and in *The Iron Chest* makes the most of the material that Godwin had shown so little interest in.

Colman's play, which was first performed at the Theatre Royal, Drury Lane, in 1796, starring Charles Kemble, closely follows

Godwin's plot, his main addition being a rather insipid love-theme. The servant-hero, Wilford (Colman's recreation of Caleb), suspects his otherwise respectable master, Sir Edward Mortimer, of having killed a local squire, a figure as brutal as Tyrrel. The plot pivots on the contents of an iron chest, which Sir Edward keeps hidden in his study and which supposedly contains incriminating evidence of Sir Edward's crime. When the trunk is finally opened, it turns out to contain a bloodstained dagger and a full written statement in which Sir Edward confesses to have murdered the squire. Colman's use of the locked-trunk motif is thus fully in line with the conventional Gothic practice of associating the dark, the unknown, and the hidden with feelings of guilt. It is Sir Edward's brother Fitzharding who at one point feels moved to address Wilford in these words, which highlight the play's moral and epitomize the significance of the image of the iron chest:

> "Harkye, young man. This smacks of mystery;
> And now looks foully. Truth, and Innocence,
> Walk round the world in native nakedness;
> But Guilt is cloak'd."[14]

Reputedly a "shrewd judge of the theatrical public's taste",[15] Colman probably thought the trunk motif was bound to succeed on the stage, but he turned out to be wrong, since the play was not a success.

The main reason why Godwin's handling of the trunk motif is more evocative and more intellectually challenging than Colman's, is that while for Colman the trunk is merely a physical given (his trunk is in fact — because it dominates the audience's span of attention — the be-all and end-all of his play), for Godwin, the mystery of the trunk is a powerful literary device that will hold the reader's attention while he unravels the real themes of the novel. To put it differently: while Colman mistakingly assumes that the meaning of the trunk is inside the trunk — that the meaning of the trunk *is* its contents — Godwin realized that the true significance of the locked trunk lies in the very act of opening it. While Colman's interest in the trunk is merely dramatic, therefore, Godwin is interested in the locked-trunk motif because it opens up possibilities for psychological and epistemological analysis and

---

14. George Colman, *The Iron Chest: A Play*, London, 1796, 90.

15. Peter Thomson, Entry on George Colman in *Restoration and Eighteenth-Century Drama*, London, 1980, 39.

speculation.[16] It is this aspect of the novel that accounts for the continuing appeal of *Caleb Williams*. It makes the novel a key text in the development of Gothic fiction, because it moves away from mainstream, sensationalist Gothicism.

One of the first to respond to the epistemological implications of Godwin's novel was the American Charles Brockden Brown. In his early twenties, when he first encountered Godwin's work, Brown was immediately enthusiastic: he called himself a radical for a while, and made several attempts to produce imitations of *Caleb Williams*. Like Colman, Brown was particularly struck by Godwin's treatment of the locked-trunk motif, and there is an impressive array of trunks in Brown's work. While trunks figure quite prominently in such works as *The Man at Home* and *Ormond*, the place and function of the trunk in *Edgar Huntly; or, Memoirs of a Sleep-Walker* is unique in Gothic fiction.

---

16. Commenting on Brown's narrative design, notably on his tendency to leave his works in an "unfinished state," Brown's first biographer, Paul Allen, touches upon an aspect of Brown's work that we would nowadays interpret as a conscious effort to resist the presiding logocentric urges and literary conventions that produce meaning. Allen writes:

All his works of imagination which he has given to the public, remain in [an] unfinished state. The author in such cases always delighted to have an opening to prosecute his subject still further, as his leisure or inclination might dictate. The reader accompanies him step by step throughout the whole labyrinth of his mysteries, with an expectation of finding them eventually cleared up. As he proceeds, however, his attention is arrested by still further novelties, which are brought forward to explain the proceeding, and which themselves require the same explanation. At the end he closes the volume with a mind still unsatisfied. The author was often asked by his friends, when he proposed to elucidate the mysteries with which his works of fancy abounded, to which he would give some sportive reply, plainly intimating that he considered it a matter of perfect indifference whether this task was ever accomplished or not. He seemed to consider the curiosity of his readers as an engine in his hands which he might play upon for his amusement merely, and relinquish when he was tired of such sport.

From this cause, all his works of a fanciful character present to the eye this chequered and motley appearance. One mystery gives hint to another, and the reader is finally left in the lurch wondering how the last was intended to have been elucidated (*The Life of Charles Brockden Brown*, ed. Charles E. Bennett, 1975, 387-88).

Although Brown's notorious narrative vagueness makes it hard to summarize the story (let alone establish its exact meaning), there appears to be little doubt that the essential plot pattern in *Edgar Huntly* is modelled on that of Godwin's novel. The narrative is in the form of a distracted first-person account of the bewildering events following the mysterious assassination of the narrator's friend, Waldegrave, by a person or persons unknown. As in the case of *Caleb Williams*, what sets the narrative going is the juxtaposing of the narrator/protagonist's excessive fascination with an enigma. While in Godwin's novel the narrator/hero is immediately confronted with his master's remorseful preoccupation with the secret contents of a mysterious strongbox, Brown opens his *Edgar Huntly* with a scene no less puzzling. Passing the scene of Waldegrave's murder during one of his nightly rambles, Edgar observes a half-naked man wailing remorsefully while digging in the ground. Filled as he is with feelings of grief and revenge, Edgar unsurprisingly assumes a connection between the stranger's midnight digging and Waldegrave's murder, and interprets the man's wailing as a sign of his guilt. Edgar starts following the man, who turns out to be a neighbour's servant, an Irishman called Clithero Edny. In pursuit of Clithero, Edgar discovers the entry to a secret cave, where (on top of a hill, across a deep ravine) Clithero appears to have found a safe retreat. Puzzled by the whole situation, Edgar returns to his neighbour Inglefield to spend the night. There, in the room which the murdered Waldegrave used to occupy, Edgar discovers a secret box which Clithero had left behind. At this point (again, as in *Caleb Williams*, roughly half-way through the novel) Brown has led the reader so deep into the mystery of Clithero and his involvement in the murder of Waldegrave, that he — along with Edgar — cannot but assume that the opening of the box must reveal at least part of the truth.

What immediately strikes one about the trunk scene in *Edgar Huntly* is the exuberance of descriptive detail and the sheer length of the scene (113-18, chapters 11 and 12). Brown carefully creates the impression that what we are faced with here is by no means a common box:

> [The box] stood in a corner, and was easily distinguished by its form .... Its structure was remarkable. It consisted of six sides, square and of similar dimensions. These were joined, not by mortice and tenon; not by nails, not by hinges .... The means by which they were made to cohere were invisible.
>   Appearances on every side were uniform, nor were there any marks by which the lid was distinguishable from its other surfaces (114).

This circumstantial description of Clithero's box, which is obviously meant to excite the reader's desire for disclosure and which therefore functions as an element of Barthesian *jouissance*, emphasizes that, as in the case of *Caleb Williams*, the meaning of the trunk is ultimately in the opening of it. Significantly, while delaying the reader's desire for textual fulfilment, Brown has his protagonist embark on a lengthy analysis of the moral implications of opening Clithero's secret box — of attempting to reveal painstakingly concealed information. The outcome of Edgar's soul-searching is a conspicuous attempt to rationalize his curiosity and to exonerate himself from blame:

> I intended not a theft. I intended to benefit myself without inflicting injury on others. Nay, might not the discoveries I should make, throw light upon the conduct of this extraordinary man, which his own narrative had withheld? Was there reason to confide implicitly on the tale which I had heard?
> In spite of the testimony of my own feelings, the miseries of Clithero appeared in some degree, phantastic and groundless. A thousand conceivable motives might induce him to pervert or conceal the truth. If he were thoroughly known, his character might assume a new appearance, and what is now so difficult to reconcile to common maxims, might prove perfectly consistent with them. I desire to restore him to peace, but a thorough knowledge of his actions is necessary, both to shew that he is worthy of compassion, and to suggest the best means of extirpating his errors. It was possible that this box contained the means of this knowledge (115).

Although he has kept the reader on tenterhooks long enough already, Brown is determined to protract his textual deferral, carrying over the actual opening of Clithero's trunk to the next chapter. When the trunk *is* finally opened, the result is even more sobering than the trunk-opening in *Caleb Williams*:

> I surveyed it with the utmost attention. All its parts appeared equally solid and smooth. It could not be doubted that one of its sides served the purpose of a lid, and was possible to be raised ....
> .... A touch, casually applied at an angle, drove back a bolt, and a spring, at the same time, was set in action, by which the lid was raised above half an inch. No event could be supposed more fortuitous than this. An hundred hands might have sought in vain for this spring ....

> I opened the trunk with eagerness. The space within was
> divided into numerous compartments, none of which contained
> any thing of moment. Tools of different and curious
> constructions, and remnants of minute machinery, were all that
> offered themselves to my notice (117).

From a narrative point of view the opening of the trunk may be
anticlimactic, but the scene is interesting for other reasons. There is
something peculiarly self-conscious about Brown's handling of the trunk
motif, and the passage quoted confirms this impression. Thus the fact
that the mysterious trunk turns out to beget further mysteries (what
tools? and what minute machinery?) suggests that Brown's trunk is a
kind of postmodern Chinese-box construction *avant la lettre*: each new
revelation merely defers the meaning which we expect to find.

This aspect of Brown's work signals an important development in
eighteenth-century Gothic fiction. More than any other Gothic writer
before him, Brown flagrantly manipulates the readers' responses to the
text: *not* with the purpose of titillating or shocking them (the prime
concern of mainstream Gothic novelists), *nor* to make them critically
review their moral or political beliefs (as Godwin and the other
"novelists of purpose" did), but to undermine the readers' imaginative
effort to read the text as an epistemological unit of meaning, purpose
and design. The reading-process in the Gothic tale of mystery (that is,
the opening of the "closed" text) being a metaphor for man's belief in a
teleological universe, Brown's Gothic fiction ultimately aspires to
subvert the reader's "will to knowledge". Not containing "any thing of
moment", Clithero's trunk, like Melville's empty sarcophagus (in
Pierre), "highlights the painful truth that the center of things is
hollow".[17] The painful truth, to be more specific, is that in the face of
epistemological crisis and ontological indeterminacy, man invariably
conceives of a box, puts a message in it, locks the box, throws away
the key, and pretends to have forgotten the message. Subsequently, all
his philosophical efforts are directed towards opening the box and
revealing its contents, which, when found, will affirm the ontological
status of the searcher (man), as well as the validity of the search (man's
existence). In *Edgar Huntly*, Brown — the trickster artist — has
tampered with the familiar Gothic box (the text) before he offers it to
his reader; he has opened the box with a spare key, removed the

---

17. Roland Hagenbüchle, "American Literature and the Nineteenth-Century
Crisis in Epistemology: The Example of Charles Brockden Brown", *Early
American Literature*, 23 (1988), 136.

message and locked the box again, carefully hiding all traces of the fraud. This explains why the guileless reader coming to Brown's novel is bound to feel like "the Trojan Hero attempting to embrace the shade of his father".[18]

When Edgar's expectations concerning the secret contents of Clithero's box have been frustrated, he tries to hide the traces of his having tampered with it. Much to his chagrin, however, the lid refuses to be closed again, no matter how hard he tries:

> I now perceived that Clithero had provided not only against the opening of his cabinet, but likewise against the possibility of concealing that it had been opened. This discovery threw me into some confusion. I had been tempted thus far, by the belief that my action was without witnesses, and might be forever concealed. This opinion was now confuted. If Clithero should ever reclaim his property, he would not fail to detect the violence of which I had been guilty. Inglefield would disapprove in another what he had permitted to himself, and the unauthorized and clandestine manner in which I had behaved, would aggravate, in his eyes, the heinousness of my offence (118).

This appendix to the trunk opening scene — unique in Gothic fiction — is remarkable in that it effects a radical reversal of the outside/inside dichotomy. Significantly, the trunk-scene opens with a person guilty of no crime (Edgar), who, by wrongfully opening Clithero's trunk, hopes to be able to prove that its owner, who in the eyes of the world is guilty of the murders of Wiatte and Waldegrave, is actually innocent. The scene ends, however, with the innocent person (Edgar) confessing himself guilty of a double breach of confidence and trust, while the allegedly guilty party turns out to be innocent.

The reversal of the inside/outside dichotomy as dramatized in the trunk opening scene is symptomatic of a whole series of similar reversals in the novel, causing the book's moral and epistemological compass to pivot continuously. One of the most prominent manifestations of the outside/inside reversal is Brown's use of the doubling device. Thus it is very difficult after a while to distinguish between Edgar Huntly and his mirror image Clithero Edny. Whereas Edgar, for instance, is a narrator/hero who is innocent and yet guilty (of Mrs Lorimer's death), victim (of the natives) and yet oppressor (of Clithero), Clithero is a hero/narrator (or at least co-narrator) who is

---

18. *The Life of Charles Brockden Brown*, 388.

guilty (of the death of Wiatte) and yet innocent (of Waldegrave's death, and also, in a sense, of Wiatte, since he killed the latter in self-defence, not knowing that it was Wiatte), oppressor (of Mrs Lorimer) and yet victim (of Huntly's inquisitiveness and of Sarsefield's vindicativeness). With Brown thus upsetting the outside/inside dichotomy, the seat of truth itself is radically displaced, so that it becomes impossible for the reader to discriminate between innocence and guilt, order and chaos, justice and anarchy. In this way, the reader of Brown's tale gradually becomes immersed in a state of ontological uncertainty, which becomes even more daunting as soon as he discovers that it is not only Clithero who is a sleepwalker, but that Edgar, too, belongs to that category. This implies that Edgar's account of the life Clithero may in fact be no more than the "wakeful dream" of a guilt-ridden somnambulist (161).[19] Somnambulism in *Edgar Huntly*, then, is by no means a mere element of a sensationalist Gothic setting: it is employed as a metaphor for the temporal and spatial indeterminacy of the human condition.

The key to a correct understanding of the locked-trunk motif in Brown's fiction is the self-conscious way in which he employs it. This is not to say that his fiction is metafictional or self-reflective; rather, it is self-conscious in its effect upon the reader, in that it seems deliberately to thwart the reader's suspension of disbelief. More than a mere expression of his awareness of the epistemological crisis of his age, Brown's use of the discourse of Gothic fiction — with all its proclivity to ellipsis, repetition, paradox, inconsistency and mystery — is an instrument of *conscious* subversion, causing all prevailing value-systems to be in in abeyance. While it may be true that Gothic fictions in general implicitly "assault ideological conditionings" and question "the limits of art, social organization, politics, psychology and metaphysics",[20] Brown's Gothicism not only signals — in Foucault's phrase — the discontinuity of traditional historical discourse, but *actively* seeks to undermine, or dismantle, the metaphysical tradition of

---

19. As a matter of fact, Huntly — like Caleb Williams before him — explicitly calls attention to the fact that he is not really a reliable narrator. Thus at one point, having just become aware of the bodies of the three Indians he killed, Huntly says: "In spite of the force and uniformity with which my senses were impressed by external objects, the transition I had undergone was so wild and inexplicable; all that I had performed; all that I had witnessed since my egress from the pit, were so contradictory to precedent events, that I still clung to the belief that my thoughts were confused by delerium" (194).

20. *Gothic Fictions: Prohibition/Transgression*, 262.

logocentrism and historical cognition. Unlike Radcliffe's (ideologically reactionary) Gothic mode of the "explained supernatural", Brown's Gothicism, which is sometimes aptly referred to as "rational fiction", is an attempt to create an internal disturbance in Western metaphysics and the literary and historical discourses that support it. Brown's subversive Gothic fiction, therefore, makes most sense, I suggest, when seen in the light of the Foucauldian agenda for a poststructuralist historiography: "it is a matter ... of strategic questioning of reason by reason, of the metaphysical tradition with the very tools that that tradition has given us." Brown generates a kind of writing that "exceeds, by questioning them, the values most dear to the tradition".[21] While it is true that, in the closing movements of *Edgar Huntly*, *Ormond* and other novels Brown restores the moral and epistemological *status quo* through the timely deaths of his nihilistic villains and the last-minute re-union of long-parted friends and lovers, this does not necessarily detract from his being a writer who challenges the presiding logocentric modes in Western metaphysics. Even though to all intents and purposes he retains the will to knowledge and the pursuit of historical cognition, Brown poses fundamental questions concerning the epistemological basis of meaning, identity and purpose before he arrives at the moment of perfunctory closure.

In terms of the generic development of Gothic fiction, this puts Brown in a different category from Colman, and even from Godwin. Colman's treatment of the locked-trunk motif in *The Iron Chest* puts him firmly in the Radcliffe/Reeve school of the "explained supernatural". Godwin's *Caleb Williams* is basically a "novel of purpose" and merely employs discursive strategies pertaining to the Gothic in order to challenge the dominant value-systems in contemporary society. Ideologically speaking, *Caleb Williams* is therefore anti-bourgeois, in contrast to Colman's and Radcliffe's tales of the "explained supernatural", which really confirm the presiding value systems and the existing distribution of power. Taking its cue from Godwin's radicalism, Brown's *Edgar Huntly* proposes a Gothic mode which opens up possibilities for epistemological speculation and for the radical displacement of meaning. I cannot, therefore, agree with Fiedler in identifying Brown's fiction as intrinsically bourgeois and conformist. To my mind, Brown's Gothic fiction constitutes a mode of revolutionary writing not matched by any European predecessors or followers, with the notable exception of Shelley.

---

21. Frank Lentricchia, *After the New Criticism*, Chicago, 1980, 209 and 210.

PULEX DEFIXUS, OR, THE SPELLBOUND FLEA:
AN EXCURSION INTO PORNO GOTHIC

ROBERT DRUCE

> *"... but are they all horrid?*
> *Are you sure they are all horrid?"*[1]

> *The final belief is to believe in a fiction, which you*
> *know to be a fiction, there being nothing else. The*
> *exquisite truth is to know that it is a fiction and that you*
> *believe in it willingly.*[2]

On 19 April 1933, William Hamilton, aged 43, a bookseller of Phoenix Street, Charing Cross Road, appeared before Sir Rollo Graham-Campbell at Bow Street Police Court, charged with selling two obscene books. Mr C.R.V. Wallace, for the Director of Public Prosecutions, stated that the books had been bought by a police officer, and could only be described as "absolute filth". Mr Laurence Vine defending, said that the books were not stocked by Hamilton but were obtained specially by him for a young policeman who had represented himself as an army officer and had paid no fewer than six visits to the shop, in the role of *agent provocateur*. He had put great pressure on the defendant, and it was only after great persuasion that Hamilton had agreed to procure the books. The Magistrate said that nothing could be worse than the two books before him, and it was not a case for a pecuniary penalty alone. Hamilton was sentenced to 3 months' imprisonment in the second division and in addition ordered to pay a fine of £100 and 10

---

1. Catherine Morland to Isabella Thorpe: Jane Austen, *Northanger Abbey*, ch. 6.

2. Wallace Stevens, "Adagia", *Opus Posthumus* (1957).

guineas costs. The works in question were entitled *Flossie*, and *The Autobiography of a Flea*.[3]

One evening twelve years later, a fledgling sixth-former, I was on my way home from school. As I sat in the railway waiting-room, a member of the Upper Sixth came in and thrust the faint carbon copy of a number of typewritten pages into my hand. "If you're quick", he said, "you can read it before the train comes. I've got to give it back tonight." He stood on guard at the door, while I found myself reading part of the excerpted seventh chapter of *The Autobiography of a Flea* (hereafter referred to as "the *Flea*"), and *in medias res*:

> Father Ambrose, however, was fully alive to the necessity of caution, and the good man let no opportunity pass by, while the young lady was in his confessional, of making direct and pertinent enquiries as to her conduct with others, and theirs to his penitent. It was thus Bella came to confess to her spiritual guide the feelings engendered within herself by the amatory proceedings of M. Delmont.
>
> Father Ambrose soon set about, with his usual astuteness, to turn the fact he had just acquired to his advantage.
>
> Nor was it long before his sensual and vicious brain conceived a plot which, for criminality and audacity I, as a humble insect, have never known equalled ... (47).[4]

---

3. See *The Times*, 20 April 1933, 7; *News of the World*, 23 April 1933, 10. *Flossie*, by an unknown hand, and subtitled with typical facetiousness: *Social Studies of the Century: Flossie, a Venus of Fifteen by one who knew this charming Goddess and Worshipped at her Shrine*, bears the spurious imprint: "Printed at Carnapolis for the Delectation of the Amorous and the Instruction of the Amateur in the Year of the Excitement of the Sexes MDCCCXCVII." The date, however, is likely to be accurate.

4. In the carbon-copy pages I saw in 1945, typing errors were frequent and so, almost certainly, were omissions, additions, and other corruptions of the text. The extracts cited here, are retrieved from a paperback edition which I have to hand, but which is not listed in the British Library Catalogue; page references for what they are worth (since they vary with every printing, even between superficially identical editions sharing a common imprint) are to this edition. It lacks date and imprint, other than "Printed in Great Britain", on its back cover, but is *circa* 1960. *Autobiography of a Flea* occupies pages 7-102 of a 188-page volume, which also contains *Lady Pokingham; Or, They All Do It*. The text has been considerably abridged. In quoting from it, I have silently restored a few minor excisions revealed by comparison with the original? edition [BL: PC 31.1.15: see note 6, below].

If it was my first encounter with pornographic writing, it was also a first plunge into comparative literature.

Even on such fragmentary first acquaintance it was impossible not to be struck by the facetious tone: a tone in essence ironic and contemptuous. Distant echoes of it are still to be found today in the captions to pictures of nude models in "adult" publications: "a charmful armful", "our toothsome twosome". It was impossible to ignore the archaism, and the frolicksome circumlocution. "A Flea", the narrator points out as the chapter opens, "cannot well be supposed to describe personal beauty, even in those on whom they feed". Bella's "heaving bosom", nevertheless, "whence peeped two white, exquisitely-formed and strawberry-tipped 'pomettes'", did not escape his compound eye. But above all there was the relentless authorial attention to the "stalwart weapon", the "terrible instrument" and, all passion momentarily spent, "the lolling member" of each male actor in the drama. Virgil's *"monstrum horrendum, informe, ingens"* did not seem far away in my imagination. Nor, in reality, were the elegant obscenities of Catullus: but this was a Catullus not to be encountered among our expurgated Higher Certificate texts.

Closer at hand lay the delicious horrors of the Gothic, with its trembling heroines and their fatal fascination with tales of crime and the forbidden: a fascination as compelling as mine, no doubt, as I raced through the handful of pages, fearful of being caught in the act, anxious to reach the end before my train arrived. And perhaps between the copy of *Northanger Abbey* in my school satchel and the typewritten sheets I held in my hand there was a further and closer connection, although I was not fully conscious of it at the time. But I had read *The Turn of the Screw* more than once, and knew that its fascination and horror, even if never-named, was rooted in sexuality somehow corrupt; although in what way corrupt, I could not then have said or, indeed, understood.

For Catherine Morland, that impressionable reader, horror might seem to lie alike within the ivied walls of Udolpho and Northanger; but was there not also a hint of something darker, perhaps, for those who plunged into Mrs Radcliffe's delightfully "horrid" pages? Of dangers to the innocent intruder which were specifically sexual in nature? Of being helpless within the clutch of others: of enforced seduction, perversion, incest, and multiple rape behind doors barred and padlocked against the quivering innocent — and for that reason doubly inviting. Of evil lurking in monkish cells, and in the shadows of Bluebeard's chamber? Fantasied dangers only distantly to be glimpsed through and beyond Jane Austen's ironic text, but perhaps paraded in daylight here, in the ill-typed pages? Horrid and nameless orgies, here named? Luxury as threatening and corrupt as it might be made to seem briefly delicious?

> The evening was cold, but a pleasant warmth was imparted to the luxurious apartment by a stove, while the soft and elastic sofa and ottomans with which the room was furnished gave an air of listless repose. In the brilliant light of a deliciously perfumed lamp, the two men appeared like the luxurious votaries of Bacchus and Venus, as they reclined only lightly clad, and fresh from a sumptuous repast.
>
> As for Bella, she surpassed herself in beauty. Habited in a charming "negligee", she half disclosed and half revealed those budding sweets of which she might well be proud .... These and other beauties lent their several attractions to make up a delicate and delicious whole, with which the pampered Deities might have intoxicated themselves, and in which two lustful mortals now prepared to revel (48).

The "two lustful mortals" are Bella's uncle, and Father Ambrose.

In due course, the revellers pause for "a revivifying glass of wine round"; after which the three sit down, and concert "a devilish plot for the defilement and enjoyment of the beautiful Julia Delmont". They will trap Monsieur Delmont into violating his own daughter. Then, with the threat of exposure hanging over him, Delmont will be helpless to deny the conspirators access to Julia. The prospect, like the wine, revivifies the men, and they lead Bella to the couch once more.

A paragraph or so later, the chapter, and the crudely-typed carbon copy, came to an end.

The signs all indicated that this was a "gentlemanly" text, and seemed to place it somewhere in the eighteenth or nineteenth century. In point of fact, if nothing else might, the word "ottoman" is likely to fix the date of the fragment at no earlier than the first decade of the nineteenth century; and so explode the British Library's first-recorded edition's false imprint date of 1789.[5] The talkative Flea is an implied author with, clearly, a respectable education: he was bred at a public-school, no doubt. If his text is obscene, his authorial diction — in his seventh chapter, at any rate — is never crude nor vulgar. The Flea has a sense of style, and seems anxious to share his enjoyment in it with the reader. As a close eye-witness — it would be hard to come closer — he

---

5. The earliest usage recorded in *OED*, is 1806; Byron used the word three years later, in a letter.

paints his scenes with gusto, and counterpoints the gusto with irony. His tale, he insists, is all too deplorably true: on a Flea's word of honour.

If the fragment was provocative for a fifteen-year-old schoolboy in 1945, it was all the more so because it was contraband, an obscene publication, a matter — even in its fragmentary and typewritten state — for the police to deal with. Today, in a generally, if not universally, altered climate of public opinion, with seven editions to date of the *Flea* listed in the British Library open catalogue and other editions available elsewhere, it is possible to take a more detached view of the work as a whole. And in the present context, to ask whether it does not stand within — and, if so, how close to the centre or the fringes of — a Gothic tradition.

This essay is a necessarily brief attempt to explore that question, and further questions which arise out of it.

As is commonly the case where clandestine publication is concerned, the work is anonymous and the imprints, if any, of successive editions spurious. In the absence of an identifiable original, I take here as *ur*-text the large hand-made paper edition which stands at the head of the list to be found in the British Library catalogue.[6] With an imprint and date of "Cytheria, 1789", its conjectured year of publication is 1887.

---

6. Details of listings in the British Library Catalogue are as follows:
The Autobiography of a Flea, told in a Hop, Skip and Jump (etc.); L[arge] P[aper]. Cytheria 1789. 8vo. One of 10 copies on handmade paper. The Imprint is fictitious. London 1887? [PC 31.1.15]
- do - L[arge]. P[paper]. 1789 (1887). One of 20 copies printed on large paper [PC 29.2.47]. *[Despite the 8vo page size, the print area centred on each page is closer to 24mo.]*
- do - [With Plates], pp. 190. The Phlebotomical Society; Cytheria 1789 (1890). 8vo. The Imprint is fictitious. Printed in Brussels. [PC 13.d.2]. *[This copy is annotated in a manuscript hand: "Published by Charles Carrington, part of the Davies Bequest."]*
- do- pp. 220; Literary Press, London 1901. 8vo. [PC 26.c.10]
- do- pp. 210; W. Gayda & Co, Philadelphia, 1915. 8vo. Imperfect, wanting pp. 32-52. [PC 14.ee.26]
- do - Atlanta: Pendulum Book, 1968,9. vol 2-4; 17 cm. Imperfect; wanting vol 1. [PC 22.ad.34]
The Autobiography of a Flea: An Intimate Memoir of the Victorians at Play. pp. 176; Star Books [W.H. Allen], London, 1983. [Cup 358/263]. *[This copy lacks the extended title and epigraph verses of the 1887 edition; the text has been modernized and vulgarized.]*

The facetious tone of the *Flea* is set on the extended title page (not featured in every edition) where the work announces itself as:

The Autobiography of a Flea, told in a Hop, Skip and Jump,
and Recounting all his Experiences of the Human and Superhuman
Kind, both Male and Female; with his Curious Connections,
Backbitings, and Tickling Touches; the whole scratched together
and arranged for the Delectation of the Delicate, and for the
Information of the Inquisitive.

In the 1890 edition, published — if the British Museum cataloguer's pencilled-in attribution is accepted — by Charles Carrington, the "Phlebotomical Society" imprint continues the joke. In certain editions, my reference-text included, a verse epigraph occupies a further page: of this, more later.

The incidents recounted in the book, being variations on a theme, are soon enumerated. The Flea's earliest recollections are of finding himself within a church where Bella, a fourteen-year-old beauty, is handed a *billet-doux*. The story, it should be noted, beginning in a church and ending in a monastery, remains in hailing distance of the clergy throughout. Bella is seduced by Charlie, her young admirer. The fact becomes known to Bella's confessor, Father Ambrose, who, dismissing Charlie with threats of divine retribution, continues Bella's seduction.

In due course, and with increasingly unbridled enthusiasm, Bella passes from orgy to orgy in the company of Father Ambrose, Father Clement (his fellow-monk), the Superior of their order, Monsieur Verbouc (her uncle and guardian), and — once the plot unfolded in Chapter 7 has reached its consummation — Julia Delmont and Julia's father. Along the way, Ambrose exploits the secrets of the confessional in seducing other parishioners, Mme Verbouc among them, and Bella pleasures a farm-hand and his father, in a rustic interlude.

In Chapter 12, Bella and Julia, alone in the world after the deaths of M. Verbouc and M. Delmont, are "received into the arms of Holy Mother Church upon the same day" and when their novitiate is complete, both take "the vows and the veil". After the ceremony, they are privately conveyed to a room in which "some fourteen" priests await them. But at this juncture, as the Flea remarks, "if it is out of the power of a Flea to point a moral, at least it is not beyond his ability to choose his own pastures". The scene which ensues is too much for its pulicid author:

> The cries of those who discharged, the hard breathing of those
> labouring in the sensual act, the shaking and groaning of the
> furniture, the half-uttered, half-suppressed conversation of the
> lookers-on, all tended to magnify the libidinous monstrosity of
> the scene, and to deepen and render yet more revolting the
> details of this ecclesiastic pandemonium.
>   Oppressed with these ideas, and disgusted beyond measure
> at the orgy, I fled. I never stopped until I had put some miles
> between myself and the actors in the hateful drama, nor have I
> cared to renew my familiarity with either Bella or Julia (101).

The Flea departs for pastures new — the Miltonic echo will not be lost
on the work's intended audience — and the memoir ends.

     The tongue-in-cheek moral indignation of the Flea, like his self-
mocking authorial stance and his addiction to hyperbole, is part of the
joke, part of the concordat between the anonymous human author and
his readers. It parodies that cast of thought in which moral indignation
masks a prurient interest, an attitude not unknown among those who
take it upon themselves to censor and suppress. And if the Flea is a
hypocrite, a pornographer pimping for his readers, how much greater is
the hypocrisy of the male protagonists which the Flea is at such pains to
expose? Whether his readers turn the pages in shared horror or
delighted empathy, the human author has them in a subtle double-bind.

     "The novel", Leslie Fiedler points out, "is fiction pretending to be
truth, the marvellous pretending to be the probable. One can scarcely
open an early example of the genre without finding ... on the title-page
the claim 'founded in truth' or 'a tale of truth'".[7] Consequently, the
title and the opening paragraphs of the *Flea*, with its initial quibble on
"cannot say" and "accept ... *per se*", are a parody of such double-
dealing:

> Born I was — but how, when or where, I cannot say; so I must
> leave the reader to accept the assertion *per se*, and believe it if
> he will. One thing is equally certain, the fact of my birth is not
> one atom less veracious than the reality of these memoirs, and if
> the intelligent student of these pages wonders how it came to
> pass that one in my walk — or perhaps I should have said jump
> — in life, became possessed of the learning, observation and
> power of committing to memory the whole of the wonderful
> facts and disclosures I am about to relate, I can only remind him

---

7. Leslie Fiedler, *Love and Death in the American Novel*, New York, 1966, rpt.
Paladin, 1970, 42-43.

that there are intelligences, little suspected by the vulgar, and
laws in nature, the very existence of which have not yet been
detected by the advanced among the scientific world (7).

And the comedy continues into a metaphor of self-disculpation not
entirely *malapropos*, perhaps, in an author-pornographer:

> I have heard it somewhere remarked that my province was to get
> my living by blood sucking. I am not the lowest by any means of
> that universal fraternity, and if I sustain a precarious existence
> upon the bodies of those with whom I come into contact, my
> own experience proves that I do so in a marked and peculiar
> manner, with a warning of my employment which is seldom
> given by those in other grades of my profession. But I submit
> that I have other and nobler aims than the mere sustaining of my
> being by the contributions of the unwary ....
> It is the attainment to learning which I shall evoke in
> describing the scenes of which I have been a witness — nay,
> even a partaker (7-8).

And indeed, he partakes, and with frequent shifts of authorial stance
and tone. He denounces a protagonist, in an indignant aside to the
reader:

> It is time to lift the veil from the real character of Father
> Ambrose. I do so with respect, but the truth must be told. The
> man was the living personification of lust. His mind was in
> reality devoted to its pursuits, and his grossly animal instincts,
> his ardent and vigorous constitution, no less than his hard,
> unbending nature, made him resemble in body, as in mind, the
> Satyr of old (22-23).

In applauding the action, his modesty is tempered with amazement:

> I do not think I ever felt my unfortunate infirmity in the matter
> of a natural inability to blush more acutely than on the present
> occasion.... Well might I have exclaimed with the poet of old:
> *"Moses!"* or with the more practical descendant of the Patriarch:
> *"Holy Moses!"* (26).

He is seduced into empathy:

> Reader, I am only a flea. I have but limited powers of
> perception, and I fail in ability to describe the gentle gradations

and soft creeping touches by which this enraptured ravisher approached his conquest .... I closed my eyes, the sexual instincts of the male flea arose within me, and I longed — yes! how ardently I longed to be in M. Delmont's place (79-80).

But he is equally ready to frustrate the activities of his human puppets:

> Never had I longed so ardently to contribute to the discomfiture of a champion as on the present occasion and, moved with the complaints of the gentle Bella, with the body of a flea and the soul of a wasp, I hopped at one bound to the rescue.
>
> To dig my proboscis into the sensitive covering of the scrotum of M. Verbouc was the work of a second. It had the desired effect. A sharp and tingling sensation of pain made him pause. The interval was fatal (39).

If the Flea's protagonists are lay-figures, gross embodiments of insatiable lust, it is the Flea — the paradox is calculated — who is most human. At moments such as when he springs to Bella's defence, he is an engaging rogue.

In defining a literary genre or sub-genre, it is almost always impossible to draw hard and fast lines. What constitutes "obscenity", or "pornography" has always and inevitably been notoriously difficult to define: as a history of criminal prosecutions shows. The *Autobiography of a Flea,* the sale of which earned a bookseller a swingeing fine and three months in jail in 1933 could, precisely a half-century later, be openly marketed in an uncut version by the reputable publishing house of W.H. Allen. But that the book is indeed pornographic, a masturbatory fantasy, could hardly be in doubt.

Nor can its "Gothicity": for it stands directly in an anti-clerical Gothic tradition of which Matthew Gregory Lewis's enormously popular *The Monk* of 1796, is an early English example. We might perhaps call this species "Monkish Gothic", in double tribute to Lewis and to "Maria Monk", the no doubt pseudonymous author of *Monks and their Maidens.* Subtitled *Awful Disclosures by Maria Monk of the Hotel Dieu Nunnery of Montreal, Monks and their Maidens* was published in London in 1837, in a second and revised edition with an Appendix and a Supplement displaying a Plan of the Nunnery, by the Reverend J.J. Slocum of New York. As Henry Spencer Ashbee, a leading connoisseur of erotica, was to point out, "immense editions" of this work "were sold in rapid succession, and gained, to an astonishing degree, belief among all classes of readers."[8]

An advertisement for Maria Monk's *Monks* can be found — alongside advertisements for *Nunneries and the Confessional*, by Priest Hogan [*sic*], Foxe's *Book of Martyrs*, Sister Lucy's *Disclosures of New Hall Convent*, and Doctor Armstrong's *The Confessional Must be Unmasked* — on the back cover of *The Morality of Romish Devotion, Or the Confessional Unmasked*. This latter publication is an 80-page pamphlet, priced one shilling, and circulated by the Protestant Evangelical Mission & Electoral Union in a printing claiming to be its 50th thousand, in January 1869.[9]

Of the Protestant Evangelical Mission & Electoral Union and their publications, I will have more to say. But at this point a number of questions immediately arise, some answers to which are specific to the trade in *erotica*.

Who was the author of the *Flea*? What audience did he have in mind, and what response did he hope for? Can other responses, intended or not, be observed in the history of its reception?

And again, what vicissitudes are works such as his likely to undergo, and with what consequences to the integrity of the text?

It is not known who wrote the *Flea*, and the date of its first publication is conjectural; as is so often the case of a trade in contraband, where "everything with it [is] involved in obscurity, and surrounded with deception".[10] Since the work is not mentioned in Ashbee's *Index Librorum Prohibitorum* (1877), *Centuria Librorum Absconditorum* (1875), or *Catena Librorum Tacendorum* (1885), it is reasonable to assume that it was first published after 1884 or 1885;

---

8. See Pisanus Fraxi (Henry Spencer Ashbee), *Centuria Librorum Absconditorum*, London, 1875. Ashbee's *Centuria* is reproduced as Volume II of the *Encyclopaedia of Erotic Literature*, New York, 1962; Ashbee's comments on and quotations from *Monks and their Maidens* are to be found on pages 149-56 of this edition.

9. A copy [Cup 365.1.47] in the British Library has been annotated by "RS" (almost certainly Robert Steele, secretary to the Society): "PS This pamphlet was first published in Dublin about the year 1835 and was republished in a somewhat different form in 1857." The Introduction, dated December 1868, is corrected in holograph by RS to January 1869.

10. H. Montgomery Hyde, *History of Pornography*, London, 1966, 25.

Montogomery Hyde suggests 1887,[11] as does the British Library catalogue. The author is an educated and often stylish writer. But the assertion on the back cover of the Star Books edition of 1983 that "this ingenious and witty tale has been credited to a renowned English lawyer" seems to offer little more than an inspired guess, not to be found elsewhere. (The front-cover claim of the same edition that it is "An Intimate Memoir of the Victorians at Play" is, of course, nonsensical.)

The production of "*curiosa*", "*erotica*", and works of "*galanterie*" was considerable in the first and second halves of the nineteenth century: in England the output was "prodigious", particularly from 1820 to 1840, and from 1860 onwards, while the authorship was almost exclusively male:

> Extremely little was produced by females. It is true that a considerable portion of erotic publications pretend to be the work of women, who are allegedly recounting their personal experiences, but in many instances the authors are known to be male and in nearly every instance internal evidence points to male authorship.[12]

The *Flea*'s first audience was clearly one of like-minded, and almost certainly male, connoisseurs of *curiosa*: men of some education, and wealthy enough to indulge their interest. The two British Library copies issued under the "Cytheria" imprint are expensively bound, printed on hand-made paper, and stem from editions of ten and twenty respectively. Obviously, the audience for later editions, and particularly for those in paperback, has been a much wider one: compared with what the earliest editions must have cost, the latterday copies are of easy access and relatively cheap.

With many such works — as was certainly the case with the *Flea* — somewhere along the line crudely produced and often fragmentary versions of the original are likely to emerge, recopied — as no doubt was the carbon-copy text I saw in 1945 — surreptitiously and after hours on an office-typewriter: texts literally and inevitably corrupt.

Yet professionally printed and published editions may be no more faithful to an original, for adulteration of the contraband he sells is part of any criminal dealer's game. Hence, despite the claim on its cover

---

11. *Ibid.*, 113.

12. *Ibid.*, 25.

that it is an "authentic and unexpurgated" version of "the Sensational Forbidden Victorian Underground Classic", the 1960? edition of the *Flea* which is my page-reference text has been severely abridged and, while descriptions of incest abound, the many original references to and descriptions of "perversions" (cunnilingus, fellatio, and sodomy among them) have been carefully excised. Here, obviously, there has been a deliberate intention to mislead on the part of the publisher (and a safe one, since the buyer of *his* version is unlikely to know what he has been cheated of).

At any moment, a copyist may choose to enter a contraband text just as, before the enforcement of laws of copyright, plagiarists might enter any text; not only tinkering with words and phrases, but splicing into it passages stolen from elsewhere, or adding material of their own. Indeed, at times the first edition of a supposedly original title may constitute adulterated merchandise from the outset, being itself in part or entirely a gluing-together of plagiarized fragments, translations and back-translations.

If the date and authorship of a proscribed work is uncertain, and its literary provenance dubious, so its chance of physical survival: if offered for sale, it is liable to seizure and destruction by the Police; on an owner's death, it is likely to be destroyed by his executors or heirs.

Or indeed, it may perish at the hands of its satiated and now ashamed reader. We may turn to the diary of Samuel Pepys for the tale of such an outcome:[13]

> 13 January 1668 stopped at Martins, my bookseller, where I saw the French book which I did think to have had for my wife to translate, called "L'escholle des Filles"; but when I came to look into it, it is the most bawdy, lewd book that ever I saw, rather worse than *putana errante* — so that I was ashamed of reading in it ....[14]

But on 8 February he was back at Martin's:

---

13. *The Diary of Samuel Pepys*, eds Robert Latham and William Matthews, *Vol VIII: 1667*, London, 1975, 21-22, 57-59.

14. The work of Michael Millot and Jean L'Ange, *L'Escholle des filles* was first published in Paris in 1655. Millot was condemned and the book was burned. Despite this, further editions followed in 1659, 1667, and 1668. English translations were the subject of prosecutions in 1677, 1688, and 1774-5 (see David Foxon, "Libertine Literature in England, 1660-1745", *The Book Collector*, XII (Spring 1963), 21-36, where extracts from Pepys' text are cited and annotated).

... away to the Strand to my bookseller's, and there staid an hour, and bought that idle, roguish book, *L'escholle des Filles*, which I have bought in plain binding (avoiding the buying of it better bound) because I resolve, as soon as I have read it, to burn it, that it may not stand in the list of books, nor among them, to disgrace them if it should be found.

On the morning of the 9th he read a little:

9 Lord's day ... attending business and also reading a little of *Lescholle des Filles*, a mighty lewd book, but yet not amiss for a sober man once to read over to inform himself in the villainy of the world.

That evening he entertained three friends to dinner:

We sang till almost night, and drank my good store of wine; and then they parted and I to my chamber, where I did read through *L'escholle des Filles*; a lewd book, but what doth me no wrong once to read for information sake (but it did hazer my prick para stand all the while, and una vez to decharger); and after I had done it, I burned it, that it might not be among my books to my shame; and so at night to supper and to bed.

In its offer of an alluring escapist fantasy, pornography invites the reader into a world of make-believe where wishes are instantly granted, where power over others is unlimited, while any price that may have be paid in satiation or remorse can be forgotten in the pleasures of the moment. Fantasies of violence can be acceded to: "in the pornographic fantasy, as in the comic cartoon, one can be destroyed or dismembered without being hurt."[15] In Pornotopia (the word is Steven Marcus's apt coinage), it is always bedtime. The supplies of drink and delicious viands are inexhaustible. Neither beds nor bodies smell of sweat, and both are infinitely accommodating. In Pornotopia, libido knows no limits.

The first, immediate, and certainly sought-for effect is aphrodisiac; the text is an invitation to masturbation, as Pepys's diary makes clear it was for him. A pornographic romance stands in the precisely similar relationship to a treatise on sexual techniques, as culinary writing stands to a book of recipes. It is not analytic, but pragmatic. Charged with emotion, it fleshes out the list of ingredients and the diagrams, and is

---

15. Steven Marcus, *The Other Victorians*, London, 1966, 69.

intended to make the reader's mouth water. In just such a way the Gothic novel invites the reader to empathize an active role within the fantasy, to share the palpitations and the dry mouth and the goose-flesh of a fascinated terror. When both elements run together, as they do in what I call here "Monkish Gothic", and in another sub-genre that I have called elsewhere "Mutiny Gothic",[16] they powerfully combine.

Moreover, being illicit, themselves the immediate object of a voyeuristic quest, documents (as they were for Pepys) to be hidden away once acquired, and given rein to behind locked doors, the pornographic texts become in a sense part of the sin itself and not only the vehicle of the sin. As C.H. Rolph points out: "in so far as the enjoyment of pornography is one form of extra-marital sexual activity the infraction of the laws in obtaining the material is part of the inherent pleasure."[17]

The author of verses which appear on the final page of nineteenth-century editions of the *Flea* (but not since then) takes the narrative beyond the Flea's reminiscences and into an outer, editorial frame. There he envisions a previously modest reader, now "aghast" before the text, yet moved irresistibly by the Flea's recital (the discrete blanks in the text are not mine, but his):

> Aghast the modest reader stands,
> His — firm grasped in both his hands:
> The red blood o'er his visage steals;
> His eyes display the lust he feels;
> His parted lips, his veins on fire,
> Show how a Flea can raise desire;
> With snorting nostrils all aflame,
> He flies to find some willing dame;
> Enters her house,— pays down the "blunt";
> And blind with lust, calls out for —.

And then, uncalled-for but inevitable, post-copulatory or post-masturbatory *tristitia* is at last likely to supervene. After the cries for madder music and stronger wine, and a more frenzied dance of the flesh, the reader's response is quite likely to end, as for Pepys — and as

---

16. "'And to think that Henrietta Guise was in the hands of such human demons!': Ideologies of the Anglo-Indian Novel, 1859-1957", in *Shades of Empire in Colonial and Post-Colonial Literatures*, eds C.C. Barfoot and Theo D'haen, Amsterdam and Atlanta: Ga., 1993.

17. C.H. Rolph, *Does Pornography Matter?*, London, 1962, 35.

indeed the Flea's own memoir does — in a grey awaking into a Dowsonian mood of regret and self-disgust.

Perhaps also into a shudder of distaste for the "hapless innocent", now seen as a cold and alluring succubus, a *Belle Dame sans Merci*. Or perhaps into a mood of pity for *her*, and extrojected loathing of those very assailants with whom the reader has so readily empathized until the moment of detumescence. It is precisely such a response which in "Monkish Gothic" and "Mutiny Gothic" alike can often be seen to be harnessed to a darker purpose.

The act of writing or acquiring a forbidden text is not only likely to be fraught with a delicious sense of danger, to be "horrid" in Isabella Thorpe's sense of the word, but in itself is a deliberate act of rebellion: a fact which official suppression and proscription may attempt to grapple with:

> Since sexual activity and writing of it is a revolt against authority, authority from time to time takes action against the revolt — or else authority is so repressive that revolt is the result .... On the side of literature, too, one can see that the writer becomes increasingly hostile to authority; by the 17th century the writing of sexual licence is linked with explicit attacks on religious and social conventions, and in the 18th century pornography has become obsessed with sexual orgies in religious or pseudo-religious orders, with the attack on the family in the theme of incest, and with the anarchism of de Sade.[18]

Thus it is that, while providing the vehicle for an attack on established moral belief, the traffic in pornography can provide the cash for revolution.[19] Conversely, it may be harnessed to the forces of reaction and suppression, and fuel the hatred of what is seen as an alien creed, or race. "Monkish Gothic" fomented anti-Catholicism; "Mutiny Gothic" offered a potent argument against giving India self-rule. Both sub-genres are worth a moment's consideration.

In the 1850s, the pamphleteers of the Protestant Evangelical Mission & Electoral Union began to intensify their campaign to "maintain the

---

18. David Foxon, "Libertine Literature in England, 1660-1745", *The Book Collector*, 12 (Winter 1963), 303-304.

19. See, on this point, Iain McCalman, *Radical Underworld: Prophets, Revolutionaries, and Pornographers in London, 1795-1840*, Cambridge, 1988.

Protestantism of the Bible and the Liberty of Britain". Their principal and much-publicized aim was to get the Parliamentary grant to Maynooth College of £30,000 a year withdrawn, and to this end they invoked a tradition of anti-clericalism and pornographic horror.

Their pamphlet, *The Confessional Unmasked, showing the Depravity of the Romish Pristhood, the Iniquity of the Confessional and the Questions put to Females in Confession; and exhibiting in part the ATROCITY and ABOMINATIONS of THE TEACHING OF THE GOVERNMENT COLLEGE OF MAYNOOTH*, was first issued in this form from the headquarters of the Protestant Mission & Electoral Union, Strand, London, in 1857. In 1865, a copy was sent to each member of both Houses of Parliament. Ironically, in striving to depict the atrocity and abominations which so much disturbed them, the writers had over-reached themselves, and in 1867 the pamphlet was successfully prosecuted under the Campbell Act. In that same year, it was reissued in an amended version, under the title *The Morality of Romish Devotion, Or The Confessional Unmasked*. It is this edition which carries the advertisements quoted on page 230 above. The revised version was itself to be the subject of further prosecutions. In 1871, George Mackey was prosecuted at Winchester for selling it. In turn, a report of Mackey's trial, in which report *The Morality of Romish Devotion* was reproduced in its entirety, was itself the subject of criminal prosecution. On 30 April 1872, an appeal in the Court of Common Pleas against the order of Sir Thomas Henry, Bow-street Magistrate, for the seizure and destruction of copies of Mackey's trial, was dismissed with costs.[20]

In mounting their attack, the pamphleteers of the Protestant Mission & Electoral Union insisted upon the moral degradation of the Roman Catholic priesthood:

> I now declare most solemnly and seriously, that after twenty-five years in full communion with the Roman Catholic Church, and officiating as a Romish priest, hearing confessions and confessing myself, I know not another reptile in all animal nature so filthy, so much to be shunned, and loathed, and dreaded by females, both married and single, as a Roman Catholic priest or bishop who practises the degrading and demoralizing office of auricular confession.[21]

---

20. See *The Times*, Wednesday, 1 May 1872, and *Pall Mall*, 30 April 1872.

21. Thus the lapsed "Priest Hogan", in *The Confessional Unmasked*, 50th thousand, London, 1867, 37.

And again, an inner-cover advertisement for the Mission & Union's anonymous fourpenny pamphlet, *Doctrines of Christianity and Dogmas of Romanism*, cites an extract from that work:

> A Romish priest ... is a moral Skunk, whose offensive properties and destructive habits make the creature at once an object of dread, loathsomeness, and aversion. He is an embodiment of brute and demon combined in one character, the Cobra that defiles and destroys. He is an unscrupulous *mesmerist*, exposing the nakedness and perverting the faculties of those who put themselves under his influence. He is a most venomous nondescript, and agent of Satan, for transforming men and women into useless or malignant beings.

Here are the elements of a sub-genre which can be traced in part from Boccaccio's satire via Jean Barrin,[22] de Sade, and Monk Lewis, to the revelations of sometime nuns, advertisements for whose memoirs are flown on the cover pages of *The Confessional Unmasked*. The *Disclosures of New Hall Convent,* by the hand of "Sister Lucy", and Maria Monk's *Awful Disclosures ... of the Hotel Dieu Nunnery of Montreal,* in *Monks and their Maidens*, are of a piece, and lie in the same tradition of Monkish Gothic as the *Flea* which, fifty years later, was to follow them:

> ... in a private apartment, he [Father Dufrèsne] treated me in a brutal manner; and from two other priests I afterward received similar usage that evening. Father D. afterward appeared again, and I was compelled to remain in company with him until morning .... The Superior of the Seminary would sometimes come and inform us, that he had received orders from the Pope, to request that those nuns who possessed the greatest devotion and faith, should be requested to perform some particular deeds, which he named or described in our presence, but of which no decent or moral person could ever endure to speak. I cannot repeat what would injure any ear, not debased to the lowest degree. I am bound by a regard to truth, however, to confess,

---

22. *Vénus dans le cloître, ou la religieuse en chemise: Entretiens curieux... par l'abbé du Prat* (1683) is usually ascribed to Barrin. A translation by Robert Samber, under the title *Venus in the Cloister, Or, the Nun in her Smock*, had a wide circulation in England. Its prosecution is recorded in Cobbett's *State Trials*, Volume 17.

that deluded women were found among us, who would comply with those requests.[23]

Maria Monk goes on to a graphic description of how the newborn infants conceived during these orgies were baptized by the Father who was their natural father, and then suffocated by the Mother Superior.

Thus there is a continual inter-traffic between pornography, Gothic horror, and anti-Papism, each feeding the other. Perhaps by the time the *Flea* came to be written, the Monkish setting had become more a matter of convention than significance. But that it should have become so, merely emphasizes how vital an ingredient the imagined horrors of the confessional, the convent and the monastery had become within the Gothic tradition. The effect of the popular prejudices which Monkish Gothic both fed upon and traded in was clear enough to Cardinal John Henry Newman:

> The popular demand is for the prodigious, the enormous, the abominable, the diabolical, the impossible. It must be shown that priests are monsters of hypocrisy, that all nunneries are dens of infamy, that all bishops are the embodied plenitude of savageness and perfidy. Or at least we must have a cornucopia of mummery, blasphemy and licentiousness ... if the great Protestant tradition is to be kept alive in the hearts of the population. The great point in view is to burn into their imagination, by a keen and peremptory process, a sentiment of undying hostility to Catholicism. Who cares for the story itself? it has done its work; time stops for no man; it has created or deepened the impression in the minds of its hearers that a monk commits murder or adultery as readily as he eats.[24]

What of "Mutiny Gothic"?

In the course of the hundred years between 1857 and 1957, at least 87 "Mutiny" novels were to be written by British authors. Novels, that is, in which the writer's plot is centred on events occurring immediately before, during, or immediately after the sepoy rebellions of 1857. The Mutiny theme steadily grew in popularity, reaching its peak around the

---

23. Maria Monk, *Monks and their Maidens*. The passage, among others, is cited in *Centuria Librorum Absconditorum* (*Encyclopaedia of Erotic Literature*, 152).

24. "Lectures on the present condition of Catholics in England: Addressed to the Brothers of the Oratory in the Summer of 1851", *Works*, London, 1913, 140-41.

turn of the century: at least 40 titles first appeared between 1886 and
1903; of those, 21 appeared in the six years between 1893 and 1899.

As the stuff of romance, the Mutiny theme was irresistible, Gothic
of the purest water. If a very few authors strove to take a cool,
historically accurate view — writing, as it were, more in sorrow than in
anger — even in *their* accounts the bias is inevitably towards Gothic
horror. Most practitioners of the genre are less scrupulous. Substituting
paranoid fantasy for historical research, they fill their pages with lurid,
often long-drawn-out accounts of the sepoys' betrayal, the murder and
mutilation of Englishmen, the rape of English women and children and,
with the reassertion of British rule, condign revenge.

The ideological thrust of "Mutiny Gothic" is all too apparent. India,
its climate, its peoples, and their heathen creeds, are equally treacherous
to the white man whose thankless duty it is to govern and convert. Self-
government for these "new-caught, sullen peoples, /Half devil and half
child" (Kipling exactly caught the Imperialist mood of 1899)[25] is a
hopeless and perilous cause, now and in the future. Gothic horror can
be relied upon to strike directly at the reader's emotions, and inner
fears. As in the anti-Catholic cause, a rehearsal of terror is likely to be
powerfully persuasive — both in 1874, seventeen years after the
historical events:

> The secret and long-pent-up hatred of generations and of race,
> caste, creed and colour were there. Their eyeballs gleamed and
> blazed; their white teeth glistened as they ground them; they
> hissed and hooted, yelled and shrieked in the madness of their
> rancour and loathing, the Mohammedan vying with the Hindoo,
> the Bheel, the Kholee, and the Khond, who worship the cattle
> goddess.
>
> And to think that Henrietta Guise was in the hands of these
> human demons![26]

And, half a century later, in 1924:

> ... a perfectly fiendish chuckle here broke in on the speaker as
> the tall, burly figure of the Maharaj rose to its feet with a
> horrible leer. "Yea! Hand her over to me, and I warrant I'll

---

25. "Take up the White Man's Burden" (1899), *Rudyard Kipling's Verse 1885-
1926*, Inclusive Edition, London, 1927.

26. James Grant, "Fairer than a Fairy", *Tinsley's Magazine*, London, 1874,
111-12.

teach her what women were made for! Hand her over — I can
kill her when I've done with her."[27]

And now (as George Orwell remarked of Mickey Spillane's *No
Orchids for Miss Blandish*)[28] for a header into the cesspool.

C. Lestock Reid's *The Masque of Mutiny* was published in 1947,
the year of the Indian Independence Act. In the author's Preface, the
Mahatma Ghandi is pointedly compared with the corrupt and fictional
Brahmin Biji Rao, who will be encountered in the novel:

> Ghandi, though by birth of the Vaisya Caste, made up of
> moneylenders, lawyers and merchants, may be said to have been
> promoted to a kind of honorary Brahmin-hood, to have become
> the Biji-Rao of today: and all the clamour for Swaraj, for
> "democratic elections," Dominion Status and all the rest of it is
> simply a smoke-screen to blind the eyes of the British public and
> the British politicians — as indeed it has — to their true aim, the
> same old unswerving purpose — a Brahmin domination of India,
> which would be autocratic beyond Hitler's wildest dreams ...
>
> To hold and rule India is absolutely essential to our
> continued existence not only as an Empire, but even as a nation.
> We can do so, as the Mutiny abundantly proved — provided we
> do not attempt the impossible task of defeating the Brahmins in
> argument.[29]

But within the novel, it is not argument (however much based on
special pleading) which Reid offers in his last-ditch attempt to frustrate
the cause of Independence, but the invidious special pleading of porno-
Gothic:

> With one jerk he wrenched the baby from her arms, hurled it
> over the rail.
>
> "Here is tender meat for thy skewers."
>
> Half a dozen bayonets were raised, but by some miracle the
> hurtling body evaded them all, fell on the hard-beaten earth of
> the compound where it lay, its tiny limbs jerking spasmodically.
> Instantly the disappointed bayonets were at work, pitching it into
> the air, catching it, tossing it up again, till nothing was left but a

27. Flora Annie Steel, *The Law of the Threshold*, London, 1924, 256.

28. *Collected Essays, Journalism and Letters*, Penguin, 1970, III, 251.

29. *The Masque of Mutiny*, London, 1947, ii.

sodden shapeless bundle abandoned in favour of better sport
(60).

And the white women, the wives and daughters of the
conquerors, while treating him with the cool courtesy due to his
rank, had repelled his mildest advances with a scarcely veiled
contempt that made him writhe. Their words of denial might be
polite, the looks — it was all too obvious to them that he was a
"native," a coloured creature, impossible as a friend,
unthinkable as a lover .... But ah! Their desirability! Their fair,
smooth skins, the spun gold of their hair, the soft swell of their
bosoms, urgent and alluring. He longed to crush their white
bodies to him in ineffable ecstasies, he longed to tear and mangle
their white limbs in unspeakable tortures (87-88).

Gratified by their compliments, rendered generous by satiety and
hatred, he waved a careless hand towards the shrinking group in
the corner.
      "Lo, there are others. I desire them not; they are pale and
passionless .... Take your choice."
      Then, as the men rushed forward he halted them with a
gesture, struck by a sudden, brilliant idea.
      "Nay, not here. Take them into the street. Show to the
world how these accursed *memsahibs* should be treated."
      Howls of applause greeted this monstrous suggestion. Once
more his followers rushed forward; and this time were not
stayed. The pitiable victims were dragged from the house. Some
were almost torn to pieces in the process, for there were far
more men than women. Some, luckier than their sisters, were
dead before they reached the street. But the rest —
      Prince Abool Bukr watched the orgy for a few moments,
sniffing delicately at a flower; he found the contrast of white and
brown limbs, mingling inextricably, writhing in passion of
agony, very stimulating (89).

It would be going beyond the scope of this brief study to assume — as I
believe to be the case — that *every* Gothic novel is characterized by
undercurrents of "horror" which are sexual in origin. Freud was
satisfied that this was so:

      It is easy to establish, whether by contemporary observation or
      by subsequent research, that all comparatively intense affective
      processes, including even terrifying ones, trench upon sexuality
      .... The sexually exciting effect of many emotions which are in
      themselves unpleasurable, such as feelings of apprehension,

fright or horror, persists in a great number of people throughout their adult life. There is no doubt that this is the explanation of why so many people seek opportunities for sensations of this kind, subject to the proviso that the seriousness of the unpleasurable feeling is damped down by certain qualifying facts, such as its occurring in an imaginary world, in a book or in a play.[30]

But that there can be seen to exist at least two sub-genres of Gothic — "Monkish Gothic" and "Mutiny Gothic" — which may usefully be grouped together as "porno-Gothic", both of which have been exploited in the service of political propaganda, seems to me to be indisputable.

---

30. Sigmund Freud, *Three Essays on the Theory of Sexuality* (1905), Penguin, 1977, 123.

THE SPLIT PERSONALITY AND OTHER GOTHIC ELEMENTS IN DAVID LINDSAY'S *A VOYAGE TO ARCTURUS*

WIM TIGGES

The most successful novel by the Scottish author David Lindsay (1876-1945), *A Voyage to Arcturus* (1920),[1] has been variously qualified as science fiction, (metaphysical or symbolical) fantasy, romance, allegory and dream-novel. Its "message" is usually considered to be mysterious if not misty and messy, its style has been designated awkward, amateurish and even appalling. In spite of its lack of canonical status, the book has had a considerable amount of critical discussion devoted to it.[2]

---

1. David Lindsay, *A Voyage to Arcturus*, New York, 1968.

2. For the most substantial of these, see Joanna Russ, "Dream Literature and Science Fiction", *Extrapolation*, 11 (1969), 6-14; John B. Pick et al., *The Strange Genius of David Lindsay*, London, 1970, esp. 45-64; Jack Schofield, "Cosmic Imagery in *A Voyage to Arcturus*", *Extrapolation*, 13 (1972), 146-51; John Derrick McClure, "Language and Logic in *A Voyage to Arcturus*", *Scottish Literary Journal*, 1 (1974), 29-39; Colin Wilson, "Introduction" to David Lindsay, *The Violet Apple* and *The Witch*, Chicago, 1976, 1-18; Eric S. Rabkin, "Conflation of Genres and Myths in David Lindsay's *A Voyage to Arcturus*", *The Journal of Narrative Technique*, 7 (1977), 149-55; Melvin Raff, "The Structure of *A Voyage to Arcturus*", *Studies in Scottish Literature*, 15 (1977), 262-7; Gary K. Wolfe, "Symbolic Fantasy", *Genre*, 8 (1977), 194-209; Kathryn Hume, "Visionary Allegory in David Lindsay's *A Voyage to Arcturus*", *Journal of English and Germanic Philology*, 77 (1978), 72-91; Joy Pohl, "Dualities in Lindsay: A Voyage to Arcturus", *Extrapolation*, 22 (1981), 164-70; Bernard Sellin, *The Life and Works of David Lindsay*, trans. Kenneth Gunnell, Cambridge, 1981, esp. 138-73; Harold Bloom, *Agon: Towards a Theory of Revisionism*, New York and Oxford, 1982, 200-23. See also the excerpts from critical articles and reviews in *Twentieth-Century Literary Criticism*, eds Dennis Poupard and James E. Person Jr., Detroit: Mich, 15 (1985), 215-44. I have been unable to consult *David Lindsay*, ed. Roger C. Schlobin, Starmont Reader's Guide, No. 9, Starmont House, 1982. Further references to these works will be in the text by page number whenever the writer is mentioned, or in the text by surname of writer and page number, or in footnote.

Although it has never, to my knowledge, been discussed in terms of or in connection with the Gothic novel, it has been related to the works of (amongst others) Novalis, Shelley, E.T.A. Hoffmann, Mary Shelley, Thomas Carlyle, Edgar Allan Poe, Lewis Carroll and Walter Pater. On this basis, a possible association with the Gothic genre is at least arguable.

In this paper I will investigate into two thus far neglected aspects of the novel, both derived from or closely related to the Gothic mode. Firstly, I will discuss its relationship with the dialogic novel (along the lines of Mikhail Bakhtin's *Problems of Dostoyevsky's Poetics*)[3] in alignment with the theme of a dream-quest and the prominence of the Split Personality or Double topos. Secondly, I will try to demonstrate the appropriateness of the style to the subject matter.

The very titles of most of Lindsay's six other novels, *The Haunted Woman* (1922), *Sphinx* (1923), *The Adventures of M. Mailly* (1926), *Devil's Tor* (1932), *The Violet Apple* (1976) and *The Witch* (1976), attest to their author's interest in the supernatural and the macabre, as do indeed the contents of these works. Lindsay's thus far most authoritative biographer, Bernard Sellin, does not inform us of Lindsay's interest in or even familiarity with the Gothic tradition,[4] but we are told that his favourite authors were Jules Verne, R.L. Stevenson and H. Rider Haggard, and in particular George MacDonald, the author of such fantasies as *Phantastes* and *Lilith* (51-52). Sellin also records that Lindsay considered Dostoyevsky "perhaps the greatest of all writers" (55). This is of particular relevance in view of the special

---

3. This book originally appeared in 1929 and was reissued in 1963 under the title *Problemy poetiki Dostoevskogo*. In what follows I make use of the new English translation of this second edition by Caryl Emerson: Mikhail Bakhtin, *Problems of Dostoevsky's Poetics*, Minneapolis, 1984, which supersedes the earlier translation by R.W. Rotsel, Ann Arbor, 1973.

4. In discussing Lindsay's works, Sellin does make some concrete references to the Gothic novel. The houses in the novels show "quite distinct architectural features, just as, at the beginning of the 'Gothic novels', the reader is almost invariably confronted with the structure of the castle" (75); moreover, in each case "its name isolates it" (*ibid.*), which could also be said of Starkness in *A Voyage*. Cf. references on 92, 95 (where certain aspects of *Devil's Tor* are compared to the *Mysteries of Udolfo*), 175 (in connection with the Sublime), and 199. Sellin also remarks that "the plots of his books have retained an archaic aspect that is reminiscent of the tradition of the eighteenth-century novel" (176). Rabkin notes that "Maskull's northward journey brings to mind the deadly search of Victor Frankenstein" (155).

position assigned to Dostoyevsky by Mikhail Bakhtin in his famous discussion of the "carnivalesque" type of literature, known more technically as the dialogic novel or menippea. While, in many ways, Lindsay's works can be securely placed within this genre, the question that remains to be addressed is in what way this dialogic mode can be related to the Gothic, a link which is not explicitly made by Bakhtin himself.

First of all, it can be argued that many of the characteristics enumerated by Bakhtin for the menippea are eminently shared by the Gothic: freedom of invention, the depiction of exceptional situations, the relationship of fantasy and symbolism with the world of the sordid (cruelty, sexual perversion, crime, indoctrination and imprisonment, murder and suicide), the struggle between Good and Evil, pleasure and pain, the presence of dreams and of unusual and abnormal moral-psychic human situations, the theme of the double, eccentric or scandalous behaviour and cynical statements, a picaresque shifting of scenes, a mixture of prose styles and of genres, often in the form of the "chinese box" structure of tales within tales, and even humour.

Secondly, it may be helpful to recall Bakhtin's original qualification of the dialogic novel as basically "carnivalesque". William Patrick Day, in his discussion of Gothic fantasy, repeatedly stresses its essentially parodic nature:

> In the space between the worlds of religion and myth and science, between romance and realism, between soul and psyche, between inner and outer life, nineteenth-century readers saw the source of their anxiety and fear, that is, in the failure of religious, scientific, and philosophical systems to create a sense of wholeness and unity in the self and in the world, which would have allowed individuals to define their own existence. The Gothic fantasy occupied this empty space, filled it through parody of these systematic visions that did not quite account for the world, and turned anxiety and fear in that cultural gap into pleasure, articulating and defusing the anxiety and fear that called it into existence. As parody, it could articulate, reflect, invert, but it could not create a mythology of its own. But in its fertile suggestiveness, the Gothic fantasy could be used in the creation of empowering mythologies.[5]

---

5. William Patrick Day, *In the Circles of Fear and Desire: A Study of Gothic Fantasy*, Chicago and London, 1985, 10-11; cf. 13, 59-62.

The point to be taken is that Day's description would seem to cover the dialogic novel in general equally well, and I think that *A Voyage* is to be recognized at once as a "parody" of the real world in this very sense. Just as in the Gothic novel the protagonists are provided with the paraphernalia of medievalism or orientalism by way of carnivalesque "masks" to hide perhaps the emptiness of their inherent vulgarity but perhaps also the too solid flesh of their very real fears and desires, so in *A Voyage* the "mask" plays a vital role.

It need not be emphasized that the skull is a Gothic prop, and that Lindsay's hero has an almost-parodic portmanteau name: Maskull. If carnival is a reversal of everyday life, as it is originally of the mass, so is the Gothic novel, with its reminiscence of the "Black Mass".

A major motif in both Gothic and dialogic modes is that of the Double. Day, however, calls the Double "a central motif in the genre" (76). Its relationship with the dialogic novel is that the dialogue is an externalized form of an internal dichotomy or *aporia*, and as such it enables its author to multiply split-offs or doubles of the protagonist in a manner which can be traced back to medieval romance.[6] There, however, the "dialogue" remains largely on a symbolic level, as indeed it often does in the Gothic novel, whereas the dialogic novel distinguishes itself mainly by raising the dualities to a more abstract and philosophical level.[7]

To some extent the artistry of *A Voyage* lies in the fact that the symbolic representation of dialogic or dialectic attitude is partly retained. Arcturus itself is presented as a double star system (27), which is astronomically incorrect, and, as Schofield has noted, "the double protagonist parallels the double star".[8] Maskull and Nightspore, the primary Double in the novel, enter it simultaneously (17), and when Maskull dies, Nightspore at once reappears and assumes Maskull's identity. Whenever Maskull and Nightspore are together as separate

---

6. Unambiguous examples of the Double in Middle English literature are Floris and Blauncheflour and Eger and Grime in their eponymous romances, the Green Knight and Sir Bertilak de Hautdesert in *Sir Gawain and the Green Knight*, Palamon and Arcite in Chaucer's "Knight's Tale", and many more examples could be adduced. Readings from Freudian and particularly Jungian points of view have revealed interesting insights into this matter.

7. Cf. Alice, who likes to play at being two persons in Carroll's *Alice's Adventures in Wonderland*, and the way the narrator's soul "Joe" splits off from the protagonist in Flann O'Brien's *The Third Policeman*.

8. Schofield, 147-48; see also Pohl, 165.

characters, Krag, who informs Maskull early on that "Nightspore and I
are old friends" (24), is never far off, as in the vision Maskull has in
the Wombflash Forest of himself, Krag and Nightspore marching in line
to the drum taps of Surtur (153-54). Already at Starkness, Maskull tells
Nightspore: "I'm beginning to regard you as a second Krag" (34). He
is himself more closely associated with the despised and vulgar
Crystalman, whose grin he assumes when Krag strangles him as the
apparition at the seance (22) — as it turns out later, Krag hereby
actually sends Maskull back into Tormance, where the woman Tydomin
was threatening to kill him and assume his gender (122-23). In the
"double" account of this event, Lindsay introduces the dualities of
apparition and reality, of time and space, and of male and female, all of
which are well-known Gothic features.

The complementarity of Krag-Surtur and Crystalman-Shaping can
thus be seen as being closely related to that of Nightspore and Maskull
— as Krag tells Maskull when the latter is about to die: "You are
Nightspore", so he also informs Nightspore immediately afterwards:
"Maskull was his [Crystalman's], but Nightspore is mine" (277).

The dualities in *A Voyage* have been aptly discussed by Pohl and
more succinctly by Sellin (109-13). That these dualities are particularly
appropriate in *A Voyage* is confirmed by Robert Rogers's assertion that
"decomposition tends to occur wherever an artist feels moved, however
unconsciously, to depict Manichean extremes of good and evil within a
single personality".[9] The decomposition that takes place in *A Voyage*
is, however, of the most complex kind. In fact, we have all the varieties
that are distinguished by Rogers. The first of these is the "Mirror
Image", which occurs when Maskull sees himself externalized, first as
an apparition at the seance, then in the vision in Wombflash Forest after
Dreamsinter has given him a disagreeably tasting nut to eat, and finally
when he has become Nightspore and sees Maskull's dead body on
Gangnet's raft. Secondly, Maskull and Nightspore are examples of the
"Secret Sharer" type of decomposition, with Maskull as the "monster"
to Nightspore-Krag's "Frankenstein", and thirdly Krag and Crystalman
are implementations of the "Opposing Self", the double as a set of
mutual enemies. In addition, Rogers's distinction between subject and
object decomposition is present as well: Maskull and Nightspore are
split-offs of one subjective character, the two sides of the omnipresent
protagonist, whereas the Crystalman-Surtur double is experienced by
this protagonist as an object division (albeit only to the extent that they

---

9. Robert Rogers, *A Psychoanalytic Study of the Double in Literature*, Detroit,
1970, 46.

are not themselves equated with the decomposition of the protagonist). That the object division is a "divine" set is appropriate in view of Rogers's argument that "most object doubles are parent figures" (110). The relationship between Krag-Surtur and Maskull-Nightspore-Crystalman is indeed that between father and son. Krag is both Maskull's (mostly absent) guide and his killer (in the Wombflash Forest vision he stabs Maskull in the back).

Harold Bloom, whose reading of *A Voyage* is a Gnostic one, sees the quaternio of Maskull, Nightspore, Crystalman, and Krag as that of the Freudian libido, id, superego and achieved ego respectively.[10] Bloom assumes that the outcome of the quest in *A Voyage* is psychologically satisfactory, but I doubt whether this is true. After all, Nightspore's conclusive remark to Krag after his final vision is "The struggle is hopeless", and in the concluding sentence of the novel Krag and Nightspore proceed "into darkness" (287). It would, moreover, be possible to read *A Voyage* as a "deconstruction" of the superego in the shape of the various Tormantians and their philosophies. That Lindsay does not in the end provide us with a very clear resolution is confirmed by C.N. Manlove, who writes that the novel "set[ting] out to show all the pleasures of life as empty and corrupt, does so through a series of images so vivid, striking and abundant that the impression at least equally conveyed is a love of creation".[11]

As in most Gothic novels, the writing of *A Voyage* undercuts what it suggests is its own philosophy — that reality is illusionary and of a lower order. In *A Voyage*, the effect of this is to create a strong overtone of agony, a word which is etymologically derived from the Greek "agon", meaning "struggle". The aesthetic value of *A Voyage* lies, in my opinion, not so much in the outcome of the struggle, or even in its nature, but in the way Lindsay has "masked" it by means of the style he applies. It is in his choice of mode that the influence of the Gothic upon Lindsay becomes particularly evident.

An important duality in *A Voyage* is the "male/female dichotomy", and another vital one is that of pleasure and pain.[12] Both complexes

---

10. Bloom, 214.

11. C.N. Manlove, *The Impulse of Fantasy Literature*, London, 1983, 14.

12. About the male/female dichotomy see Pohl, 166. About the dichotomy pleasure/pain, in his *Philosophical Notes* Lindsay wrote: "the Sublime is split into pleasure and pain" (quoted in Sellin, 187). This is perhaps the reason why Joiwind survives, since for her, as for the archetypal mother, pleasure and pain are inseparable.

have been regarded as typical of the Gothic novel as well. In allowing Day to speak for Gothic fantasy's basic concerns, we can see at once where the relationships lie. "The pattern of all relationships in the Gothic fantasy", he argues, "operates on the dynamic of sadomasochism. One asserts one's power either by inflicting or enduring pain, or both" (19). A few pages before, this argument began on the premiss that "the Gothic world cannot allow for a character who is both capable of significant action and truly heroic" (16) — and indeed Maskull is never the initiator of his adventures so much as the plaything of circumstances. His "success", if it can be called that, is frequently said to be a matter of "luck" (see 67, 159, 205, 230). Maskull, who is forced to make moral decisions or to arrive at moral insights each of which subsequently turns out to be an illusion of Crystalman, is indeed the "ambiguous, egocentric, self-destructive antihero" of Day's account rather than the romantic quest-hero of pre-Gothic fantasy. The Gothic hero,

> a version of the Faust character, an overreacher seeking power, pleasure, even godhood ... always enters the Gothic world of his own free will, even though he surely does not understand what he is getting into. His attempt to assert his power leads him to this world, and his actions there lead to his destruction (Day, 17).

"Most important, though", Day continues,

> is the fact that the protagonist is always alone. The fantasy defines its world as a place where there exists one self; everything else in that world is Other, an enemy to the desires and integrity of the self, whether that self wishes to become a god or simply to escape and get married. Everything and everyone else conspire against the protagonist, and victimization and isolation are the central features of both the masculine and the feminine self in the Gothic fantasy (19).

The hero's submission to events, which he only imagines he can influence but in reality passively suffers (see Sellin, 150), reminds one once again of the protagonists of Carroll's *Alice* books and O'Brien's *The Third Policeman*. Sellin repeatedly characterizes Maskull as "ingenuous" (155, 164, 165), and his plight is indeed not much different from that of Alice or of O'Brien's nameless narrator, both whose Wonderlands are ultimately ruled by the exigencies of language. Staggered by the thought "that he was a man of destiny ... that he could not be here for his own purposes, but must be here for an end" (79), Maskull also discovers that he is "a slave to words", as Tydomin tells him (130). Later on he wonders: "But what is luck — a verbal expression, or a thing?" (159), and he tells Polecrab that "reality and falseness are two words for the same thing" (165). "Anything can be said in this place and it will be true and will have to be believed", the nameless narrator in *The Third Policeman* realizes.[13] "To be a free man", Krag tells Maskull shortly before the latter's death, "one must have a universe of one's own" (266), but even Nightspore must share Muspel with Krag.

Just as in *Alice's Adventures in Wonderland* and *Through the Looking-Glass* survival is reduced to a matter of eating or being eaten and playing or being played with, so in *A Voyage* the protagonist often finds himself having to destroy or absorb his opponents' identities or be destroyed or absorbed himself. The nature-worshipping and pure Joiwind may appear to be an altruistic and beautiful person, but her self-sacrifice in sharing Maskull's "awful blood" (40) just after his arrival makes her into a demanding mother-figure who extorts a promise Maskull will never be able to keep, "never to raise your hand against a living creature, either to strike, pluck, or eat, without first recollecting its mother, who suffered for it" (75). Putting this super-egoistic moral bond on Maskull she ironically undercuts her own pious assertion that she does not have children of her own because she prefers loving all to loving some (57). Maskull, however, instead of promising as she desires, promises never to lift his hand against a living creature without first recollecting her (75), thereby turning the pledge into a sexual one, as Joiwind does not fail to recognize. Needless to say, Maskull never once gives evidence of recalling this vow, except possibly when he "sorbs" Joiwind's brother Digrung, thus indirectly introducing the common Gothic motif of incest. Actually, what he wants from Digrung is concealment of his misdeeds from Joiwind, which Digrung refuses to agree to (116-20).

A Voyage to Arcturus is Gothic also in its protagonist's relationship to the world he finds himself in; Day speaks of a "state of enthralment, first to the possibilities of the Gothic world, then to its horrors" (23), which is precisely what befalls Maskull. "The vision of the Gothic world", he goes on to say, "evokes in the protagonist both fear and desire" (23), and this leads him to conclude that "the descent into the Gothic underworld becomes a descent into the self in which the

---

13. Flann O'Brien, *The Third Policeman*, London, 1976, 86.

protagonists confront their own fears and desires and are transformed, metamorphosed, doubled, fragmented, and destroyed by this encounter. However, the conventions of the genre always externalize this process, presenting the psychic experience of the protagonists in terms of their encounters with exotic places, creatures, and events" (27),[14] precisely, I would say, Maskull's plight. Another striking correspondence lies in the illusionary nature of the protagonist's actions, a point hammered by Day: "Action can never be progressive, only circular" (44). Using *Melmoth the Wanderer* by way of illustration, Day also enlarges upon the juxtaposition of viewpoints and the "multiplicity of voices" in the Gothic novel, whose narrative structure is "not a sequence of actions, but a sequence of stories" (47). Although this "Chinese boxes" structure of the Gothic novel is not so prominent in *A Voyage*,[15] it is not entirely absent either. Early on in the novel we are given "Panawe's Story" (68), and the apparition at the seance is curiously connected to events in a cave on Tormance some hundred pages later.

To summarize, then, *A Voyage* shares with the Gothic fantasy major conventions such as the Faustian hero, the use of the Double, the supernatural, transformation and metamorphosis, and the use of remote and exotic setting (Day, 198, n.4). The question that remains to be addressed is to what extent these Gothic motifs of agony enhance the aesthetic quality of *A Voyage*. Putting on the agony, has Lindsay also succeeded in putting on the style? If one is to go by the judgment of earlier critics, the outcome would appear to be negative, as they unanimously appear to agree with Krag's cynical remark that "there's nothing worth seeing on Tormance" (263). Joanna Russ, whose article is presumably the first to appear after the 1968 paperback reissue of *A Voyage*, sets the tone, using a phrase from Lindsay's admirer C.W. Lewis in her epitaph: "the style is appalling".[16] Already in 1940 and 1947 Lewis had referred to Lindsay's style as lacking "sound taste in language" and "often laughably crude". An outspoken despiser of Lindsay's novel, Brigid Brophy, called it "aesthetically of the same

---

14. Cf. 177: "the Gothic fantasy is the expression of the fears and desires created, but unacknowledged by conventional culture."

15. But cf. Wilson (1976, 11): "it [*A Voyage*] is a masterpiece — in form as well as content, being constructed like a series of Chinese boxes, one inside the other."

16. Russ, 6. References in the following lines are to Lewis, quoted in Poupard and Person, 217; Brophy, 218; Wilson, in Pick, 35, and Wilson, 5; McClure, 37, 37-38, 33.

order as an embryo pickled in a bottle". Colin Wilson, who in 1970 called the style of *A Voyage* "stiff and awkward" in 1976 adds that it is the work of "a genuinely incompetent writer". McClure, however, argues that its "oddities" are intentional and concludes by asking his readers: "would it not have been a gross inconsistency if a book which suggests that all pleasures are delusions and traps had been written with grace and elegance?". His suggestion that Lindsay "deludes the reader ... into thinking that he has heard something very profound", apart from coming very close to the intentional fallacy, hardly renders Lindsay a good service, and one would almost prefer the judgment of Harold Bloom, who advises the reader to "try to imagine *Through the Looking Glass* as it might have been written by Thomas Carlyle, and you will not be far from the verbal cosmos of David Lindsay" (201).

One could, of course, retort to all this by stating that everything that can be held against Lindsay's style can be held *a fortiori* against the styles of Walpole, Mrs Radcliffe and Maturin, to mention only a few distinguished Gothic novelists. In Maskull, I would argue, Lindsay has created a literary character who remains "true to his own self". The means to this end are largely stylistic. Maskull's first three utterances are questions, the first one a counter-question to Krag, who at the seance asks Maskull about the apparition: "Wouldn't you like to see the land where this sort of fruit grows wild?" (22). Maskull retorts: "What sort of fruit?", without realizing that the apparition is Maskull himself on Tormance. It has been noted that the fruit-image recurs throughout the novel, setting a Miltonic tone without labouring it.[17] Nightspore, Maskull's double, "consumed by an intense spiritual hunger" (18), is repeatedly described as biting or gnawing his nails or his lip (see 18, 34, 278, 279, 283). Maskull's dying words are again a question, the last of three: "Who are you?", he asks Krag (277), echoing his second question at the seance: "Who are you, and how did you come here?" (23).

Lindsay's naming is admitted to be "brilliant" even by Russ (11). With characteristic modesty, he makes Joiwind declare: "I don't think our names are very poetic, but they follow nature" (51). Being English-based portmanteaux, they create a simultaneous effect of familiarity and alienation. Tormance, the name of Arcturus's planet, is undoubtedly a composite of "torment" and "romance", heterogeneous ideas yoked together, to indicate duality and agony. Similarly, names like Joiwind

---

17. For a reference to the influence of Milton on Lindsay, see Visiak in Pick *et al.*, 1970, 101. For the reference to the fruit-symbolism in *A Voyage*, see Hume, 1979, 80.

and Corpang express what their bearers stand for without completely solving the riddle of their identity.

The descriptive style of *A Voyage* is not so much awkward or stiff as precise and clinical, which creates an appropriately "agonistic" distance between what is observed and how it is observed.

A scene on Tormance must serve as example:

> The man led him a little way into the forest, and walked straight up to a certain tree. At a convenient height in its trunk a hole had been tapped and plugged. Polecrab removed the plug and put his mouth to the aperture, sucking for quite a long time, like a child at its mother's breast. Maskull, watching him, imagined that he saw his eyes growing brighter.
>
> When his own turn came to drink, he found the juice of the tree somewhat like coconut milk in flavor, but intoxicating. It was a new sort of intoxication, however, for neither his will nor his emotions were excited, but only his intellect — in a certain way. His thoughts and images were not freed and loosened, but on the contrary kept laboring and swelling painfully, until they reached the full beauty of an *aperçu*, which would then flame up in his consciousness, burst, and vanish. After that, the whole process started over again. But there was never a moment when he was not perfectly cool, and master of his senses. When each had drunk twice, Polecrab replugged the hole, and they returned to their bank (162).

Not only does this description catch the tone of wonder appropriate to a new experience, it also serves to elucidate, by means of the child-imagery, the nature of an *aperçu*. Moreover, the images are not isolated. In a much later scene, where Maskull has a discussion on the nature of love with Sullenbode, with whom he has a brief love-affair, he says: "Love is a strong drink. Perhaps it is too strong for human beings. And I think that it overturns our reason in different ways" (257). At first sight, nothing could be more trite and sentimental, and the additional information that Maskull has somewhat earlier loosened his inhibitions by drinking "raw spirit" in Haunte's cavern does not change this impression. However, when we realize that already at Starkness Maskull had been finishing off a bottle of whisky, and that the "gnawl water" on Tormance has a buoyant effect on his personality, we may begin to see how Lindsay, rather than trying to formulate the ineffable or leaving the reader entirely in the dark by the use of empty formulas, simply has his hero express his emotions and thoughts in terms of the familiar. At the beginning of the same conversation with Sullenbode, Maskull had said about love that it is "restlessness —

unshed tears — thoughts too grand for our souls to think..." and "too wonderful a thing to remain uncompleted" (257). By toning down the way he does, he is made to show a sense of reality which is more admirable than Sullenbode's suggestion that love "is completed by anguish". The whole scene is at once romantic and moving, and disillusioning — a scene, in fact, of agony, which is adequately supported by style.

"AN IMMENSE SNAKE UNCOILED": H. RIDER HAGGARD'S HEART OF DARKNESS AND IMPERIAL GOTHIC

BART WESTERWEEL

It may be something of an exaggeration but it is not far off the mark to suggest that the reasons for the exclusion of H. Rider Haggard from the canon of English literature and those for incorporating Conrad are uncomfortably similar. F.R. Leavis conveniently summarized a particular critical response to Conrad in a passage explaining why he (Leavis) was prevented by a sense of exasperation from writing an announced article that was to be entitled "Conrad, the Soul and the Universe":

> [Conrad] has, of course, long been generally held to be among the English masters; the exasperation records a sense that the greatness attributed to him tended to be identified with an imputed profundity, and that this "profundity" was not what it was taken to be, but quite other, and the reverse of a strength.

What had discouraged Leavis from writing the proposed article was a note on Conrad by E.M. Forster, quoted by Leavis:

> These essays do suggest that he [Conrad] is misty in the middle as well as at the edges, that the secret casket of his genius contains a vapour rather than a jewel; and that we needn't try to write him down philosophically, because there is, in this direction, nothing to write. No creed, in fact. Only opinions, and the right to throw them overboard when facts make them look absurd. Opinions held under the semblance of eternity, girt with the sea, crowned with stars, and therefore easily mistaken for a creed.[1]

In *The Great Tradition* Leavis uses *Heart of Darkness* (1899) as a witness for the prosecution. What Leavis blames Conrad for — the lesser Conrad, that is — is that he borrowed

---

1. F.R. Leavis, *The Great Tradition* (1948), Penguin, 1962, 192-93.

the arts of the magazine-writer (who has borrowed his, shall we say, from Kipling and Poe) in order to impose on his readers and on himself, for thrilled response, a "significance" that is merely an emotional insistence on the presence of what he can't produce. The insistence betrays the absence, the willed "intensity" the nullity. He is intent on making a virtue out of not knowing what he means. The vague and unrealizable, he asserts with a strained impressiveness, is the profoundly and tremendously significant ....

"Consider, for instance, how *Heart of Darkness* is marred", Leavis pronounces to the court (where he serves conveniently as both prosecutor and judge).[2]

What Leavis admires in Conrad's masterpiece is the "overpowering evocation of atmosphere" by means of "objective correlatives" in the "details and circumstances of the voyage to and up the Congo", but he objects strongly to the "adjectival and worse than supererogatory insistence on 'unspeakable rites', 'unspeakable secrets', 'monstrous passions', 'inconceivable mystery' and so on", where these phrases do not seem to be attached to anything experienced by the narrator of the story or to contribute significantly to the tone of the narrative.[3]

The aspects of Conrad's fiction that Forster and Leavis object to thus strongly will be readily recognized by students of the Gothic mode in literature as combining some of its basic ingredients: *horror* and *mystery*. In G.R. Thompson's succinct but lucid description of these terms in Gothic discourse *horror* suggests "the perception of something incredibly evil or morally repellent", while *mystery* suggests "something beyond this, the perception of a world that stretches away beyond the range of human intelligence — often morally incomprehensible — and therefore productive of a nameless apprehension that may be called religious dread in the face of the wholly *other*.[4] The horror, it should be added, is embedded in an aesthetic based on pleasurable fear.[5]

"Morally incomprehensible", "nameless apprehension": it is not surprising that a great critic writing an important book on the major

---

2. *Ibid.*, 199.

3. *Ibid.*, 194, 198.

4. *The Gothic Imagination: Essays in Dark Romanticism*, ed. and introd. G.R. Thompson, Washington DC, 1974, 3.

5. See Eve Kosofsky Sedgwick, *The Coherence of Gothic Conventions*, New York, 1980, rpt. 1986, 11.

English novelists (Jane Austen, George Eliot, Henry James, Joseph Conrad) has little patience with those aspects of one of these canonized authors that would put him in a less formidable category, on a par with Mrs Radcliffe, Poe, Stevenson, Kipling and Rider Haggard. As Thompson points out:

> ... classic works of fiction which employ Gothic conventions and subjects ... tend not to be critically examined in the tradition of a developing Gothic mode but in some other, more acceptable tradition of the novel (1).

What Thompson calls the kind of high Gothic as represented by such novels as *Moby Dick*, is the "embodiment of demonic-quest romance, in which a lonely, self-divided hero embarks on insane pursuit of the Absolute" (2).

Whereas in the case of Conrad important aspects of his style are dismissed for their anomalous and low-brow nature in an otherwise high-brow aesthetic and moral context, H. Rider Haggard never attained the status of a serious writer, largely because of the Gothic nature of his romantic tales of adventure, notably the most popular of them all, *She* (1887).

In view of what was said before it is interesting to note that one of the earliest critical responses to Rider Haggard's bestseller is based on similar critical assumptions as those of Forster and Leavis regarding Conrad. Criticizing the uneven style in which passages of sublime grandeur alternate with "ill-timed touches of flippancy", the journalist writes:

> A style alternately flat and flamboyant, cheap philosophy, shallow sentiment .... If Dante had been accompanied on his tour through the "città dolente" by a special correspondent of the *Daily Telegraph*, the result would have been just such a book as "She".[6]

At this point a brief account of the main events of this "dread tale", called by Haggard himself a "History of Adventure", is in order. The narrator of the story is Horace Holly, a solitary Cambridge scholar and misogynist — "he was popularly supposed to be as much afraid of a woman as most people are of a mad dog", physically very strong and

---

6. *Pall Mall Gazette*, No. 6802, 4 Jan. 1887, 5; quoted in H. Rider Haggard, *She*, ed. Daniel Karlin, Oxford, 1991, xviii.

extremely ugly. The first we hear of him he is said to be "shortish, rather bow-legged, very deep chested, and with unusually long arms" (2). When one adds to the list of Holly's attractions the dark hair covering most of his face and the small-set eyes it comes as no surprise that the Editor of the story compares him with a gorilla. Holly becomes guardian of Leo Vincey, the only son of his one friend. Leo is the exact counterpart of Holly. He is very goodlooking, tall, his head "was covered with little golden curls growing close to his scalp" (1) and he is as much attracted to the opposite sex as they are by him. His graceful demeanour is compared with that of a wild stag. When Leo comes of age he is allowed to open the casket his father left him. It contains a scarab, a potsherd covered with inscriptions and a number of manuscripts, all of which are dutifully reproduced in the book. The potsherd was manufactured and inscribed by Haggard's sister-in-law, and Sir John Evans, the antiquary, commented on its quality: "All I can say is that it might *possibly* have been forged." The Greek inscription was composed by Haggard's former headmaster. To the one and a half page long inscription in uncial Greek Haggard adds, for "general convenience in reading", a transcription into the cursive character and a complete translation into English. Other inscriptions on the sherd, in medieval Latin and its black-letter English translation, were produced by a committee member of the Norfolk and Norwich Archaeological Society.[7] The sherd and the manuscripts trace back Leo's family history to an Egyptian priest of Isis — "though he was of Greek extraction" (10) — who was called Kallikrates ("the beautiful-in-strength"). Kallikrates broke his vows of celibacy and fled with his bride to the coast of what today is called Mozambique. Leo's family name Vincey means "avenger", appropriate because Kallikrates was murdered by a powerful and beautiful white Queen of an African tribe, who had fallen in love with him and was jealous of his married state. This mysterious Queen knows the secret of Life and has reigned over her people for more than two thousand years, hiding her unaging beauty behind a veil. This is where the story proper begins.

Leo and Holly go on a revenge-quest to Africa, accompanied by their servant Job; on their arrival they are nearly killed by the Amahaggar tribe, whose custom it is to place red-hot pots upon the

---

7. I derive the information about the origins of the artefacts from Karlin's highly useful notes (321-23). The emphasis on knowledge and learning in general and Cambridge University in particular may perhaps be explained partly by the fact that H. Rider Haggard, the eighth of ten children, was considered to be the family dunce, according to his father. He never went to university.

heads of strangers. They are conveyed to the caves of Kôr, where they meet the mysterious queen: Ayesha or She-Who-Must-Be-Obeyed.[8] While Leo is fighting an almost fatal illness, Holly is allowed into the private quarters of Ayesha and when she unveils herself for him he falls hopelessly in love with her. His love is not returned, however, because Ayesha cures Leo and recognizes in him the reincarnation of Kallikrates and a reward for her patience in waiting twenty centuries for his return. After several adventures involving visits to a ruined city and underground tombs adorned with thousands of mummies, prepared with some highly inflammable substance and therefore serving for torches on festive occasions, Holly is allowed by Ayesha to look into the "seeds of time" in the magical basin of water kept in her bedchamber.

Holly, Leo and Job are then taken by Ayesha on a perilous journey to an underground cavern, where they see the Pillar of Life, a revolving column of fire. Ayesha tries to persuade Leo to enter the flames and thus gain eternal life and youth and, to demonstrate that the fire is harmless, she steps into it first. To the horror of the three men she loses her beauty, and dies after a few moments of agony, an aged woman, shrunk and shrivelled up like "a hideous little monkey frame" (295).[9]

With a superhuman effort Holly and Leo manage to regain the upper world of ordinary life, shattered and transformed by their experience. So much for the story of this "History of Adventure".

The book was and is a bestseller. It was filmed eleven times and Rider Haggard records in his diary that the movie made by H. Lisle Lucoque, starring Alice Delysia and first shown in February 1916, had attracted nearly two million people by 5 June of that year.[10]

The book has been interpreted in many different ways. Carl Jung saw it as a striking example of the anima concept and cites it as a representative instance of an "extroverted" or ignorantly intuitive myth. Leo Michael regarded it as a religious allegory; Sandra Gilbert and Susan Gubar place it in the tradition of the *femme fatale* and as a combination of the colonial pessimism of the late nineteenth century

---

8. In his autobiography, Haggard tells us with some relish that in the Haggard household there was a doll called She-who-must-be-obeyed, kept in a nursery cupboard to frighten the brothers and sisters (see Karlin, xxii).

9. It is noteworthy that Holly and Ayesha, the two most intelligent characters in the novel, are both described by the monkey metaphor. It reflects Haggard's response to Darwinian theory.

10. See Karlin, xiv, and D.S. Higgins, *The Private Diaries of Sir H. Rider Haggard, 1914-1925*, London, 1980, 65.

with male dread of female domination. Alan Sandison and Wendy Katz studied the novel in the context of British imperial fiction, although their respective books are not in agreement as to Haggard's place in that tradition.[11]

I would like to approach the novel from a slightly different angle, that of Imperial Gothic, a term suggested by a chapter in Patrick Brantlinger.[12] It is difficult not to notice the Gothic elements in Haggard's novel. They surface on virtually every page of the book and extend to every novelistic aspect. In characterization there is the idea of the split personality, exemplified in Holly and Leo Vincey. The first time we encounter them they are walking arm in arm on the streets of Cambridge. Although Leo is ostensibly the hero of the book, we should not forget that the narrative focus is with Holly. Holly maintains firm control over the language in which Leo is presented to us. Leo is to a large extent Holly's creation and the latter takes care not to be outdone by his pupil. Holly has considerable intellectual powers and Leo is said by Holly to be "brilliant and keen-witted but not a scholar" (21). But the lines Leo gets to say in the book are slightly inane and more often than not of a "By golly, uncle Holly" kind. As Daniel Karlin puts it, "Leo is represented with relentless consistency as a dumb blond", while Holly is "in charge of the production" (xxvi). During many of the most awe-inspiring events in the book Leo is either ill or asleep, and even in hunting, the male sport *par excellence*, Leo misses an easy target and is outdone by his guardian. All in all, Leo's passivity and vulnerability are emphasized, also in his relations with Ayesha, the dominating, active and destructive anti-heroine. Leo's relationship with Ayesha represents some of the Victorian male's deepest fears: the roles of the Beauty and the Beast are played by the two male protagonists and both are made subservient to a powerful female.

Let us quickly survey some of the other Gothic elements: there are the reflecting surfaces of the basin in Ayesha's chamber and the mirror in Holly's bachelor room at Cambridge. There is Ayesha's subterranean

---

11. Carl Jung, *The Development of the Personality*, trans. R.F.C. Hull; *Collected Works*, XVII, London, 1954; Leo Michael, *She: An Allegory of the Church*, New York, 1889; Sandra M. Gilbert and Susan Gubar, *No Man's Land*, vol. 2: *Sexchanges*, New Haven and London, 1989; Alan Sandison, *The Wheel of Empire: A Study of the Imperial Idea in Some Late Nineteenth and Early Twentieth-Century Fiction*, London, 1967; Wendy R. Katz, *Rider Haggard and the Fiction of Empire: A Critical Study of British Imperial Fiction*, Cambridge, 1987.

12. Patrick Brantlinger, *Rule of Darkness: British Literature and Imperialism, 1830-1914*, Ithaca, 1988, 227-74.

abode and the ruined city as reflections of her mythical existence; there are objects of the past influencing the present. There is the monomyth of an ancient culture giving meaning to the meaningless materialism of late nineteenth-century civilization.[13]

The myth of Isis and Osiris is present in the killing of Kallikrates, and the unveiling of Ayesha recalls the influential book by Madame Blavatsky: *Isis unveiled* (1877). The influence of the Cambridge school of mythography that produced Frazer's *The Golden Bough* (1890) is noticeable, for instance, in the contrast between the underworldly life of dark-haired Ayesha (very unlike Ursula Andress in the Hammer Film of *She* of 1965, who is what some people still dare to call a stunning blonde and who for obvious reasons is seen unveiled right from the start) and Leo, whose beauty and golden curls make him a sun god of the upper world. He is called "the Greek god" in the book while Holly who helps Leo to reach Ayesha's underworld is appropriately called "Charon" (2). Analysed from a Jungian perspective this explicitly chthonic (underworld) element is symbolic of the spiritual transcendence that the union between Leo and Ayesha is supposed to bring about.[14]

As will become clear below there are more reasons to allow for a psychological reading of this kind. And there is the non-referential discourse in which what is *not* said, what is *not* understood, contains as much truth or a higher truth than can be attained by the rational mind.[15]

Mystification and amazement accompany the traveller on his way into the unfathomable and unknowable regions of the spirit and of his subconscious fears and desires. There is, finally, the strange mixture of high idealism and low impulses, of the celestial and the infernal, that

---

13. See Barton Levi St Armand, "The 'Mysteries' of Edgar Poe: The Quest for a Monomyth in Gothic Literature", in Thompson, 64-93.

14. See Carl G. Jung, *Man and His Symbols*, London, 1964, 154 ff. The term "chthonic" is used extensively throughout Camille Paglia's *Sexual Personae*, New York, 1991, and defined by her as "a substitute for Dionysian": "What the west represses in its view of nature is the chthonian, which means 'of the earth' — but earth's bowels, not its surface" (5).

15. Leaving things unsaid or half-said is also, of course, a convenient ploy, if one wants to write, as Haggard did, a popular novel in six weeks.

makes the characters experience a "mysterium tremendum", that fills the mind "with blank wonder and astonishment".[16]

This last aspect, the mixture of lofty ideals and unholy desires, is but one of the elements that makes a comparison between *She* and *Heart of Darkness* a useful undertaking. And, once the Gothic framework is recognized as a common denominator for both books, however different they are in other respects, many more likenesses leap to the eye. As we saw before, Conrad, like Haggard, uses the language of mystification. This is the way Marlow describes the agony of Kurtz's soul: "I saw the inconceivable mystery of a soul that knew no restraint, no faith, and no fear, yet struggling blindly with itself",[17] and this is how Holly spies on Ayesha like a true voyeur: "... the agony, the blind passion, and the awful vindictiveness displayed upon those quivering features, and in the tortured look of the upturned eyes, were such as surpass my powers of description" (163); when he returns to his own quarters "along the pitch-dark passage", Holly felt that he had seen "a vision of a Soul in Hell" (166). The passage reminds one of Marlow's fascination with the mysterious black woman the search party encounter at the edge of the river:

> Her long shadow fell to the water's edge. Her face had a tragic and fierce aspect of wild sorrow and of dumb pain mingled with the fear of some struggling, half-shaped resolve .... Suddenly she opened her bared arms and threw them up rigid above her head, as though in an uncontrollable desire to touch the sky, and at the same time the swift shadows darted out on the earth, swept around on the river, gathering the steamer into a shadowy embrace (103).

When the steamer leaves, with Kurtz on board, the woman is the last figure seen by Marlow:

---

16. Cf. a passage in *Private Diaries*, where Haggard is considering writing another sequel to *She* : "I had thought of some celestial — or infernal — scenes" (121). The term "mysterium tremendum" was coined by Rudolf Otto and adopted in an article by S.L. Varnado, "The Idea of the Numinous in Gothic Literature", in Thompson, 11-21.

17. Joseph Conrad, *Heart of Darkness and The Secret Sharer* (1910), New York, 1971, 113.

Only the barbarous and superb woman did not so much as flinch, and stretched tragically her bare arms after us over the sombre and glittering river (115).

The narrator's role is an interesting point of comparison anyway. Neither in *She* nor in *Heart of Darkness* is the focalizer the main character of the novel. Holly and Marlow are essentially observers rather than protagonists of their respective stories. This is a characteristic aspect of the Gothic discourse. In the Gothic novel the mythical world gains in credibility exactly because it is entered by and seen through the eyes of an average man of common sense, who is not easily amazed or deluded and not susceptible to superstitious sentiments. By means of a focalizer such as Marlow and Holly the reader's share is increased and his wonder and astonishment grow as he looks at the unfolding events over the shoulder of these sound men of sense.

Another shared feature is the journey towards the goal. In both cases the journey begins in England and takes the travellers across the sea and up a river far into the continent of Africa. But here an interesting and significant point of difference may be observed. Marlow's journey up the river is an active search, described in a metaphor that is both sexual and colonial: "The reaches opened before us and closed behind .... We penetrated deeper and deeper into the heart of darkness" (68). Much earlier Marlow had characterized the river as "a mighty big river, ... resembling an immense snake uncoiled, with its head in the sea, its body at rest ... and its tail lost in the depths of the land. And as I looked at the map of it in a shop-window, it fascinated me as a snake would a bird — a silly little bird" (11); and about the place of the river on the map he says, "I was going into the yellow. Dead in the centre. And the river was there — fascinating — deadly — like a snake" (15).

In *She* the journey up the river seems fairly straightforward. The men have to struggle up an ancient canal, overgrown with weeds, but are then caught by the Amahaggers and carried first to their village and later across the swamps to the ancient city of Kôr, the abode of She. In *She* it is not the river that is compared with a snake about to swallow up any traveller that comes near but the swamp surrounding the mountain in which *She-who-must-be-obeyed* resides. The pools of the swamp or quagmire are full of alligators and "large quantities of a hideous black water-snake, of which the bite is very dangerous ...". The swamp's worst feature is "... the awful smell of rotting vegetation that hung about it, which was at times positively overpowering ..." (116). The men camp overnight on a bit of elevated dry land in the middle of the swamp. The next day they travel on, the white men and Billali, the leader of the Amahagger, the "People of the Rocks", still carried in litters. An accident occurs, when one of the bearers is bitten by a snake and falls into a "slimy pool" (122), never to be seen again, possibly because "the snake-bite paralyzed him". Billali is saved by Holly who overcomes his disgust and jumps into the "horrid slimy-looking pool" (123).

For a Jungian there is a unified explanation for the scene. Animals that can live in two environments, in water and on the earth, are symbols of transcendence, according to Jung:

> These creatures, figuratively coming from the depths of the ancient Earth Mother, are symbolic denizens of the collective unconscious. They bring into the field of consciousness a special chthonic (underworld) message.

And Jung goes on to mention specifically lizards, snakes and other such animals as examples: "these are intermediate creatures that combine underwater activity and the bird-flight with an intermediate terrestrial life. The wild duck or the swan are cases in point. Perhaps the commonest dream symbol of transcendence is the snake ....." Apart from frogs, snakes, and alligators Rider Haggard mentions a whole catalogue of "aquatic birds", "Geese, cranes, ducks, teal, coot, snipe, and plover swarmed around us, many being of varieties that were quite new to me" (116).

Viewed from a Jungian perspective the snake-river in *Heart of Darkness* and the water-snakes in *She* carry the same chthonic message. In *She* there is the additional feature that the water-snakes find their counterpart in Ayesha herself whose snake-like qualities of fatal attraction and elusiveness are emphasized by the repeatedly mentioned double-headed snake of solid gold that fastens her white kirtle (155, 162, etc.), by the movement of her body when she strips for Holly (*excusez le mot*, but that is what happens): "she stood up and shook the white wrappings from her, and came forth shining and splendid like some glittering snake, when she has cast her slough" (189), or when she holds Leo in her arms at last, "Suddenly, with a snake-like motion, she seemed to slip from his embrace" (230). Her voice sounds "like the hiss of a snake" (197; also 163, 164).

Actually the image of Ayesha as the Fatal Serpent is the perfect counterpart of the water-snakes in the swamp. As Camille Paglia argues, "Bog and quagmire are my chthonian swamp, that dank primal brew of earth and water that I identify with the female body ....":

The horror film uses rot as a primary material, part of the Christian west's secret craving for Dionysian truths. The horror film blunders about, seeking, without realizing it, the chthonian swamp of generation, the female matrix.[18]

In *She* the (male) struggle is against the (female) swamp and against a powerful serpent-woman. It is significant in this respect that the male protagonists are carried across the swamp in litters and are equally helpless in the face of the transcending majestic beauty of the woman. Both instances evince the Victorian male's fear of female domination, particularly sexual domination.

Although there is no immediate counterpart in *Heart of Darkness* of the serpent-woman, there is a structural parallel in the fact that Marlow's journey up the river also leads to a male vision of an impressive female figure, whose appearance is described in far greater detail than that of any other character in the novel. The struggle against the Congo, the snake-river in *Heart of Darkness*, shares several elements with the journey in *She*. There is the repeated reference to the hippopotamus, the chthonic river animal "that had the bad habit of getting out on the bank and roaming at night over the station grounds" (46). When it takes to the river at night, the noise of "mighty splashes and snorts reached us from afar, as though an ichthyosaurus had been taking a bath of glitter in the great river" (49). The hippo is primeval, like the "primeval mud" in which the wrecked steamer is stranded, waiting for repairs, "like a carcass of some big river animal" (43). The mud smells and later the hippo meat that was taken aboard as food for the cannibals, goes rotten, making "the mystery of the wilderness stink in my nostrils" (57; cf. also 68), the smell of rot underlining the rift between the Earth Mother and the white intruders. Whereas in *She* the white men lose their manhood and are helplessly conveyed to where She lives, in *Heart of Darkness* it is the steamer that loses its energy the nearer the search party comes to the heart of darkness; it "seemed at her last gasp, the stern-wheel flopped languidly …. It was like watching the last flickers of a life" (64). And then, when they arrive at Kurtz's place at last, there is the magnificent black woman. She is described not as a serpent but as an Amazon, another type of the male-dominating female:

She walked with measured steps, draped in striped and fringed clothes, treading the earth proudly …. She carried her head

---

18. Paglia, 92 and 268-69.

high; her hair was done in the shape of a helmet; she had brass
leggings to the knee, brass wire gauntlets to the elbow .... And
in the hush that had fallen suddenly upon the whole sorrowful
land, the immense wilderness, the colossal body of the *fecund*
and mysterious life seemed to look at her, pensive, as though it
had been looking at the image of its own tenebrous and
passionate soul (103, italics added).

Clearly the black woman is yet another representative of the fertile
Earth Mother, like the hippopotamus and the snake river itself,
unsettling the male intruders and ultimately sending them back, with the
emaciated body of Kurtz, bewildered and in awe of her female
power.[19]

It is hardly accidental to find the snake image represented in two
novels written around the turn of the century. The snake is not just an
attribute of the *femme fatale* of the *fin de siècle*; it is an aesthetic ideal
that pervaded all aspects of the culture. *She* was published in 1887, at a
time when the serpentine line of Rossetti and Burne-Jones was in
fashion. As Camille Paglia puts it:

> The Rossetti woman rebels against Victorian convention, her
> unpinned hair and unstructured medieval gown flowing with
> lyrical freedom. The heavy head swags on a serpentine neck.[20]

Rossetti's brooding figure of *Astarte Syriaca* (1877) could indeed have
stood model for Haggard's Ayesha, with her dark hair and flowing,
semi-transparent gown against a dark, mysterious background that
suggests an atmosphere not unlike that of the Caves of Kôr. We find the
same aesthetic ideal represented in many of the portraits and
photographs of the greatest stage personalities of the age, Sarah

---

19. There is a contrast in the way the journey ends in the two novels. In *Heart
of Darkness* the way back to sea is easy, "The brown current ran swiftly out of the
heart of darkness, bearing us down towards the sea with twice the speed of our
upward progress" (115), whereas in *She* the journey away from the Place of Life is
the most arduous and hazardous of the whole book. The snake-river regurgitates
the unwanted trespassers; the snake-woman (now turned into a monkey) does not
let go so easily of her prey.

20. Paglia, 491.

Bernhardt, Eleanora Duse and Isadora Duncan.[21] The snake-like qualities attributed to Sarah Bernhardt even found their way into the English novel of the period. In Mrs Humphry Ward's *Miss Bretherton* (1884), whose heroine is an actress, the Royal Academician Forbes speaks disparagingly of "your thin, French, snake-like creatures".[22] Dramatically this figure probably reached its histrionic and expressive climax in the figure of Salome, not so much as depicted in Wilde's play (published in English in 1894, though first performed in its original French version in Paris in 1896), but in Richard Strauss's opera first presented in Dresden in 1905.[23]

The very first time Ayesha appears to the reader, through the amazed eyes of Holly, the narrator, the description is perfectly in accordance with the aesthetic ideal of the serpentine line:

> ... a tall and lovely woman, instinct with beauty in every part, and also with a certain snake-like grace which I had never seen anything to equal before. When she moved a hand or foot her entire frame seemed to undulate, and the neck did not bend, it curved (142).

Late nineteenth-century Gothic fiction found its model for the snake motif in Coleridge's *Christabel*, the poem in which innocence

---

21. In the *Mémoires* by Sarah Bernhardt (Paris, 1907), for instance, there is a photograph of the famous actress in her coffin in which the serpentine neck is a prominent feature (between 336 and 337). Bernhardt's own sculpture of the drowned Ophelia also features the serpentine line (between 328-29). Cf. also the photographs in Isadora Duncan's autobiography *My Life* (London, 1928) and in the biography (or, rather, hagiography) of Eleonora Duse by E.A. Rheinhardt (I consulted the Dutch translation by T.J. Bergmann-Jelgersma, published in Arnhem in 1929). John Stokes refers to Sarah Bernhardt's "serpentine shape" in "Aspects of Bernhardt", *The Yearbook of English Studies*, 11 (1981), 143-60.

22. Mrs Humphry Ward, *Miss Bretherton*, London, 2nd edn, 1891, 29 (see C.C. Barfoot, "The Actress as Surrogate Author and Marginalized Woman in Mrs Humphry Ward's *Miss Bretherton*", in *Studia Patriciae Shaw Oblata*, eds S.G. Fernández-Corugedo *et al.*, Oviedo, III [1991], 31-52).

23. For a discussion of the representative significance of the figure of Salome in the period, see Frank Kermode, *Romantic Image*, London, 1957, esp. ch. 4, *passim*. Paradoxically in Wilde's text, it is Salome herself who gloats on the snake-like attributes of John the Baptist: his hair that writhes like "a knot of black serpents" round his neck, and his tongue "like a red snake darting poison ... that scarlet viper that spat its venom upon me" (*The Annotated Oscar Wilde*, ed. H. Montgomery Hyde, London, 1982, 311 and 323).

(Christabel) is represented by the dove; experience (Geraldine) by the serpent.[24] Coleridge himself had been influenced strongly by M.G. Lewis, whose classic tale of horror and sexual transgression *The Monk* (1796) contains an androgynous representation of Lucifer with a Medusa head.[25] In *Christabel* Geraldine with her "snake's small eye" (1. 583) looks at the eponymous heroine:

> One moment and the sight was fled!
> But Christabel in a dizzy trance
> Stumbling on the unsteady ground
> Shuddered aloud, with a hissing sound
>
> (ll. 588-91)

Geraldine's brief look makes a lasting impression on poor Christabel:

> The maid, devoid of guile and sin,
> I know not how, in fearful wise
> So deeply had she drunken in
> That look, those sunken serpent eyes,
> That all her features were resigned
> To this sole image in her mind
>
> (ll. 599-604)

What Harold Bloom observes with regard to *Christabel* may be applied to *She* and *Heart of Darkness* with equal force:

> ... *Christabel* seems to offer no *catharsis*, no release from the intense suffering it so vividly depicts, the fear it seeks to arouse .... Where Blake defied the demonic and sought to use it for his apocalyptic ends, Coleridge indulged his Imagination by it and came to distrust Imagination in consequence.[26]

This is not the place to discuss the idea of the Fatal Woman at length, but one text, much closer in time and spirit to the novels under discussion than Coleridge's poem, seems particularly relevant in this

---

24. *Coleridge's Poems*, ed. J.B. Beer, London, 1963, 195-210.

25. In a review of *The Monk*, the reviewer, probably Coleridge, says that "the temptations of Ambrosio are ... described with libidinous minuteness" (*The Critical Review*, XIX [February 1797], 197).

26. Harold Bloom, *The Visionary Company: A Reading of English Romantic Poetry*, rev. and enlarged edn, Ithaca and London, 1971, 217.

context, a passage from Swinburne's *Notes on Designs of the Old Masters in Florence* (1868), where the poet discusses some studies of female heads by Michelangelo:

> ... her hair, close and curled, seems ready to shudder in sunder and divide into snakes. Her throat, full and fresh, round and hard to the eye as her bosom and arms, is erect and stately, the head set firm on it without any droop or lift of the chin; her mouth crueller than a tiger's, colder than a snake's, and beautiful beyond a woman's .... Here also the electric hair, which looks as though it would hiss and glitter with sparks if once touched, is wound up to a tuft with serpentine plaits and involutions; all that remains of it unbound falls in one curl, shaping itself into a snake's likeness as it unwinds, right against a living snake held to the breast and throat. This is rightly registered as a study for Cleopatra ... an encounter between the woman and the worm of Nile ... so closely do the snake and the queen of snakes caress and cling.[27]

Swinburne suggests that Shakespeare expressed his awareness of the idea of proximity of the snake-queen and the snake-river in Antony's question: "Where's my serpent of old Nile?" In its combined emphasis on the chthonic images of the snake of the river and the Fatal Woman the quoted passage may serve as a sub-text for both *She* and *Heart of Darkness*.

As far as the imperial aspect is concerned, the novels have more in common than appears at first sight. In both there is colonial domination of an indigenous tribe by a white outsider, who is the Other both to the tribe and to the narrator. In both novels the penetration of the country is described in terms of trespassing, of an infringement, and the natives try to keep out the strangers. In both novels, too, there is a sense of despair about the state of civilization. Patrick Brantlinger formulated the following three distinctive features of what he calls imperial Gothic: "individual regression or going native; an invasion of civilization by the forces of barbarism or demonism; and the diminution of opportunities for adventure and heroism in the modern world".[28] All three play a role in the two books. There is also the comparison between the heart of darkness and England. In *She* it is suggested that Ayesha will

---

27. The passage is quoted in Mario Praz, *The Romantic Agony*, Oxford, 1970, 249-51.

28. Brantlinger, 230.

accompany Leo back to England and rule over it (the reflection of
another deeply lodged fear of the Victorians: the invasion of England by
the Other). In Conrad a comparison is made between the domination of
the Romans over England and the domination of the colonists over
Congo: as in *She* the supremacy of an ancient Imperial power is held up
as an example for the situation in the present. Finally, the imperial
theme is gender-dominated in both novels: by Ayesha in *She* and by the
black woman and Kurtz's Intended in *Heart of Darkness*. Marlow is
rendered powerless in the face of these two women. To the male
narrator both the black woman and the white lady represent the Other.
Praz, writing about the Fatal Women of Swinburne and D'Annunzio,
remarks that, "like the Byronic superman, the superwoman also
assumes an attitude of defiance to society"; "Men behave in her
presence like the youthful lover of Pantea, like the desperate lovers of
Swinburne: they burn with masochistic desire", but the Fatal Woman
also "offers power and empire to the man who is fascinated by her"
and, Praz concludes:

> woman represents the active principle not only in the giving of
> pleasure, but also in the ruling of the world. The female is
> aggressive, the male vacillating.[29]

It seems justified on the basis of the evidence presented to add to
Brantlinger's list a fourth, gender-oriented characteristic of late
nineteenth-century Imperial Gothic fiction: it undermines male
supremacy, unquestioned until then, in its representation of the
imperialistic rule of the world. *She* can be regarded as precursor of
Heart of Darkness, and a recognition of the Imperial Gothic element in
Conrad's novel makes us understand more about one of the sources for
both the matter and the literary style he adopted for it than the
"two-handed engine" of Leavis's critical apparatus that "stands ready to
smite once and smite no more".

29. Praz, 271, 273 and 274.

DRACULA IN FILM

N.J. BREDEROO

The Gothic Novel, with all its dark hidden eroticism, has had a strong influence on the film industry of the twentieth century. The film-going public enjoyed shivering in the dark, and many novels and short stories written in the nineteenth century provided ready plots. It must, of course, be realized that a book is hardly ever rendered into a film in its entirety, since the director, and more particularly the producing company, always rework the story. In addition, public decency required that Hollywood intervened to censor any overly erotic theme.[1] As a consequence of a number of catastrophic scandals in the early days of Hollywood, self-censorship was applied from the Twenties onwards.[2] The conservative Republican Will Hays came to the head of an organization which was given the authority to cut films, on the basis of the Production Code.

It is in this way that Mary Shelley's *Frankenstein* (1818) and Robert Louis Stevenson's *The Strange Case of Dr Jekyll and Mr Hyde* (1886) were reproduced on screen many times.[3] What is interesting here is to see how the story changed structure, and influenced our current vision of Frankenstein and Dr Jekyll. Hardly anybody still associates Shelley and Stevenson with these names; everyone thinks of Boris Karloff and Spencer Tracy. Also, the awareness of the homo-erotic import of the

---

1. Kevin Brownlow, *Behind the Mask of Innocence, Sex, Violence, Prejudice, Crime: Films of the Social Conscience in the Silent Era*, London, 1990.

2. L.J. Leff and J.L. Simmons, *The Dame in the Kimono, Hollywood, Censorship, and the Production Code from the 1920s to the 1960s*, New York, 1990.

3. N.J. Brederoo, "Hollywood und die englische Romangattung des 'Gothic Novel'", in *Interbellum und Exil*, ed. Sjaak Onderdelinden, Amsterdam, 1991.

books has disappeared as an effect of popular Hollywood film versions.[4]

The erotic aspects of Bram Stoker's *Dracula* have been pointed out many times. The vampire appears in the book not in the form of a monster, but as a man who, in spite of his monstrous qualities, remains attractive. And it is not necessary to be a psychoanalyst to see that the sucking of blood has erotic overtones, particularly since the vampire applies this treatment mostly in bedrooms. Moreover, the comparison which has been made between blood and the male sperm is, in my view, correct.[5] In this way the vampire follows from the much older tradition of the demonic female succubus which was presumed to drain male potency during sleep.

The belief in the male vampire occurred particularly in Eastern Europe and it appears that people there still follow rituals to drive off the vampire. The Catholic Church classed vampires under the general category of witches, and treated them as such, but the Greek Orthodox Church takes vampirism very seriously. To be rid of the vampire, according to Eastern European beliefs, it is necessary either to burn the body of the un-dead, or behead it, or drive a stake through the heart. It is possible to defend oneself against the vampire with garlic or the cross.[6]

The picture which Eastern European people had of the vampire was based to a great extent on the historical aristocrat Vlad Dracula, who, like the later book and film hero, lived in Transylvania. There, he conducted a reign of terror, not only against the Turks, whom he fought, but also against his own population. He was particularly famous for impaling his enemies to death. Lurid sixteenth-century engravings reproduce these executions in every detail. His enemies' belongings were committed to the fire.[7]

This story has little to do with Stoker's novel, although the wooden stakes and the fire reoccur, more or less. Much closer come the many stories that circulated after the death of Vlad. People began to see him

---

4. William Veeder, *Mary Shelley: Frankenstein. The Fate of Androgyny*, Chicago and London, 1986; and William Veeder and Gordon Hirsch, *Dr Jekyll and Mr Hyde after One Hundred Years*, Chicago and London, 1988.

5. David Pirie, *The Vampire Cinema*, Leicester, 1977, 12.

6. Documentary, *Die blutig ernste Geschichte des Grafen Dracula*, ZDF, 5-9-1987.

7. Pirie, 11-31.

Fig. 8: Countess Elizabeth Bathory, "The Bloody Countess".

Fig. 9: The historical Dracula, Vlad Dracul.

as the great leader of the vampires, and rumours were rife that his grave was found to be empty. In the eighteenth century particularly, a great fear of vampirism possessed the land of Dracula's birth. Many graves were opened in order to search for vampires.[8]

Stoker was able to form a picture of this tyrant because a contemporary portrait has transmitted his appearance to us. But his cruel head can hardly be solely responsible for the attractive aristocrat in the novel. A second source was certainly the controversial figure of Lord Byron. In May 1819 a novella, *The Vampyre*, had been published in the *New Monthly Magazine* under his name and ever since then rumour had regularly connected him with vampirism.[9] His charm, perversity, and highly-coloured sexual reputation contributed to turning him into the figure of the "Satanic Lord" who both attracts and repels.

Sexuality, which, in the Victorian period, was even more repressed, found its outlet in bizarre renderings of this theme. One has only to think of the women who inhabit the paintings of the Pre-Raphaelites, or of Oscar Wilde's *Salome*, with Aubrey Beardsley's illustrations. Stoker's *Dracula* fits in well in this company. There is no question of sex between the English characters of the book, unless we attach a symbolic significance to the stake which is driven through Lucy's heart. All the erotic attraction is attributed to the foreign count. He operates like a drug on women, who are clearly more susceptible to his charm than men. In this way, the suggestion of sexuality remains legitimate, for, after all, women were weak and had to be protected against strange powers. The fact that people were actually aware that this sexual obsession resided in one's own spirit is proved by the rise of sexology in the Nineties.

The first film version of the blood-sucking count was made in Germany in 1922 by Wilhelm Friedrich Murnau,[10] which is hardly surprising when one considers the increasing popularity of the Expressionist film, a film school which had started with another horror film, Wiene's *Das Kabinett des Dr Caligari*[11] dating from 1919.

---

8. See K. Brokaw, *A Night in Transylvania*, New York, 1976, 17-60.

9. See Mario Praz, *The Romantic Agony*, London and New York, 1970, 78-81. As Praz makes clear, the actual author of the story was John Polidori, Byron's secretary and physician.

10. Lott Eisner, *Murnau*, London, 1973, 108-19.

11. Wolfgang Kaul, *Caligari und Caligarismus*, Deutsche Kinemathek, Berlin, 1974.

Fig. 10: Bela Lugosi as Dracula.

Horror stories could be filmed excellently in the Expressionist style, and were often about a satanic individual who terrorized the area he lived in. *Dracula* offered all kinds of possibilities for this new German movement.

Unfortunately we know very little about Murnau's private circumstances, so that much concerning the production of this film remains in the dark. Two things are clear. Firstly, Murnau was not given the rights to film the book, and so he changed the story and eventually called the film *Nosferatu*. Secondly, Murnau reworked the story in the light of his own homosexuality, which explains the explicit treatment of the obsessive desire of the count for the blood of the male clerk who visits the castle at the beginning. Another testimony to the effect of Murnau's own leanings on his version is that the relation between the lovers remains somewhat sterile.

Nosferatu, or Count Orlock, as he is called in Murnau, possesses none of the demonic attraction of Dracula. He is a phantom who disturbs our night's sleep. At the end of the film, the heroine offers herself to something which literally disappears into smoke. On the other hand, the set design and the camerawork are sublime. The shots with the shadow of the count remain impressed in the memory much more than the later, more substantial, presence of Bela Lugosi or Christopher Lee in the American and British productions of *Dracula*.

A few years after the appearance of Murnau's film, there was a stage production of *Dracula*, upon which Tod Browning based his film version (1931). The character of Dracula was first going to be played by Lon Chaney, popularly known as "Mr Horror", but his early death meant that another choice had to be made. The Expressionist actor Conrad Veidt was mentioned as a possibility, but eventually the choice fell on Bela Lugosi.[12] The choice of a foreigner was without doubt in accord with the Production Code, which kept a strict eye on the moral import of the American film. There were many "Don'ts" and even more "Be Carefuls" which censored the contents of the film, and naturally, the producers tried to get round the prohibition, for the public was always drawn by risky topics. A common method was to dress "the bad" in a moralistic jacket. In this way it was possible to show many sins, as long as they were punished in the end. The possibilities widened if the sinners were foreigners. Thus, Garbo and Dietrich could interpret many *femmes fatales* and Von Stroheim was able, as a director, to film decadent subjects for a long time, as long as America

---

12. Pirie, 50-54.

Fig. 11: Max Schrêck as Count Orlock in *Nosferatu*.

was not involved. The choice of Lugosi, with his terrible accent, made it possible to film "The Strangest Love Story of All", as it was then called. Lugosi is anything but a Latin Lover; indeed he is the personification of Evil. In this way, the erotic import of the Dracula story is weakened, and everything revolves around Dracula's hypnotic powers.

The count's bites into the necks of young women were kept carefully out of the picture. The first *Dracula* suggests much more than it actually shows. The women provide the information that the treatment takes place on a bed, but in the case of the clerk in Dracula's castle the spectator remains in doubt whether any blood-sucking really occurs. This film therefore became a more prudish version of the book. Later Hollywood versions followed the same trend.

The female vampire does occur in Stoker in the characters of Dracula's three wives and in the transformed Lucy, but their descriptions are not very explicit. For this topic, it is preferable to turn to the story of *Carmilla* written by Sheridan Le Fanu in 1872. This tale contains a hint at lesbian love. Here, too, the later product is derived from a historical figure, the countess Elizabeth Bathory,[13] who became notorious as a woman who was sexually aroused by the torture of virgins.

The first female vampire to be the central figure of a film appears in *Vampyr* (1932) by Carl Dreyer,[14] a Dane. Here, the vampire is an old woman who endangers the life of a young woman, but there are no erotic complications. Dreyer has indeed made a purely artistic film which follows the Scandinavian preference for topics connected with the occult. This is probably one of the reasons why the film is so little known. It is suitable for art-houses, and does not, on the whole, appeal to the general public.

Hammer Studios and the sex vampire

The genre was reborn in Britain's Hammer Studios, which began to make vampire films in 1957. The first *Dracula* to be filmed here bestowed on Christopher Lee immortal fame as a fascinating demon. His Dracula returned many times in follow-up stories, and so he was able to deepen and extend his reading of the count with all its erotic overtones. The count's bite became more and more explicit and the colours of the film emphasized the bloody treatment; while the sexual

---

13. *Ibid.*, 17-18.

14. Tom Milne, *Carl Dreyer*, New York, 1971, 107-19.

Fig. 12: Christopher Lee as Dracula.

excitement experienced by his victims — all women — leaves little to the imagination. The British public sometimes expressed shock, but this did not stop them from thronging to see the films.[15]

In the Seventies, a general relaxation of attitudes to the portrayal of sexual themes enabled the vampire film to become openly erotic. France stood in the vanguard of this development. The lesbian theme of Le Fanu's *Carmilla*, in particular, inspired many directors, and became for a time the most popular version of the story, represented in such cult films as Harry Kumel's *Daughters of Darkness*, and even in more pornographic productions. The lesbian vampire overshadowed the old count, as the heroine of plots which became ever more bloody and sadistic. The genre reached the limits of possible development in this mode, and transformed itself into the zombie movie.

In this new climate of sexual explicitness combined with an ever more trivial approach to the story, it became possible to make parodies of the vampire film. The best of this group is perhaps *Dance of the Vampires*, also called *The Fearless Vampire Killers*. Roman Polanski made this film in 1967 as a comic parody of the classic Hammer Studio vampire film, a decade old by that time. Here for the first time we come across a homosexual male vampire, who reads romantic love poems. The character who inspired his bloody love was played by Polanski himself. So, by the late Sixties nothing was too crazy for a vampire film.

A parody that has nothing to do with humour was produced by the Warhol Factory, under the title of *Blood for Dracula*. In fact, Morrissey was responsible for this failure. The plot of this film, produced in a milieu which saw itself as a vanguard of the sexual revolution, is about a vampire who can only digest the blood of virgins. All kinds of perverse, and anything but virginal, women offer themselves as victims, with the result that the poor vampire is always sick and vomiting.

The way was now open for Black vampires, South American vampires, etc., all of them developments which have nothing to do with Stoker.

---

15. Documentary, *The Hammer Studio that Dripped Blood*, BBC 2, 26-6-1987.

POSTMODERN GOTHIC

THEO D'HAEN

My thesis is simple: the Gothic exists in postmodernism. In fact, there is even such a thing as a return of the Gothic in postmodernism. Until now, this phenomenon has only been acknowledged in passing. I think this is a pity, as in my view the Gothic, as part of the fantastic, in postmodernism fulfils a particular function, and the recognition of the role it plays has rather far reaching implications for the entire discussion on postmodernism.

Postmodernism is with us to stay. So much seems certain, given the ubiquity of the term in contemporary critical parlance. But what is postmodernism? Some critics, often of a neo-Marxist tendency (Jameson) use the term, often negatively, to refer to all fiction (or even literature) produced *after* Modernism.[1] Others (Hassan, Hutcheon, Lee, Alexander, and many others) use it positively to refer to a particular kind of fiction, primarily but not necessarily contemporary, characterized by a common set of techniques, conventions and themes (self-reflexiveness, metafiction, eclecticism, redundancy, multiplicity, discontinuity, intertextuality, parody, pastiche, the dissolution of character and narrative instance, the use of minor or popular genres, the erasure of boundaries, and the de-stabilization of the reader).[2] The problems of both the one and the other approach are legion. Used as a period term postmodernism rules out all discrimination or differentiation

---

1. Fredric Jameson, *Postmodernism, or, The Cultural Logic of Late Capitalism*, Durham: NC, 1991.

2. Ihab Hassan, *The Postmodern Turn: Essays in Postmodern Theory and Culture*, Athens: Ohio, 1987; Linda Hutcheon, *A Poetics of Postmodernism: History, Theory, Fiction*, New York and London, 1988 and *The Politics of Postmodernism*, London and New York, 1989; Allison Lee, *Realism and Power: Postmodern British Fiction*, London, 1990; Marguerite Alexander, *Flights from Realism: Themes and Strategies in Postmodernist British and American Fiction*, London, 1990.

beyond that implied by the chronological boundary chosen. This choice itself, by the way, is in itself reason for violent disagreement, with some dating postmodernism from the publication of Joyce's *Finnegans Wake*, and others preferring the mid-fifties or even the sixties. Used as a category, postmodernism pits a huge mass of literary works often widely divergent among themselves against other works both contemporary and earlier. As postmodernism in the latter sense has grown increasingly more inclusive during the last decade or so, it now includes Walter Abish but also Margaret Atwood, Richard Brautigan but also John Banville, Robert Coover but also Julio Cortázar, Don DeLillo but also Samuel Delaney, Stanley Elkin but also Alfredo Bryce Echenique, Raymond Federman but also Carlos Fuentes, and so on through the alphabet, with some critics talking of Laurence Sterne, Melville, and Yeats as (proto-)postmodernists. The question is whether such blanket use of the term, either in the chronological or the classifying sense, is doing any good. Perhaps things might look up if we did not speak of a single and monolithic "postmodernism" but of a number of postmodernisms in the postmodern period?

Recently, Hans Bertens has distinguished between an "avant-garde", a "poststructuralist" and an "aesthetic" postmodernism, and he links these various postmodernisms both to different historical stages in the use of the term, roughly speaking the 60s, 70s and 80s, and to different stances, inspired by opposing socio-political convictions, toward contemporary literature and culture in general.[3] These stances, moreover, are perceptually defined; in other words, they depend upon how one *reads* a particular work rather than upon any "objective" quality of the work itself: an avant-garde reading foregrounds the work's technical features distinguishing it from works in a previous mode, and specifically from Modernism; a poststructuralist reading focuses on the decentring of the (bourgeois) subject, the deferment of meaning, and the problematical status of the text; and an aestheticizing reading stresses the artificiality, the emptiness, the lack of depth, the purely formal interests of the postmodern work. This last way of reading, ironically, unites both old-fashioned moral critics and their neo-Marxist colleagues, the former accusing postmodernism of being anti-humanistic, the latter stigmatizing it as neoconservative. As Bertens cautions, none of these postmodernisms appears in unadulterated form; that is, it is quite possible and even probable to "find" features of any one of these postmodernisms in most texts that are usually branded as

---

3. Hans Bertens, "Postmodern Cultures", in *Postmodernism and Contemporary Fiction*, ed. Edmund J. Smyth, London, 1991, 123-37.

"postmodern". Depending upon the reading strategy adopted, one or another set of features will be foregrounded. However, it is clear that each reading strategy will tend to favour a particular core of texts from the generally available pool as its postmodern "canon".

As Bertens indicates, the various ways of reading postmodernism he discerns are historically successive. It seems safe to say that in our day the avant-garde reading has in itself become historical, dependent as it was upon, or corollary to, the conscious will of the earliest practitioners and critics of postmodernism to legitimize their own artistic practice or academic interest. Still, it is this avant-garde reading of postmodernism that provided the initial space for both the poststructuralist reading and the moral conservative and neo-marxist aesthetic reading, thus repeating in the last third of our century the discussions with regard to the historical avant-gardes of the first third of our century. These two ways of reading postmodernism are still very much with us. I would argue, though, that instead of dividing the field between them, as Bertens seems to argue, they are the reverse sides of one single coin, and that concentrating on them exclusively obscures our view of yet another postmodernism which defines itself, depending upon one's point of view and the vehemence of one's convictions, either in opposition or as complementary to the poststructuralist/aesthetic one. This "other" postmodernism foregrounds the fantastic elements, and among them the Gothic, in postmodern texts. Obviously, as is the case with the other postmodernisms, this one too will come up with a canon of its own of texts that most easily allow themselves to be read in the way advocated. Let me tackle these issues one by one.

Jameson and his fellow neo-Marxists blame postmodernism for having sold out to the culture-industry of late capitalist consumer society, and for failing to raise the true issues of class and economic deprivation. The poststructuralists praise postmodernism for problematizing all givens of present-day society, and specifically man's position in his world. What both fail to see or to admit is that the society they are speaking of is Western society, and that the world they mention is that of Western *man*. The neo-Marxists fail to see that in contemporary multinational capitalism the dividing line no longer runs between capital and labour in the traditional sense, but between those intimately involved with late capitalism — in the sense of either working it or being worked by it, running it or serving it, in any case perceiving it and being perceived by it as mutually influential in productive terms — and those excluded by it. Poststructuralist and aesthetic postmodernism could then be two ways of relating to late capitalism from within. The latter directly translates late capitalism's commodifying influence into an "aesthetic" experience, reduplicating as it were the very personality (or non-personality) make-up multinational capitalism needs: functional man, broken up in disparate units, without any essence to him, man as malleable putty, what Gerhard Hoffmann has called "situational" man.[4] The former reflects upon "situational" man and his world. This is postmodern self-reflexiveness with a vengeance. However, as I indicated, this is the postmodernism of the centre, foregrounding late capitalism's central categories in terms of productive involvement with itself. In this sense this postmodernism, I would argue, continues in the main line of the various -isms that have taken up the centre of the literary system in Western society and culture since the eighteenth century. Or rather, and quite paradoxically, it has to be seen as continuing this line precisely by radically attacking the tenets that have upheld it over a two-hundred year period. I will expand upon this hypothesis, and at the same time move into my discussion of postmodern Gothic, by way of two recent publications summarizing the most commonly held positions on the Gothic and the fantastic: Neil Cornwell's *The Literary Fantastic: From Gothic to Postmodernism*[5] and José B. Monleòn's *A Specter Is Haunting Europe: A Sociohistorical Approach to the Fantastic.*[6]

Most theorists of the fantastic start from the assumption that it originated as a complement or foil to the discourse of rationalism enshrined by the Enlightenment. For Rosemary Jackson "fantasy characteristically attempts to compensate for a lack resulting from cultural constraints: it is a literature of desire, which seeks that which is experienced as absence and loss".[7] She claims that "the fantastic traces the unsaid and the unseen of culture: that which has been silenced, made invisible, covered over and made 'absent'". As such, "literary fantasy is a telling index of the limits of (the dominant cultural) order," and "its introduction of the 'unreal' is set against the category of the 'real' — a category which the fantastic interrogates by its difference"

---

4. Gerhard Hoffmann, "The fantastic in fiction: its 'reality' status, its historical development and its transformation in postmodern narrative", in *REAL (Yearbook of Research in English and American Literature)* 1 (1982), 267-364.

5. Neil Cornwell, *The Literary Fantastic: From Gothic to Postmodernism*, London, 1990.

6. José B. Monleòn, *A Specter Is Haunting Europe: A Sociohistorical Approach to the Fantastic*, Princeton: NJ, 1990.

7. Rosemary Jackson, *Fantasy: The Literature of Subversion*, London, 1981, 3.

(4). In this relationship, it is the literature of the "real" that is perceived as mainstream, whereas the literature of the "unreal" acts as its "shadow" in the guise of minor or popular genres, or as subordinate elements in mainstream genres. Obviously, these categories shift over time. Therefore, fantastic literature develops in a dialectic relationship with main line literature. Linda Hutcheon sees fantasy as "the other side of realism" and as "represent[ing] historically a parallel and equally valid literary tradition".[8] Jackson and Hutcheon, along with many other critics, argue for the fantastic in literature as having a subversive effect with regard to Western bourgeois or capitalist society, though they admit that in its more extremely escapist forms it can also work to uphold the status-quo of the dominant cultural order. Cornwell summarizes this position by saying that "there would ... appear to be a fairly extensive consensus for seeing a more prominent, if not autonomous, role for the fantastic element in the history of prose literature, in interlocking and mutual dependence on 'reality' within the fictionality of fictional worlds, and given to the expression of — and perhaps at times making an impression upon — particular social and psychological tendencies".[9]

At variance, Monleòn argues against the subversive potential of the fantastic in literature, even in its non-escapist forms. Specifically, he sees it as a system for the dominant order to *name* its victims, and in particular as a means for the bourgeoisie to demonize or "monster-ize" its opponents in the economic and political arena depending upon the changing make-up of that arena; that is why in the Gothic the locales (ruins, castles, monasteries, etc.) and the figures of the fantastic are associated with the older feudal order, and why in the course of the nineteenth century there is a shift to co-eval locales and figures inspired upon the lower classes, branding them as criminal, demented, etc. That is also why, when according to the bourgeoisie's own progressive and historical logic of "reason" in matters political and economic they have become dethroned, or at least are in danger of becoming so, by the rising lower classes, "higher" art turns to an attack on reason itself in the guise of language or of consciousness — as is the case with most avant-garde -isms of the early twentieth century, and in the realm of politics the bourgeoisie turns to the fantastic as a means of control, as in fascism.

---

8. Linda Hutcheon, *Narcissistic Narrative: The Metafictional Paradox*, New York and London, 1984, 77.

9. Cornwell, 27.

According to Monleòn, then,

> A central, crucial paradox, therefore, dominated the cultural
> panorama at the turn of the twentieth century: the discourse of
> reason that had served to promote and justify the ascent of the
> bourgeois world now articulated its own negation. The premises
> of that discourse were used precisely by that sector that had been
> excluded from the rational world to build an alternative society.
> The discourse of reason would shape the voice of the working
> class; unreason, on the other hand, would be adopted by the
> dominant sector precisely and paradoxically as a means of
> avoiding the collapse of order. Bourgeois epistemology,
> immersed in this exchange, was left floating in a universe
> apparently without meaning. The fantastic abandoned its
> confining frame and invaded the entire cultural landscape,
> bringing its representation of paradox, of antinomy, to all
> corners of artistic activity.[10]

For Cornwell, too,

> From a position of lurking around the Gothic and baroque
> margins of "minor" works and genres in the eighteenth and
> nineteenth centuries, the literary fantastic in its broader sense,
> cross-fertilizing and evolving new forms, has marched steadily
> towards the mainstream of literature. In the twentieth century, in
> the age of modernism and postmodernism and under progressive
> impact from the ideas generated by (or encapsulated in)
> psychoanalysis, existentialism and dialogism (Freud and dreams,
> Sartre and being, Bakhtin and carnival) the fantastic has,
> arguably, reached a position in which it is increasingly itself
> becoming "the dominant", as it continues to develop not only its
> dialogical, open and unfinished styles of discourse but also a
> strong social, political and ethical thrust.[11]

Monleòn and Cornwell offer these observations as concluding remarks
to their respective books. However, it seems to me that both are a bit
hasty in lumping together Modernism and postmodernism here. Indeed,
when Monleòn argues that in the process of gradual self-recognition of
bourgeois society the fantastic had become ever further internalized to
the point, precisely, where the distinction between the "real" and the
"unreal" blurred at the historical moment of crisis of bourgeois cultural

---

10. Monleòn, 98-99.

11. Cornwell, 211.

logic, he must also allow for the naturalization of all unnatural or supernatural events in fiction as psychological, and not necessarily material, phenomena. As exceptions to this I can only think of the works of Franz Kafka, an author who repeatedly has been claimed as a (proto-)postmodernist. In other words: in most modernist works the "unreal" is recuperated by the fact that the world sketched in these fictions is a function of the characters' psychology rather than an "objective" description of their physical surroundings. On the whole, this seems a rather neat confirmation of Brian McHale's thesis that the dominant in modernism is epistemological.[12] Concretely, it seems to be a correct evaluation of the epistemological problems facing a bourgeoisie traversing the turbulence caused by the transition from late bourgeois capitalism to early corporate capitalism in the sense sketched by Lucien Goldmann in his *Pour une sociologie du roman*.[13] It is only in this sense, then, that I can accept Monleòn's remark that

> fantastic art and the avant-garde would share the same basic principles, making it almost impossible to separate them. Starting with the twentieth century, the analysis of the fantastic requires the study of the central cultural expressions of modernism.
> Unreason became a quotidian magic, an ordinary occurrence in which the natural and the supernatural appeared at the same level, hence forgoing any claims to representation and ultimately to meaning.[14]

Put another way, if the supernatural has no "meaning" in modernism it is because it has no function. I would argue, though, that things are different in postmodernism. Specifically, I would argue that in postmodernism we witness the reintroduction of the "unreal" as a meaningful category or element. Even more precisely, I would argue for the fantastic in postmodern literature as the counter-axial counterpart of present-day forms of (social) realism in opposition to poststructuralist/aesthetic postmodernism. This is also the moment where I can pick up on my earlier remarks with regard to poststructuralist/aesthetic postmodernism being a continuation of mainstream Western literature by way of a negation of the tenets of that literature. Monleòn argues that "when the fantastic expands in

---

12. Brian McHale, *Postmodernist Fiction*, New York and London, 1987.

13. Lucien Goldmann, *Pour une sociologie du roman*, Paris, 1964.

14. Monleòn, 100.

modernism it attacks the last refuge of reason: language" and that "the destruction of representation through representation ... will be the new paradox that will haunt the twentieth century" (140). These remarks read like a definition of poststructuralist/aesthetic postmodernism: a "deconstruction" of the orthodox categories that had maintained, firmly as in realism or hesitantly and tenuously as in modernism — depending upon the historical circumstances, mainstream Western fiction in its various -isms since its emergence in the eighteenth century. In other words, poststructuralist/aesthetic postmodernism comes down to a deconstruction — inevitable in the historical situation in which postmodernism finds itself — of the various forms of accommodating the Western discourse of "reason" as legitimized by whatever "scientific" underpinnings, whatever Lyotardian master or metanarratives, valid at any given time. This postmodernism, then, reveals itself as the heir to all other central -isms in mainstream Western literature. Fantastic postmodernism, on the other hand, falls heir to the "parallel tradition", as Linda Hutcheon called it.

Just like its counterparts, fantastic postmodernism favours a particular selection from among the generality of works covered by the blanket term "postmodernism". This "canon" is heavily slanted towards what in most recent critical usage has come to be subsumed under "the post-colonial". As Helen Tiffin notes in her introduction to *Past the Last Post: Theorizing Post-Colonialism and Post-Modernism*, the post-colonial in writing covers two "archives". The first archive "constructs it as writing ... grounded in those societies whose subjectivity has been constituted in part by the subordinating power of European colonialism — that is, as writing from countries or regions which were formerly colonies of Europe".[15] The second archive, Tiffin claims, is "intimately related to the first, though not co-extensive with it". In this second archive "the post-colonial is conceived of as a set of discursive practices, prominent among which is *resistance* to colonialism, colonialist ideologies, and their contemporary forms and subjectificatory legacies" (vii). This pretty exactly covers the discourse, with a few extensions, of what Rosemary Jackson has called "the shadow on the edges of bourgeois culture", which is "variously identified as black, mad, primitive, criminal, socially deprived, deviant, crippled, or (when

---

15. Helen Tiffin, "Introduction", in *Past the Last Post: Theorizing Post-Colonialism and Post-Modernism*, eds Ian Adam and Helen Tiffin, London, 1991, vii-xvi.

sexually assertive) female".[16] In short, the list includes all groups, both geographically and socially, marginalized by the economic and political power structures of bourgeois capitalism, its dominant cultural order and its mainstream literature. As Monleòn concludes from this and another passage from Jackson in which she argues that during the Victorian age, "evil was basically assigned to very concrete figures, such as the worker/revolutionary, the foreigner, the madman, or the active woman," "it is clear, then, that norms in fantastic literature (as in dominant ideology) were determined by the image of a bourgeois man".[17] Monleòn uses this in support of his thesis that the class struggle in Western society is reflected in fantastic literature from the eighteenth to the turn of the twentieth century from the point of view of the dominant culture and power group. However, it seems to me that Monleòn here stops short of drawing the full implications from his own thesis. If it is true that Gothic literature, and the fantastic in literature throughout the eighteenth and nineteenth centuries, externalized the fears of bourgeois society and thus literally laid its ghosts for it, it also *did* put up some form of resistance to the dominant ideology from the margins. After all, it cannot be a coincidence that so many of the authors of Gothic and fantastic literature were "peripheral" in geographical or social terms: Scots, Welshmen, Irishmen, and women. For the contemporary period at least Monleòn seems to be willing to concede this possibility:

> After World War II, the international panorama changed drastically. New relations of power, the creation of a hierarchy of first, second and third worlds, the supremacy of corporations, the existence of a nuclear threat — all would be elements that would contribute to a different social order. The rich production of the fantastic that invades our most recent past thus requires the tracing of another history.[18]

In fact, we could argue that in this post-war panorama the postmodern fantastic fulfils both the functions Cornwell *et al.* and Monleòn see for the fantastic: at the same time to express the fears of the dominant cultural order and subvert that order. For Western society the postmodern fantastic serves as complement to poststructuralist/aesthetic

---

16. Jackson, 121.

17. Monleòn, 92.

18. *Ibid.*, 139-40.

postmodernism. Whereas the latter postmodernism expresses the reality of contemporary corporate society both as desired by the system and as perceived by those productively involved with it from a Western point of view — roughly speaking, that much-maligned cliché: Western white heterosexual male — the fantastic postmodern expresses the fears of this society for, and the pressures exerted upon it by, those it has traditionally excluded from participation or has made subservient to the interest of making its "central" character into its present shape. This at one and the same time explains why poststructuralist/aesthetic postmodernism has largely remained a matter of the so-called first world, and why fantastic postmodernism flourishes in the third world and with minorities and marginalized groups in the first world. From a wider perspective, this distribution is in itself a telling illustration of the globalization of the Western economic system. For non-Western society and for the marginalized in Western society — roughly speaking: Western "non-society" — the postmodern fantastic signals resistance to the hegemonic discourse of Western society.

It is in this framework, then, that the postmodern Gothic needs to be read. As is generally the case in postmodernism, it is not to be expected that the Gothic will appear in a generically "pure" form. Rather, it will manifest itself in the form of generic debris, of quotations, parody and pastiche, incorporated in the multi-layered structure of what Cornwell has baptized a *portmanteau* novel (154). At variance with poststructuralist/aesthetic postmodernism, though, in fantastic postmodernism such debris is not without meaning or content, merely pointing at the void of Lyotard's master narratives.[19] Rather, it serves to counter-write the dominant order's discourse, to (re)(w)ri(gh)t(e) wrongs, to redress the balance of history as unfinished business. An example of how this might work is to be found in Robert Rawdon Wilson's article "SLIP PAGE: Angela Carter, In/Out/In the Post-Modern Nexus".[20] Wilson analyses Carter's story "Lady of the House of Love" as a counter-discourse rewriting of a traditional Gothic vampire story. Tracing the various generic and intertextual echoes resonating in Carter's story he demonstrates how it is "about the fate of women in a patriarchal world" and "about power, and who, in such a world, normally possesses power" (120). Summarized like this, the point Wilson makes seems trite. Yet, he makes a convincing case. A

---

19. Jean-François Lyotard, *La condition postmoderne*, Paris, 1979.

20. Robert Rawdon Wilson, "SLIP PAGE: Angela Carter, In/Out/In the Post-Modern Nexus", in *Past the Last Post*, 109-23.

similar case could be made for Carter's use of Gothic elements in
Nights at the Circus. To be sure, Carter's rewritings are often done
tongue-in-cheek, they are parodic in the general sense Linda Hutcheon
has given to this term in her *A Theory of Parody*,[21] but they are
certainly *not* without content or meaning. In *Nights at the Circus* they
serve to uphold the more general thrust of the book as a rewriting of all
of Western literature, starting with Homer, from a feminine — or
feminist — point of view. As far as the fantastic is concerned, Cornwell
has argued similar cases for John Banville's *Birchwood* and *Mefisto*,
Salman Rushdie's *The Satanic Verses*, and Toni Morrison's *Beloved*, all
of which contain Gothic elements. The list could easily be expanded.
Obviously, the specific use each of these fictions makes of Gothic
elements will depend upon the particular wrong they are aiming to
(rew)ri(gh)t(e), upon the particular unfinished business of history they
are trying to wind up, or which our postmodern reading of them
perceives them as trying to do. What is similar in all of these novels,
though, is that the Gothic elements are used in combination with what
has come to be called magic or magical realism, and which Amaryll
Chanady has explained as a mode of narration in which "the
supernatural is not presented as problematic" and in which the reader is
prevented "from even considering a rational solution".[22] Here,
precisely, is where the difference with the original Gothic formula
comes to rest. In the generic Gothic novel the dominant cultural order is
finally reconfirmed — the supernatural explained — and the ghosts of
unreason are laid to rest. The Gothic as used in combination with magic
realism does not allow for any such explained resolution. Instead of
being reduced in the final analysis to the world of the dominant cultural
order's "reality", therefore, the Gothic in fantastic postmodernism
creates one or more alternate "realities" on a par with that of the
dominant cultural order's. The thrust of the fantastic postmodernist use
of the Gothic is truly ontological in McHale's sense: to create a clutch
of worlds. Whereas poststructuralist postmodernism sees this multitude
of worlds as "problematizing" the "real" world of the dominant cultural
order, and aesthetic postmodernism sees it as an escapist manoeuvre of
that dominant cultural order selling itself via the culture industry,
fantastic postmodernism — in a truly post-colonial vein — sees it as

21. Linda Hutcheon, *A Theory of Parody: The Teachings of Twentieth-Century
Art Forms*, New York and London, 1985.

22. Amaryll Chanady, *Magical Realism and the Fantastic: Resolved versus
Unresolved Antinomy*, New York and London, 1985, 23.

effectively *challenging* the dominant cultural order. This also explains why from a post-colonialist point of view the theorization of the postmodern along exclusively poststructuralist/aesthetic lines is resented as an attempt at re-inscribing counter-discourses into a Western hegemonic paradigm and thus to "defuse" any possible resistance-effect. In the final analysis, such theorization only reveals that in our postmodern age it is precisely poststructuralist/aesthetic postmodernism that has come to stand for the discourse of the dominant cultural order. In this situation, only fantastic postmodernism can speak of what its postmodern counterparts must needs be silent: of what it means to be the dominant culture's, or late capitalism's, "other".

NOTES ON CONTRIBUTORS

Chris Baldick, Goldsmiths College, University of London, edited *The Oxford Book of Gothic Tales* (1992), and his other books include *In Frankenstein's Shadow* (1987). He is currently editing, with Robert Morrison, a selection of tales from the early years of *Blackwood's Edinburgh Magazine*.

C.C. Barfoot, English Department, Leiden University, published *The Thread of Connection: Aspects of Fate in the Novels of Jane Austen and Others* (1982); has most recently edited, alone or with others, *The Great Emporium: The Low Countries as a Cultural Crossroads in the Renaissance and the Eighteenth Century* (1992), *Theatre Intercontinental: Forms, Functions, Correspondences*, and *Shades of Empire in Colonial and Post-Colonial Literatures* (1993), *In Black and Gold: Contiguous Traditions in Post-War British and Irish Poetry* (1994), and *Ritual Remembering: History, Myth and Politics in Anglo-Irish Drama* (1995).

Michel Baridon, English Department, University of Burgundy, Dijon, has published *Gibbon et le mythe de Rome* (1977), *Le Gothiques des lumières* (1991), and articles on garden history, the Gothic revival and the relation of science to literature and the arts. He is currently completing an *anthologie raisonnée* presenting the great garden texts of the three great traditions: the western garden, the islamic garden and the gardens of the Far East.

N.J. Brederoo, Art History Department, Leiden University, specializing in Modern Art and New Media; in 1990 appointed to an personal chair of film history, an area in which he mainly publishes, at the University of Amsterdam.

E.J. Clery, Department of English, University of Keele, is about to publish *The Rise of Supernatural Fiction, 1762-1800*, which provides a more extensive account of the Cock Lane ghost and its relation to the development of a Gothic genre.

Neil Cornwell, Department of Russian Studies, the University of Bristol, is the author of *The Literary Fantastic: From Gothic to Postmodernism* (1990); *James Joyce and the Russians* (1992); and Russian literary studies on Vladimir Odoevsky, Pasternak and Pushkin; as well as the translator of volumes of fiction by Odoevsky (*The Salamander and Other Gothic Tales*, 1992) and Daniil Kharms (*Incidences*, Serpent's Tail, 1993).

Marysa Demoor, English Department, University of Gent, and National Fund for Scientific Research, has published *Friends over the Ocean: Andrew Lang's Letters to J.B. Matthews, J.R. Lowell, F.J. Child, William James and H.H. Furness* (1989) and *Dear Stevenson: The Letters of Andrew Lang to Robert Louis Stevenson* (1990); edited *De Kracht van het Woord: Honderd Jaar Germaanse Filologie aan de R.U.G.* (1890-1990), 2 vols (1991); recent articles in *Victorian Periodicals Review*, Edwardsville, 1990, in *Belgian Essays in Language and Literature*, Liège, 1993, and in *Cahiers Victoriens et Edouardiens*, Montpellier, 1994.

Theo D'haen, English Department, Leiden University, has published extensively on modern European-language literatures. He is the author of *Text to Reader* (1983), and co-author of *Windows on English and American Literature* (1991). He has edited and co-edited several collections of essays, including *Convention and Innovation in Literature* (1989), *History and Post-War Writing* (1990), *Postmodern Fiction in Canada* (1992), and *Shades of Empire in Colonial and Post-Colonial Literatures* (1993).

Robert Druce, English Department, Leiden University, published *The Eye of Innocence: Children and Their Poetry* (1965 and 1972); *Firefang*, a novel (1972); *This Day Our Daily Fictions: An Enquiry into the Multi-Million Status of Enid Blyton and Ian Fleming* (1992); edited *A Centre of Excellence* (1987), and the "Poems on Pictures" issue of *Word and Image* (1986). Articles on the theoretical relationship of poems to paintings, the changing role of letters in paintings, the practical problems of composing a sestina, and the relationship of verbal texts to graphical texts have appeared in other issues of *Word and Image*, and in *Verbal/Visual Crossings, 1880-1980* (1990).

Helga Hushahn, currently working on a dissertation on the reception of Schiller in Britain, has published an article on *"The Rovers; or, the Double Arrangement*: The Anti-Jacobins and German Drama" (1991).

Anthony Johnson, English Department, Åbo Akademi University, Finland; has recently completed *Ben Jonson: Poetry and Architecture*, and is currently preparing an edition of William Cavendish's *The Country Captain* for the Malone Society. He is also editing two volumes, *Literature and the Alchemical Imagination: A Symposium*, and *Inigo Jones: The Annotations — I. Plato, Plutarch, Vasari*.

Gudrun Kauhl, Aachen University from 1982 to 1988, has written a contextual study of Joseph Conrad's *The Secret Agent* which was accepted as a Doctoral dissertation and published in 1985. She is currently working on psycholanalysis and the gothic tradition (Matthew Lewis, the Brontës and Jean Rhys).

Thomas Kullmann, English Department, Heidelberg University, published *Abschied, Reise und Wiedersehen bei Shakespeare; Zu Gestaltung und Function epischer und romanhafter Motive im Drama* (1989) and *Vermenschlichte Natur: Zur Bedeutung von Landschaft und Wetter im englischen Roman von Ann Radcliffe bis Thomas Hardy* (1994), as well as several articles on Elizabethan literature and twentieth-century fiction.

Claire Lamont, Department of English Literary and Linguistic Studies, University of Newcastle upon Tyne, specializes in late eighteenth- and early nineteenth-century English and Scottish literature, and has published in particular on Dr Johnson, Jane Austen, Sir Walter Scott, and ballads.

Douglas S. Mack, English Department, University of Stirling is General Editor of the Stirling/South Carolina edition of James Hogg, and his publications include the editions of James Hogg's *Selected Poems* (1970), of Sir Walter Scott's *The Tale of Old Mortality* (1993). He has recently published an edition of James Hogg's *The Shepherd's Calender*.

David Punter, English Department, University of Stirling. His publications include *The Literature of Terror: A History of Gothic Fictions from 1765 to the Present Day* (1980); *Romanticism and Ideology: Studies in English Writing 1765 to 1830* (1981); *The Hidden*

Script: Writing and the Unconscious (1985); *The Romantic Unconscious: A Study in Narcissism and Patriarchy* (1989), as well as numerous articles on Gothic and romantic topics.

Alan Shelston, English Department, University of Manchester, has edited Thomas Carlyle's *Selected Writings* (1971) and Elizabeth Gaskell's *The Life of Charlotte Brontë* (1975) and *Ruth* (1981). He is editor of *The Gaskell Society Journal*, and has written on a number of nineteenth-century novelists. He is joint General Editor of the "Ryburn" edition of the individual volumes of the poetry of Thomas Hardy, for which he has just prepared *Moments of Vision* (1994); he has also completed a new edition of *Mary Barton*, for Everyman, which will be appearing shortly.

Elizabeth Tilley, English Department, University College Galway (National University of Ireland). Her publications include essays on twentieth-century British and Canadian fiction; an edition of papers on Gender and Colonialism is currently being prepared. She is also working on a volume of essays and resource materials on nineteenth-century Gothic literature.

W.M. Verhoeven, English Department, University of Groningen, published *D.H. Lawrence's Duality Concept: Its Development in the Novels of the Early and Major Phase* (1987), and essays on William Godwin, Charles Brockden Brown, Fenimore Cooper, Melville, Anne Tyler, Michael Ondaatje, and others; edited *Rewriting the Dream: Reflections on the Changing American Literary Canon* (1992) and *James Fenimore Cooper: New Historical and Literary Contexts* (1993).

Peter de Voogd, English Department, Utrecht University, published *Henry Fielding and William Hogarth: The Correspondence of the Arts* (1981) and articles on British Modernist writers; edits *The Shandean*; has broadcast a radio series on Commonwealth literature.

DAVID FAUSETT

Images of the Antipodes in the Eighteenth Century
A Study in Stereotyping

Amsterdam/Atlanta, GA 1995. VIII,231 pp.
(Cross/Cultures 18)
ISBN: 90-5183-814-X   Hfl. 75,-/US-$ 46.50

How did Europeans view the unknown region at their antipodes in early times, before the explorations of Captain Cook and others made it well known? Throughout the ages it has evoked fantastic images which affected the arts and sciences, and the evolution of the novel in the century prior to the major discoveries was influenced in the same way. The eighteenth century was also a critical phase in European social history, a time when many modern patterns of economic life and international relations were formed. Distant explorations and discoveries bore implications for that process, which tended to be worked out in fictional voyages mingling fact with fiction. *Images of the Antipodes* asks what these can tell us about Europe's expansion to the limits of the New World - about the first contacts between cultures with very different worldviews, about the colonial relations that followed, and about the geopolitics of the region since then. They offer a perspective on cross-cultural relationships generally - nowhere more apparent than in their use of ancient images of the antipodes.
This is the third part of a study on the intellectual history of travel fiction, and deals with the period from the 1720s to the 1790s, focusing on an issue that is as vital now as it was then: cultural or racial stereotyping, and the link between this and the differing politico-economic aspirations of peoples. It is a dual problem of exploitation, which has been associated with the antipodes since the beginnings of Western literature. The book discusses teratological fantasies, the literary background in utopias and Robinsonades, *Gulliver's Travels* and other travel fiction from mid-century onwards, the parallels between real and imaginary voyages, and the way the latter often prefigured the rise of modern anthropology and of colonial relationships in the austral regions. Particularly relevant was the odd blend of arcadianism and horror inspired by, or projected onto, these places in the later eighteenth century - as it had long been in the past. The works discussed are chiefly English and French, but include other European examples of the type.

USA/Canada: Editions Rodopi B.V., 233 Peachtree St., N.E., Suite 404, Atlanta, GA 30303-1504, Telelephone (404) 523-1964, *Call toll-free* (U.S.only) 1-800-225-3998, Fax (404) 522-7116, Internet e-mail: F.van.der.Zee@rodopi.nl
All Other Countries: Editions Rodopi B.V., Keizersgracht 302-304, 1016 EX Amsterdam, The Netherlands. Tel. + + (0)20-622-75-07, Fax + + (0)20-638-09-48, Internet *e-mail:* F.van.der.Zee@rodopi.nl

STAMOS METZIDAKIS

Difference Unbound
The Rise of Pluralism
in Literature and Criticism

Amsterdam/Atlanta, GA 1995. 250 pp.
(Faux Titre 94)
ISBN: 90-5183-767-4   Hfl. 80,-/US-$ 50.-

This is the first book to examine the precise relationship between pluralism and the production of modern Western literature and criticism from the eighteenth century to the present. Unlike other recent studies of pluralism's role in interpretation (by Wayne Booth, Ellen Rooney, and K.M. Newton, for instance), it underscores the historical rather than exclusively epistemological reasons behind what might be called "the rise of literary pluralism." The latter term entails two different types of phenomena: critical pluralism and aesthetic pluralism. The critical type, the one more often studied by theorists, results from the co-existence of more and more readings of the same canonical works. The aesthetic variety refers instead to the ever-growing number of modern texts that have been intentionally written differently, i.e., in different styles or forms, and about different kinds of people, situations, and things.
Reviewing a wide range of authors - from German, French, and English Romantics to contemporary Anglo-American and European poststructuralists - this polemic shows how and why the current literary emphasis on difference derives from an oftentimes unquestioned allegiance to the notion of cultural pluralism. Once the "problem" of literary pluralism is defined, the second chapter indicates how its historical rise is properly studied by shifting back and forth between differences in texts to differences in and among readers. The third and fourth chapters illustrate through numerous textual examples that modern literature and criticism have become pluralistic because European and American writers and critics have increasingly sought to be original and progressive, respectively. The book's conclusion calls for a renewal of critical approaches to literature based on a given society's values, all the while recognizing the evolutionary nature of such values.

USA/Canada: Editions Rodopi B.V., 233 Peachtree St., N.E., Suite 404, Atlanta, GA 30303-1504, Telelephone (404) 523-1964, *Call toll--free* (U.S.only) 1-800-225-3998, Fax (404) 522-7116, Internet *e-mail:* F.van.der.Zee@rodopi.nl
All Other Countries: Editions Rodopi B.V., Keizersgracht 302-304, 1016 EX Amsterdam, The Netherlands. Tel. + + (0)20-622-75-07, Fax + + (0)20-638-09-48, Internet *e-mail:* F.van.der.Zee@rodopi.nl

MARTYN CORNICK

French Intellectuals and History
The *Nouvelle Revue Française* under Jean Paulhan, 1925-1940

Amsterdam/Atlanta, GA 1995. 232 pp.
(Faux Titre 93)
ISBN: 90-5183-797-6   Hfl. 65,-/US-$ 40.50

This work aims to fill a gap in our knowledge of French cultural history between the wars. The contribution of the *Nouvelle Revue Française* to the intellectual history of this period. He has not been studied before. The current study, based on the archives of the editor, Jean Paulhan, examines the subject thematically.

USA/Canada: Editions Rodopi B.V., 233 Peachtree St., N.E., Suite 404, Atlanta, GA 30303-1504, Telelephone (404) 523-1964, *Call toll--free* (U.S.only) 1-800-225-3998, Fax (404) 522-7116, Internet e-*mail:* F.van.der.Zee@rodopi.nl
AllOther Countries: Editions Rodopi B.V., Keizersgracht 302-304, 1016 EX Amsterdam, The Netherlands. Tel. + + (0)20-622-75-07, Fax + + (0)20-638-09-48, Internet e-*mail:* F.van.der.Zee@rodopi.nl

HENDRIK SMEEKS
The Mighty Kingdom of Krinke Kesmes

Presented by David Fausett
with a translation of the Dutch text by Robert H. Leek

Amsterdam/Atlanta, GA 1994. ca. 200 pp.
(Atlantis 10)

ISBN: 90-5183-695-3   Hfl. 60,-/US-$ 37.50

This is the first English edition of a novel that is little known outside Dutch literary circles, but is an interesting example of popular fiction and radical thought about science and society in its day - not only in the Netherlands, but throughout Western Europe. It formed a bridge between the rationalist seventeenth century and the Age of Enlightenment, and was also a lively story in itself. It was rather less than imaginary, moreover, being linked to seventeenth to seventeenth-century Dutch activities in Australia and the first real knowledge about the legendary southern continent. Among the novels based on such exploits, this was one of the most remarkable. The dominance of classics like Defoe's *Robinson Crusoe* has tended to obscure many such works, but they can be better appreciated today as a result of changing views about literary genres. Defoe, in particular, built on an earlier tradition in which *Krinke Kesmes* played a vital role.

The text is translated from the original edition, and the author's handwritten additions to it are included or discussed in the introduction. A glossary explaining obscure terms and a full bibliography are given along with the introduction, which outlines the background and significance of the work. This is by David Fausett, an authority on early travel fiction and, in particular, that relating to exploration in the austral regions.

USA/Canada: Editions Rodopi, 233 Peachtree Street, N.E., Suite 404, Atlanta, GA 30303-1504, Telephone (404) 523-1964, Call toll-free 1-800-225-3998 (U.S. only), Fax (404) 522-7116
And Others: Editions Rodopi B.V., Keizersgracht 302-304, 1016 EX Amsterdam, The Netherlands. Telephone ++ (0) 20 622 75 07, Fax ++ (0) 20 638 09 48

INTERTEXTS
IN BECKETT'S WORK et/ou
INTERTEXTES
DE L'OEUVRE DE BECKETT

Ed. by Marius Buning, Sjef Houppermans

Amsterdam/Atlanta, GA 1994. 135 pp.
(Samuel Beckett Today / Aujourd'hui 3)
ISBN: 90-5183-796-8   Hfl. 40,-/US-$ 25.-

Internet *e-mail:* f.van.der.zee@rodopi.nl
USA/Canada: Editions Rodopi, 233 Peachtree Street, N.E., Suite 404, Atlanta, GA 30303-1504, Telephone (404) 523-1964, Call toll-free 1-800-225-3998 (U.S. only), Fax (404) 522-7116
And Others: Editions Rodopi B.V., Keizersgracht 302-304, 1016 EX Amsterdam, The Netherlands. Telephone ++ (0) 20 622 75 07, Fax ++ (0) 20 638 09 48

LITERATURE AND THE GROTESQUE

Ed. by Michael J. Meyer

Amsterdam/Atlanta, GA 1995. 195 pp.
(Rodopi Perspectives on Modern Literature 15)
ISBN: 90-5183-793-3   Hfl. 60,-/US-$ 37.50

Contents: RALPH CIANCIO: Laughing In Pain With Nathanael West. MICHAEL QUIGLEY: Excavations of The Grotesque in Peter Schaffer's Equus. MARY CATANZARO: Disconnected Voices, Displaced Bodies: The Dismembered Couple in Beckett's *Krapp's Last Tape, Happy Days and Play*. BRIAN RAILSBACK: Uncomfortable Reflections in John Steinbeck's Grotesques. ZITA M. MCSHANE: Steps: Mapping a Grotesque Universe or a Universal Grotesque. TIMOTHY P. TWOHILL: Flimsy Masks and Tortured Souls: Luigi Pirandello and The Grotesque. JACK SLAY, JR.: Delineations in Freakery: Freaks in The Fiction of Harry Crews and Katherine Dunn. LEONARD CASSUTO: Jack London's Class-Based Grotesque. KELLY ANSPAUGH: Jean qui rit and Jean qui pleure: James Joyce, Wyndham Lewis and The High Modern Grotesque. GREG METCALF: The Soul In The Meatsuit: Ivan Albright, Hannibal Lecter and The Body Grotesque. TIM LIBRETTI: What A Dirty Way To Get Clean: The Grotesque in The Modern American Novel.

Internet *e-mail:* **F.van.der.Zee@rodopi.nl**
USA/Canada: Editions Rodopi, 233 Peachtree Street, N.E., Suite 404, Atlanta, GA 30303-1504, Telephone (404) 523-1964, Call toll-free 1-800-225-3998 (U.S. only), Fax (404) 522-7116
And Others: Editions Rodopi B.V., Keizersgracht 302-304, 1016 EX Amsterdam, The Netherlands. Telephone ++ (0) 20 622 75 07, Fax ++ (0) 20 638 09 48

FINNEGANS WAKE
"Teems of Times"

Ed. by Andrew Treip

Amsterdam/Atlanta, GA 1994. 212 pp.
(European Joyce Studies 4)
ISBN: 90-5183-604-X   Hfl. 70,-/US-$ 43.50

This is a collection by diverse hands on the thematic, conceptual and contextual impact of time in and around Joyce's *Finnegans Wake*. In keeping with the practice of the Zürich James Joyce Foundation workshops, from one of which, over Easter 1992, the collection developed, many essays emphasize the local temporal textures of *Finnegans Wake* through close readings of individual passages. However, this does not preclude fruitful interaction with wider contexts and theoretical concerns. Two articles are detailed studies of social and political contemporary contexts with which Joyce's last work was in dialogue. Three more explore philosophical, psychological and scientific theories of time which Joyce exploited and transformed in his text. Two essays relate *Finnegans Wake* to discussions of time in French feminist and deconstructive theory: and finally, four essays concentrate on the temporality of composition - two apiece on each of the chronology of Joyce's early note-taking and draft processes. The collection should prove interesting to all readers and critics of Joyce as well as to critics concerned with the problem of historicizing and contextualising the temporally disruptive texts of high modernism and early postmodernism.

Internet *e-mail:* F.van.der.Zee@rodopi.nl

USA/Canada: Editions Rodopi, 233 Peachtree Street, N.E., Suite 404, Atlanta, GA 30303-1504, Telephone (404) 523-1964, Call toll-free 1-800-225-3998 (U.S. only), Fax (404) 522-7116

And Others: Editions Rodopi B.V., Keizersgracht 302-304, 1016 EX Amsterdam, The Netherlands. Telephone ++ (0) 20 622 75 07, Fax ++ (0) 20 638 09 48

LITERATURE AND SCIENCE

Ed. by Donald Bruce and Anthony Purdy

Amsterdam/Atlanta, GA 1994. 179 pp.·
(Rodopi Perspectives on Modern Literature 14)
ISBN: 90-5183-762-3   Hfl. 55,-/US-$ 34.-

Taking as a starting point the embeddedness of all disciplinary and interdisciplinary inquiry - since interdisciplinarity is itself not a unitary phenomenon but encompasses many different knowledge practices embedded in widely differing political, economic and ideological constituencies - the essays in this volume explore in different ways some of the conversations currently taking place across disciplinary boundaries in the exciting new field of literature and science. Like literature, science is seen as a site of competing ideological constructions, as a complex (and richly ambiguous) element of modern (and postmodern) social discourse, circulating in a wider cultural community where its currency fluctuates according to complex changes in social and epistemic conditions, including the relative prestige or cultural capital of 'science' (or 'literature') within professional and disciplinary hierarchies at any given time.

USA/Canada: Editions Rodopi, 233 Peachtree Street, N.E., Suite 404, Atlanta, GA 30303-1504, Telephone (404) 523-1964, Call toll-free 1-800-225-3998 (U.S. only), Fax (404) 522-7116
And Others: Editions Rodopi B.V., Keizersgracht 302-304, 1016 EX Amsterdam, The Netherlands. Telephone ++ (0) 20 622 75 07, Fax ++ (0) 20 638 09 48

LIMINAL POSTMODERNISMS
The Postmodern, the (Post-)Colonial
and the (Post-)Feminist

Ed. by Theo D'haen and Hans Bertens

Amsterdam/Atlanta, GA 1994. 357 pp.
(Postmodern Studies 8)
ISBN: 90-5183-756-9   Bound Hfl. 180,-/US-$ 112.-
ISBN: 90-5183-772-0   Paper Hfl. 50,-/US-$ 31.-

USA/Canada: Editions Rodopi, 233 Peachtree Street, N.E., Suite 404, Atlanta, GA 30303-1504, Telephone (404) 523-1964, Call toll-free 1-800-225-3998 (U.S. only), Fax (404) 522-7116
And Others: Editions Rodopi B.V., Keizersgracht 302-304, 1016 EX Amsterdam, The Netherlands. Telephone ++ (0) 20 622 75 07, Fax ++ (0) 20 638 09 48 / Internet *e-mail:* F.van.der.Zee@rodopi.nl

THEMATICS RECONSIDERED
Essays in Honor of Horst S. Daemmrich

Ed. by Frank Trommler

Amsterdam/Atlanta, GA 1995. 278 pp.
(Internationale Forschungen zur Allgemeinen und
Vergleichenden Literaturwissenschaft 9)
ISBN: 90-5183-787-9   Hfl. 90,-/US-$ 56.-

Responding to a new interest in thematic studies, the volume features essays by some of the leading scholars from the United States and Europe. In honor of Horst S. Daemmrich, the co-author with Ingrid Daemmrich of the handbook *Themes and Motifs in Western Literature*, the contributors reassess, both in theory and in case studies, the viability of thematics as part of contemporary literary criticism. They demonstrate the broad scope of methodologies between strict systematization of themes and motifs and reader-response conceptions of 'theming.' Special topics include a thematology of the Jewish people; motifs in folklore; a cluster on madness, hysteria, and mastery; the story of Judith; Cinderella; thematics in Dürrenmatt and Isaac Babel; chaos as a theme. A concluding chapter illuminates aspects of nineteenth-century literary history.

USA/Canada: Editions Rodopi, 233 Peachtree Street, N.E., Suite 404, Atlanta, GA 30303-1504, Telephone (404) 523-1964, Call toll-free 1-800-225-3998 (U.S. only), Fax (404) 522-7116

And Others: Editions Rodopi B.V., Keizersgracht 302-304, 1016 EX Amsterdam, The Netherlands. Telephone ++ (0) 20 622 75 07, Fax ++ (0) 20 638 09 48 / Internet *e-mail:* F.van.der.Zee@rodopi.nl

DAVID FAUSETT

The Strange Surprizing Sources of Robinson Crusoe

Amsterdam/Atlanta, GA 1994. 240 pp.

(Textxet 3)

ISBN: 90-5183-705-4   Hfl. 70,-/US-$ 43.50

Robinson Crusoe is the archetypal tale of marooning on a desert island, whose sensational success in 1719 set off a craze for "Robinsonades". This book re-examines the sources of the story, and traditional views about them. It has been assumed that Defoe's novel was prompted by Britain's overseas activities and refers allegorically to Defoe's own culture. Others have thought that an earlier Dutch novel, *The Mighty Kingdom of Krinke Kesmes*, might have been Defoe's model. Although this theory was refuted in the 1920s, it is reviewed here in relation not only to *Krinke Kesmes* but also to broader literary, social and religious developments in the seventeenth century. Opinions about the origins of *Robinson Crusoe* have a considerable bearing upon its interpretation, so it is ironical that Defoe's sources for the "Strange Suprizing Adventures" of Crusoe prove to themselves be "strange and surprizing", and largely non-British. To trace them one needs to abandon that prejudice, and to question certain modern literary categories. What was perceived as fact or fiction in reports of distant events? How did early utopian fantasies relate to the description of foreign peoples? David Fausett's book re-examines the story as commentary on social developments in its own time (and ours), and looks beyond Defoe's own culture in a more sustained way than has been done before.

USA/Canada: Editions Rodopi, 233 Peachtree Street, N.E., Suite 404, Atlanta, GA 30303-1504, Telephone (404) 523-1964, Call toll-free 1-800-225-3998 (U.S. only), Fax (404) 522-7116

And Others: Editions Rodopi B.V., Keizersgracht 302-304, 1016 EX Amsterdam, The Netherlands. Telephone ++ (0) 20 622 75 07, Fax ++ (0) 20 638 09 48

HENK SLAGER

Archeology of Art Theory

Amsterdam/Atlanta, GA 1995. 195 pp.
(Lier en Boog Studies 5)
ISBN: 90-5183-788-7   Hfl. 60,-/US-$ 37.50

This study is an archeological investigation into the historically changing relationship between words and images. The result is an encyclopedia of interpretative techniques in which language functions as a model of thought.

Three periods come to the fore. In the classical one, grammatical structures are responsible for the dominance of describing and identifying activities. Thought about art departs from the idea, that classificatory systems (words) represent images. *Art criticism* is the form of interpretation in this period.

In the modern period time moves to the foreground. Now attention is focused on changes in grammatical forms instead of changes in constant structures. A hermeneutic form of interpretation comes into being: *Art History*.

In the postmodern period one realizes that words fail to establish a consistent relationship with visuality. New, semiological theories of interpretation now explain what images can signify.

This volume is of interest for philosophers of art and art theoreticians, as well as for students and professionals in both fields.

USA/Canada: Editions Rodopi B.V., 233 Peachtree St., N.E., Suite 404, Atlanta, GA 30303-1504, Telelephone (404) 523-1964, *Call toll--free* (U.S.only) 1-800-225-3998, Fax (404) 522-7116, Internet e-*mail:* F.van.der.Zee@rodopi.nl
All Other Countries: Editions Rodopi B.V., Keizersgracht 302-304, 1016 EX Amsterdam, The Netherlands. Tel. + + (0)20-622-75-07, Fax + + (0)20-638-09-48, Internet e-*mail:* F.van.der.Zee@rodopi.nl